Guide to ORACLE

Guide to ORACLE

Tim Hoechst
Oracle Corporation

Nicole Melander
Oracle Corporation

Christopher Chabris
Harvard University

Intertext Publications
McGraw-Hill Book Company

New York St. Louis San Francisco Auckland Bogotá
Hamburg London Madrid Mexico Milan Montreal
New Delhi Panama Paris São Paolo
Singapore Sydney Tokyo Toronto

Library of Congress catalog card number 90-83338

10 9 8 7 6 5 4 3 2 1

ISBN 0-07-020631-7

Intertext Publications / Multiscience Press, Inc.
One Lincoln Plaza
New York, NY 10023

McGraw-Hill Book Company
1221 Avenue of the Americas
New York, NY 10020

Composed and typeset by Christopher Chabris, Castle Productions Limited. Edited by Jamie Hamilton.

Table of Contents

Foreword   ix
Preface   xi

1 Overview   1
  1.1 Introduction   1
  1.2 Audience   2
  1.3 Conventions   3
  1.4 How to Read This Book   5
  1.5 Organization   5
  1.6 Conclusion   7

2 Preparing to Build the Application   9
  2.1 Introduction   9
  2.2 Developing a Data Model   10
    2.2.1 Entities   11
    2.2.2 Attributes   12
    2.2.3 Relationships   13
  2.3 Our Data Model   15
  2.4 Using the Data Model   18
  2.5 Going Beyond the Data Model   21
    2.5.1 Table relationships in the physical model   22
    2.5.2 Column definitions in the physical model   29
  2.6 Conclusion   33

3 Overview of SQL   35
  3.1 Introduction   35
  3.2 Data Manipulation   36
    3.2.1 The SELECT statement   36
    3.2.2 The INSERT statement   45
    3.2.3 The UPDATE statement   46
    3.2.4 The DELETE statement   47
    3.2.5 Commit and rollback   48
  3.3 Data Definition   49
  3.4 Data Control   51
  3.5 Conclusion   53

4 Building the Database   55
  4.1 Introduction   55
  4.2 Software Management   55
  4.3 ORACLE Application Development Environment   58
  4.4 Naming Conventions   62
  4.5 Domain Definition   64
  4.6 Software Development Standards   65
  4.7 Definition of a Goal   66
  4.8 Sizing the Application Tables   67
  4.9 Building the Application Tables   68
 4.10 Conclusion   74

5 Building the Online Applications   77
  5.1 Introduction   77
  5.2 Understanding SQL*Forms   78
    5.2.1 Making the transition to a
           nonprocedural language   78
    5.2.2 Using SQL*Forms   79
    5.2.3 The SQL*Forms modules   79
    5.2.4 The Designer   82
    5.2.5 Saving versus generating   86
  5.3 Writing Specifications for SQL*Forms   91
  5.4 SQL*Forms Design Review   92
  5.5 Creating Standards for SQL*Forms   93
  5.6 Creating Skeleton Forms   97
    5.6.1 The HELP system   98
    5.6.2 The APPL form   101
    5.6.3 The dynamic MENU system   103
    5.6.4 The skeletons   111
  5.7 Building the Application   122
    5.7.1 The LFV forms   122
    5.7.2 Default application forms   124
    5.7.3 Generic functions and the code library 127
    5.7.4 Application-specific techniques   141
  5.8 Conclusion   160

6 Building the Reports   161
  6.1 Introduction   161
  6.2 Understanding SQL*Plus   161
  6.3 Understanding SQL*ReportWriter   165

6.4 Preparing to Write Report Specifications   168
    6.4.1 Report design review   170
    6.4.2 Creating standards for reports   170
6.5 Developing Report Skeletons   173
    6.5.1 SQL*ReportWriter skeleton   173
    6.5.2 SQL*Plus skeleton   175
6.6 Building the Reports   178
    6.6.1 SQL*Plus reporting techniques   179
    6.6.2 SQL*ReportWriter reporting techniques   189
6.7 Conclusion   196

7 Putting It All Together   197
7.1 Introduction   197
7.2 Looking Back   198
    7.2.1 The menu system   198
    7.2.2 The help system   201
    7.2.3 An application skeleton   201
7.3 Calling Reports   202
7.4 Portability Review   209
7.5 Migrating Old Data   211
7.6 Integrating Existing Systems   218
7.7 Moving the Software   221
7.8 Conclusion   222

8 Testing and Tuning   225
8.1 Introduction   225
8.2 Inside the ORACLE RDBMS   226
8.3 Tuning SQL   232
    8.3.1 Understanding query execution   233
    8.3.2 Understanding the optimization process   243
    8.3.3 SQL tuning techniques   254
    8.3.4 Using Oracle's SQL analysis tools   263
    8.3.5 Interpreting the tuning information   271
    8.3.6 A methodology for tuning SQL   272
8.4 Tuning the Rest of the Application   275
    8.4.1 Tuning SQL*Forms applications   276
    8.4.2 Tuning SQL*ReportWriter applications   279
8.5 Application Testing   279
8.6 Tuning and Testing the MegaMarket Application   281
8.7 Conclusion   282

9 Documenting the System   283
  9.1 Introduction   283
  9.2 Documentation Overview   283
    9.2.1 User documentation   284
    9.2.2 Technical documentation   285
  9.3 Easing the Technical Documentation Burden   287
    9.3.1 Documentation using CASE*Dictionary   287
    9.3.2 Documentation using the data dictionary   288
    9.3.3 Documentation using tool tables   292
    9.3.4 Cross reference reports   295
    9.3.5 Data integrity reports   297
  9.4 Documenting Reference Tables and Data   299
  9.5 Conclusion   305

10 Additional Development and Software Topics   307
  10.1 Introduction   307
  10.2 Distributed Processing   307
  10.3 Distributed Databases   309
  10.4 Security Management   310
  10.5 Auditing   311
  10.6 Archiving   312
  10.7 Executive Information Systems   312
  10.8 Reporting Databases   314
  10.9 Future Oracle Software   314
    10.9.1 PL/SQL   315
    10.9.2 SQL*Forms 3.0   317
    10.9.3 SQL*Menu 5.0   321
    10.9.4 The CASE*Tools   323
    10.9.5 ORACLE*Graphics   324
    10.9.6 ORACLE Version 7.0   325
  10.10 Conclusion   326

Appendices
  1 Development Checklist for an ORACLE Application   327
  2 MegaMarket Forms Standards   329
  3 MegaMarket Naming Conventions   335
  4 MegaMarket Tables   339
  5 Sample MegaMarket Form Design Document   345

Index   347

Foreword

As our society enters the fourth decade of the Information Age, information systems professionals face several dilemmas. Perhaps the most important is to determine the optimal method of utilizing the myriad hardware and software components that are available to meet the seemingly insatiable information needs of computer users.

The wide range of technological advances within the computer industry of the past three decades has been extraordinary. One of the most significant achievements has been in the field of database management. Oracle Corporation, founded in 1979, has been an innovator and leader in the development of *relational technology*. The ORACLE Relational Database Management System (RDBMS) is one of the most widely used products of its kind in the industry today. I have had the unique opportunity of being among the first in the industry to utilize ORACLE technology in a real world environment. Over the past eight years, I have personally experienced the phenomenal improvements within the ORACLE product line as well as its overwhelming acceptance by the marketplace.

While the benefits of information systems have been promised for many years, implementation of information systems which span multiple hardware devices and physical locations throughout an organization or enterprise has proven difficult to achieve. Products such as ORACLE provide complete solutions for successfully implementing Enterprise Wide Information Systems. Delivering on the promise of the benefits of relational technology and the ORACLE product line is what this book is all about.

Guide to ORACLE uses a "results oriented" approach to rapidly implementing everything from small, standalone applications to large, distributed, mission critical applications using ORACLE. While the approach taken by this book is firmly grounded in relational theory, it does not lose sight of the fact that in practice, organizations use technology such as Oracle's to solve critical information management issues that are essential to the corporation's success and bottom line.

I have had the privilege of working with Tim Hoechst and Nicole Melander on a wide variety of large scale, mission critical, ORACLE-based systems. The years of hands-on experience and unequaled expertise including the insight of both authors is effectively summarized and presented. The authors present the material in a manner which focuses on transferring their knowledge and expertise of ORACLE technology to the reader.

This book will undoubtedly serve as an invaluable guidebook and reference for any information systems professional who needs to deliver successful ORACLE-based systems on the first try.

Barry A. Leffew
Director, Professional Services
Oracle Federal Group
Bethesda, MD
May 1990

Preface

We have helped countless people with their ORACLE application development efforts. Over and over again, we have run into the same problems and questions. And each time we give an interesting tip or trick in response, we hear the same refrain, "Why isn't that written down anywhere!?!" In this book we've tried to write it all down.

We found that the undocumented tips and techniques were only one part of the solution, though. Most of the development teams that we encountered had never had the opportunity to perform a full development life-cycle using ORACLE, and therefore had never learned many of the procedures and methods for effectively managing large projects. We share suggestions that will not only organize your ORACLE projects, but save you valuable time.

The basis of this book is a realistic application that we design, develop, test, tune, and document. And along the way, we discuss the difficulties we encounter and alternatives for resolving them. We've tried not to make any decisions without discussing our justifications for the choice. In this way, we hope that you will be able to make informed decisions at critical points in your own ORACLE development projects.

Because we wanted to portray a realistic application, we had to make it very large. We included examples from our application throughout the book, but naturally, we could not put *all* of the application modules into the text. If you're interested in the details of the application itself, refer to the card in the back of the book that will tell you how you can receive a disk that includes everything we built. We welcome any comments that you have about the book at the address listed on this card, although we can't promise a written response.

Finally, this book includes our experiences as well as those of many others. With this in mind, we would like to thank Barry Leffew, Mike

Price, Todd Weatherby, Greg Foudray, Rudy Corsi, Scott Sherman, Bill Smith, Denise Fleming, Chris Connolly, Tim Danison, Ken Jacobs, Stuart Read and David Richardson. And of course, thanks to Jamie Hamilton, who edited the manuscript, and Alan Rose, who published it. And most importantly, we would like to thank our parents for their encouragement and Lorie and Emily for putting up with our unending computer talk.

Bethesda, MD
Cambridge, MA
June 1990

1

Overview

1.1 Introduction

During the past several years, the relational database management system (RDBMS) has become one of the premier software tools in the computer industry. It has opened the world of data management to all sorts of computer users and developers by providing both access to large amounts of data and to the structures in which that data is stored. Now, professional quality database applications can be constructed easily and maintained without cumbersome programming support. This sort of flexibility in a data management tool has brought the RDBMS to the forefront and there are now several commercially available RDBMSs on the market.

Because the RDBMS provides such a flexible and intuitive environment, developing simple applications very quickly is now possible. However, despite the simplified development process, building large applications can still be difficult. Many concepts come easily and can be quickly put into practice. As with anything, though, some of the more difficult concepts take longer to grasp. Most of the RDBMS literature available today concentrates only on the first step: introducing the new user to the concepts of relational database theory and building small applications. This book will take you beyond that stage and discuss the issues and techniques involved in building large and complicated data management applications.

Among the vendors who currently produce relational database management systems, Oracle Corporation has led the industry in many ways with its product of the same name: ORACLE. Because of its success ORACLE has become the product against which the others are judged. There are, of course, many other relational database management products available, but they cannot deliver the power and flexibility offered by ORACLE. ORACLE has always remained at the leading edge of database technology, providing outstanding performance as well as transparent connectivity across hardware and operating system platforms. It is, in our opinion, the best relational database management software available today.

We understand, however, that most of you do not have the luxury of choosing the database software that you want to use. Most often, software purchases are not made by those who will develop applications. Take heart, then, because this book is for you. We will not be trying to convince you to use ORACLE. Rather, we will show you what you need to know to build bigger and better ORACLE applications.

Because RDBMS technology and ORACLE are relatively recent inventions, knowledge about using them for software development is still evolving every day. Only after long exposure to the products will these ideas coalesce in your mind. As professional ORACLE application developers, we have had the opportunity not only to build large database systems but also to watch other programmers work with ORACLE. By gathering these experiences in this book, we hope to take you beyond the introductory stages of application development and show you some of the extra techniques needed to produce "industrial strength" applications. This is a book on *using* ORACLE. After reading it, you will understand how the ORACLE products work and how to take advantage of our experiences to utilize the ORACLE tools more effectively.

1.2 Audience

This book is not intended for the beginner. By beginner, we mean someone who has never used ORACLE or who has only used it to a limited extent. The focus of this book is to build on basic concepts to introduce more advanced ones. Consequently, we must assume that you are familiar with the ideas behind relational databases. To properly understand many of the examples, you should also have several months of experience with SQL, SQL*Plus, and SQL*Forms. If you are new to ORACLE or even to relational databases in general, we think that you will still be able to learn quite a bit from this book—but the first time through may be slow. If you try to spend as much time as possible actually working with the product while you go through this book, we think you'll be off to a tremendous start.

In writing this book, we found in several cases that clear fundamentals were required to explain properly the more advanced topics. As a result, you will find that some sections start at a relatively basic level. We encourage you to read these sections with a view towards reestablishing a foundation upon which to build more advanced ideas. For example, we discuss the fundamentals of SQL in order to provide insight into how the language is *structured*, rather than simply how it is used. Do not misinterpret these introductory sections as having been written below your level of ORACLE experience. Familiarity with the basics is an integral part of the advanced user's knowledge.

We believe that the people who will gain the most from this book are database analysts, application developers, and database administrators. We will introduce techniques to help all three of these groups perform their jobs more effectively. The analyst will see how the database should be designed, the programmer will learn development techniques that make it possible to implement complex applications, and the database administrator will learn how to manage the data as well as how to optimize the database environment.

1.3 Conventions

Several conventions are used throughout this book. First, Oracle is both a company and a product. The company is referred to with just the first letter capitalized: Oracle. The product is shown in all capitals: ORACLE. We will present SQL statements and application code exactly as they would appear in a program except for words shown in italics, which should be replaced by an appropriate value. For example, consider this SQL statement:

```
SELECT 'X'
FROM tablename
WHERE some condition is true
```

This statement shows the words SELECT, 'X', FROM, and WHERE as literals that must appear exactly this way, while the *tablename* would be the name of one of your tables and the *condition* would be an appropriate one for that table.

Whenever you see a "hint box," it will contain a little helpful trick or technique that is not an integral part of the text, but is appropriate to the discussion.

Hints

As you read through this book place a small sticker on the pages that have hints that you like. This will help you find the trick later (when you desperately need it).

In Chapters 2 through 9, we will take you through a complete database development effort. Along the way we will compile a *checklist* of important tasks and decisions. These points are marked in the text and the entire list is given in Appendix 1.

The ORACLE software set consists of several different tools, each with many versions. Most of what we discuss in this book is independent of the software versions being used. There are, however, many cases where our examples will not apply to older versions of the ORACLE products. Because of this, you should be aware of the versions that we are using:

- RDBMS Version 6.0
- SQL*Plus Version 3.0
- SQL*Forms Version 2.3
- SQL*ReportWriter Version 1.1

These are the versions that were available when we started the book in the summer of 1989. By the time we finished, of course, newer versions were in sight. With this in mind, we have included a discussion in Chapter 10 that provides an up-to-the-minute description of the ORACLE product line.

One of ORACLE's technical advantages is its portability—it runs on most of the popular hardware and software platforms. Everything we discuss in this book should apply directly to your work regardless of the platform that you are using. For purposes of consistency, we have chosen the UNIX operating system and the C programming language for our examples. Remember, however, that virtually everything we do also applies to VMS, MS-DOS, and VM, as well as to many other environments. Any inconsistencies among platforms will be noted; for example there are cases in SQL*Forms applications where block- and character-mode environments must be treated differently. We will point out these instances and explain the alternatives in each environment.

1.4 How to Read This Book

Start at the beginning. Although it will become a useful piece of reference material, you will get the most out of this book if you follow it like a story, reading from front to back. That's exactly the way we wrote it, because it's a chronological account of an application development effort. We tell the story of the project as it evolves. Decisions made in one chapter might be based on facts discussed in a previous chapter. The rationale behind such decisions will only make sense if you know all the facts.

We recommend that you follow along with our development effort with your own ORACLE system if you have one. You do not need to implement every SQL statement that we discuss, but pausing occasionally to test things out and experiment will greatly improve your overall understanding.

1.5 Organization

This book has ten chapters, the first of which you have almost finished, as well as five appendices. Each chapter is briefly described here to illustrate the overall direction of the book.

Chapter 2:Preparing to Build the Application. This chapter introduces you to the application that we will be implementing throughout the rest of the book: the MegaMarket Inventory Management System. There is a brief overview of the data modeling technique that we used for this application as well as a discussion of how to best move from this logical model into the physical model. After this chapter, we will be ready to begin building our application.

Chapter 3: Overview of SQL. In this chapter, we review many of the basic concepts underlying SQL in order to provide a greater understanding of its structure. This discussion does not provide a complete lesson in SQL, but acts as a good review for those who haven't used it in a while or who have some misunderstandings about its structure.

Chapter 4: Building the Database. In Chapter 4, we begin implementing the database for our application. We will accomplish this by setting up the development environment, establishing standards and naming conventions, and sizing and constructing the application tables designed in Chapter 2.

Chapter 5: Building the Online Applications. Chapter 5 focuses on the development of the SQL*Forms applications in the MegaMarket system. We will not only present ways of managing a development effort like this one, but also discuss complex SQL*Forms issues by presenting real examples from our development of the MegaMarket application.

Chapter 6: Building the Reports. In this chapter we will build the reports that will support our MegaMarket application and we will discuss the many factors involved in choosing the right reporting tool. We will suggest techniques for developing reports that are both complex and efficient.

Chapter 7: Pulling It All Together. This chapter discusses the final steps involved in turning a good application into a superior one. These include packaging all of the application software with a consistent user interface, as well as tying the reports into the SQL*Forms applications. It is here that we will put most of the finishing touches on our application.

Chapter 8: Testing and Tuning. Once the system is built, how can it be tested to ensure that it is functioning properly and at peak performance? Although this question is undoubtedly one of the most important in large system design efforts, it is very difficult to find extensive reference material on performance tuning and testing. We will discuss ways of refining your applications so that they more effectively utilize indexes, memory, and disk space. We will also present some important guidelines for testing applications to help ensure that no errors go uncorrected.

Chapter 9: Documenting the System. This chapter presents some interesting techniques for documenting the database and the applications based on the information stored in its data dictionary. These techniques will show you how you can effectively use the database and SQL to generate a large portion of your documentation automatically. Although documentation standards are largely a matter of personal taste, we will describe our own preferences and offer some suggestions for simplifying the documentation task.

Chapter 10: Additional Development and Software Topics. This chapter describes some important aspects of application development, including distributed data, executive information systems, and networking, that are not covered elsewhere in the book. Because many of these topics can (and do) fill books of their own, we will cover them only briefly, addressing the particular issues and problems that ORACLE users are likely to encounter. In this chapter, we will also provide a glimpse of where the ORACLE software is going. Since Oracle Corporation is continually striving to stay at the forefront of database technology, new versions of its software appear almost daily. In this book, we cover the versions that were current in mid-1989 when we began to write. In this final chapter, we provide an up-to-the-minute account of what is available as well as some hints of what is next on the horizon including Version 7.0 of the RDBMS and Version 3.0 of SQL*Forms. We will describe what to expect and what not to expect from these forthcoming products, as well as how to prepare for their arrival in your current application development projects.

1.6 Conclusion

We urge you to take all the time you need to get involved in the examples and discussions presented in this book. When a SQL statement piques your interest, take the time to try it out in SQL*Plus and experiment with it—this is by far the best way to learn SQL. If a SQL*Forms application that we write reminds you of one with which you've been having trouble, stop and try to make it work. A habit of experimentation and an eagerness to understand will ultimately give you greater control over the ORACLE development environment.

Although much of this book can be used as a cookbook for your applications, take the time to be a philosopher and think about the concepts, rather than simply copying from our examples to your programs. We believe that by thinking about how SQL and the ORACLE tools function, you will be able to use them in your own applications far more effectively. Good luck!

2

Preparing to Build the Application

2.1 Introduction

Getting started is the hardest part of any process. Yet each time you successfully (or even unsuccessfully) complete a procedure you learn new techniques to use the next time. To help you master ORACLE with fewer trips through this cycle, we will share our techniques and strategies for developing ORACLE applications by taking you along as we develop a complete application. We think that the tricks we use and the traps we avoid in the process will be applicable to your development efforts as well. We have chosen a complex application that is challenging enough to provide realistic examples but simple enough to eliminate the need for long explanations.

The relational database application we will develop over the course of this book will be designed to automate the business functions of a fictitious corporation called MegaMarket, a national retail sales chain that sells everything from food to hardware supplies to clothing. MegaMarket's slogan is "If we don't sell it, you don't need it." The CEO of MegaMarket has called us in because the business has grown and diversified so much that it has become difficult to keep track of anything. Products that are top sellers in one store can't be given away in others, the number of various suppliers is growing out of control, and managing the distribution of products from the warehouses to stores is becoming impossible. The national headquarters can barely manage its own employees, the regional offices can't control the stores in their region, and customers are complaining that they receive several copies of the same advertising flyers, each addressed to a different spelling of their name.

We will set up a plan to not only make suggestions about how business operations might be improved, but also automate those operations with an ORACLE database system. We will design and construct an inventory management system that will control the stocking and maintenance of warehouses and stores, the tracking of transactions in each store, and the management of personnel information.

To define our application requirements, we used a subset of Oracle's CASE*Method, which is not a product, per se, but a formal *methodology* for developing relational database systems. Literally, the term "CASE" stands for Computer Aided Systems Engineering, and it has become a buzzword in the computer industry. CASE is simply a concept that helps systematize the tools used in database systems design, whether they are computer applications or the step-by-step procedures performed during the design and implementation of a database application. Oracle's method, the CASE*Method, includes its own strategy and diagramming techniques, but the relational theory upon which it is based has become quite standard in the industry. Although Oracle's methodology emphasizes these theoretical aspects of application development, the newest facet of the CASE*Method is not theory at all, but tools to support it. These products are discussed in more detail in Chapter 10.

As we proceed through this effort, we will tell you more about the requirements of the MegaMarket inventory system, but we will start by discussing the first component of any database application: the data model.

2.2 Developing a Data Model

A *data model* is a set of diagrams and textual descriptions that illustrate the primary components of an application and the relationships between them. The data model is certainly one of the most important aspects of any database development effort, since without it there is no guarantee that the information stored in the database will accurately represent the real world. It not only aids in the development process, but also provides a means of validating the analyst's understanding of the user's requirements. The theory of data modeling is largely outside the scope of this book. It's an extensive topic by itself and applies not specifically to

ORACLE, but to database development in general. As a result, we will only be discussing some of the essential aspects of data modeling while we present part of the data model for our MegaMarket application.

A data model developed using the CASE*Method consists of several diagrams and reports, the most important of which is the *Entity/ Relationship Diagram* (ERD). This diagram succinctly depicts the basic data elements in a system and describes the relationships between them; if this diagram is complete, the database structure can be derived directly from it. Other diagrams produced during the data modeling process include *Function Hierarchies* and *Data Flow Diagrams*. Function hierarchies detail each function supported within the system. Data flow diagrams document the path that a piece of data follows as it is passed throughout the system and are used within the CASE*Method primarily to validate that the ERD is complete. Because the ERD provides all the essential information about the data to be stored in the system and includes all the basic components of a relational database model, our discussion here is limited to it.

2.2.1 Entities

The first step in building an Entity/Relationship Diagram is the definition of entities, the basic *things* in a system about which the user wants to track information. If there's something that you are interested in storing information about, it's an entity. Employees, purchase orders, requisitions, customers, products, and organizations could, for example, all be entities. Notice that in each of these cases, there is something interesting to record about the entity: An employee's phone number, the date of a purchase order, the individual who authorized a requisition, the salesman assigned to a customer, the price of a product, and the manager of an organization. The existence of such information is a sure sign that something is an entity. The important entities in a system are referred to as the *major entities*.

Generally, a system will also include several *minor entities*, whose identities are often less obvious than those of the major entities discussed above. These entities represent not the major components of the system, but rather those data elements that are driven by a list of valid values. For example, perhaps the most common minor entity is the STATE entity. Because our system will include addresses, we would like to store something about each state, namely the two-letter state code and the full name of the state. By storing a table of this information in the database, we will be able to provide the name for a given state code as well as ensure that a state code is valid. Another example might be a TRANSACTION TYPE entity, which would include a code that describes the method of payment for a customer purchase as well as a description of that code. Quite often, minor entities are not included in the ERD unless they apply specifically to the application. For example, while the STATE entity may not appear in an ERD, the TRANSACTION TYPE entity will. Note that if states were an integral part of the application (a demographics application, for example), then the STATE entity is a major entity and should appear in the ERD.

In an ERD, an entity is depicted by a rounded rectangle with the capitalized, singular entity name in the center. Figure 2.1 shows how some of the entities from our data model would appear in an ERD.

2.2.2 Attributes

Entity names and rounded rectangles by themselves do not suffice to properly depict the data in a given system. Each entity must be defined in detail. To do this, we list each entity's *attributes*, the individual data elements that describe the entity. In the examples above, we saw that we might like to track information about a customer. The entity would be called CUSTOMER, and its attributes might include the name of the customer, the date the customer was obtained, the customer's telephone number, and so on. Every entity has attributes—in fact, an entity is actually defined by its attributes.

Each attribute in a data model is defined by the entity that it describes and the set of appropriate values that it may assume. This set of values is called the *domain* of the attribute. It is important not to confuse domain with *datatype*. The domain is the set of valid values for an attribute, while the datatype describes the way those values will physi-

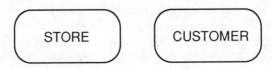

Figure 2.1 Sample MegaMarket entities

cally be stored. So, although a state code attribute and a first name attribute might both be stored in the database as characters, the set of valid first names is not the same as the set of valid state codes. This concept of domains is important for two reasons. First, if we want to compare the values of two attributes, their domains must intersect. Physically, we can compare any two values of the same datatype, but logically, we don't want to compare state codes and first names because such a comparison has no meaning. Even if someone has a first name of MD or CA and the comparison succeeds physically, it means nothing logically. Second, the domain of an attribute often helps us validate a value by comparing against all possible values. In the case of states, this is easy because the entire domain contains only 50 distinct values. This does not, of course, apply to all domains. But remember that although defining all of the distinct values for the first name domain is impractical, the domain still exists in a logical sense as "the set of all valid first names." We will present some conventions for choosing domains in Section 4.5. At this point, it is only important to understand that an entity is defined by its attributes and an attribute is defined by its domain and the entity that it describes.

After all of the entities have been identified, detailed attribute lists are produced. These attribute lists are generally not part of the ERD, although it is not uncommon to list some of the attributes directly on the entities themselves. In our model, we have simply listed the attributes for each entity in outline form (see Figure 2.5). In older physical file-based systems, this portion of the model was referred to as the file or record layout.

2.2.3 Relationships

The third step in building an ERD is defining the relationships between entities. In any system, virtually every entity will be related to the others in some way. We need to store information about these relationships in the database. For example, we've seen already that a customer can purchase something in a store; this means that there is a relationship between the STORE entity and the CUSTOMER entity. Once a relationship like this one is recognized, its type must be determined. There are three types of relationships: *one-to-one*, *one-to-many*, and *many-to-many*. These reflect exactly what their names suggest—how many of one entity are related to another entity. Using our customer example from above, we might say, "Each store may be visited by one and only one

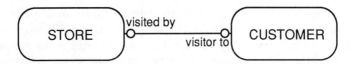

Figure 2.2 One-to-one relationship

customer and each customer may visit one and only one store." This, of
course, would be a one-to-one relationship. It is depicted in the ERD with
a single line running between the two entities along with a textual
description of the relationship. The relationship can be further qualified
by using a small circle on the line to represent that the relationship is
optional—to say "each customer *may* visit one and only one store" rather
than "each customer *must* visit one and only one store." (We refer to this
type of relationship as a MAY BE relationship.) A one-to-one relationship between customers and stores is depicted in Figure 2.2.

One-to-one relationships are very rare but they do occur. The relationship between customers and stores is actually not one-to-one—we would
certainly hope that not just one but rather many, many customers can
visit each store. An actual one-to-one relationship might exist some-
where else in our application. For example, each of the employees in a
MegaMarket store is given a locker in which they can keep their personal
belongings. Each employee may use one and only one locker and each
locker must be used by one and only one employee. Although this one-to-
one relationship actually exists, we aren't tracking any information
about lockers, so you'll notice that it is not depicted in our diagrams.

The second and most common relationship type is one-to-many. In this
case, we might say, "Each customer may visit one and only one store
while each store may be visited by many customers." So, for each store,
there are many customers. One-to-many relationships like this one are
depicted by a single line that branches into many lines as can be seen in
Figure 2.3.

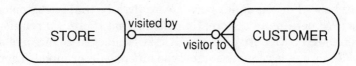

Figure 2.3 One-to-many relationship

This one-to-many relationship more fully describes the actual relationship between customers and stores, but is still not complete, since each customer should be able to visit more than one store. An actual one-to-many relationship in our application exists between the stores and the employees because each employee may work in one and only one store while each store must be staffed by one or more employees.

The third relationship type is many-to-many. With this we could say, "Each customer may visit one or more stores and each store may be visited by one or more customers." This is not an uncommon situation at all; in fact, this is the actual nature of the relationship between customers and stores in our model. A many-to-many relationship is diagrammed as shown in Figure 2.4.

2.3 Our Data Model

Given an Entity/Relationship Diagram and list of attributes, it should be relatively easy to understand the various data elements in a system and how they are related. They should, in a way, be self-explanatory. Figure 2.5 contains a subset of the attribute list for our application and Figure 2.6 shows the full Entity/Relationship Diagram. These two should fully describe the various pieces of information that we plan to store in the database.

By simply taking a look at our ERD, you should be able to glean at least the following information, if not more:

- Each supplier produces one or more shipments for our business and can be classified by many inventory classifications.
- Each shipment is sent to one warehouse and is made up of many inventory items.

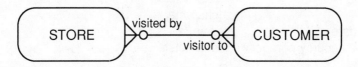

Figure 2.4 Many-to-many relationship

FACILITY

Facility number	number	(PK)
Name	character	
Address street1	character	
Address street2	character	
Address city	character	
Address state	character	
Address zip	character	
Phone number	character	
Fax number	character	
Number of customers	number	
Square footage	number	

INVENTORY ITEM

Item number	number	(PK)
Item comment	character	

SUPPLIER

Supplier number	number	(PK)
Name	character	
Address street1	character	
Address street2	character	
Address city	character	
Address state	character	
Address zip	character	
Phone number	character	
Fax number	character	

EMPLOYEE

Employee number	number	(PK)
Last name	character	
First name	character	
Middle initial	character	
Userid	character	
Title	character	
Hire date	date	
Social security number	character	

Figure 2.5 Attribute list

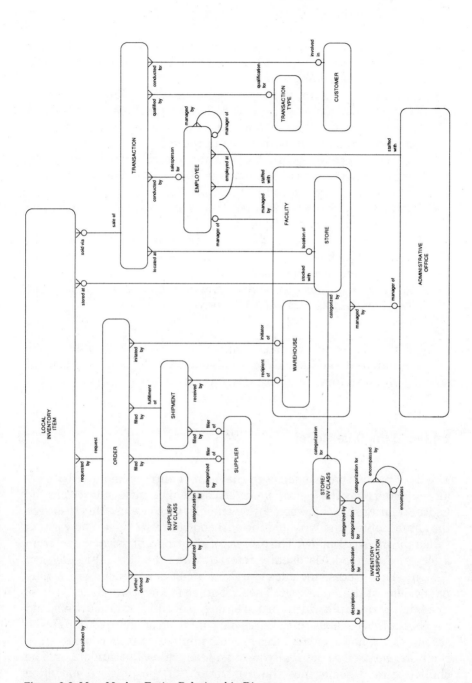

Figure 2.6 MegaMarket Entity Relationship Diagram

- Each inventory item is classified by an inventory classification, is sold in a transaction, and is stored in a facility which is either a warehouse or a store.
- Each facility is managed by one administrative office.
- Each transaction might involve many inventory items, but is classified by one transaction type and has one customer, one employee, and one store involved in the sale.
- Each employee works in either a facility (store or warehouse) or an administrative office and is managed by another employee.
- Each facility is managed by one employee.
- Each administrative office manages many stores and warehouses and employs many employees.
- Each store can be classified by many different inventory classifications and, as a facility, can house many inventory items. Each store also can have several transactions.
- Each customer may be involved in more than one transaction, but a transaction has only one customer.

The ERD will not only help us document our system and validate our understanding of the user's requirements, but also aid us when we actually sit down and create our database structures.

2.4 Using the Data Model

The data model that we depict in the form of entities and attributes is also referred to as the *logical model* of a system because it describes the logical relationships between data elements. Once we use this to design the actual tables that will hold the data, however, we have a new model called the *physical model*. The process of creating a physical model from a logical data model is usually referred to as the "logical-to-physical design." This process includes two separate stages, which may or may not be done at the same time. The first stage follows established "rules" in a fairly straightforward way to refine the entities, relationships, and attributes into database structures (i.e. *tables*, *views*, and *columns*). The second stage, however, requires specific implementation choices, since the rules we use are not really hard and fast rules, but guidelines. The challenge (and sometimes the frustration) of the physical modeling process lies in these choices.

The derivation of database tables from an ERD is a three-step process. First, *each entity will become a table*. Most of the columns for the table have been defined through the attributes. One column in particular, however, will play a special role in the use of the table because it will uniquely identify each row in the table. This is called the *primary key*. This key may be comprised of more than one column, but it must be unique for each row in the table. Occasionally a primary key for an entity is obvious and already exists. If you are absolutely certain that this key is always unique, and that it will not change over time, then you should use it. It is our preference, however, to use system-generated numerical keys whenever possible because unique values are easily created and no integrity problems arise when the old coding scheme changes.

Second, entities joined by *one-to-one relationships may be combined into a single table*. Since for each row in one table there is exactly one row in the other table, the two can be combined into one larger table. Although it is sometimes justified to keep the two tables separate to maintain a logical breakdown of the data, this is generally not recommended for performance reasons. This is based on the assumption that when you go after a record in one table, you will want to see the related information in the other table. ORACLE uses slightly more time to retrieve information from two tables than to retrieve it from one. So, if you want to see all of the information together anyway, why not store it all in one table where it can be accessed more quickly?

Third, *many-to-many relationships must be broken into three tables*. There is no way to represent many-to-many relationships in just two tables because every row in a table must be unique. If we tried to represent our CUSTOMER to STORE relationship in two tables, we would have to have one customer record in the customer table for each store that that customer visits. This means that one customer would appear in the customer table several times. It is a basic rule of relational theory that no rows in a table be duplicated this way. So, to represent many-to-many relationships, a third table, called an *intersection table*, is added. In the intersection table, data is stored about the relationship between the two entities rather than about the entities themselves. Figure 2.7 shows how the many-to-many is thus broken into two one-to-many relationships.

It is not unusual to discover that the intersection table represents an entity in and of itself—that there is something about the intersection that you want to track. In our model, for example, the intersection between CUSTOMER and STORE is an entity that we call TRANSAC-TION. A transaction represents a customer/store relationship and

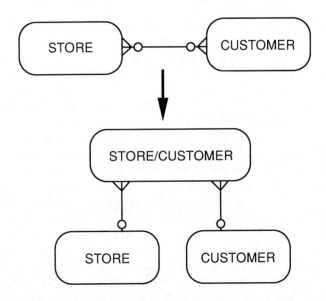

Figure 2.7 Representing many-to-many relationships

carries specific information of its own such as the amount, date, and salesperson, that we would like to record. Therefore, it becomes not just an intersection table but an entity as well.

Having removed the one-to-one and many-to-many relationships, we are left with tables joined only by one-to-many relationships. On an ERD, all relationships were represented by lines. In the tables, however, something more tangible, called a *foreign key*, is necessary to represent a relationship. Foreign keys occur when the primary key of one table is listed as a column in another table. So, for each record in the transaction table, we list the primary key of the store involved in the transaction. Since the same store can be listed in the transaction table several times with different customers, but each transaction only has one store listed, we see that the one-to-many relationship is preserved. Foreign key assignments are made based on the ERD by following a simple rule: The primary key of the "one" end of the relationship is stored as a foreign key in the "many" end of the relationship. So, in Figure 2.7, we would place the primary keys of both STORE and CUSTOMER into the TRANSAC-TION table as foreign keys. Such a combination of two foreign keys will usually become the primary key for the intersection table.

Next, we define each table in detail by using its primary key, attributes, and foreign keys as columns. In Section 3.3, we will discuss the syntax required to actually create an ORACLE table with these columns. We will also see that we can enforce our relational rules by creating tables that prohibit blank or duplicate primary keys. This will be the first step toward guaranteeing that the data we store in our database is valid.

Now that we have completed our data model, we can begin to implement our application. However, we cannot build any SQL*Forms applications until we make several important decisions. Until now, we have been looking only at the high-level, theoretical aspects of developing our database. Before continuing, however, we must consider some issues that apply specifically to our application.

2.5 Going Beyond the Data Model

The result of the first stage of physical design is a model that implements the logical design without any modification. Although this may seem acceptable and even desirable, in reality it is neither. In fact, implementing the pure logical model directly from this stage often results in an application that performs poorly. How, then, do we get from this logical design to an actual application? There are many different ways to make to this jump, but ultimately they all result in a physical design. For example, many people choose to prototype the application based on the logical design, making design changes whenever necessary based on the problems they encounter during implementation. The result of this process is indeed a physical design. We prefer to approach physical design in a more organized fashion, however. By carefully looking at the logical model and the physical implications, we use our experience to find problem areas and we make modifications to the model before any applications are built. In this way, we produce a physical model based on careful consideration of the logical design and the physical constraints rather than a physical model based on "fixes" to quick and dirty application development. (Despite this approach, we think that prototyping can be a valuable tool. We generally use it only to test specific solutions to problems that we have not encountered.) In this section, we will describe some of the decisions that we made while moving from the logical design to the physical design of our application.

There are many junctures in the process where we need to make choices. These choices will directly affect the difficulty of implementing and the overall performance of the application. We try to make the right choices by thinking carefully about the actual application, perhaps even creating realistic sample data in handwritten versions of the tables. We concentrate on two main areas: The complexity of the SQL required for typical requests (made via SQL*Plus or other reporting tools) and the operation and feasibility of the SQL*Forms applications. In short, we need to know how the application will be used. We need to know the distribution and amount of data and we must always keep sight of performance and flexibility. And finally, in some cases, we make an intuitive decision based on our experience.

2.5.1 Table relationships in the physical model

The physical design of the Inventory Management data model was very typical. We had many decisions to make and we used a combination of instinct and knowledge to make our choices. Our first consideration was the FACILITY entity pictured in Figure 2.8.

The FACILITY entity encloses two *subentities*, STORE and WARE-HOUSE. Although a store and a warehouse are very similar (which is why they are both modeled as FACILITY entities), each has specific attributes. For instance, we are interested in the number of customers that patronize a given store but for a warehouse we are concerned with the overall square footage.

So how do we *physically represent subentities* like store and warehouse? Should we create two tables, one for stores and one for warehouses, or should we make one table for both? If we decide on one table, how will we know whether a facility is a store or a warehouse? The relative merits of these alternatives depend on the relationships between the facility table and other tables. For instance, the SHIPMENT table is related ONLY to a warehouse, and the TRANSACTION table is related ONLY to a store, but the EMPLOYEE table is related to BOTH a store or a warehouse.

With one table, the BOTH relationship can be represented with a simple query, or question. The ONLY relationships, however, require first checking a "facility type" to produce a subset of ONLY stores or ONLY warehouses. This subset may be selected by a stored SQL statement (in a view) or via real time SQL within the applications. We must also take the time to validate the data entered into columns relating ONLY to a specific facility type by checking that the facility type entered is correct. These additional validations are usually enforced by the application. We could meet this particular need by validating

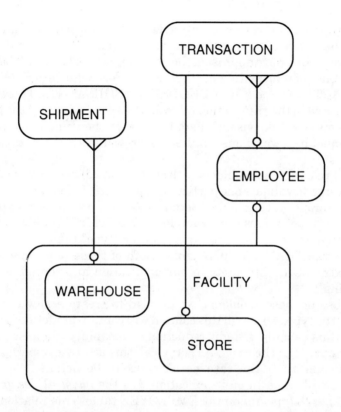

Figure 2.8 The FACILITY entity

columns based on the facility type. We could also create two separate applications, one for stores and one for warehouses.

Using two tables, on the other hand, facilitates the ONLY relationships. However, the BOTH relationship becomes very difficult. According to the rules of relational theory, a foreign key must always describe one primary key. Yet, in this scenario the foreign key of EMPLOYEE implies two different primary keys (to WAREHOUSE and STORE), a clear violation of the relational rules.

For our purposes, we decided that this particular rule is important, so we chose to create one table for the FACILITY entity. Now we have one more question to answer. How do we indicate the "type" of a FACILITY (store or warehouse)? An obvious solution would be to create a column with predefined values, perhaps "S" and "W," which would be hard-coded into the application rather than retrieved at run-time from a look-up table. The rules of relational databases denounce the use of such "indicators." In a pure approach, the determination of a type is based on the existence of information in other tables. For instance, a STORE has TRANSACTIONs and a WAREHOUSE has SHIPMENTs. Therefore, if there is a row in the transaction table for the specific facility, the facility must be a store. Likewise, if there is a row in the shipment table, the facility must be a warehouse. If there is a row in both, the data must be corrupt.

There are two basic problems with such strict adherence to relational theory. First, to validate one particular type (store, for instance) we must query one or more other tables. Second, every time a row is inserted into one of the "type" tables (for example, the SHIPMENT table) we must ensure that rows do not exist in the other "type" table or tables (for example, the TRANSACTION table). Both of these requirements will mean extra SQL statements in our application and therefore slower processing.

Because of these problems, we decided to create a new column to indicate the type. Although this column will contain predefined codes as values, thus causing a slight reduction in flexibility, the performance benefits outweigh the costs. As is typical, this is a case of performance versus flexibility. In this case, performance is the victor.

Another dilemma in our application was the *physical design of the "either/or" relationship* on the EMPLOYEE table. This relationship is depicted in Figure 2.9.

We can implement this relationship by creating two different columns, one representing the FACILITY relationship and one representing the ADMINISTRATIVE OFFICE relationship. Since only one of these relationships can exist, only one of these columns would have a value. This integrity constraint would be enforced within the application. A second implementation strategy is to create one column for both relationships and an indicator column to identify the relationship (to FACILITY or to ADMINISTRATIVE OFFICE). This option, as with the FACILITY entity options, requires one foreign key to denote two different primary keys. Since this breaks an important rule without offering significant performance benefits, we chose the two-column solution.

The management relationships between employees and facilities demand the next set of decisions. There are two distinct relationships, one for the manager of other employees and another for the manager of a facility (store or warehouse). These relationships are shown in Figure 2.10. *Controlling and validating relationships* like these require addi-

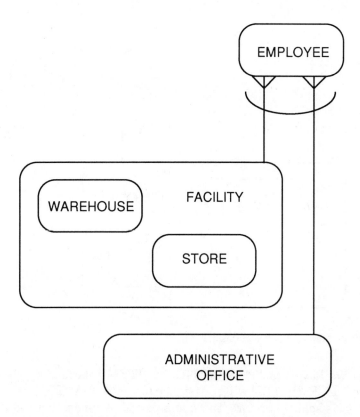

Figure 2.9 Either/or relationship

tional consideration because there are potential integrity issues. For instance, must the manager of a facility work at the facility (as determined by the relationship between EMPLOYEE and FACILITY)? And does it make sense for one employee to be subordinate to another further down the management hierarchy?

The details for these relationships are not part of the data model, so they require additional information from the end-user. For our application the constraints of the relationship are contained in the specifications for the SQL*Forms applications that will manage the EMPLOYEE and FACILITY tables. Note that these constraints are not automatically enforced by SQL*Plus or any other Oracle tool. Chapter 5 provides more details on these specifications and integrity issues.

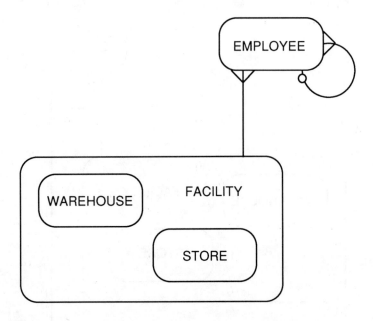

Figure 2.10 Management relationships

Next we have the TRANSACTION to ITEM relationship shown in Figure 2.11. Each ITEM will be assigned to a TRANSACTION only when the item is sold. Therefore, there is a period of time when the item is sitting on the shelf in the store (or the warehouse). This relationship does not appear difficult until we consider the operation of the application. How will the operator want the application to look and operate? He

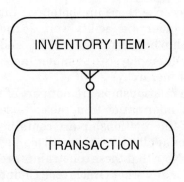

Figure 2.11 Transaction/item relationship

(probably a cashier) would typically want to record the purchase of several existing items and would not be overly concerned with the concept of a transaction. The operator would use the form much as a data entry form.

This is an important nuance. SQL*Forms requires that a record first be selected before it can be updated. Therefore, to record the transaction number, the operator must first query each item individually. This requirement would make the application extremely cumbersome. You can see from this example that *the application will sometimes drive the design* of the database. We believe that this is acceptable as long as the important relational rules and the integrity of the database are not violated in the quest for functionality and maintainability.

We decided to resolve this issue by refining the database tables. Following the rules we placed the transaction number into the INVENTORY ITEM table and we added the inventory item number to the TRANSACTION table. We also added this latter column to the primary key for the TRANSACTION table (the combination of transaction number and inventory item number are unique). Both of these changes do not affect the logical model, though they do bend the rules.

While considering the application needs, we should also examine the ORDER table. Each satisfied order is composed of many individual items, but the items are received in bulk. Although our data model properly represents this, we should think about how we will "create" separate INVENTORY ITEMs from one satisfied order. We decided that this requirement can probably be handled through SQL*Forms without changing the current design. Since we know the number of items and the appropriate primary key information, we can develop SQL*Forms application code to create the necessary items. Chapter 5 provides all of the detailed information for this process. Although we did not need to change the data model to support this requirement, we should always think about the applications (both online and batch).

Sometimes we inadvertently have *extra, or redundant, relationships* in our data model and sometimes we intentionally add them during the logical to physical design. Study the relationships shown in Figure 2.12 between TRANSACTION and EMPLOYEE, EMPLOYEE and STORE, and TRANSACTION and STORE.

Following the first two relationships, we can determine the store where the transaction occurred (based on the employee). We can do this since an employee only works at one store. Yet it seems more intuitive that a transaction should occur at a store, rather than with an employee. So, we can either keep the logical design redundancy or eliminate it in

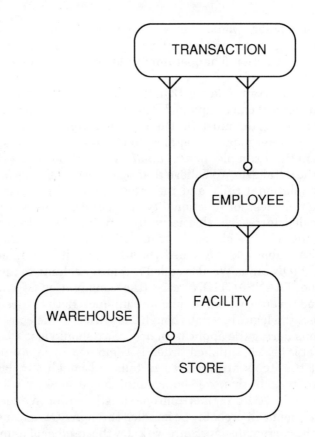

Figure 2.12 Redundant relationships

our physical design. Keeping it will require extra validation upon the entry of a transaction (checking the relationship between EMPLOYEE and STORE). Eliminating it will require a change to the data model and mean the loss of a relationship that is logically important. Some of our more sophisticated users will be utilizing the end-user tools. The intuitive nature of this relationship for our users prompted us to decide to retain the additional relationship (by keeping the STORE column in the TRANSACTION table).

Another interesting case that we have is *a table with a relationship but no other attributes*. Examine the CUSTOMER and TRANSACTION entities depicted in Figure 2.13. We might like to have the customer name, address, and buyer preferences, but we know we cannot ask for them at the time of a transaction. Imagine if every time you made a

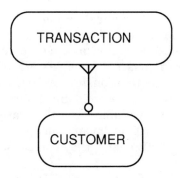

Figure 2.13 An entity with no attributes

purchase you had to spell your name and wait for a query to execute. Yet we might want to provide a mechanism for recording this sort of mailing list information, which could be gathered through surveys and other means.

This leads us to wonder whether the customer entity belongs in our model. Is it outside of the scope of an Inventory Management system? If it were, we could either expand the data model to include additional entities, thus expanding the scope, or eliminate the customer entity. In order to prevent software cost and scheduling problems, we decided that the data about customers will be handled in a future application, so we removed the customer entity.

A similar observation might be made about intersection tables that have no attributes other than the relationship (such as SUPPLIER to INVENTORY CLASS). We might think that these tables are outside of the scope of our system, but we must retain this kind of table because the relationship itself is crucial to the application.

2.5.2 Column definitions in the physical model

All the problems we have encountered so far involved complete tables and/or the relationships they hold. Now we will consider some of the more subtle decisions to be made, relating to the actual content of specific column "types."

For instance, how do we handle any "type" of *MAY BE relationship*? When we have a MAY BE, we always have a foreign key column that may be NULL. One case of this in our data model is the ITEM to STORE relationship shown in Figure 2.14.

An item may have been created in a shipment but remains in the warehouse. Therefore it has not been "assigned" to a store and the column representing the relationship is NULL. This is a problem because a NULL value can represent many different conditions. In some cases it may mean "not available." In other cases it may mean "unknown." And in still others it may mean "not applicable." Although these may seem like trivial distinctions, they can cause many integrity and programming nightmares.

For example, consider the effect of NULL values on a NUMBER column. If we attempt any type of calculation (such as addition) on that column, we must be sure to use the NVL function to get correct results. NVL temporarily replaces the NULL value with the value it represents (in the case of addition, zero). Every application program, online or batch, must contain this substitution. This leaves too much room for error, resulting in too many opportunities for report totals to be incorrect.

The alternative is to actually store the value that the NULL represents. We can accomplish this by storing zeros in number columns

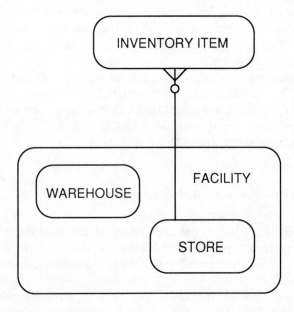

Figure 2.14 MAY BE relationship

whenever they do not contain a valid value. Although this means more storage (which nowadays is relatively cheap) and additional SQL at insert time (to set the column value to its default), it eliminates the integrity risk. In our STORE to ITEM dilemma, we can avoid the NULL foreign key by creating a special STORE value that means "still in warehouse." Then, we can use this value as our foreign key.

A second benefit of this approach, in addition to the integrity clarification, is that we reduce searches for IS NULL or IS NOT NULL. This applies to our STORE to ITEM relationship when we make requests like, "Find an available item of a specific INVENTORY TYPE." If we followed all the rules and did not create a "still in warehouse" store this request would be WHERE INVENTORY TYPE = 'some-type' AND STORE IS NULL. In ORACLE, NULL searches do not use an index. Note that an index on INVENTORY TYPE *would* still be used (for additional indexing tips refer to Chapter 8). Whenever ORACLE sees the NULL operation in the WHERE clause predicate of a SELECT statement, it assumes that an unindexed search, commonly referred to as a "full-table scan," will be the fastest access to the data. In some cases, ORACLE is correct. In others, we want to use the NULL column index (STORE in the example above). To do this we must store a value in the column, thereby also storing it in the index.

We must be careful when we consider taking this approach. It requires us to store values in a primary key that do not represent the real world (there is no actual store named "still in warehouse"). And it renders meaningless some of the other columns for the NULL representation (what is the address of our dummy store?). Keeping these concerns in mind, but recognizing the frequency of this type of request, we decided to use this method. We defined the column as NOT NULL and defined a bogus STORE to represent the NULL value.

After further consideration, though, we recognized an even more elegant solution—we decided to always store the actual location for the item. Since an item is physically located at either a store or a warehouse, we can simply store the FACILITY for an item versus only the STORE.

There are many other column "type" decisions to be made. One is the use of *multi-column primary keys*. The rules say that all prime tables must have a single column, preferably a number column, as the primary key. However, since we are storing a "meaningless" number instead of the real data, this can result in many additional *joins* (SQL queries that combine two or more tables by relating foreign and primary keys) and sequence number generations (to produce the "meaningless" number). We decided to handle this for each table on a case-by-case basis. For

Physical ERD

Notice that this final solution does not conform with our data model. In the ERD, we see that an INVENTORY ITEM is related to a STORE, not a FACILITY. Is this a flaw in the data model that should make us worry about its integrity in other places? No, it is merely an example of how the *physical* model can differ from the *logical* model. Deviations from the model are perfectly acceptable, but they should always be documented. If there are just a few small changes, they can simply be mentioned in the physical design documentation. If there are many such changes, it is often appropriate to develop a *physical ERD*. This is simply an additional ERD that shows all of the changes made during physical design. Figure 2.15 shows how we might represent this example in our logical and our physical ERDs.

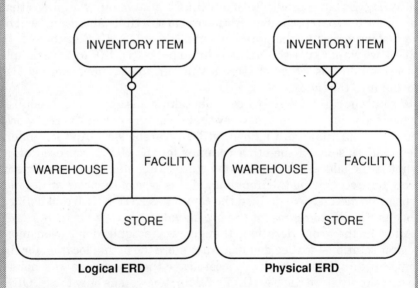

Logical ERD   **Physical ERD**

Figure 2.15 Logical ERD versus physical ERD

Remember that the physical ERD is an *additional* ERD. You should not change the logical ERD at this stage of the development.

example, in the many-to-many table SHIPMENT/INV CLASS we allowed the two foreign key columns to be the primary key of the table instead of creating an additional system-generated column.

Another consideration is the *physical storage of numbers versus characters*. Should we always store numbers as NUMBERs (ORACLE's numeric datatype)? Or should numbers be stored as CHAR (ORACLE's character datatype)? Remember when making this decision that ORACLE drops leading zeros in NUMBER columns (consider the implications when storing a zip code of 02014). To stay flexible, we chose to store everything as CHAR, unless the column will be used in calculations, since the application can enforce the "real" datatype.

A related choice is whether or not to *store "boilerplate,"* such as the hyphens in a social security number. Due to the leading zeros issue, SSN must be a CHAR column of nine positions. Perhaps all of our SQL*Forms applications that use SSN will either expect dashes in entry or format the SSN to add the dashes. In both cases the user would like to view the SSN field with dashes. If we store them in the SSN column, we would eliminate the need to format the entry at query time. Although this may yield a fairly insignificant improvement in response time, the advantage will compound with each additional column stored with boilerplate. We decided to store the boilerplate in general, but to review the costs and benefits in each case.

2.6 Conclusion

We started this chapter by defining the logical data model and quickly migrated beyond this model into the physical data model. While it is difficult to provide a generalized method for this process, we hope that we have provided markers to keep you from making a wrong turn. We admit that we must often rely on experience to make database design decisions. However, a complete understanding of the ORACLE toolkit is an important element of this experience. The next chapter focuses on one of the most powerful tools of any relational system: SQL.

3

Overview of SQL

3.1 Introduction

In this chapter, we will begin building our database. This means, of course, that we will be talking to ORACLE for the first time. Naturally, if we expect ORACLE to understand what we are saying, we must learn to speak its language. ORACLE's native language is called SQL, which is pronounced "sequel" and stands for *Structured Query Language*. In any language, there is a great difference between knowing a few phrases and being fluent. Although it is nice to know how to order a cheese omelette in French, it is hardly sufficient if you plan to live and work in Paris. The same is true with SQL. Although simply asking for all of the rows in a table may be useful once in a while, learning to ask intricate questions of ORACLE is where the real art lies. With this in mind, we hope to accomplish three things in this chapter. First, we will provide a general overview of the whole language. Second, we will show you some of the more subtle SQL constructs that make answering even the most difficult questions possible. Third, and most important, we will show you how to *use* SQL. After completing this chapter, you will not only know the constructs and syntax of SQL, but also understand its power as a tool and as a means of conveying information. In short, you will know not only know how to speak SQL, but also what to say.

Before we rush off to become poets, however, we must first learn our vocabulary. In computers, this means syntax, and SQL has a very specific syntax that must be followed. The next three sections detail the various components of a SQL statement. Taken literally, our examples will show you how to construct valid SQL statements. We encourage you, however, to look beyond the formalities of the syntax—*what* the statements do—and attempt to understand *how* the language works. In English, for example, although there are infinitely many sentences you have never actually said, you have no problem composing new sentences because you understand how the language works. We will study SQL in the same way: Rather than simply list example statements for you to plug into your own applications, we will explain how the commands are constructed so that you will have no problem building statements of your own.

Why do we need SQL? Well, very simply, ORACLE stores information. We need a way to give it new information, remove information from it, change information in it, and find out what information it contains. SQL provides us with a means of communicating these needs. Using it, we can do all of the things described above and more with ORACLE. We can add new rows to a table. We can delete rows from a table. We can modify the values in a particular column of a given row. And we can pose questions that return just the piece of information that we need. In addition, we can use SQL to create and maintain database objects (tables, views, indexes) and regulate access to our data by particular users. All of these tasks can be broken into three functional categories: *data manipulation, data definition,* and *data control.*

3.2 Data Manipulation

The most frequently used set of SQL commands are those that manipulate the data stored in ORACLE. With them, we can modify and retrieve the data stored in a table. These statements are referred to as *Data Manipulation Functions.*

3.2.1 The SELECT statement

Perhaps the most important of all the data manipulation functions is the SELECT statement. It is important because in most applications, it is used far more than anything else, and because the construction of SELECT statements can directly affect the performance of an application. One SELECT might take minutes or hours while another that returns the same result takes only seconds. These performance issues will be discussed in detail in Chapter 8, but to appreciate them, you must first understand the SELECT statement in depth. Mastering the SELECT statement is a theme throughout this book. In this section, we will discuss the basic structure and syntax variations of the statement; in later chapters we will demonstrate the versatility of the SELECT statement with real examples.

The purpose of the SELECT statement is to issue *queries* to ORACLE. In other words, a SELECT statement asks ORACLE to return a specific combination of data values from the tables in the database. These values may come from many columns, many rows, and many tables. The output of a SELECT statement is simply a set of columns and rows—not a table, per se, but data in a tabular format. Since it is easier to describe an actual table, for convenience we will refer to the output of a SELECT statement as a virtual table with the understanding that no table actually gets created by ORACLE for this output. Why the great distinction? If ORACLE actually did create a table for this output, we could perhaps go back later and examine or modify it. This is not the case. The output "table" of a SELECT does not exist in the database and has no life span beyond the execution of the SELECT statement. (We will see later how real database tables *can* be created from the output of a SELECT statement.)

To construct a SELECT statement, we must determine exactly what columns and what rows will make up the output table we wish to retrieve. Naturally, the simplest case is to ask for all of the columns and all of the rows of a table:

```
SELECT   column1, column2, column3, ..., columnN
FROM     tablename
```

The SELECT keyword in this statement is followed by the *select list*, a list of columns that should make up the output table. Since the table definition is stored in ORACLE (via the Data Dictionary), we can ask ORACLE to list the columns for us (if we are specifying all of them) by saying:

```
SELECT   *
FROM     tablename
```

ORACLE can break the asterisk down into the select list very easily.

The Asterisk

This does not need to be an all-or-none proposition—you can use an "*" as well as individual columns if you specify the table name:

```
SELECT   tablename.*, column1, column2
FROM     tablename
```

ORACLE will list all of the columns in the table and the ones you request explicitly will be listed again.

We can, of course, choose not to list *all* of the columns in a table. So, to select a particular set of columns from a particular table, you would say:

```
SELECT   column1, column3
FROM     tablename
```

This will work as long as columns 1 and 3 are both columns in the table *tablename*. So, in this way, we have begun to dictate the contents of the output table by defining exactly which columns we would like to see. In any query, we can also reference a column more specifically by preceding it with the tablename and a period (.). So, the above query could be written as:

```
SELECT   tablename.column1, tablename.column3
FROM     tablename
```

We will see that it is generally not necessary to reference columns this way, but sometimes it is essential to eliminate ambiguity. Similarly, the table can be referenced more specifically by preceding it by the userid of the table's owner (i.e. *userid.tablename.column*).

The select list in a query is our first example of *lists* in SQL. This concept is one you will see throughout the language. A list is simply an ordered set of values that is distinctly separated, usually by commas. These values can be column names, expressions, and literals (strings and numbers). We will begin to see the importance of lists below when we discuss the WHERE clause.

Since the select list only defines the columns for the *output* table, its values may or may not correspond to actual database tables. We may, for example, wish to display a literal value as a column in our output table:

```
SELECT   column1, 'HELLO', column2, 523
FROM     tablename
```

The output table for this statement will have the word HELLO and the number 523 in the second and fourth columns respectively for every row that is returned (in this case, all rows). The value that we place into a column could be even more complicated, such as an entire expression:

```
SELECT   3*(5+6)/17, column1
FROM     tablename
```

This statement will put 1.94 into the first column of each row returned by the query. Extending this idea, we can mix columns, literals, and expressions in the select list:

```
SELECT   (column1*17)+11, column2
FROM     tablename
```

For each row returned, the expression will be evaluated and placed into the appropriate columns of the output table. Expressions can also include functions. SQL includes many built-in functions that operate on columns and literals. For example, the function UPPER takes one argument, a character string, and converts each of its letters to upper-case:

```
SELECT   UPPER('Hello'), UPPER(column1)
FROM     tablename
```

This statement puts the word HELLO into the first column of our output table and the capitalized version of *column1* into the second column for each row. Functions like this one are called *single-row* functions because they operate on one row at a time. We will discuss some of the most interesting functions at various points throughout the book. A list of all of the single-row functions is available in *The SQL Language Reference Manual*, which is part of your ORACLE documentation.

The FROM clause in the SELECT statement is the only other keyword that is required. The list of tables in the FROM clause simply defines those columns that are available for use in the SELECT statement. If you want to use a column, it must be part of a table in the FROM clause. Similarly, if you do not want any columns from a table, there is no need to list the table in the FROM clause. In fact, you should *not* list a table in the FROM clause if the rest of the statement does not reference any of its columns. For example, if you wanted to evaluate the expression (3*4)+(5*6), you could put it into the select list of a query. Remember, however, that expressions in the select list get evaluated *for each row returned by the query.* Consider this statement:

```
SELECT  (3*4)+(5*6)
FROM    table_with_a_million_rows
```

It is a perfectly valid SQL statement, but it will return an output table with a million 42s in it! More important than the size of the output is the fact ORACLE will evaluate the expression separately for each of the million rows, wasting considerable time. A solution to the problem is to select the expression from a very small table, preferably one with just a single row. Since this is a common technique for evaluating expressions in the ORACLE tools, there is a special table called *DUAL* that is always available just for this purpose. DUAL exists in every ORACLE database, it is owned by the SYSTEM user, everyone has access to it, and no one can change it. It is as small as a table can get—one row and one column. Since DUAL has only one row in it, we could have answered our arithmetic question like this:

```
SELECT  (3*4)+(5*6)
FROM    SYSTEM.DUAL
```

We know how to pick the columns that we want to make up our output table, but how do we pick the rows? This is done by including a *WHERE*

SYS(TEM).DUAL

In Version 5.0 of the RDBMS, DUAL was owned only by the SYSTEM user. In Version 6.0, however, this changed and ownership of this table was given to SYS. Since so many existing applications references SYSTEM.DUAL, this was a problem. The software is now generally distributed with a copy of DUAL in the SYSTEM account as well. If, for some reason, you do not have SYSTEM.DUAL in your Version 6.0 database, we recommend that you create one rather than changing all of your applications or creating synonyms that point to SYS.DUAL.

clause in the SELECT statement. This portion of the SELECT statement is also referred to as the *predicate* of the statement. In the predicate, we specify one or more conditions that may or may not be true for a row in the table. ORACLE will test the condition for each row in the table specified in the FROM clause; if the condition is satisfied, then the row will be part of the output table. The syntax for a simple statement predicate is:

```
SELECT   column list
FROM     tablename
WHERE    column1 = value1
```

There is an endless list of available variations on this basic WHERE clause, so we will cover just a few of the more frequently encountered ones here. You will see more examples of interesting WHERE clauses throughout the application that we build in this book. In the example above, the expression in the WHERE clause is simply a comparison between a column in the table and some value—either another column, an expression, or some literal. This is the most common way of using WHERE. Note, however, that the WHERE clause does not have to contain any columns from the tables in the FROM clause. Similarly, the columns in the WHERE clause need not be the same as the columns in the select list. For example, in the following query, the select list has nothing to do with the FROM clause and nothing to do with the WHERE clause:

```
SELECT   3+4
FROM     tablename
WHERE    75+(13–2) = 86
```

Although this statement is perfectly valid, remember that it will return "7" for all of the rows in the table that satisfy the WHERE clause. And which rows satisfy the WHERE clause? All of them, of course, because for each row, 75+(13–2) is equal to 86. So, the table that we use makes no difference, except for the number of 7s that will be returned. (Remember that for statements like this one, SYSTEM.DUAL is generally used because it contains only one row.)

The expressions in the WHERE clause can utilize standard logical operators as well as some interesting other operators such as BE-TWEEN, LIKE, and IS NULL. The BETWEEN operator lets you compare a value against a range:

```
SELECT   column list
FROM     tablename
WHERE    column1 BETWEEN 1 AND 10
```

This comparison is inclusive, so the values 1 or 10 would satisfy this example. LIKE is used to perform character pattern matching with '%' and '_' used as wildcard characters. The '%' wildcard will match any number of characters and the '_' wildcard will match any single character:

```
SELECT   column list
FROM     tablename
WHERE    column1 LIKE 'A%W_R_'
```

Finally, IS NULL lets you check for columns that have no value stored in them:

```
SELECT   column list
FROM     tablename
WHERE    column1 IS NULL
```

There are several other operators like these and they are also listed in *The SQL Language Reference Manual*.

The evaluation of WHERE clause expressions that use these operators can be reversed as well by using the keyword NOT. With all of the operators except IS NULL, the word NOT is simply placed in front of the operator name: WHERE *column1* NOT BETWEEN 1 AND 10 or WHERE *column1* NOT LIKE 'A%W_R_'. With IS NULL, the word NOT is placed differently: WHERE *column1* IS NOT NULL. With these operators and and the keyword NOT, you can test for all kinds of different conditions.

Any of the expressions in a WHERE clause can be joined together with the set operators AND and OR. So, for a given row to be part of the output table, it must fulfill this condition AND that condition OR some other condition. For example:

```
SELECT   column list
FROM     tablename
WHERE    (column1 = value1
  AND     column2 > value2 + 17)
  OR      column3 + column4 = 31
```

We've parenthesized these expressions to force the precedence that we have in mind. In this case, the parentheses are unnecessary because AND has higher precedence than OR anyway. As always, it is recommended that you over-parenthesize rather than under-parenthesize.

As we will see when we start building more sophisticated queries in our application, the WHERE clause can also contain expressions that include functions and even other queries. For example, the following query illustrates how you can use a function and *nested select* statement to find the particular answer you need:

```
SELECT   column list
FROM     tablename1
WHERE    SUBSTR(tablename1.column1, 1, 4) = 'ABCD'
   AND   tablename1.column2 =
   (SELECT tablename2.column3
    FROM    tablename2
    WHERE   tablename2.column4 = 'WXYZ')
```

In this statement, the value that is returned by the inner SELECT statement (also referred to as a *sub-query*) will be compared to the column value of the main SELECT statement. The main query checks each row to see if the WHERE clause is true, or, in this case, if the value of a column is the same as the value returned by a SELECT statement. This query will only work if the nested SELECT statement returns a single row because it would be impossible for one column value to be equal to many column values. To solve this problem, let's look back for a moment at the concept of a list that we discussed briefly above.

Remember that a query returns a list of column values for each row. The IN operator gives us a means of comparing a single value to a list of values to see if any match. Because ORACLE handles lists rather generically, these two types of lists can be compared when we use nested SELECT statements in a WHERE clause. If we say,

```
SELECT   column list
FROM     tablename1
WHERE    tablename1.column1 IN
   (SELECT tablename2.column2
    FROM    tablename2)
```

we can compare a column value (tablename1.column1) to each row returned by the nested SELECT statement. We can do the same type of comparison with column lists as well:

```
SELECT  column list
FROM     tablename1
WHERE  (tablename1.column1, tablename2.column2) IN
   (SELECT tablename2.column3, tablename2.column4
    FROM     tablename2)
```

In this example, we have compared a list of values to a list of lists of values!

Another way that the nested SELECT statement can be used is in the form of a *correlated sub-query*. A correlated sub-query is just like a regular sub-query except that it references the table in the outer query. So, for each row in the outer query, the inner query is executed again referencing the current row of the outer query. To eliminate ambiguity, always reference columns by their table name in correlated sub-queries:

```
SELECT  column list
FROM     tablename1
WHERE  tablename1.column1 =
   (SELECT tablename2.column2
    FROM     tablename2
    WHERE  tablename1.column3 = tablename2.column4)
```

Although we have only scratched the surface of the WHERE clause here, in general, the WHERE clause is the most important part of a SELECT statement. What is important at this point is that you understand its purpose and its many basic forms. Throughout this book, you will see all sorts of different WHERE clauses. Take the time to examine each one carefully to see exactly how it works.

We hope these examples have given you some insight into exactly how ORACLE goes about processing a query. First, it examines the statement predicate (its WHERE clause), validating that the columns referenced are part of the tables in the FROM clause. Next, based on the conditions in the predicate, it decides which rows will be part of the output table. Then, for each such row, it breaks down the expressions in the select list by substituting column names with the appropriate values from the row and evaluating any functions. (As we have seen, it doesn't matter if the expressions do not reference any columns.) The final result is an output table consisting of one column for each expression in the select list and one row for each row that satisfies the predicate.

3.2.2 The INSERT statement

The second of the data manipulation functions is the INSERT statement. We use the INSERT statement to add new data to a table. With a single statement, we can add one or more rows to a given table. We can insert into only one table with a single INSERT command.

The basic format for an INSERT statement is:

INSERT INTO *tablename*
VALUES (*column1 value, column2 value, ..., columnN value*)

This format requires that all columns from the table have corresponding values in the *values list*, or the portion of the statement enclosed in parentheses. Once again, we see the concept of a list in a SQL statement. Here the elements of the list correspond to the columns as they are defined in the table. Lists in SQL statements almost always have corresponding lists with the same number of elements, each matching one-to-one. For example, an alternate form of the insert statement allows you the flexibility of modifying the list that matches the values list:

INSERT INTO *tablename (column1, column2, ..., columnN)*
VALUES (*column1 value, column2 value, ..., columnN value*)

In this form, not every column in the table is part of the values list since a *column list* has been specified. This allows a row to be inserted that does not have a value for every column. Notice, though, that the column list and the values list must match one-to-one and the corresponding elements in each list must be of the same datatype (as defined in the CREATE TABLE statement which we will discuss below).

The concept of lists is especially important because it can also be usefully applied to the SELECT statement. As we saw above, the SELECT statement returns a list of column values (which we have been describing as a table for convenience), so we can use the following syntax to insert from one table into another:

```
INSERT INTO tablename1 (column1, column2, ...)
SELECT  columna, columnb, ...
FROM    tablename2
```

Just like the other INSERT statements, this statement contains two lists that match one-to-one. As the rows from the output table generated by the SELECT statement are returned, they are inserted into the table listed in the INSERT clause.

You should be growing familiar with this idea of breaking a statement into its components. Just as English sentences can be broken into nouns, verbs, adjectives, etc., an INSERT statement can be broken into the insert clause, the column list, and the values list. This allows us to see more clearly how different components can be interchanged to produce new SQL statements—just as we substituted one list for another in this example.

3.2.3 The UPDATE statement

The third important data manipulation function is the UPDATE statement. The UPDATE statement is like the INSERT statement in that it modifies the data in a table. The difference, of course, is that the UPDATE statement modifies existing rows rather than adding new ones. As with inserting, only one table can be updated in a single statement.

Since UPDATE modifies rows already in a table, it must first find the rows. Thus, the UPDATE statement is really composed of two parts: the columns with their new values, and a WHERE clause that determines which rows are to be updated:

```
UPDATE tablename
SET     column1 = value1, column2 = value2, ...
WHERE   some condition is true
```

This statement says, then, that for each row in table tablename that satisfies the condition in the where clause, set column1 to value1 and column2 to value2, etc. The WHERE clauses used in an UPDATE statement are just like those used in a select statement. As a matter of fact, the process for finding the rows is exactly the same. When an UPDATE statement is issued, ORACLE must first perform the equivalent of a SELECT statement to find the appropriate rows. It is important to understand that virtually any WHERE clause that works in a SELECT statement will also work in an UPDATE statement. Also remember that just as a SELECT statement with no WHERE clause returns all the rows in a table, an UPDATE statement with no WHERE clause will modify all of the rows in the table!

Notice that the SET clause of the update statement contains several comma-separated columns. What should this suggest to us? That's right—a list! We'll see lists popping up more and more throughout SQL. For example, the following statement is certainly possible:

```
UPDATE tablename1
SET (column1, column2, column3) =
  (SELECT columnA, columnB, columnC
  FROM    tablename2
  WHERE  condition_that_returns_one_row)
WHERE some_condition
```

Again, looking for these alternate ways of combining SQL statement components will help you increase your understanding of how SQL operates.

3.2.4 The DELETE statement

The fourth of the data manipulation functions in SQL, the DELETE statement, is the final way of modifying data. While INSERT adds rows and UPDATE changes rows, DELETE removes rows. You cannot delete just part of a row—to do this, you must update some of the columns in the row to NULL. So all that we must specify in a DELETE statement are the rows to delete and the table from which to delete them:

```
DELETE FROM tablename
WHERE some condition is true
```

As always, we specify a particular set of rows through the use of a WHERE clause. In this case, each row that satisfies the conditions in the WHERE clause will be removed from the table. And since omitting the WHERE clause implies "all of the rows," a DELETE statement without a WHERE clause will remove all of the data from the table. The

WHERE clause can be as simple or complex as you like. All of the considerations mentioned in the construction of SELECT statement predicates apply to DELETE statements as well.

3.2.5 Commit and rollback

Whenever you issue a data manipulation command that actually changes the information in the database, the change will appear to you right away. In other words, when you insert a row into a table and then immediately select from the table, the row will be there. Anyone else, however, who is looking at that table, will not see your changes until you explicitly save them to the database. This process is called *committing* the change. None of your changes actually affect the database until you commit them. If, on the other hand, you decide that you do not want your changes saved to the database, you can perform a *rollback*. This essentially tells ORACLE to forget about all of the changes that were made since your last commit.

The concept of commit and rollback is based on the idea of a *logical transaction*. When we issue a data manipulation statement, we are performing a *physical transaction*. Each change is a transaction. Generally, we might think that we would like to see each transaction committed to the database immediately so that everyone could use this data. A problem arises, however, when we consider a logical transaction that is made up of more than one physical transaction. The most commonly used example of this is a transfer of money from checking to savings. Although this involves two physical transactions (delete from checking, insert into savings), the whole transfer represents one logical transaction because we don't want just one of these two to occur. If, for example, you performed the deletion, committed it, and then the system came down, what happens to the accounts? Money was removed from checking but not added to savings. If, on the other hand, you deleted the money from checking but did not perform a commit until after the insertion into savings, then everything would be okay. This is because ORACLE automatically performs a rollback if the database comes down. (Actually, ORACLE performs a rollback when the database comes back up.) So the moral is to commit your data only after a *logical* transaction is complete.

3.3 Data Definition

The data definition statements in SQL are used to create, modify, and delete database objects such as tables, indexes, and views. The syntax for these statements is relatively straightforward. In most applications, these statements play a small role because they are used only at the beginning when the database is created. Their performance, for example, is usually of little concern because they are not run on a regular basis. One thing to keep mind is that these statements automatically perform a commit when executed, so that any outstanding transactions are made permanent.

The first of the data definition commands that concerns us is the CREATE statement. This one keyword is actually used to create tables, views, and synonyms. The CREATE TABLE statement takes a table name and a column list:

```
CREATE TABLE tablename
(column1 datatype1, column2 datatype2, ...)
```

The most commonly used datatypes are CHAR, NUMBER, DATE, and LONG. Notice that the column list is a comma-separated list of column definitions much like the lists we have seen before. So, if we want to create a new table from the output table of a SELECT statement, we can just substitute the list:

```
CREATE TABLE tablename1
AS SELECT   column1, column2, ...
FROM        tablename2
WHERE       some condition is true
```

This is in fact the only means of copying a table in ORACLE. Notice, however, that the new table need not match the old one exactly; we can control exactly which columns and which rows are used and in what order the columns appear. So if, for some reason, we wanted to reorder the columns in a table definition, we would have to do it like this (remember that if we leave out the WHERE clause, all rows will be copied):

```
CREATE TABLE tablename1
AS SELECT column5, column2, column7
FROM tablename2
```

RENAME

Quite often, ORACLE users use this method to rename tables—they CREATE a new table based on the old one and then DROP the original. There is, however, a RENAME command available in SQL that can be used to rename tables:

```
RENAME old_table_name new_table_name
```

The CREATE command can also be used to create *views*. Views are database objects that are based on the output tables of a SELECT statement. When we associate a view with a SELECT statement, we can then treat the output table as if it were a table itself. Remember that the table does not exist per se (there is no copy of the data), but the view can be queried as though it were a table. To create a view we say:

```
CREATE VIEW viewname
AS SELECT   column1, column2, column3, ..., columnN
FROM        tablename
WHERE       some condition is true
```

(Any SELECT statement that does not include an ORDER BY clause will work.) The new view can be queried as though it were a table, and when that happens, ORACLE creates a new SELECT statement that combines the two queries and operates on the original table.

The third object we can make with the CREATE command is a *synonym*. A synonym is an alias that we can use to reference other database objects. For example, if a user gave you access to his table called *tablename*, you would have to reference it in the following manner:

```
SELECT *
FROM    userid.tablename
```

Since this can be cumbersome, you might decide to create a synonym called *tablename*:

```
CREATE SYNONYM tablename FOR userid.tablename
```

Now, whenever you refer to *tablename*, ORACLE will use the synonym to reference the appropriate table. The database administrator can also create public synonyms, which let everyone use common names for given tables in given accounts.

Each of the three database objects that we have discussed can be removed from ORACLE with the DROP command:

DROP TABLE *tablename*

DROP VIEW *viewname*

DROP SYNONYM *synonymname*

Once a database object is dropped, it is gone. There is no way to get it back, so make sure you maintain backups of your tables and views if you can't risk losing them.

3.4 Data Control

The third type of SQL statement that we will discuss now is *data control*. Data control statements allow you to control access to specific database objects or the entire database itself. One of the most significant data control statements is the *GRANT* command, which is used to regulate the degree of access available to a particular user.

The first version of the GRANT command allows you to provide various types of access to a particular table:

GRANT [SELECT, UPDATE, INSERT, DELETE, ALTER, DROP]
ON *tablename*
TO *userid*

You can specify one or more of the options in the brackets for a given table. It is also possible to specify that you would like to give the other user permission to grant access to others, as follows:

GRANT [SELECT, UPDATE, INSERT, DELETE, ALTER, DROP]
ON *tablename*
TO *userid*
WITH GRANT OPTION

This will not, of course, allow the user to grant a level of access that he does not possess. Finally, if you specify the word PUBLIC in the TO clause in place of a userid, then everyone can access the table. The REVOKE command is used to remove any level of access given to a user through a GRANT statement.

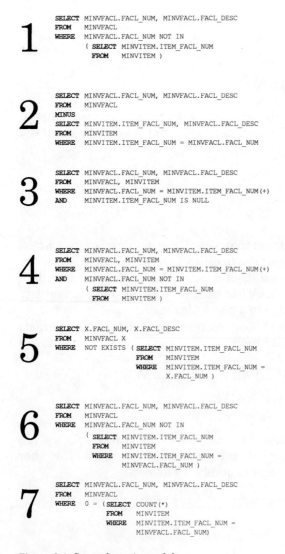

```
1   SELECT  MINVFACL.FACL_NUM, MINVFACL.FACL_DESC
    FROM    MINVFACL
    WHERE   MINVFACL.FACL_NUM NOT IN
            ( SELECT  MINITEM.ITEM_FACL_NUM
              FROM    MINVITEM )


2   SELECT  MINVFACL.FACL_NUM, MINVFACL.FACL_DESC
    FROM    MINVFACL
    MINUS
    SELECT  MINVITEM.ITEM_FACL_NUM, MINVFACL.FACL_DESC
    FROM    MINVITEM
    WHERE   MINVITEM.ITEM_FACL_NUM = MINVFACL.FACL_NUM


3   SELECT  MINVFACL.FACL_NUM, MINVFACL.FACL_DESC
    FROM    MINVFACL, MINVITEM
    WHERE   MINVFACL.FACL_NUM = MINVITEM.ITEM_FACL_NUM(+)
    AND     MINVITEM.ITEM_FACL_NUM IS NULL


4   SELECT  MINVFACL.FACL_NUM, MINVFACL.FACL_DESC
    FROM    MINVFACL, MINVITEM
    WHERE   MINVFACL.FACL_NUM = MINVITEM.ITEM_FACL_NUM(+)
    AND     MINVFACL.FACL_NUM NOT IN
            ( SELECT  MINVITEM.ITEM_FACL_NUM
              FROM    MINVITEM )


5   SELECT  X.FACL_NUM, X.FACL_DESC
    FROM    MINVFACL X
    WHERE   NOT EXISTS ( SELECT  MINVITEM.ITEM_FACL_NUM
                         FROM    MINVITEM
                         WHERE   MINVITEM.ITEM_FACL_NUM =
                                 X.FACL_NUM )


6   SELECT  MINVFACL.FACL_NUM, MINVFACL.FACL_DESC
    FROM    MINVFACL
    WHERE   MINVFACL.FACL_NUM NOT IN
            ( SELECT  MINVITEM.ITEM_FACL_NUM
              FROM    MINVITEM
              WHERE   MINVITEM.ITEM_FACL_NUM =
                      MINVFACL.FACL_NUM )


7   SELECT  MINVFACL.FACL_NUM, MINVFACL.FACL_DESC
    FROM    MINVFACL
    WHERE   0 = ( SELECT  COUNT(*)
                  FROM    MINVITEM
                  WHERE   MINVITEM.ITEM_FACL_NUM =
                          MINVFACL.FACL_NUM)
```

Figure 3.1 Several versions of the same query

3.5 Conclusion

This has been a whirlwind tour of SQL. If you have more detailed questions about the exact SQL syntax, you should refer to *The SQL Language Reference Manual* that is part of your ORACLE documentation. If you have questions about how to effectively use SQL, however, just keep reading because, basically, that is all there is to ORACLE application development. Throughout the rest of this book, we will be presenting all of the interesting SQL statements that we developed to complete the MegaMarket system. In fact, we will present the first one right now.

NAME	NULL?	TYPE
MINVFACL		
FACL_NUM	NOT NULL	NUMBER(10)
FACL_DESC	NOT NULL	CHAR(60)
FACL_EMPL_NUM_MGR		NUMBER(10)
FACL_OFFC_NUM_MGR	NOT NULL	NUMBER(10)
FACL_TYPE_HCV	NOT NULL	CHAR(1)
FACL_ADDR_STREET1	NOT NULL	CHAR(40)
FACL_ADDR_STREET2		CHAR(40)
FACL_ADDR_CITY	NOT NULL	CHAR(30)
FACL_ADDR_STATE	NOT NULL	CHAR(2)
FACL_ADDR_ZIP	NOT NULL	CHAR(10)
FACL_ADDR_PHONE_NUMBER		CHAR(10)
FACL_ADDR_FAX_NUMBER		CHAR(10)
FACL_NO_OF_CUSTOMERS		NUMBER(9)
FACL_SQUARE_FOOTAGE		NUMBER(8)
MINVITEM		
ITEM_NUM	NOT NULL	NUMBER(10)
ITEM_ORDR_NUM	NOT NULL	NUMBER(10)
ITEM_ICLS_CODE	NOT NULL	CHAR(5)
ITEM_FACL_NUM	NOT NULL	NUMBER(10)
ITEM_TRAN_NUM		NUMBER(10)
ITEM_COMMENT		CHAR(60)

Figure 3.2 Table descriptions for MINVFACL and MINVITEM

The question that we are trying to ask with this query is quite simple: *Which facilities in our system do not have any inventory?* In other words, which records in the FACILITY table (which as we shall see in the next chapter is called MINVFACL) do not have corresponding records in the INVENTORY ITEM table (MINVITEM)? This request could be written several different ways. To help demonstrate this fact we have listed seven of them in Figure 3.1. Study each of these statements carefully and try to see if you can tell how each works. If you can't, don't worry, since we will discuss them all in great detail in Chapter 8. When you are reviewing these SELECT statements, also try to think about which one you think is the best solution. That, too, is discussed in Chapter 8. We have also included descriptions of MINVFACL and MINVITEM in Figure 3.2 for your convenience.

Building the Database

4.1 Introduction

Now that we have reviewed the tools that we need to create and
manipulate database structures, we are ready to begin constructing the
database for the MegaMarket application. In this chapter, we discuss
some guidelines for preparing an effective development environment as
well as techniques for implementing our physical database design.
There are many examples in this chapter that you will be able to "plug
in" to your own environment. Many of these techniques have become
second nature to us because they are simple and they work. Use them as
the basis for your good development habits.

4.2 Software Management

Before beginning to use SQL to build our database structures, we must
address several remaining issues. The first consideration, *software
management*, is an important issue whether you have just one master
technician or 50 analysts, programmers, and quality assurance professionals developing your application. If 20 different programmers all
develop applications on their own, you can imagine some of the problems
that will arise when all the pieces must be put together: Two developers
may inadvertently choose the same name for their programs, with the

result that one is overwritten by the other, or two developers may come upon the same stumbling block and resolve the problem in different ways, resulting in unnecessary duplications of time and effort.

To help avoid these problems, you can create a central storage area to be shared by all technicians. All stages of the application implementation, from development through testing and production, can be contained within this one location. This approach provides a stable and consistent development environment.

The storage area may be physically implemented via directories under the UNIX, VMS, or MS-DOS operating systems, via partitioned data sets (PDSs) in MVS, or via minidisks in VM. For our application, which we developed in the UNIX environment, we decided to call the repository SOFTLIB and created a main directory with this name. Within this directory we created the subdirectory INVMGT for our inventory management application. Below the INVMGT directory we created directories to contain development (DEVL), testing/integration (TEST), and production (PROD) software. These last three directories are typically referred to as *staging directories*.

Next, we created specific directories under each staging directory for different types of software. We divided the software into five categories: Online applications using SQL*Forms or possibly a 3GL such as C (FORM); reports written in SQL*ReportWriter, SQL*Report, SQL*Plus, or a 3GL (REPORT); installation/environment creation software (INSTALL); user/programmer documentation (DOCUMENT); and operating system specific software (BATCH).

This directory structure can be enhanced conveniently later in the development process only by adding new subdirectories and not by rearranging what has already been established. Therefore, before continuing, we must be sure that our overall staging strategy is both flexible and complete. Let's step back for a moment to review our strategy.

A critical success factor in staging plans is the eventual need for multiple applications to share software. This possibility is often overlooked completely and cannot later be incorporated into the established directory structure. Our plan shares this deficiency. To overcome it, we will add a second subdirectory structure below SOFTLIB called SHARED. The structure of the SHARED subdirectory parallels that of the INVMGT subdirectory.

Another common shortcoming that also applies to our staging plan is the failure to consider future releases of our software. We have no way of determining which release of the software is contained within the INVMGT and SHARED directories. We can handle this requirement by renaming the subdirectories INVMGT and SHARED to INVMGTV1 and SHAREDV1 for version one of the software. This new structure can be indefinitely expanded for future versions by creating INVMGTVn and/ or SHAREDVn.

After these changes, our structure passes the flexibility test—it allows for future releases and future applications. Yet we still have one problem: Finding all of the software that is at the same stage (TEST, for instance) is a cumbersome process. In order to do this, we would have to search through each application directory, in this case INVMGTV1 and SHAREDV1, looking for a TEST subdirectory.

Since this type of request is very common, we will "invert" the top two layers of the directory structure to make the process less involved. Whereas our old structure started with the application subdirectories and moved down to the staging directories, our new structure starts with the staging directories and moves down to the specific applications. Figure 4.1 shows the final complete directory structure for our development process.

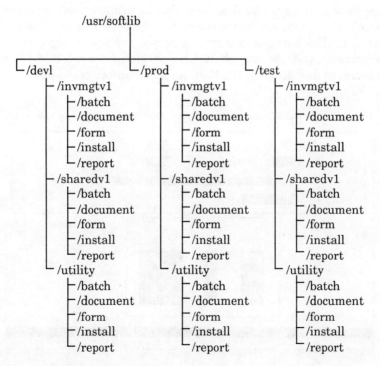

Figure 4.1 Software directory structure

Unfortunately, establishing the structure is only half the battle. We must also develop a set of rules and policies to control the movement of software between various subdirectories. These policies can be enforced by something as simple as written guidelines or something as complex as a special software package. For our project, we will use the small SQL*Forms application shown in Figure 4.2. This process is also formalized in a document containing a description of the software management structure definition and guidelines for moving software between directories. An application like this one is useful not only in large development efforts, but also even if you are the only developer, because it helps you to maintain a record of your environment when you return to perform further development in the future.

4.3 ORACLE Application Development Environment

Now that we have decided on the application environment used to manage operating system files, we are ready to start thinking about the ORACLE development environment where we will manage database structures. The same issues we discussed for operating system file management and staging should be considered for ORACLE table management and staging. If we allow each member of the development

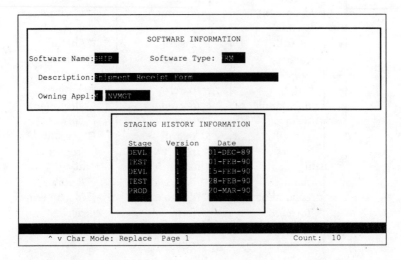

Figure 4.2 Software staging form

team to create tables at will, duplicated table names and inconsistent column definitions are likely to present problems.

Before looking at the choices for table staging, let's review some terminology and concepts. The generic term *database* is typically defined as a collection of tables. The meaning of those tables usually defines the *name* of the database. For example, all of the database tables that make up the INVMGT application might be referred to as the INVMGT database. A database may be implemented as a physical barrier or only a conceptual boundary. In the former case, the INVMGT database would be physically separate from all other databases, whereas in the latter, the databases would be physically combined yet conceptually distinct.

ORACLE allows both types of implementation. This is possible because there is a layer above a database called an *instance*. The instance is the physical boundary that may contain one or many databases. The meaning—and therefore the name and contents—of an instance is determined by the database administrator. There might be a single instance named INVMGT containing only the INVMGT database, the INVMGT instance might contain the DEVL, TEST, and PROD databases, or there might be three instances named DEVL, TEST, and PROD, each containing a INVMGT database. Figure 4.3 shows a conceptual diagram of these options.

The boundary of each database within the instance is defined by an *owner*. The owner is the ORACLE account used to create all of the tables for a particular application (or database). This account's *userid* controls all changes and accesses to the database tables. In the scenarios above, there would be a different ORACLE userid for each database identified. All other ORACLE userids would access the application tables owned by this userid. These other users could be application developers accessing development tables or end users accessing production tables. Figure 4.4 diagrams this structure.

As you can see, in this scenario there is one owning userid, INVMGT, within the DEVL instance. Each of the other users accesses INVMGT's tables. Since this is the DEVL instance, we can assume that all of the users in this environment would be developers of one type or another. Figure 4.5 shows an alternative scenario.

In this environment there are three Oracle userids (MINVDEVL, MINVTEST, MINVPROD), each owning a complete set of the INVMGT application tables. Since all stages of the development process are contained within this instance, the users might be technicians, testers, integrators, and end users. Note that users still access these tables through their own userids.

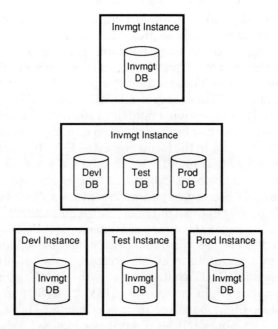

Figure 4.3 Database organization option 1

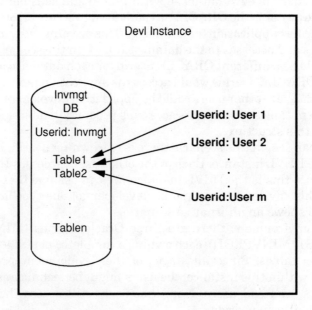

Figure 4.4 Database organization option 2

In all of the scenarios described, each user is defined to "point" to one set of application tables at any time. Developers and other technical users can change these pointers easily. The pointer is implemented by the use of synonyms (as discussed in Chapter 3) that translate a synonym name into the owner and table name. For example, the synonym MINVTOT might be translated into MINVTEST.MINVTOT, meaning MINVTEST is the owner of the table named MINVTOT.

There are two types of synonyms available, *public* and *private*. Public synonyms allow references to MINV... by any user (hence, the term *public*) to be translated. For example, this could be used to move all users from one stage to another by changing all of the public synonyms from owner MINVDEVL to owner MINVTEST. Private synonyms, on the other hand, allow individual users to point to a specific owner's tables. USERA may be a quality assurance person working with the MINVTEST tables while USERD is a developer working with MINVDEVL tables. There might even be a USERG who is working with some MINVTEST tables and some MINVDEVL tables.

You can choose any of these alternatives, or some combination, for your ORACLE environment strategy. There are a few things to consider when making these choices. One thing to keep in mind is that an instance is

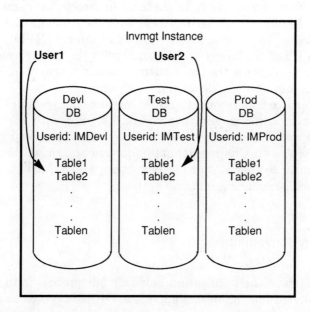

Figure 4.5 Database organization option 3

started (made available) and shutdown (made unavailable) in its entirety. This means that all databases within that instance must be controlled (started and shutdown) together. This also means that if a developer writes a program that causes an infinite loop (which never happens to us, of course ...), the entire instance could "hang." This possibility is a persuasive argument for separate production and development instances.

However, switching between instances and getting information across instances requires special networking software (SQL*Net). If we decided to create separate instances for the INVMGT and SALES applications, we could not easily work with data from both, nor could we readily share common data between the two applications.

When designing our environment strategy, we should ask ourselves the same questions we asked about our staging strategy earlier: Will it be flexible enough for future applications and future releases?

In our application, stability and sharing of data among applications are very important. We decided on three instances named TEST, PROD, and DEVL. Within each of these instances we have two databases (and two Oracle userids) called INVMGTV1 and SHAREDV1. These userids will create and own the INVMGTV1 and SHAREDV1 application tables.

Note that the structure of our ORACLE environment closely parallels that of our file system. We have three main directories named DEVL, TEST, and PROD, and three instances with the same names. We have two subdirectories within each directory named INVMGTV1 and SHAREDV1, and we have two databases with the same names within each instance. Aligning the two environments in this way enhances the overall consistency of the development environment.

This structured approach to object management should be documented for each technician involved and shared with the database administrator. This strategy need not be shared with end users. Although we will see in Chapter 9 that this documentation will become part of the technical documentation for the system, it is also an important tool for the developers during implementation.

4.4 Naming Conventions

The next step in the application development process is to establish naming conventions for objects outside of ORACLE (such as files) and objects within ORACLE (such as tables). The specific naming conventions you decide upon are not as important as the fact that you commit to a set of conventions and create a naming standards document that describes them. Again, while developing these conventions, try to envision future system requirements.

In addition to promoting consistency within the application, file naming conventions allow us to quickly identify the usage and function of an individual file. Figure 4.6 shows some of the file naming guidelines we will adopt for our project.

Naming conventions for ORACLE objects are equally crucial. Thorough guidelines provide for a high degree of consistency and allow developers or analysts to quickly identify and define table and column names. ORACLE allows up to 30 characters for the name of any database object (tables or columns, for instance). Although long object names require additional typing, they enable the function of the object to be easily interpreted from its name.

All file names will be eight characters long to allow for portability of the application (VM and MS-DOS are restricted to eight characters). The file names will be in the format Xyyyzzzz.ext as follows:

X   is the *application title*
Example:
      M for all MegaMarket applications
yyy   is the *subapplication within the application*
Examples:
      INV for Inventory applications
      GEN for General applications
      MEN for Menu applications
      LFV for "Lookup" applications
zzzz   is the *function within the subapplication*
Examples:
      SHIP for shipment function
ext   is an *extension specific to the particular tool used*
Examples:
      FRM for SQL*Forms
      REP for SQL*ReportWriter

Figure 4.6 File naming standards

For our application, we compromised by spelling out table names and abbreviating column names. Figure 4.7 lists some of our object naming guidelines.

Naming for Lookups

We decided to include the four character abbreviation used in the file naming standards (zzzz above) in our column name standards for use in SQL*Forms applications. We know that we will be creating "lookup" forms for all minor tables (discussed in Section 2.2.1). A "lookup" form is a multi-row display of a minor table containing valid choices. For example part of the form SLFVSTAT might look like this:

STATE CODE	STATE DESC
MD	MARYLAND
NJ	NEW JERSEY
NY	NEW YORK

Any application form containing a lookup column can call the lookup form to allow the user to review the valid choices and make a selection. Our naming convention for these lookup columns will allow us to create a generic SQL*Forms LIST FIELD VALUES trigger to call the appropriate lookup form. The triggers for this example will be discussed thoroughly in Chapter 5.

4.5 Domain Definition

Naming conventions are just part of the uniformity requirements of an application. Another essential ingredient is column characteristic consistency. For example, the names of all columns that hold descriptions should end in _DESC (not _DESCR or _DESCRIPTION) and have a certain length and datatype. This type of information should either be included in the overall naming guidelines document or kept as a separate document (some of ours are shown in Figure 4.8). It is interesting to note that in the future this domain information will become part of the actual database definition, eventually allowing for the storage of information like common validations and range checks. Thus, like drawing ERDs, defining domains is more than a documentation exercise.

For now, we will use the domains listed in Figure 4.8; this list will probably grow as we continue development.

4.6 Software Development Standards

The last step, and probably the most obvious of all, is the creation of software development standards to be used by all developers. The details

---

Table Names: Xyyyzzzz

Xyyyzzzz are the same as the file naming conventions
associative all associative tables (many-to-many relationships) will contain the abbreviations that describe the relationship
Examples:
    MINVSUPP is the prime table
    MINVICLS is the prime table
    MINVSCLS is the associative table

Column Names: zzzz_DESCRIPTION

zzzz is the 4-character abbreviation of the table description from the table name
DESCRIPTION is the description of the field.
foreign keys all foreign key column descriptions will be the primary key's column name.
Examples:
    SUPP_NUM is the primary key
    zzzz_SUPP_NUM is the foreign key
    ICLS_CODE is the primary key
    zzzz_ICLS_CODE is the foreign key

Index Names: Xyyyzzzz_PKn
                    Xyyyzzzz_FKn
                    Xyyyzzzz_ACn
PK   is a primary key index (unique)
FK   is a foreign key index
AC   is an access index
n   is the number of the index (beginning with 1)

Figure 4.7 ORACLE object naming standards

NAME	Description	Datatype
ADDR	Address information	
ADDR_CITY	City	CHAR(30)
ADDR_STREETn	Street line n	CHAR(40)
CODE	Table based look-ups	CHAR[2]
DATE	Date information	DATE[1]
DESC	Description	CHAR(30)
HCV	Hard-coded values	CHAR[2,3]
IND	Indicator (Y/N/null)	CHAR(1)
NAME	Name information	
NAME_FIRST	First name	CHAR(20)
NAME_LAST	Last name	CHAR(60)
NUM	System-generated keys	NUM(9)
QUANTITY	Quantity	NUM(3)
TIME	Time information	DATE[1]

1. Standard Oracle date format, including time.
2. Size will vary.
3. Any column that will have predefined values that are NOT stored in a minor table.

Figure 4.8 Domain Definition

contained in these standards will include SQL*Forms cosmetic and operation standards to promote a consistent "look and feel" throughout the applications. Also included are help message formats, error message formats, and SQL statement formats. For reporting there may be report heading standards and variable naming conventions. All of these standards will be discussed in later chapters when we discuss the various specific software development processes, such as building online applications.

4.7 Definition of a Goal

We must add one final ingredient before we begin development: The definition of a goal for the application. Although establishing goals may seem like a worthless exercise, without them you will recognize that something is missing.

An obvious goal is to develop a quality application. But what does that mean? What is "quality"? Quality may mean maximum performance or it may mean maximum flexibility. It may mean 100 percent bug-free or it may mean minimum testing with maximum results. Many of these goals conflict with one another, requiring us to constantly make trade-offs. For instance, increased flexibility (as in a rule-based system) typically results in decreased performance. Making a firm commitment to a set of goals early in the development process will provide answers to many of the inevitable questions that will arise later in the development process. The goal of our sample application is performance, but not at the expense of flexibility. We will only sacrifice performance to maintain a high degree of functionality in the application.

4.8 Sizing the Application Tables

In order to create the application tables using SQL, we need to have some technique for determining the size of each table. This information is used in the SPACE clause of a SQL statement when creating the tables and indexes. This clause is used to allocate an appropriate number of contiguous database blocks to a table. This helps to maximize disk usage as well as performance. Our size estimates will likely be inaccurate, since we are still early in the development process, but they will be better than ORACLE's defaults.

Note for V5 users: The SPACE information within the table definition in V6 can be provided via a SPACE DEFINITION in V5.

There are two techniques typically used for these estimations: Using a spreadsheet or writing programs in a 3GL or SQL. We prefer the spreadsheet technique because it is powerful and does not require a great deal of additional coding.

A spreadsheet can also be defined to calculate the number of rows in a table based on known information about relationships. For instance, we might know that there are 20 ADMINISTRATIVE OFFICEs and 10 WAREHOUSEs per OFFICE. The spreadsheet could calculate 200 WAREHOUSEs (20 x 10) for us. Figure 4.9 shows a spreadsheet that employs this technique. By using these numbers along with average row sizes, we can also use our spreadsheet to calculate table sizes. And since several spreadsheets are available that can import data from ORACLE, we can often populate these spreadsheets from existing table definitions using SQL.

We can transfer the information from the "bytes per table" column directly into our SPACE clause when we create our tables.

4.9 Building the Application Tables

The first opportunity we have to use SQL is in the actual building of the application tables. In Chapter 2, we took the data model and refined it into table definitions. Now we can build those tables.

We might be tempted to log in to SQL*Plus and start typing CREATE TABLE statements, but in the long run, that may not be the best approach. If we interactively build our tables in SQL*Plus, how will we recreate them if they are corrupted? Also, how will we verify that all of our standards (that we worked so hard to create) are followed?

A preferable technique is to use the system editor to create one or more files. These files will have an extension of .sql and be referred to as a *SQL script*. The intent of the SQL script we will write is to capture all of the SQL commands necessary to define the application environment. These

TABLE NAME	Avg Bytes per Row	Rows per Parent	Overall Rows	Bytes per Table	K per Table
ADMIN OFFICE	80	0	10	800	1
WAREHOUSE	50	5	50	2500	2
ORDER	20	1000	50000	1000000	977
INVENTORY ITEM	25	150	7500000	187500000	183105
TRANSACTION	25	1	7500000	187500000	183105
SUPPLIER	60	1	50000	3000000	2930
STORE	50	20	200	10000	10
TOTALS			*15100260*	*379013300*	*370130*

Figure 4.9 Sizing spreadsheet

include statements for creating tables, indexes, views and synonyms and performing grants for tables and users.

If we place all of these statements in one file, we will have a very large file. For instance, consider all of the things that are needed to define just one table: the DROP/CREATE TABLE statement, at least one CREATE INDEX statement, any associated DROP/CREATE VIEW statements (views based on the table), any PUBLIC GRANTs, and any PUBLIC SYNONYMs. Notice that we included corresponding DROP commands for each CREATE command. We did this in order to be able to make changes to the data definition and rerun the script. Oracle requires that the object must be DROPped before it can be reCREATEd. Therefore, when we execute the script for the first time, we will receive many "... does not exist" messages.

This brings us to a decision point. (Are you beginning to feel that all we do is make decisions?) How do we structure our SQL scripts?

We could create one big SQL script defining the entire environment. This file would contain all of the types of SQL commands listed earlier in some specified order (probably alphabetic). The disadvantage of this approach is that the excessive size of the SQL file makes it difficult to manage. The advantage is that all of the definitions are in one spot. Thus, the database administrator can easily focus on all of the elements affected by a change (for instance, when the column width of a primary key is expanded, he must change all foreign key references to that column).

Creating separate SQL scripts for each "type" of definition is another option. These types could be TABLEs, VIEWs, INDEXes, and so on. Each type would have its own file name or file extension (following some naming convention). The benefit of this strategy is that the SQL file is smaller and thus more manageable. The drawback is that it is easier to mistakenly omit changes to objects associated with one another, such as a VIEW and the TABLE it is based on.

Another alternative is to create a separate SQL script for all of the definitions associated with each table. These would include the table creation, indexes, synonyms, etc. The advantage of this plan is that each SQL file is concise and the margin of error is small. The disadvantage is the large number of files to manage.

An additional general tradeoff for each of these techniques is between the size and complexity of the SQL script and the flexibility of the definition change process. When one table changes, we reexecute the complete SQL script. If the script contains the entire environment definition, then the entire environment will be recreated; if the script contains the definition of one table, then only that table will be recreated. In the latter case, however, if we desire to rebuild the whole environment then we must execute many separate SQL scripts.

So once again we have a wide variety of options. As with our selection of standards earlier, it is most important to make a decision and adhere to it consistently. Then we can write the SQL to create the environment.

For our application we already have a subdirectory under INVMGTV1 called INSTALL. The defined purpose of this subdirectory is to hold all of the scripts necessary for the "installation" or building of our application environment. These scripts may include both SQL scripts and operating system scripts (to generate SQL*Forms applications, for example).

We decided to use a separate file for each table and each independent view created. In addition, we will have a SQL file containing the GRANT statements for USER definitions. We also formulated a naming convention for these files. The file name will be the name of the table or view being described. Figure 4.10 shows one of these files from our application.

Note that if you plan to GRANT PUBLIC access to any of your tables, you should consider putting these GRANT statements into their own file because DBA privilege is required to issue them. If they are separate from the other statements, they can easily be passed on to the DBA for execution.

Since we must execute every SQL script separately to create our environment we also created an SQL script called MGENINST.SQL. This SQL script executes all of the application SQL scripts for our application. A portion of that file is shown in Figure 4.11.

Unfortunately, we are not quite done making choices. We still need to establish some guidelines for the process of making changes. As we mentioned earlier, we can reCREATE tables using updated SQL installation files. This approach guarantees that the table definition in the data dictionary and the SQL file are always synchronized. But it requires DROP statements and, therefore, the complete loss of all test data. The alternative, using the ALTER command (which allows us to modify a table without losing any of its data) when changes are necessary, leaves open the possibility that changes made to tables may not be referenced in SQL installation files. However, this approach may not require that existing data be deleted.

If we decide to reCREATE the tables, we can create additional SQL files (or add additional SQL to the existing files) to minimize the loss of data every time we make a change. The additional SQL would include

```
REM
REM        Table/View SQL script for MINVFACL
REM               Facility (Store/Warehouse) Table
REM
REM        Creator: Nicole and Tim
REM        Created: September, 1989
REM
REM               — Change Log —
REM
REM        Description                          Date              Name
REM        -----------------------------        --------------    --------------
REM        Original SQL script                  Sept 89           Nicole and Tim
REM
REM
REM
DROP TABLE MINVFACL;
CREATE TABLE MINVFACL (
        FACL_NUM                        NUMBER(10)        NOT NULL
                                        PRIMARY KEY,
        FACL_DESC                       CHAR(60) NOT NULL,
        FACL_EMPL_NUM_MGR               NUMBER(10),
        FACL_OFFC_NUM_MGR               NUMBER(10)        NOT NULL,
                                        REFERENCES SGENOFFC(OFFC_NUM),
        FACL_TYPE_HCV                   CHAR(1)           NOT NULL
                                        CHECK (FACL_TYPE_HCV IN
                                        ('W','S')),
        FACL_ADDR_STREET1               CHAR(40) NOT NULL,
        FACL_ADDR_STREET2               CHAR(40),
        FACL_ADDR_CITY                  CHAR(30) NOT NULL,
        FACL_ADDR_STATE                 CHAR(2)           NOT NULL
                                        CHECK (FACL_ADDR_STATE =
                                        UPPER(FACL_ADDR_STATE)),
        FACL_ADDR_ZIP                   CHAR(10) NOT NULL,
        FACL_ADDR_PHONE_NUMBER          CHAR(10),
        FACL_ADDR_FAX_NUMBER            CHAR(10),
        FACL_NO_OF_CUSTOMERS            NUMBER(9),
        FACL_SQUARE_FOOTAGE             NUMBER(8)
        )
        PCTFREE         10
        PCTUSED         60
        TABLESPACE      USER_DATA;
REM
REM     STORAGE (
REM                     INITIAL 15K
REM                     NEXT            5K
REM                     PCTINCREASE     10
REM             )
REM
COMMENT ON TABLE MINVFACL IS 'Facility (Store/Warehouse) Information';
```

Figure 4.10 Table creation SQL script

```
REM
REM         Environment  Creation  Script
REM
REM         Creator:  Nicole  and  Tim
REM         Created:  September,  1989
REM
REM
REM                   - Change  Log -
REM
REM         Description                        Date             Name
REM         ------------------------------     --------------   ---------------
REM         Original  SQL  script              Sept  89         Nicole  and  Tim
REM
REM
REM
START   sharedvl/install/sgenoffc;
REM
START   invmgtvl/install/minvfacl;
REM
START   sharedvl/install/sgenempl;
START   sharedvl/install/slfvicls;
START   sharedvl/install/slfvttyp;
START   sharedvl/install/sgenappl;
START   sharedvl/install/sgenmenu;
START   sharedvl/install/sgenhfrm;
START   sharedvl/install/sgenhblk;
START   sharedvl/install/sgenhfld;
REM
START   invmgtvl/install/minvfcls;
START   invmgtvl/install/minvsupp;
START   invmgtvl/install/minvscls;
START   invmgtvl/install/minvship;
START   invmgtvl/install/minvordr;
START   invmgtvl/install/minvitem;
START   invmgtvl/install/minvtran;
START   invmgtvl/install/minvmove;
REM
```

Figure 4.11 Environment creation SQL script

INSERT statements to repopulate the important application tables and all of the reference tables.

Such INSERT statements can be generated in many ways. The data can be kept in a "flat file" (refer to "SQL to Genrate SQL" hint for a technique to create this file) and INSERTed using SQL*Loader. Or the complete INSERT statements with the VALUEs can be stored in a script file. Another technique is the use of & *parameters* in SQL*Plus. These will prompt you at run time for the information for each parameterized column in the table. For example:

```
INSERT INTO SLFVTTYP
VALUES (&TRAN_TYPE, &TRAN_TYPE_DESC);
```

When this statement is executed in SQL*Plus, each parameter becomes a prompt; thus, we would be asked "Enter value for TRAN_TYPE: " and "Enter value for TRAN_TYPE_DESC:" We can re-execute this command repetitively to recreate the data.

&& Substitution

If we specify && instead of & we define the permanent value (for the entire SQL*Plus session) for the variable. We could use this technique if we wanted to insert into several tables for the same FACL_NUM or if we wanted to execute several different selects for the same FACL_NUM. In either case, the && causes only one request for a variable regardless of the number of times it is referenced.

SQL to Generate SQL

We may want to have a technique to query the current data in the table and automatically generate INSERT statements that would recreate the data. This technique is convenient because it eliminates the need to manually update a secondary file to record the INSERTed data. We can accomplish this using a technique called "dynamic" SQL script. The term "dynamic" is used because we use SQL to generate SQL. For example, we want to "unload" our data. This can be accomplished very easily by simply SPOOLing the queried information:

```
SET HEADING OFF
SET FEEDBACK OFF
SET PAGESIZE 1000
SPOOL DATAFILE.SQL
SELECT FCLS_FACL_ID, FCLS_ICLS_CODE
FROM MINVFCLS;
SPOOL OFF
```

Notice the SET statements we used. These modify SQL*Plus environment variables so that only the data, and not any other information, is SPOOLed to our file. We SET the column HEAD-INGs off, the "n number of rows selected" FEEDBACK off, and we increased the SIZE of our PAGE.

The output of the statements will be a variable length file of data. We could also make the data fixed length by using the RPAD function (which pads the output column with spaces to a specified length) in our SELECT. The RPAD function only works on CHAR data, so we must first convert NUMBER columns using TO_CHAR:

```
SELECT   RPAD(TO_CHAR(FCLS_FACILITY_ID, 10)),
         RPAD(FCLS_ICLS_CODE, 5)
FROM     MINVFCLS;
```

This brings us halfway to our goal. We have the data (which could be read by SQL*Loader) but we do not have the surrounding SQL. This is where the "dynamic" aspect comes in to play:

```
SELECT  'INSERT INTO MINVFCLS VALUES ('''
        || FCLS_FACILITY_ID||''','''
        ||FCLS_ICLS_CODE
        ||''');'
FROM    MINVFCLS;
```

Notice that we concatenated a text string (INSERT INTO ...) to the data returned. The output from this SELECT will then be our INSERT statement.

4.10 Conclusion

We used SQL in this chapter to build the MegaMarket database. During this process we touched on all of the various decisions that should be made very early in the development effort. We are sure you agree that there is a tremendous amount of work to be done. Hopefully, you also agree (or trust us) that the investment will be paid back in orders of magnitude.

Now that we have made all of these decisions for the MegaMarket application, we can begin the development process feeling confident that we have resolved many important issues. The next chapter addresses the first portion of the development effort: building the online applications. The second portion of the effort, building the reports, is discussed in Chapter 6.

5

Building the
Online Applications

5.1 Introduction

Building the online applications is arguably the heart of the entire development process. Today's end user works regularly on a personal computer with easy-to-use, graphical tools like Lotus 1-2-3 and is accustomed to immediate visual feedback. Thus, the applications we develop must be better than ever.

The additional challenge of the process is using a fourth-generation tool, such as SQL*Forms, to write a realistic and difficult application. Any fourth-generation tool based on a *fourth-generation language* (4GL), such as SQL, removes you one level from the tediousness and difficulty of a *third-generation language* (3GL) such as COBOL or C. It also removes you from the flexibility of the 3GL. In fact, there are still developers that lament about things they can do in a *second-generation language* (2GL) like assembly language but you can't do in a 3GL like C.

The restrictions arise because the SQL*Forms program expects you to work within the bounds of a "typical" *form* (the SQL*Forms term for a data entry screen or set of screens). If you can't, you have to find a way to make SQL*Forms do something it was not designed to do. We will show you how this can happen and talk about techniques to avoid it, but when it can't be avoided, we will show you the tricks to make it work.

In this chapter, we will take you through our application building process. Our development tool will be primarily SQL*Forms and possibly a few *user-exits* (3GL code imbedded in the form) for specialized or redundant tasks. We start out the chapter broadening your understanding of SQL*Forms, then we move into SQL*Forms standards and specifications, and finally building the MegaMarket application. We will group the techniques we will study for developing forms into three categories: those for building the default forms, those used in several different forms, and those that are specific to a particular situation in our application.

5.2 Understanding SQL*Forms

The first step in building anything, ORACLE applications included, is to gather and understand the appropriate tools for the job. In our development effort, we will be using several software tools, each of which is designed for a specific task. As we have seen already, SQL*Plus can be a powerful tool in a database development project. It is not, however, well suited for the online application interface to a database. Although SQL*Plus certainly allows for any kind of data to be entered or retrieved, the interface is less intuitive and the validation and integrity checking capabilities are limited. SQL*Plus, of course, is not acceptable for production data entry. Large and complex applications require a different kind of tool—one that provides a comprehensive set of interface and validation options. To accommodate this need Oracle developed SQL*Forms, a tool for building and running screen-oriented applications for data entry and retrieval.

Picking the most appropriate tool for the job is just a first step; you must also learn how to use the tool properly. With this in mind, the following section will discuss not just how to use SQL*Forms, but how it actually works. This should open your mind to brand new ways of utilizing the tool. Later we will see examples of SQL*Forms applications that take advantage of an understanding of the product's internal workings.

5.2.1 Making the transition to a nonprocedural language

SQL*Forms and all other Oracle tools are based on SQL. Because SQL is a 4GL, it is sometimes difficult to understand. The difficulty lies in its *non-procedural* syntax. What we mean by nonprocedural is that 3GLs allow us to visualize the steps (or procedures) necessary to achieve our goal. For example, a program might get a record, add two numbers on the record, test the result against a static value, and loop back to the beginning. In this example, each of the separate steps would be at least one line of 3GL code. Using SQL, all of these separate steps are written in one statement.

Since we are using SQL*Forms, and therefore SQL, we must try to stop thinking of a module as a series of actions or steps. Instead we should think in terms of the four SQL operations (reviewed in Chapter 3): SELECT, INSERT, UPDATE, and DELETE. This is very important if you want to get the most out of SQL*Forms (or any other SQL-based tool). We wish there was an easy way to help you make this transition, but to be honest it can be very difficult. It requires that you think about problems and requirements in a whole new way. Like anything new, though, practice and experience are all that you need, and we're sure you'll get the hang of it. If you still feel uncomfortable with SQL, you may want to take a moment now and reread Chapter 3 (Overview of SQL).

5.2.2 Using SQL*Forms

As we already mentioned, it is very important to remember that *the only way to talk to ORACLE is through SQL*. What this means is that any tool we use with ORACLE simply builds SQL statements for us. In SQL*Plus, the user actually types in the SQL to be sent to ORACLE for processing. SQL*Forms works the same way, but the program builds the SQL statements for you. For example, when you type data into a blank form and press the function key that commits the data, SQL*Forms builds an INSERT statement and sends it to ORACLE. Constructing a basic form is nothing more than telling SQL*Forms how to build those statements—what tables to manipulate, what columns to use, and what screen values to utilize. By carefully constructing our forms, we will see that we can make it very easy for SQL*Forms to build the proper SQL statements and display data in the proper fashion.

5.2.3 The SQL*Forms modules

SQL*Forms is comprised of several different program modules and database tables that act in concert to produce and execute the online applications. To understand these modules, we will discuss them from a historical point of view, since each new version of the product has just been built on top of the old ones.

At the basis of every SQL*Forms form is a text file referred to as the *INP file*, so called because the name extension ".inp" that it carries. Most ORACLE developers act as though this file carries some mystical power and it is taboo to alter the file in any way. Let's remove the taboo now, but also explain why developers tend to stay away from the file.

The INP file contains a set of parameters that describe how a SQL*Forms application will work. In a sense, the INP file acts as the "source code" for the form. One difference between the INP file and traditional source code is that the INP is not compiled into an executable program, but is *generated* into a *.frm* file. This FRM file is used at run time as a parameter file for the executable program *iap* (also called *runform*). The INP and FRM files are both simply text files that can be read without much difficulty (we say nothing about comprehension). They are not, however, intended to be edited. Nor does the developer manually create the INP file. Instead, it is created by another program—yet another way in which the INP file differs from source code. Because these files are created by programs and used by programs, their syntax must be very exact. Once the syntax is corrupted, the SQL*Forms generator cannot recognize it. For this reason, you should take caution if you choose to edit the file.

Originally (in versions of SQL*Forms before 2.0), the INP file was created by using the program called *iag* (which stood for "interactive application generator"). This program simply asked the user a series of questions, paraphrased below, about how the form should operate, such as "What is the name of the application?", "What tables would you like to use?", or "Where would you like a field positioned?". The resulting INP file, which contained the questions and answers, could then be used to generate the FRM file. The program iap would be executed and would reference this FRM file.

If the form did not run properly (a screen field displayed in the wrong location, for instance), the developer had probably answered some question inaccurately. The correction could be made in one of three ways. First, the developer could start over, answering the questions again. Considering the number of questions asked to develop even a small form, this was an impractical way to debug. Second, a "%" symbol could be added to the INP after the last correct answer. When iag was executed against this file, only the questions that follow the "%" would be asked again. The final approach required the developer to edit the INP file directly to change their answers to the questions. This method could be very tricky because many of the questions asked were dependent upon the answers to prior questions. Thus, changing one answer in the INP file could require a whole set of new questions. The developer would either manually add both the question and the answer or use the "%" character along with direct editing to build the proper questions and answers.

For all practical purposes, the process works the same way today, except that the new program *iad*, the SQL*Forms *Designer*, became available with Version 2.0 of SQL*Forms. The iad program provides a means of interactively creating a form with a screen painter and editing environment. Nowadays, nearly all SQL*Forms applications are built with the Designer. However, iad still creates an INP file and generates a FRM file exactly as in the past. Some developers continue to edit the INP file created by the Designer to make quick changes, but precise syntax is still a problem; indeed, Oracle Corporation will not provide customer support for a form once its INP file has been edited. Although we often edit the INP file, you should not try it until you are very familiar with the process.

INP Edits

Once you are comfortable with the INP file you might save time by making global changes in the editor—for instance, changing the name of a table everywhere in the INP file. You might also want to make small modifications to SQL statements in the INP file since large SQL statements are often difficult to read within SQL*Forms.

Another module in the SQL*Forms application development environment is the ORACLE RDBMS itself. The details of a SQL*Forms application can be stored in an ORACLE database. From the SQL*Forms Designer, or by using the program *iac*, the contents of an INP file can be loaded into the *iap tables*. These database tables are owned by a user called SYSTEM (this user is created as part of the ORACLE install). Although you would never modify the iap tables directly, you can certainly perform queries against them. We will learn of other uses for the iap tables in Chapter 9 (Documenting).

Even though all the programs such as iag, iap, iad, and iac are still available and used, the entire process can now be controlled from within the SQL*Forms Designer. In the next two sections, we will be discussing not how SQL*Forms applications should be built, but rather how to use the SQL*Forms designing tool most effectively.

5.2.4 The Designer

Although many veteran developers will tell you that developing SQL*Forms applications is not really difficult in the INP file, using the SQL*Forms Designer effectively can make the process very simple. In this section, we will discuss not how to build forms, but how the Designer works, focusing on the *windows* found in the tool. From these windows, commands are passed to the Designer that give the form its functionality as well as maintain the form by saving it, updating it, and so on.

First let's discuss how the windows in the Designer operate in general. Each window in the Designer represents a different level in the hierarchy of the form. A new window gets stacked on top of the previous one each time you travel deeper into the form. For example, Figure 5.1 shows the CHOOSE BLOCK window layered on top of the CHOOSE FORM window.

A form will always consist of one or more *blocks*. A block is a logical collection of fields that are associated with the same *base table*. When an

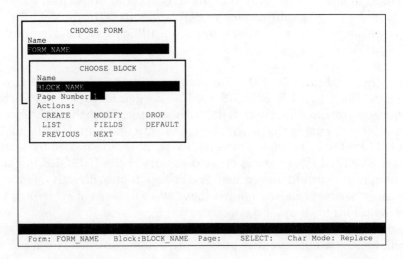

Figure 5.1 SQL*Forms Designer window layers

insertion, deletion, update, or query is performed in a block, it applies to the base table. A block is one level below a form in the basic SQL*Forms hierarchy. So, by going one level deeper from the CHOOSE FORM window, we get the opportunity to choose a block. This hierarchy metaphor is used consistently throughout SQL*Forms—whenever you select an option on a window, you travel deeper into the form and a new window appears stacked on top. Conversely, whenever you leave a window and travel higher up the hierarchy, the window disappears and leaves you where you were on its parent window.

The commands for navigating through these levels—the [SELECT] and [ACCEPT] keys—are also consistent throughout the Designer. (See the "Function Keys" hint on the next page.) These *function keys* are defined only while you are in the Designer. They are the most commonly used keys in the Designer. The way these keys operate depends on the nature of the window. Consider the common window type shown earlier in Figure 5.1, with one input area and several text menu options. When something is typed into the input area, the menu options apply to it. By moving to the menu item (with the arrow keys) and pressing [SELECT], you are saying, "apply this menu option to the word typed into the input area." So, in the CHOOSE BLOCK window, we might type the string "BLOCK_NAME" into the input area and position the cursor over the menu option NEXT. By pressing [SELECT], we give the command to display the name of the block that comes *after* the block called BLOCK_NAME. This means, of course, that if you type an invalid block name into the input area and then select NEXT, the function will fail because there is no block that follows the invalid one.

By pressing the [ACCEPT] key in a window such as this one, you are telling SQL*Forms that you have finished working at this level and that you would like to come up a level, accepting all of the changes that were made. The [EXIT] key performs the same function, but in some contexts, it implies that the changes that were made should *not* be accepted when you leave the level. Try to get into the habit of using the [ACCEPT] key to come up a level to ensure that you do not inadvertently lose any changes.

Figure 5.2 shows another type of window that you will find in SQL*Forms. In this window, there is no input area to which the functions will apply; rather, there are simply several menu options. These options are chosen by the [SELECT] key as well, but they act as binary switches that toggle on and off as they are selected. When an option is [SELECT]ed, it is highlighted and/or an asterisk appears to its left (depending on the type of terminal you are using). This generally

Function Keys

The use of brackets around function names is an Oracle convention for representing function keys. Because the ORACLE tools are portable across hardware and operating system platforms, it is important that several different terminals be supported as well. To accommodate this, ORACLE function keys are not defined by the key that is pressed, but by the function that is performed. In this way, each terminal can have its own translation from function to actual key. This is true of most of the ORACLE tools. The "mapping" of functions to keys on a particular keyboard is called a *CRT definition*, which can be modified to suit the user's needs. (We do not discuss CRT definitions in this book, but you can find more information in your ORACLE documentation.) So, when you see us refer to the [NEXT FIELD] key, that means that we are referring to "the key that you press on your terminal to perform the NEXT FIELD function." To find out which key performs a given function, press [SHOW FUNCTION KEYS]. This is, of course, the one key that you have to know before you can find out all of the others! On VT100s it's ESC-v, on PCs it's SHIFT-F1, and so on.

implies that the option is "on." So, in Figure 5.2, the field FIELD_NAME *is* a database field and it *is* displayed, but none of the other options are true. In windows such as these, [ACCEPT] leaves with the changes intact, while [EXIT] leaves without saving the changes.

These concepts of navigation also hold true in another part of the Designer: the *screen painter*. You reach the screen painter by [SELECT]ing MODIFY on the CHOOSE BLOCK window. It is here that the cosmetic changes are made to the form.

The screen painter allows you access to three things: fields, blocks, and paint. The fields can be resized, moved, or changed in format and functionality. Note that only fields in the current block (the block name is displayed on bottom line of the screen) can be modified. Block functionality, such as the number of rows displayed, can also be changed. Finally, the *paint* on the screen can be modified. The paint, or *boilerplate*, includes all text and lines (other than fields) that appear on the screen. Any printable character can be part of the boilerplate (on PCs, even the extended character set can be used to add fancy lines and borders). Since the boilerplate does not apply to a particular block, you can modify all of it on a page, regardless of the currently selected block.

*Moving SQL*Forms Fields*

Remember that the boilerplate is just paint. In other words, the label next to a field has absolutely nothing to do with the name of the field itself; changing it does not affect the field in any way. Be careful to move a field together with the associated boilerplate. Otherwise you might find yourself with completely jumbled fields and descriptions.

Navigating within the screen painter is not unlike navigating the windows. When you want to perform a function on some object, you [SELECT] it and press the appropriate function key. So, to make a field longer, you position the cursor on the field, press [SELECT], move the cursor to the *new* right edge of the field, and press [RESIZE FIELD]. This rule applies to almost everything in the painter, with one main exception: when the cursor is already positioned on a field, you do not need to press [SELECT] to perform a function on that field. For example, this means that to make a field *shorter*, you need only position the cursor on the field where you want the new right edge to be and press [RESIZE FIELD].

For another example, let's see what we must do to examine the characteristics of a field or block more closely. First, of course, you select the field or block. To select the field, you must position the cursor on the

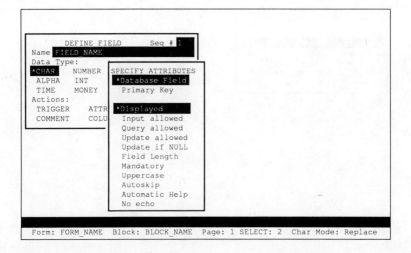

Figure 5.2 SQL*Forms Designer options window

field and (optionally in this case) press [SELECT]. To select a block, you would use the [SELECT BLOCK] key. Once the object is selected, press the [DEFINE] key. This function key knows what information to display based on what object is selected.

Finally, you should keep in mind that all changes made with the screen painter are permanent (as long as you generate or save the form as described in Section 5.2.5). Choosing [EXIT] or [ACCEPT] will bring you out one level to the CHOOSE BLOCK window, but in either case your changes will remain.

5.2.5 Saving versus generating

Before leaving the Designer, we must discuss one of the most misunderstood concepts in SQL*Forms development: *saving* versus *generating*. At the CHOOSE FORM window (shown in Figure 5.3), there are several options for working with a form. You can CREATE a form from scratch, MODIFY or LOAD an existing form, or GENERATE or SAVE a form that you have been working on. The precise meaning of these options and when it is appropriate to use them are often unclear to the SQL*Forms developer.

A SQL*Forms application can exist in one of three places. First, it is simply kept in memory while it is being created or modified within the

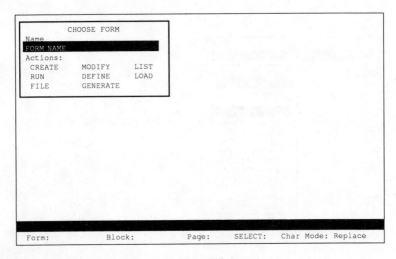

Figure 5.3 SQL*Forms Designer CHOOSE FORM window

Designer. Let's refer to this instance of the form as residing in the *workspace*. The second place for a form to exist (as we mentioned in section 5.2.3) is in the iap tables of the RDBMS. The third and final place that form can exist is in operating system files. Each of these three places has a role in the development of a form, but duplication of the same form can make it difficult to decide which version is the most up to date or to determine how to recover a damaged form. To clear up any confusion, we will describe each option and its function below.

CREATE. This option creates a brand new form in the workspace and gives it the name specified in the input area of the CHOOSE FORM window. A form cannot be created if it has the same name as a form that has already been saved to the iap tables.

MODIFY. The MODIFY option sends you deeper, to the CHOOSE BLOCK window. If a form currently exists in the workspace, it will be modified. If no form is in the workspace, the form will be retrieved from the iap tables. If it does not exist in the workspace or the iap tables, an error message will be issued.

LIST. The LIST option displays a pop-up window that contains a listing of all of the forms that are saved in the iap tables and owned by the current user. If one of the forms in the list is selected, the form name will be brought back into the input area on the CHOOSE FORM window.

RUN. This option simply executes a program called iap (or runform on some operating systems) with the form that is listed in the input area as the argument. The Designer's operation gets temporarily suspended when a form is run with this option. Control returns to the Designer when the form is finished executing.

DEFINE. The DEFINE option lets you change some of the high level attributes of a form. This is where form level *triggers* are defined. (Triggers are small scripts made up of SQL statements and built-in SQL*Forms functions that can reside at different levels of a form—form, block, or field—and that are executed based on events during runtime. We will discuss triggers throughout this chapter.)

LOAD. The LOAD option retrieves an operating system file (an INP file) which describes a form and loads it into the workspace for modification. A file cannot be loaded if a form of the same name with the same owner (ORACLE userid) already exists in the iap tables. When you [SELECT] the LOAD option, a window appears to prompt you for the name of the file that you would like to load. By default, the files that are loaded end with the extension ".inp." This is also a convenient chance to duplicate a form under a different name, because the name of the file that you specify does not have to match the name in the CHOOSE FORM input area. For example, in our project we decided to use a skeleton application (see section 5.6 for details) that we would always load as the first step of developing a new form. Then, by duplicating the form, we have created a new form that is a copy of the skeleton.

FILE. This option leads to a submenu with several database options. Each time you leave SQL*Forms, this menu will appear to make sure that you don't quit without saving the changes that you have made. The FILE submenu includes the following choices:

SAVE. This option saves the form that is currently in the workspace to the iap tables.

DISCARD. This option removes the contents of the workspace without saving your changes. The changes are permanently lost unless you have already generated—see the GENERATE option below.

SAVE AS. This option saves the contents of the workspace to the iap tables under a different name. You will be prompted to enter the new name.

RENAME. This option allows you to change the name of the form as it exists in the iap tables. This does not change the name of INP files created by previous generations of the form.

DROP. This option removes the form from the iap tables *permanently*.

GENERATE. The GENERATE option takes the contents of the workspace and writes them to an INP file and also produces an FRM file. The option actually just calls the program iag that was described earlier in Section 5.2.3.

The illustration in Figure 5.4 depicts some of the more important modules in this process and how they relate to the above menu options.

All of these options suggest that there are several ways of maintaining your SQL*Forms applications. This is true, and it is important that you make some choices about which methods you wish to employ. The most important choice is whether you wish to SAVE your forms to the iap tables or not. Many people choose to simply use the INP file as the "saved" version of their form, keeping it not in the iap tables, but only in operating system files. With this method, a form is saved by GENERATING it and modified by LOADING it. This is different from the alternative method of saving the form to the database with the SAVE option and modifying it with the MODIFY option.

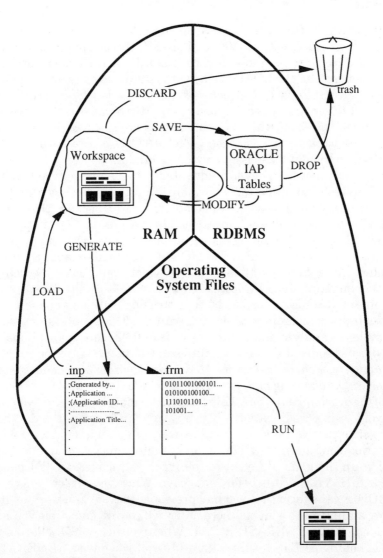

Figure 5.4 CHOOSE FORM window options

Both methods, "GENERATE and LOAD" and "SAVE and MODIFY,"
have advantages and disadvantages. First, there are several advantages
to GENERATE and LOAD, not the least of which is that it is much faster
than SAVE and MODIFY. This method also allows for easier modifica-

tion of the INP file directly because the INP file is edited and then LOADed as usual; with SAVE & MODIFY, the original must first be DROPped from the iap tables and then LOADed. The drop is necessary since a form cannot be LOADed if a form of the same name with the same owner (ORACLE userid) already exists in the iap tables. (LOADing under a different name is not a good alternative because creating several versions of the form with different names creates mostly confusion.) Finally, since a form has to be GENERATED before it can be run, SAVING to the database is somewhat redundant.

There are, however, several advantages to SAVE and MODIFY as well. This technique is better when more than one person is working with a particular form (a practice we do not advocate), because there is one central copy saved in the database. This avoids potential operating system file ownership problems with the INP files. Also, many people like the security of the SAVE and MODIFY regimen because their form is safer in the database than in a file, which could easily be deleted. Another advantage of SAVE and MODIFY is that the iap tables, just like any other ORACLE tables, can be queried using SQL. This opens a world of possibilities, including the ability to run SQL*Plus reports against the iap tables to analyze and document your SQL*Forms applications. We will discuss some of these possibilities in Chapter 9 (Documenting).

Whether you choose Save and Modify or Generate and Load is not as important as choosing one or the other and sticking with it for the entire life of the development effort. This rule is extremely important if you want to avoid losing modifications. If you save your forms to the database, make sure that you save them there every time. Imagine this common scenario: You enter SQL*Forms and create a new application. After setting up the general layout of the form, you leave SQL*Forms and decide to SAVE the form before you leave. When you return, you choose to MODIFY the form that you had previously saved. You work on it for hours, adding quite a bit of functionality. Of course, each time you RUN the form, you GENERATE it first. When you leave SQL*Forms you decide not to SAVE it this time, knowing that you have a GENERATED version, so you select DISCARD. Now there are two different versions of the form—the old one in the database and the new one in the INP file. This is exactly what you want to avoid because when you return to SQL*Forms to make the next modification, you might type in the name of your form and choose MODIFY. After making your modification (without realizing that you are looking at the *old* version from the database), you choose GENERATE so that you can RUN it. Too late do you discover that you just wrote over the existing INP file, thus destroying the new version. The only way to guarantee that you are always working with the most up-to-date version of your form is to either *always save* or *never save*.

Our preference is to use GENERATE and LOAD, because it is much faster and because we enjoy tempting fate by modifying the INP files directly. However, we will often SAVE a form to the database temporarily so that we can run queries against the iap tables. When we complete this process, however, we remember to DROP the form before making changes again. After development is complete we will SAVE all of the forms to the database for the initiation of the testing phase.

5.3 Writing Specifications for SQL*Forms

One of the large challenges in using a 4GL to build a complex application is the process of writing useful "program" specifications. When using a 3GL there are lots of diagramming choices, ranging from traditional flow charts to pseudocode. But how do we write specifications for a 4GL, in this case SQL*Forms? And since writing specifications for programs is about as exciting as writing documentation, few developers take it very seriously and it is seldom current or complete. This lack of interest often creates misunderstandings that can lead to serious bugs.

We can divide the specification process for SQL*Forms into two separate activities. The first centers around the cosmetics (the layout and the use of lines and graphics) of the form. This activity takes advantage the SQL*Forms Designer function that reads the data dictionary to create *default forms*. Thus we eliminate the need for hand-drawn screen images. These images can be printed out, or even shown onscreen, for review and acceptance by the user. The added benefit of using the built-in defaulting capability is that we can use the accepted forms (really the screen images) as the basis for the rest of the development effort.

The second activity is the specification of SQL*Forms processing. Such specifications can vary from high level functional descriptions to detailed processing descriptions. In many large organizations, analysts think through all of the necessary SQL*Forms processing in advance, and they give these process specifications to programmers who actually write the SQL*Forms applications. Smaller organizations usually have programmer/analysts doing both jobs.

Regardless of the development environment, we should have a common technique for writing specifications. When defining specifications it is very easy to get caught up in specific triggers and SQL*Forms coding. We recommend that you try to stay away from writing specifications for individual triggers and let the developer decide on the best technique. For instance, we might be tempted to specify that KEY-EXEQRY should EXEQRY in the FIRST_BLOCK, go to the SECOND_BLOCK and EXEQRY there, and then return to FIRST_BLOCK. Instead, why not specify an operation of QUERY that causes the display of every row in FIRST_TABLE and the corresponding rows in SECOND_TABLE? A similar philosophy can be used for the other operations of the form.

We like to break our specifications into the main operations of a SQL*Forms application: QUERY, INSERT, UPDATE, DELETE, COMMIT, and VALIDATE. These are very global operations that can occur in every block in the form. For each operation we specify any related actions. These actions include data validation, enforcing referential integrity, and moving the cursor around the screen.

We will not harp on the specification process since each organization has its own philosophy and its own techniques. Instead, we have included a sample of our MegaMarket specifications in Appendix 5.

5.4 SQL*Forms Design Review

Designing SQL*Forms applications appears to be a very straightforward process, but there are many nuances that should be studied. In an effort to uncover some of these subtleties, we recommend that you incorporate a design review of every SQL*Forms application into your development cycle. A thorough evaluation by a SQL*Forms "expert" will validate (or possibly invalidate) your physical design decisions and may help you avoid many potential difficulties. We consider this review system to be extremely important. Someone skilled at SQL*Forms can easily visualize the processing that is required for a specific function. If a function is going to be too complicated, it may be better to redesign it now instead of later when you are halfway through the development process.

In addition to awkward functions, there are times when you realize that your physical design makes a form very difficult to implement. In such cases, simple changes to the physical database design can often ease this difficulty. We incorporated many of these changes into our database during logical-to-physical design (discussed in Section 2.5). However, there are invariably additional changes identified during the specification process.

One general SQL*Forms design recommendation we make is that you beware of trying to force a form to be "multipurpose." Try to keep the task of each form specific and concise. It is a SQL*Forms truism that a form that attempts to do everything will perform well at nothing.

The design review should address at least these general issues:

- Keeping the functions of the form concise.
- Ensuring a close mapping of the blocks in the form to the underlying tables.
- Minimizing the number of pages in the form.
- Reviewing the intended operations of the form.

When designing for *portability* (all ORACLE-supported operating systems) or for *block-mode terminals* (specifically the large IBM and WANG environments) there are additional considerations and constraints that should be reviewed. For instance, in the latter case, you cannot depend on the use of KEY-NXTFLD or KEY-PRVFLD since the operator will probably use the TAB key. Any application that is intended to be portable must be designed with these constraints in mind. There are many junctures in the development of an application where the developer must make choices about implementation. Often these choices will be different in the two environments. When portability is not considered at the onset of development, these choices make it extremely difficult to port an application from one mode to the other (from block- to character-mode or vice-versa.) This is not a flaw in the SQL*Forms tool nor a falsification of Oracle's claim of portability. Terminal operation is completely different in a block-mode environment than it is in a character-mode environment. Thus, the forms will *run* in both environments, but they will not work the same! Throughout this chapter we will point out portability or block-mode constraints.

5.5 Creating Standards for SQL*Forms

We keep promising that we are about to start building applications and each time we throw in more preparatory "think" work! Fortunately, you will see that creating SQL*Forms standards is our first opportunity to build an application (in this case, a form called an application skeleton).

SQL*Forms standards are important for two reasons. First, the application should be consistent for the user. You can provide a user with a fully functioning and bug-free application, but just one user interface inconsistency or spelling mistake can lose you the confidence of that user. To avoid this pitfall in our project, we established guidelines for both the cosmetics (the "look") and the operation (the "feel") of our forms. These guidelines specify things such as field labels, error messages, and help text. Second, the application should be consistent for other developers. Maintenance can be a nightmare without coding standards and naming conventions (this is true of any application, not just those written with SQL*Forms).

Although many people believe that 4GLs somehow free us from the chore of setting standards, they don't. In fact, the added flexibility of high level languages can make maintenance even more of a challenge. We do not want to get sidetracked explaining the standards we developed. The details are given in Appendix 2, and in the rest of this section we will discuss the reasoning behind the standards we chose. Note that the first section of the standards document deals with all of the components of user interface, including error messages, screen field labels and alignment, and the use of graphics.

First of all, the number of error messages is an important consideration. When developing standards for error messages, keep in mind that error messages often require the execution of a SQL statement. We want to minimize error messages to reduce SQL processing overhead and improve performance. Sometimes this is not possible because we need to provide many very specific error messages. The level and detail of error messages is driven almost completely by the application user and their requirements. The MegaMarket user requirements are incorporated into our error message standards.

Another type of messaging uses the AUTOHELP facility. This facility will display a message to the user when they move into the field. These messages help the user to understand the meaning of the field. (Note that autohelp is not available in block-mode.)

The second section of the standards deals yet again with naming conventions. Our table and file naming standards provide the guidelines for the naming of the overall form. What we haven't considered are conventions for objects within SQL*Forms, such as block names, "work" field names, and user-named triggers.

Quiet Mode

The drawback of using the AUTOHELP facility is that the terminal will beep each time an AUTOHELP field is entered. We can optionally eliminate all sound effects by executing RUNFORM with the -q switch. This switch makes the form operate in quiet mode.

There are two camps on the block name issue: one group uses BLOCKn (n being a number starting with 1) and the other group uses the base table name. We fall into the second group. One reason for this preference is that we have had too many cases where we needed to add a block to a partially completed form. Using the BLOCKn technique, we would be left with two equally unacceptable choices—to leave the block names out of order by adding BLOCK3 between BLOCK1 and BLOCK2, or to rename BLOCK2 to BLOCK3 everywhere (including triggers and GOBLK/NXTBLK references) and add the new block as BLOCK2. In addition to this flexibility issue, we feel that using the base table as the block name makes block references more readable. Assuming that base table names are used for block names, we have one other block naming consideration: blocks without a base table (non-database blocks). These "work" blocks are usually called CONTROL or CTRL, yet any name is perfectly acceptable (we chose CTRL).

On a similar note, we should have guidelines for the names of "work" fields, which are non-database fields in a database block. In our experience, we have seen CTRL_, WORK_, and NONDB_, among others, used as identifiers for these fields. Again, anything is fine and we chose CTRL_.

Names for user-named triggers are probably the most difficult to formulate. The approach we used was to attempt to define the actions typically performed by triggers. We might perform general validations of data (verifying the format of a phone number, for instance). This action might be performed by many of the forms in the system. Thus, we developed a standard prefix for these triggers of VALID_. If you use this technique you will probably find that the standards will evolve with the development process, so you should make the standards document readily accessible to all developers and encourage additions.

You should also standardize the placement of user-named triggers. For example, should the triggers be placed at the form level, the block level, or the field level? If you place them at a high level (form, for example), then you improve readability because they are all centrally located but you make it difficult to cross reference triggers (where is a form level trigger used?). This is really a matter of personal taste, but again, we encourage consistency to improve the maintainability of the system.

Within all of our triggers we need to consider coding standards. For instance, do we put the SELECT and FROM clauses on the same line? Although this is a small point, readability is enhanced by choosing one method as the standard. We specified that each clause of a SQL statement (the SELECT, INTO, FROM, and each WHERE predicate) and each clause of a CASE statement (CASE, WHEN, END CASE) be aligned. We also noted that the block name be included in all form field references and the table name be included in all database field references. This makes the code more readable, simplifies future maintenance, and yields a slight performance gain (see Chapter 8 for details on performance considerations). Finally, we specified the use of GOBLK instead of NXTBLK, to improve maintainability when blocks are moved, dropped, or added to an existing form.

Another dilemma is form operation standards. We need to decide whether to take advantage of the default functionality of SQL*Forms or "hide" it through triggers. In the first case we clearly define the blocks on the form and train the user to press the appropriate keys to navigate the form (for example, KEY-NXTBLK and KEY-NXTREC). In the other case we redefine keys to perform navigation and make the divisions between blocks and rows "invisible." In the same respect, do we expect the user to press KEY-ENTQRY to determine whether a primary key exists? Or do we supply a control block to capture the primary key (or keys) and automatically query the information? In the former case the form can provide information for an unlimited number of primary keys (if the user used a LIKE operator or queried by a non-key field) and allow the user to scroll through them; in the latter, all of the information queried on the form always relates to one primary key at a time.

In many cases these decisions are provided by your user. In some cases the user will be fairly computer-literate and in others a complete novice. These different user communities require different operational interfaces.

In our application we have several different groups of users, ranging from executives to store managers to clerks. Thus, we will evaluate each form based on its expected users and develop the interface accordingly. We will not, however, forfeit any consistency. We will provide a standard

SQL*Forms Operation Prototypes

If this is your first application for a new user, you might consider developing a prototype. You can create copies of the same form with several different operational approaches and let the user decide which to use.

interface for each of the user communities (all forms used by clerks, for example).

5.6 Creating Skeleton Forms

When developing several SQL*Forms applications you will find that portions of each form are exactly the same. Thus, you will need to reference a printout of a completed form to manually copy triggers and other code that is identical. Typically the header information (titles, date/time, userid) and many of the form-level triggers (KEY-STARTUP, for instance, which is a trigger that fires when the form is first started and is generally used to set up the form's environment) apply to every form in the system. To promote consistency and reduce redundant efforts, we could create a document containing all of these "generic" triggers. Or there is an even better solution—we can create *skeleton forms* that contain triggers and other code common to all SQL*Forms applications.

These skeletons are created and then used as the basis for every form created. This provides a high degree of consistency and immense time savings for developers. We can develop a set of generic triggers and provide documentation to ensure that those using the skeleton and triggers understand the processing. This documentation can be written and quickly accessed via COMMENTS in the DEFINE TRIGGER window.

SQL*Forms COMMENTS

Take advantage of the COMMENTS capabilities when building SQL*Forms applications. It is much easier to document completed and tested triggers as they are developed than to try to go back and document them later.

Prior to jumping in and developing skeletons you should consider any applications that will be called by the generic triggers. For instance, you might decide to develop a help system that can be accessed from every form in the system. The trigger, or triggers, necessary to access the help system should be part of the skeleton form. Otherwise, you would have to go back at some later point (probably during integration) and add the trigger, or triggers, to every form in the system. You obviously want to avoid this retrofit process. The only way to do that is to develop these general applications now. If time or resources make this impossible you should at least write the specifications for the applications and take a stab at the required triggers. The following sections discuss our general applications that require triggers in the skeleton.

5.6.1 The HELP system

Application users today are accustomed to accessible, online help information. We decided to build a small help subsystem containing user documentation to meet this need. This subsystem will be available from any form in the MegaMarket system. We debated how the help subsystem should be structured and finally agreed to base it on the SQL*Forms divisions among forms, blocks, and fields. This allows the user to choose APPLICATION HELP and select the level of help required: form-level, block-level, or field-level.

The help form, named SHLPHTXT, will always be called from another form in the system. The help form will display multiple lines of scrolling text for each of the levels of help available. In order to show the correct help text, the help form must determine the form, block, and field that the user was on when APPLICATION HELP was selected. This information is passed to the help form via GLOBAL variables (we will see how the GLOBAL variables are established shortly). At form initiation, in trigger KEY-STARTUP, the help form reads the GLOBAL variables for form, block, and field and then issues the MENU macro. The MENU macro provides menu selections based on the description (entered in the BLOCK DESCRIPTION field of the DEFINE BLOCK window) of each block in the form. Figure 5.5 shows this menu.

Notice that each of the menu selections represents a different level of help. The user is presented with these choices upon entering the help form. SQL*Forms will go to the block the user selects. The form-level help block is shown in Figure 5.6.

```
                    APPLICATION HELP INFORMATION FORM
1    Form-Level Help Information
2    Block-Level Help Information
3    Field-Level Help Information




Enter selection #  1
```

Figure 5.5 Multi-level help information form

As you can see, the form-level help appears to be a completely independent form but is really one block of a multi-block form. The help form is designed so that each block (representing different levels of help) is on a separate page and appears to the user to be a separate form. This

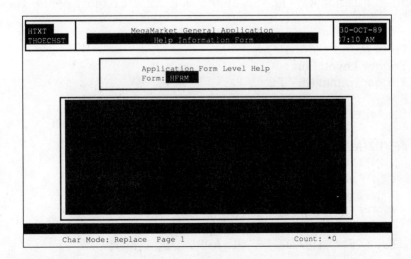

Figure 5.6 Form-level detailed help information

technique can be useful when very similar information is displayed and we wish to avoid creating separate forms. We must, however, be careful not to make the form too large by creating many similar pages. As we noted in our discussion of SQL*Forms design (Section 5.4), we want to avoid creating a form that is "overfunctional." In addition, a multi-page form can tax the memory of the system when run (we will discuss performance issues like this one in Chapter 8).

Now that we have defined the help application we can explore the other side of the help process—how to access help through an application form. As we noted, we need to pass the current form, block, and field values from the application to the help form. This is accomplished by copying SYSTEM variables into GLOBAL variables prior to calling the help form. The trigger code is shown in Figure 5.7. This trigger copies SYSTEM.CURRENT_FORM into one GLOBAL, SYSTEM.CURRENT_BLOCK into a second GLOBAL, and SYSTEM.CURRENT_FIELD into a third GLOBAL.

These trigger actions must be assigned to a specific function key. We first considered using KEY-HELP for this purpose. However, this would eliminate the standard SQL*Forms help (this help display provides field information including datatype and field length). We really wanted to give the user two different types of help: standard SQL*Forms help and application help. We decided to assign and define a function key specifically to access the help subsystem. SQL*Forms provides ten user-defined function keys for this application-specific requirements. These

Form Name: MINVSTOR
Trigger Level: Form
Trigger Name: KEY-F0

Step #2

```
#EXEMACRO COPY SYSTEM.CURRENT_FORM
   INTO GLOBAL.HELP_APPL_NAME;
  COPY SYSTEM.CURRENT_BLOCK
   INTO GLOBAL.HELP_APPL_BLOCK;
  COPY SYSTEM.CURRENT_FIELD
   INTO GLOBAL.HELP_APPL_FIELD;
  CALLQRY &HEADER.CTRL_APPL_LOCATION;
```

Figure 5.7 Passing GLOBALs to the HELP system

keys are KEY-F0 through KEY-F9 in the function key listing for triggers. We randomly choose KEY-F0 for our application help subsystem.

KEY-Fn

Some additional work is required to use KEY-F0 through KEY-F9. We must map the function to a physical keystroke. This is accomplished by running the CRT form (available only to DBAs) for the specific terminal type (IBM3101 or VT220, for instance). This process is quite simple and only requires that you modify one field value in the CRT form (a terminal escape sequence). For more information on the CRT utility refer to your ORACLE documentation.

Refer back to Figure 5.7 and note that the last statement calls the help form with the CALLQRY macro. This CALLQRY is made without a hardcoded form location (for our application the form location is the full path name /softlib/devl/sharedv1/form/shlphtxt). In step one of the KEY-F0 trigger we queried a table named SGENAPPL (which is where we store the locations of all forms) to determine the location of the help form. The next section discusses this trigger step and the SGENAPPL application.

5.6.2 The APPL form

When developing any application using SQL*Forms, whether large or small, we have many related functions. Each of these functions may be implemented in a separate form yet we still need to provide a way to navigate among the associated functions. This type of navigation is accomplished by defining triggers that use the SQL*Forms macros NEWFRM, CALL, or CALLQRY. We already saw one instance of this need in the CALLQRY to the help subsystem. We will see many other cases throughout this chapter.

When we perform any of these calling macros we must provide the name of the form that will be executed. SQL*Forms will attempt to locate that form in some default operating system location (for example, in the current directory, on the user minidisk, or in our TSO PDS). We noted earlier that the MegaMarket application forms are kept in a special set of directories. Therefore the full path name for the form must be provided to the SQL*Forms calling macro. For example, we would specify "#EXEMACRO CALLQRY /softlib/devl/sharedv1/form/shlphtxt" to access the shlphtxt form. As you can imagine, hard-coding the full path name into the call is very inflexible. Migration from devl to test in this scenario would require that we return to each form and change the CALLQRY to /softlib/test/sharedv1/form/shlphtxt.

A more flexible solution involves developing a database table that specifies the complete location of the form that correlates to the four-character form identifier (the last four characters of the form names, as per our standards). A portion of the data in this table, named SGE-NAPPL, is shown in Figure 5.8.

Once established, the trigger code that utilizes this information is fairly simple. Any application requiring access to another form executes two steps. The first step SELECTs the location of the form and puts it into a control field (this field is part of the skeleton and is named CTRL_APPL_LOCATION). Figure 5.9 shows the first step of the trigger that uses this technique to access the HTXT form.

The second step accesses the form using "#EXEMACRO <calltype> &HEADER.CTRL_APPL_LOCATION" where calltype is CALL, CALLQRY, or NEWFRM. This is the technique used in the second step of KEY-F0 (shown in Figure 5.7). Notice the "&" in front of the location field. The "&" is used in SQL*Forms to mean *the value of the field in* this

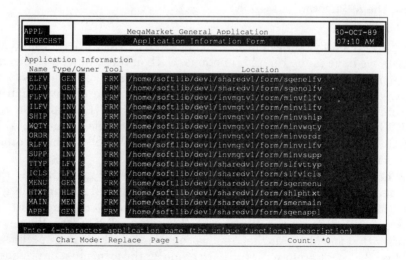

Figure 5.8 Application management data

field. In this case, we want to access the form whose name is in the field HEADER.CTRL_APPL_LOCATION. Without the "&" SQL*Forms would attempt to access a form named, literally, "CTRL_APPL_LOCATION".

We implemented procedures to ensure that any form could be called using this technique. These procedures dictate that the first step in the development of a new form is to enter the necessary information into the SGENAPPL table. This serves two functions. First, it ensures that there are no duplicate four-character form identifiers. Second, it allows for the application form to be entered into our menu hierarchy. We discuss this menu system next.

5.6.3 The dynamic MENU system

The use of a menu system provides a consistent interface for the access of any of the MegaMarket application forms. The menu system captures the hierarchy of the application forms, or the relationships among them. A menu system can be implemented using the SQL*Menu product or it can be developed in SQL*Forms. (Refer to Chapter 7 for a discussion of menu implementation choices.) We developed our own menu system using SQL*Forms. To implement this system we created a special

Form Name: MINVSTOR
Trigger Level: Form
Trigger Name: KEY-F0

Step #1

```
SELECT  SGENAPPL.APPL_LOCATION
INTO    HEADER.CTRL_APPL_LOCATION
FROM    SGENAPPL
WHERE   SGENAPPL.APPL_NAME = 'HTXT'
```

Failure Message:
SYSTEM ERROR Help form not in application table;
contact system admin.

Figure 5.9 Dynamic application location trigger

database table called SGENMENU. This table captures both the menu hierarchy (the relationships between forms) and the calls to individual application forms (using NEWFRM, CALL, or CALLQRY). A portion of the form used to enter data into SGENMENU is shown in Figure 5.10.

The two middle columns of this table are MENU_NAME (Menu Name on the screen), MENU_APPL_NAME (Appl Name). Each row in the SGENMENU table represents one selection line on a menu display. The selection could represent another level of menu or an application form. The distinction between the two types of selections is based on whether MENU_NAME or MENU_APPL_NAME have values. If MENU_NAME contains data the selection represents a menu. Otherwise, MENU_APPL_NAME will have a value representing an application form. Based on our naming standards you should recognize that MENU_APPL_NAME is a foreign key reference to the APPL_NAME column in the table SGENAPPL. As we already discussed, this foreign key can be used to construct the location of the application form.

Another important piece of information in the menu table is the name of the parent menu. This column is called MENU_MENU_NAME_PAR-ENT (Parent). You should notice from the naming conventions that MENU_MENU_NAME_PARENT is a foreign key reference back to MENU_NAME in this table. This kind of foreign key relationship is used to store a hierarchy within the table. This is appropriate since any menu

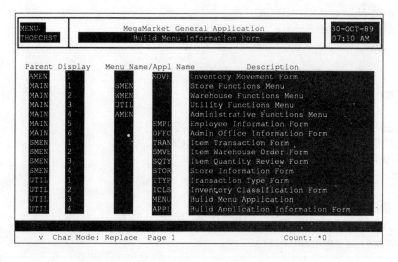

Figure 5.10 Dynamic menu data entry form

system is based on hierarchical parent-child relationships. (Every menu except the top menu will have a parent menu.) For example, in Figure 5.10 the second row is a menu named "SMEN" which represents the Store Functions Menu. Notice that the parent of this menu is a menu called "MAIN" which represents the main menu for the MegaMarket system. We will see in a moment how this information is used.

Once the information is built into the menu table we can develop the form to display the menu selections for the user. A sample of a menu in the MegaMarket system is pictured in Figure 5.11.

We refer to this menu application form as a "dynamic" menu. We use this term because the information displayed on the menu changes based on where the user is within the menu hierarchy. For example, in order to move from the highest menu in the hierarchy to any menu at the next level, the user selects an option and the menu form is simply requeried. This query is performed based on the information about parenthood in the menu table. For example, Figure 5.12 shows that each of the entries on the Main Menu has the parent menu "MAIN" and each of the entries of the sub-menu for Store Functions has a parent menu of "SMEN."

So, as we move through the menu we simply query all of the rows in the menu table that have a specific parent. When we move down the menu (to a lower level in the hierarchy) the parent is determined from the user selection. For example, on the MAIN menu we can select SMEN and

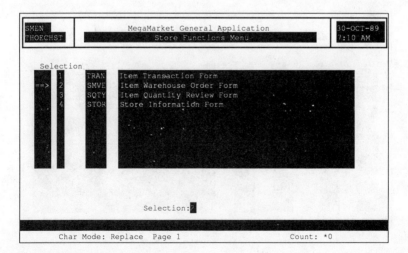

Figure 5.11 MegaMarket sample menu

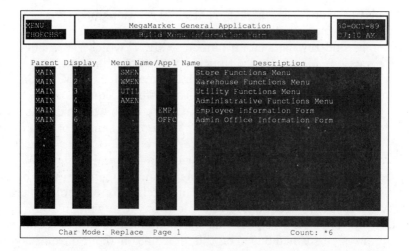

Figure 5.12a Parent-child hierarchy in menu table (MAIN MENU)

query all of the children of SMEN. Similarly, when we move up the menu (to a higher level in the hierarchy) the query is based on the parent of the current menu. From the Store Functions Menu (SMEN) we determine that the parent menu is MAIN. We can query all of the children of MAIN to show the next higher level. This process can be performed for all the

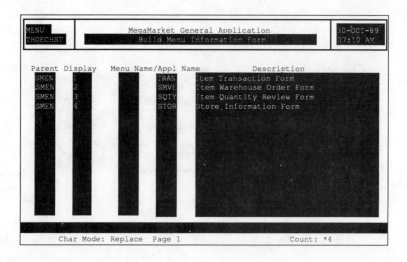

Figure 5.12b Parent-child hierarchy in menu table (SMEN MENU)

menu relationships in the SGENMENU table, including direct calls to application forms (MENU_APPL_NAME).

We implemented the menu hierarchy via a DEFAULT WHERE clause, shown in Figure 5.13, for the SGENMENU block. The query from the menu table will be restricted to the parent specified in HEADER.CTRL_FORM_NAME.

The data value in the HEADER.CTRL_FORM_NAME field is automatically (dynamically) updated via menu selections, such as entering a selection number and pressing NEXT FIELD, or pressing EXIT. Figure 5.14 is the trigger step that will determine the appropriate value for HEADER.CTRL_FORM_NAME. This trigger is fired when the user enters a selection and presses KEY-NXTFLD. The trigger first determines whether the user chose another menu (SMEN, for instance) or an application form. As we noted earlier this distinction can be made using the columns MENU_NAME and MENU_APPL_NAME. When MENU_NAME is null (the " in the trigger) an application form is called (via step CALL_APPL_FORM). Otherwise the block is requeried with a new parent by copying MENU_NAME into CTRL_FORM_NAME (used in the DEFAULT WHERE clause) and issuing EXEQRY.

Two other aspects of this form are of interest. The first is the technique we used to establish the selection numbers on the menu form. When ORACLE performs a query, each row returned is assigned a unique row number based on the order in which it was queried from the table. We can use this row number on the menu form to assign menu selection numbers and avoid the need for hardcoding them. We want to avoid hardcoding because it limits our flexibility in the future when we might want to add security to the system. For example, suppose that our security structure inhibited certain users from seeing all menu selections. If the selection number was hardcoded, the menu display might show gaps in the selection numbers: 1, 2, 5, 6, 9. This is not acceptable to the user. Using

Form Name: SMENMAIN
Block Name: SGENMENU

Default WHERE/ORDER BY clause for QUERY:

```
WHERE  SGENMENU.MENU_MENU_NAME_PARENT =
    :HEADER.CTRL_FORM_NAME
```

Figure 5.13 Menu data restriction using DEFAULT WHERE

Form Name: SMENMAIN
Trigger Level: Form
Trigger Name: KEY-NXTFLD

Step # 8   **Label**: FOUND_SELECTION

```
#EXEMACRO CASE :SGENMENU.MENU_NAME IS
    WHEN ' ' THEN GOSTEP CALL_APPL_FORM;
    WHEN OTHERS THEN
      COPY :SGENMENU.MENU_NAME
        INTO :HEADER.CTRL_FORM_NAME;
      EXETRG CENTER_FORM_DESC;
      COPY '      ' INTO &CTRL.CHOICE;
      EXEQRY; EXETRG ARROW_INIT;
      GOBLK CTRL; ENDTRIG;
    END CASE;
```

Figure 5.14 Menu selection using KEY-NXTFLD trigger

the assigned row number we can leave the door open to future menu security (or any other menu enhancements). We access the row number by simply specifying a database field named ROWNUM. This field, called a pseudo-column, will be given a value by ORACLE when the query on the menu table is performed.

The second technique uses the menu form to prevent discrepancies in form descriptions. It is very easy for the description displayed at the top of an application form to become inconsistent with the description of the form in the menu system. Understandably, such errors are unacceptable to users. To eliminate this possibility in the MegaMarket application we use GLOBAL variables to pass the form name and form description (available from the menu table) to each application form. At KEY-STARTUP, the application form reads the GLOBALs into the appropriate areas of the screen header. This process is automated by placing the necessary startup trigger steps into the skeleton (see START_FORM in the next section for more information). On the menu application side, we establish the GLOBAL variables using the trigger step shown in Figure 5.15. This trigger copies MENU_DESC into one GLOBAL and copies MENU_APPL_NAME into a second GLOBAL. The last line of the

ROWNUM

ROWNUM is not just available in SQL*Forms, but in all SELECT statements. As a pseudo-column, it is a value that can be treated like a column in a SELECT statement even though there is no physical column with which it is associated. ROWNUM has two idiosyncrasies that you should remember. First, ROWNUM values only get assigned to rows that satisfy the WHERE clause. So, if you use ROWNUM in the WHERE clause, you must be careful. For example, you can say:

```
SELECT column list
FROM tablename
WHERE ROWNUM < 10
```

This will return the first 9 rows of the table because for the first row, ROWNUM is 1 and that is less than 10. For the second row, ROWNUM is 2, and so on. For the tenth row, ROWNUM is 10 which is not less than ten. But what about the eleventh row? Is ROWNUM 11? No, because the tenth row was not returned, the ROWNUM for the eleventh (and all subsequent rows) is 10! Why is this important? Because you cannot say:

```
SELECT column list
FROM tablename
WHERE ROWNUM > 10
```

Even if there are 1000 rows in the table, this will return no rows because as each row comes up for comparison, it has a ROWNUM of 1 since no other rows have passed the comparison yet.

The second important aspect of ROWNUM is that the values get assigned before the ORDER BY is applied to the rows returned. So, if you wanted to rank the returned rows ORDERing BY a column and using ROWNUM as the rank, you're out of luck. For example, if we wanted to rank our 10 biggest transactions, we might want to say:

```
SELECT ROWNUM, TRAN_NUM, TRAN_AMOUNT
FROM MINVTRAN
WHERE ROWNUM <= 10
ORDER BY TRAN_AMOUNT DESC
```

> This won't give us what we have in mind, however, because the query will return the first 10 rows that it finds and THEN they will be ordered. We can't order them by TRAN_AMOUNT and then just select the first 10. (Actually, to get the answer that we want is difficult with SQL alone. You must use a correlated subquery that, for each row, performs a query that finds the total number of rows that have a larger TRAN_AMOUNT than this row and then order by this value.)

trigger accesses the application form using the CTRL_APPL_LOCATION that we discussed in the last section.

The last area to note in the menu form relates to the type of call used to access each of the application forms. We have two possibilities for the access, we can use CALL (or CALLQRY) or we can use NEWFRM. The main difference between the two types of call is where we end up when we exit the accessed form. For example, assume the menu form CALLs an application form. When we exit the application form we return to the menu form. If, instead, the menu form NEWFRMs to an application

Form Name: SMENMAIN
Trigger Level: Form
Trigger Name: KEY-NXTFLD

Step # 10

```
#EXEMACRO GOBLK CTRL;
  COPY :SGENMENU.MENU_DESC
    INTO GLOBAL.MENU_FORM_DESC;
  COPY :SGENMENU.MENU_APPL_NAME
    INTO GLOBAL.MENU_FORM_NAME;
  CASE HEADER.CTRL_APPL_TYPE_HCV IS
    WHEN 'LFV' THEN
      CALLQRY &HEADER.CTRL_APPL_LOCATION;
    WHEN OTHERS THEN
      NEWFRM &HEADER.CTRL_APPL_LOCATION;
  END CASE;
```

Figure 5.15 Dynamic form name and desc using GLOBALs

form, we do not ever return to the menu. The CALL and CALLQRY macros "stack" the forms in memory to allow for return to the CALLing form.

Although this is exactly what we need for a menu system, we always use NEWFRM to avoid the memory overhead involved in this stacking process. But using NEWFRM means that we must write the trigger code to return to the menu form from any application form. We developed a KEY-EXIT trigger for the skeleton form (we will discuss this in detail later) to perform a NEWFRM back to the menu form upon exit. Thus we have the best of both worlds because we simulate the CALL functionality without using the additional memory. One drawback we face with this technique is that the menu form must be loaded into memory and re-queried upon return from the application. Another minor drawback is that the cursor will always be on the first menu selection when we return from the application (in other words we will not remember the last selection).

5.6.4 The skeletons

We have performed all of the tasks in the prior sections to specify the general functions used by our MegaMarket forms. We determined all of the triggers needed by those functions to be included in our "skeleton" forms. For our application we developed two skeletons. Each of the skeletons shares a core of common triggers, but since they have different functionality there are many triggers unique to each. Depending on your user community, you may need several skeletons that provide varied functionality.

The first skeleton we developed is an application skeleton. The second skeleton is called a *list field values* (LFV) skeleton. The latter skeleton is useful since we often need to determine valid values for a field by using information from another database table. The function of displaying the valid choices for a field in SQL*Forms is called LIST FIELD VALUES. SQL*Forms provides a function key and field validation window input areas specifically for this purpose. The user can press KEY-LISTVAL and scroll through individual values. This function is useful, but limited because the user sees only one value at a time and can't scroll backwards.

We decided that this type of visual selection is much easier for the user when a full screen of values are displayed. Thus, when our user presses KEY-LISTVAL we call another form that provides multi-row selection of valid values. The user scrolls to a selection and then exits the form to "drag" the selected value back to the calling application. We call these forms LFV forms.

As we noted earlier, both types of skeleton forms share a standard "template" of information at the top (and sometimes bottom) of the form. This template is based on the cosmetic and naming standards established in Section 5.5. We physically create the template by defining the first form (we call this form skelapp) and the first block. Based on our standards this block is called HEADER. The HEADER block defines the top two lines of the form and the associated graphics. The first line contains a field for the form name (CTRL_FORM_NAME), the centered boilerplate "MegaMarket Inventory Application," and the current date (CTRL_DATE). The ORACLE userid (CTRL_USER), a field for the description of the form (CTRL_FORM_DESC), and the current time (CTRL_TIME) appear on the second line. The HEADER block is the only block we define for the skeleton forms.

We continue skeleton development by defining the triggers (referred to as core triggers) that are shared by all skeleton types. We will develop these triggers first and then add additional triggers for each skeleton later. The first core trigger we define is KEY-OTHERS at the form level. We use this trigger to turn *off* all the function keys in the entire form and to display a message (based on our standards) denoting that an invalid function key was pressed. As you can see in Figure 5.16, we display this message using the MESSAGE macro.

MESSAGE Macro

You can concatenate fields into the MESSAGE macro. For instance, you could write a trigger with #EXEMACRO MESSAGE '*ERROR*;' | | &SYSTEM.CURSOR_FIELD | | ' is invalid' to concatenate the value of the current field with the error message.

Next, we redefine (or turn *on*) each of the keys needed by the application. For example, creating a KEY-NXTFLD trigger with #EXEMACRO NXTFLD turns on the NXTFLD function key. The minimal set of keys we turn on includes KEY-EXIT (Note: this is very important—without KEY-EXIT you will not be able to exit the form!), KEY-PRINT (to allow for screen prints for documentation), KEY-NXTFLD, and KEY-PRVFLD. There may be many other keys turned on depending on the form operation. For instance, do we turn on KEY-NXTBLK? KEY-COMMIT? KEY-DELREC? The list goes on and on. We suggest that you consider

Form Name: SMENMAIN
Trigger Level: Form
Trigger Name: KEY-OTHERS

Step # 1

#EXEMACRO MESSAGE
  ERROR Invalid Key; press SHOW KEYS for valid function keys';

Figure 5.16 KEY-OTHERS to "turn off" keys

each key for each skeleton type and decide whether it applies to every block in every form in the application. If so, turn it on in the skeleton.

This KEY-OTHERs technique forces the developer to think about what keys are necessary for each form. We use this approach to minimize the possibility of a developer inadvertently leaving a key turned on. The erroneous function key will undoubtedly be found by the user and will probably uncover a bug in the form.

The next core trigger we define is KEY-STARTUP. This trigger automatically executes when the form is initiated. KEY-STARTUP is used to perform standard form initialization functions and to display information in our standard HEADER block. We originally placed all of the form start-up functions directly in the KEY-STARTUP trigger. We quickly realized, however, that these same initialization functions need to occur when the user clears the entire form using KEY-CLRFRM. To satisfy both of these needs, without duplication of code, we created a separate user-named trigger called START_FORM. This trigger is executed by both KEY-STARTUP and KEY-CLRFRM.

The START_FORM trigger contains two steps. The form name and description are retrieved from GLOBAL variables in the first step. Remember that the GLOBAL variables for the form name and form description are established by the menu application (discussed in Section 5.6.3). The values for these GLOBAL variables are also given default values in this step using the DEFAULT macro. This defaulting is necessary to display a form name and description when the form is run stand-alone (outside of the menu system). Stand-alone execution will be typical during development and testing. The second step of START_FORM issues a SELECT against SYSTEM.DUAL to fill in the remaining fields in the HEADER block. Figure 5.18 shows the two START_FORM trigger steps.

Display in Menus

We typically want only the valid keys (those turned on) to display when the user presses [SHOW FUNCTION KEYS]. To do this we can de-select "Display in Menus" in the DEFINE window of the KEY-OTHERS trigger as shown in Figure 5.17. This will cascade to all of the keys that the KEY-OTHERS trigger affects.

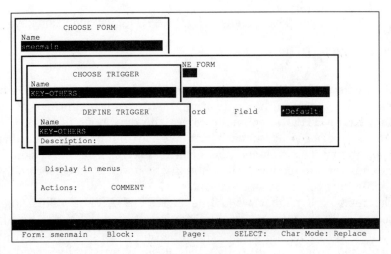

Figure 5.17 "Display in Menus" trigger attribute

We can also change the text that appears on the SHOW FUNC-TION KEYS display for a particular function key. This is accomplished by writing text in the description field in the DEFINE window.

The third core skeleton trigger also relates to the menu form. This trigger is the KEY-EXIT trigger. Extra steps are needed in this trigger because we want to return to the menu form when we exit our application. Actually, we not only need to return to the menu form, but we need to return to the appropriate menu on the form. To accomplish this we must determine the parent of the current application form. Then we can pass this information to the menu form using a GLOBAL variable. The menu form can use this parent as the basis for the menu choices displayed upon return. This selection is accomplished in the second trigger step (BACK_TO_MENU) shown in Figure 5.19.

Form Name: SKELAPP
Trigger Level: Form
Trigger Name: START_FORM

Step # 1

```
#EXEMACRO DEFAULT 'FORM NAME'
   INTO GLOBAL.MENU_FORM_NAME;
COPY GLOBAL.MENU_FORM_NAME
   INTO HEADER.CTRL_FORM_NAME;
DEFAULT 'FORM DESCRIPTION'
   INTO GLOBAL.MENU_FORM_DESC;
COPY GLOBAL.MENU_FORM_DESC
   INTO HEADER.CTRL_FORM_DESC;
EXETRG GLOBALS_IN;
```

Step # 2

```
SELECT  USER, SYSDATE, TO_CHAR(SYSDATE,'HH:MM PM'),
        LPAD(' ',(50-LENGTH(:HEADER.CTRL_FORM_DESC))/2)||
        :HEADER.CTRL_FORM_DESC
INTO    HEADER.CTRL_USER,
        HEADER.CTRL_DATE,
        HEADER.CTRL_TIME,
        HEADER.CTRL_FORM_DESC
FROM    SYSTEM.DUAL
```

Figure 5.18 Form initialization trigger

As we noted before, we also need to handle the case when the application is executed stand-alone. This is done by testing for the existence of a GLOBAL variable named MENU_FORM. This GLOBAL variable is established when the menu form initializes, thus the GLOBAL will only exist (be NOT NULL) when the application form is executed from the menu form. The first step of our KEY-EXIT trigger (shown in Figure 5.19) uses this GLOBAL to determine whether to simply EXIT or to return to the menu.

Another core trigger consideration is the use of GLOBAL values among application forms. Often a user will enter several different forms

Form Name: SKELAPP
Trigger Level: Form
Trigger Name: KEY-EXIT

Step # 1

```
#EXEMACRO EXETRG GLOBALS_OUT;
  DEFAULT ' ' INTO GLOBAL.MENU_FORM;
  CASE   GLOBAL.MENU_FORM IS
    WHEN ' ' THEN
      EXIT;
    WHEN OTHERS THEN
      GOSTEP BACK_TO_MENU;
  END CASE;
```


Step # 2 Label: BACK_TO_MENU

```
SELECT  SGENMENU.MENU_MENU_NAME_PARENT
INTO    HEADER.CTRL_FORM_NAME
FROM    SGENMENU
WHERE   SGENMENU.MENU_APPL_NAME =
        :HEADER.CTRL_FORM_NAME
```


Step # 3

```
#EXEMACRO COPY HEADER.CTRL_FORM_NAME
    INTO GLOBAL.MENU_FORM_NAME;
  NEWFRM &GLOBAL.MENU_FORM;
```

Figure 5.19 Menu form return using KEY-EXIT

in the application throughout the course of a day, or even a morning. Within each form the user may be requesting information about the exact same key value. We can provide a mechanism to "remember" the keys entered and reduce user keystrokes. We set up two triggers for this purpose named GLOBALS_IN and GLOBALS_OUT. In large applications these triggers will contain the logic to copy back and forth many stored values. The number of values depends entirely on the number of commonly used keys in the application. Our application needs are fairly simple. GLOBALS_IN and GLOBALS_OUT contain only one COPY macro that manipulates the EMPL_NUM. The user enters this number once and the system remembers the value for the remainder of the session. Each developer can add statements to GLOBALS_IN and GLOBALS_OUT for their respective applications.

Duplicate GLOBALs

You may need to establish a document containing the names of the GLOBALs passed between applications. Developers may inadvertently choose the same GLOBAL name to represent different information or choose a different GLOBAL name to represent the same information. The potential for error (for example, one GLOBAL overlaying the value of another) is high in both cases.

The remaining triggers are specific to the type of skeleton. The application skeleton (skelapp) and the list field values skeleton (skellfv) contain additional triggers. We have been working with only the application skeleton up to this point. Since the two skeletons share all of the core triggers we can create the list field values (LFV) skeleton as a copy of the application skeleton. We can then begin to develop the specific triggers for each skeleton. (You may want to save another copy of the generic skeleton in case an additional skeleton type is identified later.)

The primary trigger specific to the application skeleton deals with the code to provide the full-screen list of valid values for a field. On the application side we need to call the LFV form and accept a value from it. On the LFV side we need to pass the value back to the application. We would like to be able to make this process "generic" because we could easily have three or four LFV calls per form. Without a generic process we would need to specify essentially the same trigger steps every time we encountered a LFV field.

Our naming conventions pave the way for this kind of generic trigger. You may remember that our table and column naming standards specified that foreign key references to a "look-up" table contain CODE as the last part of the column name. This consistency in naming conventions allows us to analyze the name of the current field when the user presses KEY-LISTVAL to determine whether the field contains CODE in the appropriate position. If it does not, we can display the usual SQL*Forms message that a list of field values is not available for this field. If, however, it is a CODE field we can determine the name of the LFV form based on the column name and our naming standards. Let's walk through an example using the trigger steps in Figure 5.20.

Assume that the current field (the location of the cursor) is MINVFCLS.FCLS_ICLS_CODE. We first copy this field name into a control field in the HEADER block (CTRL_CURSOR_FIELD). We then use the SUBSTR function to determine the last four positions of the field name. If the characters are CODE, we can determine the four-character identifier for the LFV form (ICLS, in this example) using another SUBSTR function.

Note that we again query SGENAPPL for the full path name of the LFV form. (We have now seen this method used in the help system, the menu system, and LFV processing.) Once we have the application location we execute the user-named trigger LISTVAL_CALL to CALLQRY to the LFV form.

Form Name: SKELAPP
Trigger Level: Form
Trigger Name: KEY-LISTVAL

Step # 1

```
#EXEMACRO COPY SYSTEM.CURSOR_FIELD
    INTO :HEADER.CTRL_CURSOR_FIELD;
```

Step # 2

```
SELECT   SGENAPPL.APPL_LOCATION
INTO     HEADER.CTRL_APPL_LOCATION
FROM     SGENAPPL
WHERE    SGENAPPL.APPL_NAME = SUBSTR(:HEADER.CTRL_CURSOR_FIELD,15,4)
AND      SUBSTR(:HEADER.CTRL_CURSOR_FIELD,20,4) = 'CODE'
```

Failure Message:
List Field Values not Available

Step # 3

```
#EXEMACRO   EXETRG LISTVAL_CALL;
```

Figure 5.20 Automated KEY-LISTVAL trigger

Backwards SUBSTR

The SUBSTR function (and many other functions) will take a negative value as an argument. We could have determined the last four characters of the field by using SUBSTR (:HEADER.CTRL_CURSOR_FIELD,-4). This statement says to start the SUBTR four positions from the end of the string and continue to the end. Careful use of this technique could eliminate the need for cryptic naming standards.

This last step, the CALLQRY, is in a separate user-named trigger so it can be shared by forms that are similar to LFV forms, but slightly different. For example, the user might need help determining an employee number. A simple form containing the employee number and name could be developed for this purpose. Although this form would be similar to a LFV form, the foreign key column name and form name do not meet the generic trigger criteria. The user-named trigger LISTVAL_CALL allows some of the generic code for KEY-LISTVAL to be shared by these variations of LFV forms. Figure 5.21 provides all of the code for this trigger. The first three lines prepare the call to the list field values form. The remaining lines will be discussed shortly.

Form Name: SKELAPP
Trigger Level: Form
Trigger Name: LISTVAL_CALL

Step # 1

```
#EXEMACRO ERASE GLOBAL.MENU_FORM_NAME;
  ERASE GLOBAL.MENU_FORM_DESC;
  CALLQRY &HEADER.CTRL_APPL_LOCATION;
  CASE  GLOBAL.LFV_CODE_VALUE IS
    WHEN ' ' THEN
      NULL;
    WHEN OTHERS THEN
      COPY GLOBAL.LFV_CODE_VALUE
        INTO &SYSTEM.CURSOR_FIELD; NXTFLD;
  END CASE;
```

Figure 5.21 LISTVAL_CALL trigger

Once we have developed the triggers in the application form to access the LFV form, we need to create generic triggers to process the values passed back. We will put aside the application skeleton for a moment and develop the list field values skeleton. The first specific trigger step we will add to the LFV skeleton causes the form to display all of the current values in the base table at execution. This is accomplished by adding an EXEQRY to the KEY-STARTUP logic of the form.

The next specific triggers are used for passing values back to the calling form (the form where the user pressed KEY-LISTVAL and accessed the LFV form). One of these triggers allows the user to make a selection and exit, the other allows the user to exit without making a selection (to look but not touch). We decided to use KEY-EXIT and KEY-MENU for these functions. The KEY-MENU trigger copies ' ' (representing NULL) into a GLOBAL variable named LFV_CODE_VALUE and executes the EXIT macro to exit the LFV form. The user is returned to the application form without a value. The KEY-MENU trigger is displayed in Figure 5.22.

The KEY-EXIT trigger needs a little more intelligence. First, we should mention that the LFV form is used both as a query form and as an entry form. Thus each LFV form can be run stand-alone (not called from an application form) for INSERTs, DELETEs, and UPDATEs of base table data. Since we are using the same form for both of these functions, the user has many function keys available (turned on via triggers). This includes the NXTFLD function via KEY-NXTFLD. Why do we mention this? When we exit with a value, we want to copy the value in the field ending in CODE to the GLOBAL variable named LFV_CODE_VALUE. We know that the form contains a field with CODE (or we could not have called it from the application form). If we could be sure that the user's cursor was in this field, we could copy the

Form Name: SKELLFV
Trigger Level: Form
Trigger Name: KEY-MENU

Step # 1

#EXEMACRO COPY ' ' INTO GLOBAL.LFV_CODE_VALUE; EXIT;

Figure 5.22 Exiting look-up form *without* a value

value of the current field into LFV_CODE_VALUE. We could do this using &SYSTEM.CURSOR_FIELD. (The meaning of "&" is explained above in Section 5.6.2.) However, since the user can press [NEXT FIELD] and move around the row we can't be sure that the cursor is in the proper field when the user exits the form.

To account for this movement we must add some extra logic to our skeleton KEY-EXIT trigger. We need to know the entire field name for the CODE field. Once again, based on our naming conventions we can determine this field name by concatenating the form name with CODE. For example, if the LFV form name is ICLS we know the field name is ICLS_CODE. The first step in Figure 5.23 uses this information to build the CODE field name. The four-character form name (CTRL_FORM_NAME) is concatenated with _CODE into a control field (CTRL_LFV_CODE_FIELD). The second step of the trigger is a little tricky. In this step the value of the field whose name is in CTRL_LFV_CODE_FIELD (this translation is accomplished with the &) is copied into a GLOBAL variable. In our example, the value in the field ICLS_CODE is copied into the LFV GLOBAL.

We have completed the triggers for the LFV form and have established the process for copying a selected value to an application form. Now we

Form Name: SKELLFV
Trigger Level: Form
Trigger Name: KEY-EXIT

Step # 1

```
SELECT  :HEADER.CTRL_FORM_NAME||'_CODE'
INTO    HEADER.CTRL_LFV_CODE_FIELD
FROM    SYSTEM.DUAL
```


Step# 2

```
#EXEMACRO COPY &HEADER.CTRL_LFV_CODE_FIELD
    INTO GLOBAL.LFV_CODE_VALUE;
  EXIT;
```

Figure 5.23 Exiting look-up form *with* a value

must return to the application skeleton to develop the last portion of this technique. We discussed the steps taken to call the LFV form in Figure 5.21. The application form is suspended, or stacked, when the CALLQRY takes place. At that moment the user is making a selection from the LFV form. Once the selection is made, the user is returned to the application form. The trigger continues to execute from the CALLQRY. The remaining task of the application skeleton is to copy the selected value into the appropriate field on the form. The CASE statement checks whether a value was selected from the LFV form. If the GLOBAL is ' ' (denoting NULL) the trigger step is complete. Otherwise, the GLOBAL value is copied into the current field (the CODE field).

The basic triggers in our skeletons are complete. This time we are really ready to start building the MegaMarket application. No more preparations, we promise!

5.7 Building the Application

The first decision we made in the development of our application was how to divide up the work. Since we were working separately, we designed our development process to have minimum interdependencies. We accomplished this by dividing the Inventory Management application into separate functional areas. Since a store operates differently from a warehouse and a warehouse differently from an administrative office, we grouped together store functions, warehouse functions, and administrative office functions. The general functions we already discussed (including the menu and help subsystems) were also grouped together. We could give each developer or group of developers a separate function and allow them to act as a fairly autonomous unit. For our application, one developer was responsible for the warehouse and administrative office functions and the other developed the general and store functions. The first task for both developers was to create the list field values forms for their functional areas.

5.7.1 The LFV forms

The list field values forms, by their definition, will be accessed by many different application forms. They should be written early in the development cycle to allow for testing of the list field values functionality and to promote the creation of reasonable development data. These forms can be developed with minimal effort. We start the process by loading the LFV skeleton into a different name. (The steps for this duplication process were discussed in Section 5.2.5.) We then create a default form using the appropriate base table. Next, we move the fields around on the screen and add boilerplate to conform to our cosmetic standards. Then we specify an ORDER BY clause (in the DEFINE BLOCK window) to return the data in ascending order. Finally, we add triggers and field validation information.

These steps complete the development of a list field values form, with one caveat. We need to allow for the possibility of increased functionality in a list field values form. For example, we may want to provide the user with the ability to produce subsets of the rows displayed on the LFV form. By default all rows in the base table are displayed at KEY-STARTUP by a general EXEQRY. Subsets of these rows can be produced using a value passed in a GLOBAL variable as query criteria. We might need this capability, for example, on the SLFVICLS form to produce a list containing only "parent" inventory classes (remember that the ICLS table is a hierarchical table). We will further explore these types of requirements when we develop the application forms. We mention this possibility now to stress the importance of designing forms that remain open to future possibilities.

In addition to standard list field values forms, there is a special type of LFV form that is often required by the application. We discussed these special LFV forms in Section 5.6.4 for the KEY-LISTVAL trigger. These LFV forms are truly query-only forms that list application table information (rather than code table information). For example, many application forms will specify the entry of OFFC_NUM (the primary key of an administrative office). We might want to provide a LFV type form for multi-row display and selection of administrative offices. The standard entry form for offices will not be acceptable because only one, or maybe two, offices will be displayed. The entry form must display all of the fields in the SGENOFFC table. The user is not interested in all of these fields when making a selection. A few fields, perhaps OFFC_NUM and OFFC_DESC would be sufficient for the user to make a selection. A special LFV form can be developed for this purpose. These special forms are typically identified and written throughout the development process.

Developing a special LFV form is almost as simple as developing a standard LFV form. We begin, as always, by loading the LFV skeleton form into a different name. We then create a default block by designating the base table and deselecting unneeded columns. An ORDER BY clause is specified and the boilerplate modified to meet our standards. These steps are the same for a standard LFV form. The one additional step enforces query-only operation of the special LFV form. In this step we access the form level trigger list and drop all triggers that relate to DML operations (e.g. KEY-CREREC, KEY-DELREC, KEY-COMMIT).

Once the LFV forms are completed we are ready to create the application forms. We use the default forms function in SQL*Forms to start this process.

5.7.2 Default application forms

Default forms are usually developed in conjunction with the creation of forms specifications. Their cosmetics and layout can be reviewed by the user early in the design process. This technique is a simple type of prototyping that benefits both the user and the development staff. Refer to Section 5.3 (SQL*Forms Specifications) for details.

To create the default forms we begin by loading the application skeleton into a different name. We then define the default blocks on the form. This process can be made easier by taking heed of a few things. First, be aware that SQL*Forms takes the default size of number fields (the NUMBER datatype) from the data dictionary. SQL*Forms adds two positions to all number fields to allow for a plus or minus sign and a decimal point. For example, a field defined to be five digits in the database—NUMBER(5)—will default to seven positions on the form. The user will get an Oracle error if they put either six or seven digits into the screen field. This error occurs because the screen field is larger than the specified precision for the database field. In addition, a number defined without a size or precision in the database (by defining it as simply NUMBER) will default to a field length of 44 positions. To avoid these pitfalls you should always verify the field length via the FIELD VALIDATION window and remember to resize number fields.

Next, you should remember to specify an ORDER BY clause in each block (in the DEFINE BLOCK window). The ordering of data returned from ORACLE cannot be predicted and will not necessarily be constant. What this means is that you cannot be guaranteed of the display order unless you use an ORDER BY clause. It is easy to forget this requirement during development because you are working with such a small amount of data.

Also keep in mind that we are nearing the end of the millennium. The ORACLE DATE format will handle this with ease, yet you need to be careful that your forms will do the same. The easiest solution in SQL*Forms is to provide 11 character dates (DD-MON-YYYY) on all of your forms. Another option is to develop generic logic that will determine and append the current century to the date on the form. In either case, we recommend that you provide for this requirement.

You might want to remember a few keystroke savers while creating default forms. First, when changing a field to display-only you can deselect the display option in the FIELD ATTRIBUTES window. This will turn off all attributes for the field and allow you to reselect display. Also, when cutting and pasting fields you may run into a situation where the fields are out of order at execution time. This happens because SQL*Forms assigns a field the next highest field sequence number when it is cut and pasted. The movement of the cursor is determined by these field numbers. One way to correct the navigation is to DEFINE FIELD for each field on the screen and change the sequence number accordingly. A much quicker technique is to cut and paste the entire block. This is done by first selecting the top-left and bottom-right corners of the block and moving the cursor back to the top-left position. The cut and paste combination will then recreate the entire block and automatically reorder the fields left to right and top to bottom.

You might not know that when you are using the default capability you can produce a multi-row display from the start. You accomplish this by choosing to view the columns for the base table in the BLOCK OPTIONS window. Accepting the column list will display the starting screen line and the number of rows displayed. You can then increase the number of rows displayed up to the displayed maximum. Note that this technique only works if SQL*Forms calculates that there is room for more than one row on the page (including all of the default boilerplate). You can, of course, always change the block later to accommodate multiple rows, but this can often mean a lot of reorganizing on the screen

Our last comment about multi-row displays relates to the number of rows buffered option. This option specifies the number of rows that SQL*Forms will query for this block. For example, you can request that 20 rows be buffered even though only 2 are displayed. SQL*Forms will buffer the remaining 18 rows in memory. The user can scroll through all 20 rows without requesting additional data from the database. The rule

Multi-line Forms

It is possible to create a multi-line, multi-row form. For instance, Figure 5.24 shows the administrative office form.

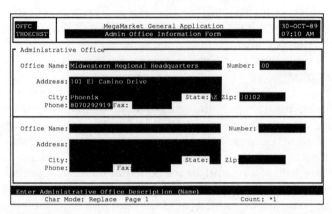

Figure 5.24 A multi-row, multi-line form

In this form, each row in the SGENOFFC table takes up more than one line on the form. Yet we want the form to display as much information as possible on one page. We can display the information for two offices on a page and allow the user to scroll the block as they would for any multi-row display. We do this in the BLOCK OPTIONS window by changing the number of lines per row to include all lines plus the heading. Figure 5.25 shows this window.

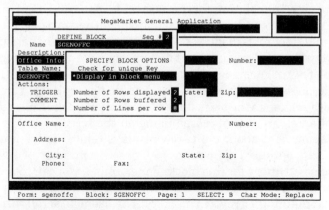

Figure 5.25 BLOCK OPTIONS for multi-row, multi-line form

of thumb is to buffer two times the number of rows displayed. Refer to the tuning information in Chapter 8 for more details on this option.

Another typical procedure during the default form development process is the placement of key fields onto page 0. Page 0 is a page on the form that cannot be displayed during runtime, so it is a good place to "hide" things. Since several blocks may share the same key, the display of this information for all blocks after the first block is redundant. Although, you cannot remove the key fields entirely from the form (because they are needed for all DML operations) you can move the fields to page 0. Page 0 placement for key fields is the simplest technique for the coordination of the blocks on a form. In addition to key fields, you may also need to put CTRL_ fields on page 0. For instance, you already saw that we put CTRL_APPL_LOCATION in the HEADER block on page 0. A complex form can actually fill page 0 with fields. To save space on page 0 you can resize the display length for all page 0 fields to 1. This will cause the field to take up only as much space on page 0 as the field label and a 1 character field require.

Page 99

Some SQL*Forms developers put all page 0 fields on a different page in the form, perhaps page 99. They then set up a "debug" key which goes to a field on that page. When they are running the form they can press this key and look at their page 0 fields to determine whether the application is functioning properly. This technique could even be included in the skeletons by adding a HEADER.CTRL_ field to page 99 and providing a KEY-F? trigger to go to that field.

Once we have developed our default forms and they have been approved by our users, we can start putting in the rest of the application code (fondly referred to as the "guts"). There are some techniques that we will use over and over in this process. The next section will discuss some of them.

5.7.3 Generic functions and the code library

Many functions and techniques are not specific to one application, but relate to many different applications, and are common issues when using

SQL*Forms. In this section we discuss these functional techniques by providing a description of the function and an example of a form from our application that uses the technique. Application specific functions and techniques are discussed in the next section.

5.7.3.1 NULL values. These cause many difficulties in a relational database. We discussed this issue during our logical-to-physical design in Section 2.5.2. Regardless of good physical database design practices, we may still have key fields that can be NULL. If so, we must make coding exceptions to handle them in our SQL*Forms applications. The crux of the issue arises when a screen field that can be NULL is used as a query criterion. In SQL*Forms, we usually specify criteria in the form "base_table.column = :screen_field." When the column we are comparing may be NULL, we must be careful when we specify our criteria. To retrieve ONLY the NULL values we must specify that "base_table.column IS NULL." This is not the same as the first query example. The first query example would bring back columns with ANY value if the screen field was NULL. The second query example would bring back the rows with NULL values in the column. This is a very important distinction. For instance, in the SGENEMPL form we can specify a query value for EMPL_FACL_NUM in the CTRL block. If we omit a criterion then we mean ANY value. To implement this requirement our DEFAULT WHERE clause (shown in Figure 5.26) will have to search specifically for NULL values if nothing was entered.

5.7.3.2 Query-only blocks. Another general technique is the implementation of query-only blocks. Although we can have a block with no enterable fields (beginning with version 2.3 of SQL*Forms), we must be able to

Form Name: SGENEMPL
Block Name: SGENEMPL

Default WHERE/ORDER BY clause for QUERY:

```
WHERE (SGENEMPL.EMPL_FACL_NUM = :CTRL.EMPL_FACL_NUM)
   OR   (SGENEMPL.EMPL_FACL_NUM IS NULL
   AND  :CTRL.EMPL_FACL_NUM IS NULL)
```

Figure 5.26 Retrieving NULL values

enter the block to be able to query the information. Thus, there is still no simple technique for implementing query-only blocks in SQL*Forms. There are several alternatives to this issue. The first approach requires the creation of one non-database field in the corner of a special control block. This field is the only enterable field in the control block and has two triggers, KEY-SCRUP and KEY-SCRDOWN. These triggers are used to allow scrolling on the query-only block without allowing the user to enter into the block (and make changes to data). The second approach is to create a non-database field for each row in the query-only block. The field is typically placed one space away from the actual data in the block. This technique provides the same basic functionality as the previous solution. The final approach is to make one of the database fields in the row enterable but not updateable. This approach provides the most appealing interface for the user since additional fields are not displayed on the screen.

Changing Field Attributes

In SQL*Forms 3.0, you can change the attributes of fields through the use of triggers. This helps with problems like this one because we can make fields enterable or nonenterable during runtime.

These last two approaches require a special trigger to prohibit the user from moving the cursor to a blank line. Without this trigger the user would be able to enter information into the blank field on the new line (since the field is enterable). We prevent this movement to a blank line

Form Name: SGENOLFV
Trigger Level: Form
Trigger Name: KEY-NXTREC

Step # 1

```
#EXEMACRONXTREC;
  CASE   :SGENOFFC.OFFC_NUM IS
    WHEN ' ' THEN PRVREC;
    WHEN OTHERS THEN NULL;
  END CASE;
```

Figure 5.27 Trigger to prevent moving past last row

by recoding the KEY-NXTREC trigger as in Figure 5.27. This trigger simply checks the value of a mandatory field (typically a primary key). If the field is NULL then the cursor must be on a new row. In this case we PRVREC to the last row in the listing.

5.7.3.3 Tracking time. We should also consider how to keep track of exactly when actions occur. For example, the transaction date and the transaction time in our application are both important for an audit trail. Thus, when we insert transaction information into the database we want to record both the current date AND the current time. Unfortunately, the DATE attribute in SQL*Forms does not contain the time (actually, it contains the default time of 12:00 a.m.). In order to store both the date and the time we must manually record the transaction time when the data is committed (inserted). Figure 5.28 from the MINVTRAN application provides the logic for this function. First the row is inserted into the database by SQL*Forms. We then update the row that was just inserted (using a POST-INSERT) and add the time information.

Since SQL*Forms considers all DATEs to be 12:00, what do you think happens when the DATE (containing the TIME) is subsequently brought back into the application? If *any* field in the row is updated, the TIME is truncated (set back to 12:00)! If your form allows both inserts and updates, you would need two more triggers to prevent this corruption of

Form Name: MINVTRAN
Block Name: MINVTRAN
Trigger Level: Block
Trigger Name: POST-INSERT

Step # 1

```
UPDATE MINVTRAN
SET MINVTRAN.TRAN_DATE = TO_DATE(:MINVTRAN.TRAN_DATE||
   TO_CHAR(SYSDATE,'HH:MI:SS'), 'DD-MON-YYHH:MI:SS')
WHERE ROWID = :MINVTRAN.ROWID
```

Failure Message:
SYSTEM ERROR Could not record time of trans. Contact Sys Admin.

Figure 5.28 Adding the current time to a row

your data. The first trigger would retrieve the date and time from the database into non-database fields on the form. This is accomplished using TO_CHAR functions in a POST-QUERY trigger. The second trigger would need to put the date and time back into the database table. Once again, SQL*Forms first performs the database operation (update, in this case). We then update the date column and add the time information using a POST-UPDATE. Figure 5.29 contains the two triggers for this process.

5.7.3.4 Validating fields that contain boilerplate. We often have a need to validate fields that contain boilerplate. For instance, we would like to

Form Name: MINVTRAN
Block Name: MINVTRAN
Trigger Level: Block
Trigger Name: POST-QUERY

Step # 1

```
SELECT  TO_CHAR(:MINVTRAN.TRAN_DATE,'DD-MON-YY'),
  TO_CHAR(:MINVTRAN.TRAN_DATE,'HH:MI:SS')
INTO MINVTRAN.CTRL_TRAN_DATE,
  MINVTRAN.CTRL_TRAN_TIME
FROM  SYSTEM.DUAL
```

Trigger Name: POST-UPDATE

Step # 1

```
UPDATE MINVTRAN
SET  MINVTRAN.TRAN_DATE =
  TO_DATE(:MINVTRAN.CTRL_DATE||
  :MINVTRAN.CTRL_TIME, 'DD-MON-YYHH:MI:SS')
WHERE  ROWID = :MINVTRAN.ROWID
```

Figure 5.29 Remaining triggers for time field manipulation

allow the user to enter a social security number with, or without, the dashes. In either case, we need to be sure that the format is correct. We can use the TRANSLATE function of SQL for this requirement. The TRANSLATE function allows us to create a mask and check the value (on the screen or in the database) against the mask. Figure 5.30 shows the validation trigger for the social security number (SOC_SEC_NUMBER) in the employee table (SGENEMPL). This trigger appears very complicated but is really quite straightforward. Let's first examine the WHERE clause. The TRANSLATE function changes any digit (the list of 0123456789) into a 9 and leaves all other characters untouched. Therefore the WHERE clause is simply checking the data entered against the masks of 999-99-9999 or 999999999.

The SELECT portion of the statement is more complicated. The INSTR function determines whether the user entered the SSN with dashes. If so, no formatting is necessary. Otherwise the SSN entry must be divided into three pieces and concatenated with dashes. The IF-THEN logic of the SELECT is performed with the DECODE function.

During physical design we made a decision to store the boilerplate with all database fields to improve performance (refer to Section 2.5.2 for

Form Name: SGENEMPL
Trigger Level: Form
Trigger Name: VALID_SSN

Step # 1

```
SELECT   DECODE(
         INSTR(:SGENEMPL.EMPL_SOC_SEC_NUMBER,'-'),0,
         SUBSTR(:SGENEMPL.EMPL_SOC_SEC_NUMBER,1,3)||'-'||
         SUBSTR(:SGENEMPL.EMPL_SOC_SEC_NUMBER,4,2)||'-'||
         SUBSTR(:SGENEMPL.EMPL_SOC_SEC_NUMBER,6,4),
         :SGENEMPL.EMPL_SOC_SEC_NUMBER)
INTO     SGENEMPL.EMPL_SOC_SEC_NUMBER
FROM     SYSTEM.DUAL
WHERE    TRANSLATE(:SGENEMPL.EMPL_SOC_SEC_NUMBER,
         '0123456789','9999999999') IN ('999-99-9999','999999999')
```

Failure Message:
ERROR Invalid Social Security Number; format 999-99-9999 or 999999999.

Figure 5.30 Validating SSN that contains boilerplate

details). Due to this general decision, we will have several forms that need the same basic SSN trigger discussed above. To allow all forms to share the developed code, we can place this SSN SQL statement into a special form called the *code library*. We implemented the code library by creating a form called "codelibr" in the /softlib/devl/utility/form directory. Any application developer can cut and paste a portion of this form into their INP file. This library will contain any triggers that might be needed by another application developer. This approach helps us avoid "reinventing the wheel."

Reusable Code

Version 3.0 of SQL*Forms provides the ability to copy triggers from one form to another. The copy can occur physically by adding the code into the application INP file or the code can be added to the executable FRM file when generated (this is similar to a COPYLIB concept in COBOL). Establishing the code library technique now will allow you to quickly take advantage of the new feature when it becomes available.

Editing an INP File

The cut and paste operation requires the application developer to edit the INP file directly. The easiest way to safely perform this edit is to build the trigger (such as VALID_SSN at the form-level) through the Designer and put some text into the trigger step (like the words "TRIGGER HERE"). Subsequent Generation of the form will cause an error (because "TRIGGER HERE" is not a valid trigger step operation) but will not destroy the trigger. You can then go into the INP file using your favorite system editor and paste in the appropriate trigger.

Another consideration when storing boilerplate in the database relates to the placement of the validation trigger (for example, VALID_SSN). Executing the validation trigger at POST-CHANGE will specify that the trigger should fire in two occasions. The trigger will fire when the field changes (this is what we expect) and the trigger will fire for each row returned by a query. The POST-CHANGE is fired at query time by SQL*Forms because the screen field value changed from nothing (NULL) to the database field value. This nuance is very important. Consider a sequence of events where we first press EXEQRY and display a row from the EMPL table on the screen. This query causes the POST-CHANGE trigger on EMPL_SOC_SEC_NUMBER to fire. The POST-CHANGE then SELECTs the EMPL_SOC_SEC_NUMBER into itself. Since EMPL_SOC_SEC_NUMBER is a database field, SQL*Forms will flag the database row as changed. When this type of circular update inadvertently occurs, you will receive many unexpected "Do you want to commit?" messages when you try to exit the form. A better alternative is to fire the validation trigger at POST-FIELD. There are a few drawbacks even with this location of the trigger, however. First, the trigger fires every time the user moves through the field (regardless of whether a change occurred). Second, POST-FIELD is not valid in the block-mode environment.

All of this discussion is necessary because we are storing the boilerplate in the database. You might think this decision was not sound. However, if we had decided not to store the boilerplate, we would have other equally difficult decisions to make during the implementation of this process. Consider, for example, the triggers needed to display a date in a format that is different from the Oracle DATE format. We would

Form Name: SGENEMPL
Block Name: SGENEMPL
Field Name: CTRL_SOC_SEC_NUMBER
Trigger Level: Field
Trigger Name: POST-CHANGE

Step # 1

```
SELECT  SUBSTR(:SGENEMPL.CTRL_SOC_SEC_NUMBER,1,3)||
        SUBSTR(:SGENEMPL.CTRL_SOC_SEC_NUMBER,5,2)||
        SUBSTR(:SGENEMPL.CTRL_SOC_SEC_NUMBER,8,4)
INTO    SGENEMPL.EMPL_SOC_SEC_NUMBER
FROM    SYSTEM.DUAL
WHERE   (SGENEMPL.EMPL_SOC_SEC_NUMBER <>
        SUBSTR(:SGENEMPL.CTRL_SOC_SEC_NUMBER,1,3)||
        SUBSTR(:SGENEMPL.CTRL_SOC_SEC_NUMBER,5,2)||
        SUBSTR(:SGENEMPL.CTRL_SOC_SEC_NUMBER,8,4)
OR      :SGENEMPL.EMPL_SOC_SEC_NUMBER IS NULL
```

Figure 5.31 Field boilerplate post-change trigger

need two fields for the DATE information. The first field would be a database field in ORACLE DATE format on page 0 and the second field would be a non-database field on the display page. The code to handle both the query and insert/update of these fields is quite complex. Examine Figure 5.31 for a simplified example of the POST-CHANGE trigger needed if the social security number is stored without boilerplate. Note that a POST-QUERY trigger would also be necessary to complete this process.

Two fields are used in this trigger. The first is the database field EMPL_SOC_SEC_NUMBER and the second is the non-database field CTRL_SOC_SEC_NUMBER. The non-database field is the data entry field on page 1 while the database field is on page 0. When the operator enters a social security number with dashes (the logic for variable entry would be the same as the prior example) the numbers from the entry are SELECTed into the database field. The WHERE clause determines whether the value in the non-database field is different from the value in the database field using the not equal operator (<>). If the values are not the same the SELECT INTO occurs, otherwise both values are untouched.

5.7.3.5 Query on a non-database field. The capability that is still missing with the POST-CHANGE trigger (and the double field alternative) is the ability to query on a non-database field. The natural mechanism in SQL*Forms for query criteria uses only database fields. Thus, we must explicitly write the code to allow the query of non-database fields. We accomplish this using a PRE-QUERY trigger. This trigger converts any non-NULL, non-database fields into the database field to be used for query. In the following example we copy the converted social security number into the database field. Once this is done, SQL*Forms will automatically use this value at query time (as though someone had typed the value directly into the field). Figure 5.32 provides these trigger steps.

5.7.3.6 Developing validation triggers. There are three alternatives for developing field validation triggers. The first uses a SELECT statement in a POST-CHANGE against the SYSTEM.DUAL table to validate the field. If the SELECT fails, so does the POST-CHANGE, and the cursor does not move. The second technique uses a CASE statement in a KEY-NXTFLD trigger. The screen field is checked against a set of pre-determined values in the CASE statement. A NXTFLD is executed if the

Form Name: SGENEMPL
Block Name: SGENEMPL
Trigger Level: Block
Trigger Name: PRE-QUERY

Step # 1

```
SELECT  SUBSTR(:SGENEMPL.CTRL_SOC_SEC_NUMBER,1,3)||
        SUBSTR(:SGENEMPL.CTRL_SOC_SEC_NUMBER,5,2)||
        SUBSTR(:SGENEMPL.CTRL_SOC_SEC_NUMBER,8,4)
INTO    SGENEMPL.EMPL_SOC_SEC_NUMBER
FROM    SYSTEM.DUAL
```

Figure 5.32 Field boilerplate pre-query trigger

value matches, otherwise the cursor does not move. The third technique also uses a CASE statement but in the POST-CHANGE trigger. The CASE statement uses the OTHERS condition with an ENDTRIG FAIL to cause the trigger to fail. All of these techniques are acceptable but the

Form Name: SGENEMPL
Block Name: SGENEMPL
Field Name: EMPL_TITLE
Trigger Level: Field
Trigger Name: POST-CHANGE

Step # 1

```
#EXEMACRO CASE :SGENEMPL.EMPL_TITLE IS
    WHEN 'Facility Manager' THEN NULL;
    WHEN 'General Manager' THEN NULL;
    WHEN 'Facility Worker' THEN NULL;
    WHEN OTHERS THEN
      MESSAGE
        '*ERROR* Invalid Empl Title; values are FM, GM, FW';
      ENDTRIG FAIL;
    END CASE;
```

Figure 5.33 Employee title validation trigger

last is the recommended approach. This technique is shown in Figure 5.33. The use of CASE statements is preferred because they execute faster than SELECT statements (because SQL*Forms does not send a SQL statement to the kernel).

CASE Commas

The syntax of the #EXEMACRO CASE statement allows for commas between fields to reduce typing. This functionality is not currently documented. For example, Figure 5.34 shows another way we could have written the CASE statement in Figure 5.33.

```
#EXEMACRO CASE :SGENEMPL.EMPL_TITLE IS
    WHEN 'Facility Manager',
         'General Manager',
         'Facility Worker' THEN NULL;
    WHEN OTHERS THEN
      MESSAGE
        '*ERROR* Invalid Empl Title; values are FM, GM, FW';
      ENDTRIG FAIL;
    END CASE;
```

Figure 5.34 Alternate CASE syntax

5.7.3.7 The use of user exits. One of the features that makes SQL*Forms so flexible is the ability to use a 3GL program to perform some function not otherwise available. These 3GL extensions to SQL*Forms are called *user exits*. Many application developers tend to shy away from user exits in their applications. Although we recognize that portability is of prime interest, there are cases in which a simple user exit can save a tremendous amount of redundant application code. The effort required to rewrite the exit for a different operating environment can be well worth the time. For instance, consider the CODE fields that we discussed for the LFV forms. Each time we run into one of these fields (and it is not unusual in a medium-sized application to have 100 or more CODE tables) we need to display the description for the code. We do this both to confirm the CODE value for the user and to conform to our standards. This means that we must write essentially the same SQL statement in a POST-CHANGE trigger for every CODE field in every application form. We could avoid this wasteful redundancy by writing one user exit to which we pass the name of the CODE field. The user exit would query the appropriate

CODE table and return the description. Figure 5.35 shows a portion of the C code for this technique. As you can see, the user exit code is fairly simple and straightforward. The time saved and the elimination of potential errors is tremendous.

```c
/* codeval - returns the description of a CODE field */
int codeval()
{
EXEC SQL BEGIN DECLARE SECTION; /*Bind variable declarations*/
  /* Variable declarations...*/
EXEC SQL END DECLARE SECTION;
...
/* Get the name of the Current Form Field */
        EXEC IAF GET SYSTEM.CURRENT_FIELD INTO :field_name;
/* Format field_name and column_name */
        field_name.arr[field_name.len] = '\0';
        strcpy(column_name.arr,field_name.arr);
        column_name.len = field_name.len;
/* If field doesn't end in CODE, return success */
        str_ptr = ((char *)field_name.arr)+strlen(field_name.arr)-4;
        if (strcmp(str_ptr,"CODE"))
                return(SUCCESS);
/* Parse out the root of the table/column name */
        column_name.arr[strlen(column_name.arr)-4] = '\0';
/* Get the value of the CODE field */
        EXEC IAF GET :field_name INTO :code_value;
        code_value.arr[code_value.len] = '\0';
/* Build table name */
        strcpy(table_name.arr,"SLFV");
        strcat(table_name.arr,column_name.arr);
        table_name.arr[strlen(table_name.arr)-1] = '\0';
        table_name.len = strlen(table_name.arr);
/* Build column name */
        strcat(column_name.arr,"DESC");
        column_name.len = strlen(column_name.arr);
/* If field is empty, return SUCCESS and blank out DESC field */
...
/* Build SELECT statement */
        strcpy(sql_stmt.arr,"SELECT ");
        strcat(sql_stmt.arr,column_name.arr);
        strcat(sql_stmt.arr," FROM ");
        strcat(sql_stmt.arr,table_name.arr);
        strcat(sql_stmt.arr," WHERE ");
        strcat(sql_stmt.arr,field_name.arr);
        strcat(sql_stmt.arr,"='");
        strcat(sql_stmt.arr,code_value.arr);
        strcat(sql_stmt.arr,"'");
        sql_stmt.len = strlen(sql_stmt.arr);
/* PREPARE statement and OPEN cursor */
...
/* Exception handling */
...
/* Fetch the description into desc_value using cursor PREPAREd cursor */
...
/* Put the description into the DESC field */
        EXEC IAF PUT :column_name VALUES (:desc_value);
        return(SUCCESS);
/* Whenever the description is not found */
...
}
```

Figure 5.35 CODE field user exit

5.7.3.8 Generating sequence numbers. Another common dilemma and concern is the approach to generating sequence numbers. With a relational database, we do not have true pointers from one table to another. We do, however, have sequential numbers that we use to relate two tables. These numbers are basically another form of a pointer. In V6, you can create SEQUENCEs for all of your system-assigned numbers. You can then write PRE-INSERT triggers to provide the next number. Optionally, you can assign the number in a POST-CHANGE trigger on a mandatory field in the block. This can be a helpful technique since users often complain that the sequence number is not assigned until commit time. Thus, in V6 the sequence number can be assigned at any time. The only potential drawback to this approach is that there will be "gaps" in the numbers. This occurs if the number is assigned at POST-CHANGE and the user does not commit. Lost numbers can also occur if the PRE-INSERT assigns the next number and the user discards the commit. We do not consider this a significant drawback since the numbers are almost purely for internal purposes.

5.7.3.9 List Field Values forms. The final generic technique relates to refining our LFV forms (either standard LFV forms or special LFV forms) to produce subsets. For example, we developed a special LFV form that displays all inventory classes. This form is usually appropriate, but there are cases where the user wishes to see a subset of inventory classes. For instance, the user may be interested only in inventory classes that have a common parent (for example, all inventory classes that have the parent COMP). We can add logic to our form to accept a GLOBAL variable and produce a subset of inventory classes. The form that calls the inventory class LFV form can pass the value for the query criteria. When the query is executed in the inventory class LFV, this value will be used. Figure 5.37 shows the necessary logic at KEY-STARTUP and the DEFAULT WHERE clause for the inventory class block.

This completes our discussion of generic functions and techniques. The next section introduces triggers that are specific to an application form. While you may not need to implement the exact function described, you will find that an understanding of the techniques will improve your overall expertise with SQL*Forms.

V5 Sequences

If we are using V5 this is a much more difficult process. We can only assign sequence numbers at PRE-INSERT and we must explicitly lock and update a separate table. Figure 5.36 contains the typical steps to select the current sequence number, lock the row holding the number, and then update the current number.

Form Name: SGENEMPL
Block Name: SGENEMPL
Trigger Level: Block
Trigger Name: PRE-INSERT

Step # 1

```
SELECT  EMPL_SEQUENCE.NEXTVAL
INTO    SGENEMPL.EMPL_NUM
FROM    EMPL_SEQUENCE
FOR     UPDATE OF EMPL_SEQUENCE.NEXTVAL
```

Step # 2

```
UPDATE EMPL_SEQUENCE
SET  EMPL_SEQUENCE.NEXTVAL =
     EMPL_SEQUENCE.NEXTVAL+1
```

Figure 5.36 V5 sequence number trigger

We recommend that a separate table be used for each sequence number needed (in this case the table is EMPL_SEQUENCE). This will reduce the amount of contention for any particular table. For those migrating to V6 there is an additional technique to save time at conversion and quickly take advantage of the new sequence generation process. You could create a small user exit called GENERATE_SEQUENCE. This user exit would be passed the name of the sequence, such as EMPL, and would return the next number. The user exit for V5 applications would execute each of the steps listed above against the appropriate sequence table. Then, as part of the migration to V6 you could simply rewrite this user exit to work with appropriate SEQUENCEs.

Form Name: SGENEMPL
Trigger Level: Form
Trigger Name: KEY-STARTUP

Step # 1

```
#EXEMACRO EXETRG START_FORM;
   DEFAULT ' ' INTO GLOBAL.ICLS_ICLS_CODE;
   COPY GLOBAL.ICLS_ICLS_CODE INTO
     HEADER.CTRL_ICLS_ICLS_CODE
   EXEQRY;
```

Block Name: SLFVICLS

Default WHERE/ORDER BY clause for QUERY:

```
WHERE   ((ICLS_ICLS_CODE = :HEADER.CTRL_ICLS_ICLS_CODE)
   OR      :HEADER.CTRL_ICLS_ICLS_CODE IS NULL)
ORDER BY ICLS_ICLS_CODE,ICLS_CODE
```

Figure 5.37 Default query of a block

5.7.4 Application-specific techniques

The first application of interest is the transaction form, MINVTRAN. This form is used to record the sale of inventory items at a store. At the point of sale, the user (in this case probably a clerk) enters in the inventory class code and the price. We would like to show the current total at the bottom of the form. Figure 5.38 contains the screen image for the transaction form.

5.7.4.1 Running totals. Implementing running totals in SQL*Forms is not easy at all. In fact, it is impossible in a block-mode environment since the total must be updated instantly (prior to any interrupt to the host in the block-mode environment). When considering the implementation of running totals, think first about the options you have for trigger placement. You could place the trigger at an individual field, at an individual record, at commit, and on specific keystrokes. Which of these

Undocumented Macros

As we have seen, there are many different macros available in SQL*Forms 2.3. There are, however, a few macros that we have not used because they are not documented anywhere in the ORACLE manuals. Some of these include:

```
#EXEMACRO FIRSTREC;
#EXEMACRO LASTREC;
#EXEMACRO GOREC FIRST;
(or #EXEMACRO GOREC LAST;)
```

There are also a few user exits that are not documented:

```
#EZ-CHKREC FIRST (or #EZ-CHKREC LAST)
#EZ-GOREC FIRST (or #EZ-GOREC LAST)
```

Experiment with these and see what they do—we think you'll be pleasantly surprised. Remember, however, that these are not documented for a reason (most likely they were never fully implemented or tested), so use them at your own risk!

should you use to display the current total? You might be tempted to add the current amount to the total field as the user moves out of the current amount field (in other words, on POST-CHANGE or POST-FIELD). This approach is difficult to implement because the user is not predictable. For example, consider one item being sold. The user enters the first item with an amount of $6.25. You add this amount to the current total of $0 and display $6.25. The user then realizes that the amount was incorrect, moves back to the field, and changes the amount to $5.25. You again add this amount to the current total of $6.25 and display $11.50! Since this type of change will not be uncommon, you probably do not want to calculate totals on the amount field.

The approach you do want to take is to calculate totals at the record level. This technique allows the user to move around within the record and change the amount field without affecting the running total. In our form, we use a POST-RECORD shown in Figure 5.39 to add the current amount to the running total when the user moves to a new record.

This technique works wonderfully as long as the user never moves the cursor backwards. Otherwise we are back in the same situation dis-

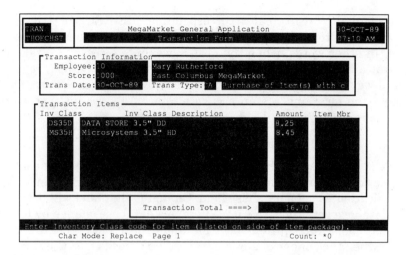

Figure 5.38 Transaction form

cussed above. Consider a user who enters one item and moves to another
row (thus firing the POST-RECORD on record one). The user then enters
another item and moves back to the first row (thus firing the POST-
RECORD on record two). Finally, the user moves back to the second row
(and fires the POST-RECORD on record one again). Once again, we have
an incorrect total. Fortunately, the solution to this scenario is fairly
simple. The POST-RECORD trigger adds the current amount to the

Form Name: MINVTRAN
Block Name: MINVTRAN
Trigger Level: Block
Trigger Name: POST-RECORD

Step # 1

```
SELECT NVL(:CTRL.TRAN_TOTAL_AMOUNT,0) +
   NVL(:MINVTRAN.TRAN_AMOUNT,0)
INTO CTRL.TRAN_TOTAL_AMOUNT
FROM  SYSTEM.DUAL
```

Figure 5.39 On-screen TOTALs post-record trigger

running total. We can create a corresponding PRE-RECORD trigger (as shown in Figure 5.40) to *subtract* the current amount from the running total. In other words, when the user moves into a record we take the current amount out of the running total and when the user leaves a record we add it back in. This technique allows the user to move freely around the form and see an accurate total of all records (except the current record, of course).

5.7.4.2 Faking a database change. The second tricky aspect of the transaction form is that one of the fields the user enters on the form, the inventory classification, is not a database field. Changing that field will not cause any database activity, so we have to fake a database change by forcing it to happen. This requirement is not unusual. In fact, there are many times when the change of a non-database field needs to cause a change to a database field. We saw one case of this dependency in the discussion of formatting fields in Section 5.7.4. In that discussion, the database and non-database fields represented the same information in different formats. In this case, the inventory classification field has no corresponding database field. Thus, we must force a change to any of the database fields in the block. In Figure 5.41 you can see that we choose to update the TRAN_NUM field by copying a zero into the field in a POST-CHANGE trigger.

The trigger shown in this figure will cause a change to the TRAN_NUM field and will subsequently cause commit triggers to fire. This is impor-

Form Name: MINVTRAN
Block Name: MINVTRAN
Trigger Level: Block
Trigger Name: PRE-RECORD

Step # 1

```
SELECT  NVL(:CTRL.TRAN_TOTAL_AMOUNT,0) -
        NVL(:MINVTRAN.TRAN_AMOUNT,0)
INTO    CTRL.TRAN_TOTAL_AMOUNT
FROM    SYSTEM.DUAL
```

Figure 5.40 On-screen total pre-record trigger

Form Name: MINVTRAN
Block Name: MINVTRAN
Field Name: CTRL_ICLS_CODE
Trigger Level: Field
Trigger Name: POST-CHANGE

Step # 1

```
SELECT   SLFICLS.ICLS_DESC,0
INTO     MINVTRAN.CTRL_ICLS_DESC, MINVTRAN.TRAN_NUM
FROM     SLFVICLS
WHERE    SLFVICLS.ICLS_CODE = :MINVTRAN.CTRL_ICLS_CODE
```

Failure Message:
ERROR Invalid Inv Class code; enter class code listed on side of item.

Figure 5.41 INV class code validation trigger

tant because we need to insert TRAN records and because we have special code that is executed at PRE-INSERT. You may recall from the physical design discussion that the item number is stored in the transaction table and the transaction number is stored in the item table. This redundancy was introduced to allow the transaction form to be strictly data entry. (In other words, the user does not need to query the item from the database in order for it to be sold.) This relationship is enforced at PRE-INSERT. An update is issued against the ITEM table to record the ITEM_TRAN_NUM.

5.7.4.3 Either/Or relationships. The employee form, SGENEMPL, demonstrates another common requirement. When we modeled the employee table, we determined that an employee can work at either a facility or an administrative office. Now how do we implement this either/or condition in the employee form? There are basically two choices. The first is to check the relationship at PRE-INSERT time. We can make sure that the user entered either EMPL_OFFC_NUM or EMPL_FACL_NUM, but not both. Figure 5.42 contains the trigger step logic for this check.

The second approach involves cursor movement. We can code the KEY-NXTFLD and KEY-PRVFLD triggers surrounding these two fields so

Form Name: SGENEMPL
Block Name: SGENEMPL
Trigger Level: Block
Trigger Name: PRE-INSERT

Step # 1

```
#EXEMACRO CASE :SGENEMPL.EMPL_FACL_NUM IS
    WHEN ' ' THEN
      CASE :SGENEMPL.EMPL_OFFC_NUM IS
        WHEN ' ' THEN
          MESSAGE
            '*ERROR* Admin Office or Facility must be entered';
          ENDTRIG FAIL;
        WHEN OTHERS THEN
          GOSTEP CREATE_EMPL_NUM;
      END CASE;
    WHEN OTHERS THEN
      CASE :SGENEMPL_OFFC_NUM IS
        WHEN ' ' THEN
          GOSTEP CREATE_EMPL_NUM;
        WHEN OTHERS THEN
          MESSAGE
            '*ERROR* Entry of BOTH Admin Office and Facility invalid';
          ENDTRIG FAIL;
      END CASE;
    END CASE;
```

Figure 5.42 Employee insert validation trigger

that the cursor will not move into EMPL_OFFC_NUM if
EMPL_FACL_NUM has something in it, or vice versa. We can likewise
enforce the entry of one of these fields. Although this technique provides
more immediate feedback to the user, we do not advocate its use. One
reason for this is that the validation process is too dependent on the
screen layout. A developer modifying this form later could easily add
fields to the form and unwittingly corrupt the either/or integrity check.
Another reason not to use this technique is that it is not portable to block-
mode environments (again because KEY-NXTFLD is not used).

MOVE_ICLS_CODE	MOVE_FACL_NUM_FROM	MOVE_FACL_NUM_TO	MOVE_QUANTITY
DS35D	3000	1000	2
DS52H	3000	1000	1
MS35H	3000	1000	1
DS35D	3000	1000	4
DT52D	3000	1000	2

Figure 5.43 Movement table

5.7.4.4 Coordinating the information in the database with the real world. An interesting dilemma we have in the automated inventory system is coordinating the information in the database with the real world. We need to track items as they are physically moved among facilities (in this case, most combinations of stores and warehouses). For instance, a store may request twenty inventory classifications with varying quantities from one or more warehouses. We support this function in the store movement form, MINVSMVE, by assigning the appropriate number and type of items to the requesting store. But how do we ensure that these items are actually loaded on a truck and delivered to the store?

We went back to our user to determine how this is done in the current paper system. We found that the shipping department of each facility receives a list of inventory items to be sent and they use this list to fill the truck(s). To accommodate this, we needed to create a table to capture an audit trail of any change to ITEM_FACL_NUM using the store movement form, MINVSMVE, or the warehouse movement form, MINVWMVE. We created a new table for this purpose called MINVMOVE. This table is used to record the FROM_FACL_NUM, the TO_FACL_NUM, and the QTY to be moved. This table will be populated throughout the day, a hard-copy produced for each warehouse in the evening, and the rows deleted. A portion of this table is shown in Figure 5.43.

On a related note, do we need to be concerned with a store selling, via MINVTRAN, an item that has not yet been received from the warehouse? Fortunately, this issue can be resolved easily because the user cannot sell something that is not physically in hand. Therefore, if a user requests an item that has not been received from the warehouse, the item will not physically reside in the store and it will not be sold.

There is one more aspect of this process that we need to consider. We view inventory items as individual items with a specific inventory classification. Each item has a unique item number within the system but we move and sell items based only on inventory classification (since, for example, we could not expect someone to gather a specific pencil from a pallet of pencil boxes). This nuance requires an interesting technique within the two movement forms. Figure 5.44 shows the screen images for these forms.

As you can see, we are recording the MINVMOVE information in the multi-row block in each of these forms. The remaining processing is to assign the TO_FACL_NUM to a set of items. For example, the first row on the form MINVSMVE shows 10 DS35Ds being moved from FACL_NUM 30 to FACL_NUM 200. The processing behind this row needs to change the ITEM_FACL_NUM from 30 to 200 for 10 individual DS35D items. Since we are not concerned with specific ITEM_NUMs, we can select any 10—purely at random—and update them.

The technique to make this happen uses the ROWNUM pseudo-column that we mentioned in the SGENMENU processing. The numbers in this column are sequentially assigned as rows are retrieved from the table. Our SELECT and subsequent UPDATE for this (QTY) number of items can be implemented as shown in the PRE-INSERT trigger of the MINVMOVE block (Figure 5.45).

5.7.4.5 Multi-selection look-up forms. Producing a multi-selection look-up form is another trick that often comes in handy. Most look-up forms (including ours) list all of the valid values and return one when exiting

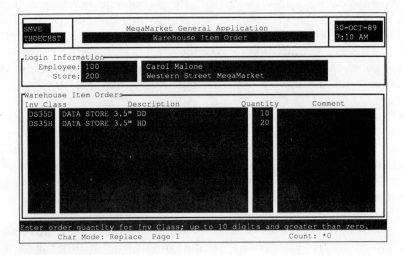

Figure 5.44 Warehouse order form

Form Name: MINVSMVE
Block Name: MINVMOVE
Trigger Level: Block
Trigger Name: PRE-INSERT

Step # 1

```
UPDATE MINVITEM
SET      MINVTIEM.ITEM_FACL_NUM =
         :MINVMOVE.MOVE_FACL_NUM_TO
WHERE    MINVITEM.ITEM_FACL_NUM =
         :MINVMOVE.MOVE_FACL_NUM_FROM
AND      MINVITEM.ITEM_ICLS_CODE =
         :MINVMOVE.MOVE_ICLS_CODE
AND      ROWNUM <= :MINVMOVE.MOVE_QUANTITY
```

Figure 5.45 Store ITEM movement trigger

the form. Many times, however, we would like to bring back several values. If the number of values brought back was fixed, then the form would operate exactly the same as a single value form with more global variables. What we really want, though, is a dynamic form that allows for any number of selected values. In our application, we needed such a form for assigning the inventory classifications to a facility or supplier. Because a given facility is likely to have several inventory classifications, we did not want our user to have to choose them one at a time from a standard look-up form, so we built the multi-selection look-up form shown in Figure 5.46.

Notice that this form looks like any other look-up form except for the single character field running down the left side. It is in this field, called SELECTION, that the user will "mark" his choices; this is the only enterable field on the form. Each time the NXTFLD key is pressed on a given record, an asterisk will be copied into this field as a marker. If the NXTFLD key is pressed again, the asterisk will be removed. In this way, selections can be "toggled" on and off. At the same time some work is going on behind the scenes to keep track of the selections in a single control field that can be returned as a global. This field will contain a list of values separated by a vertical bar (the "|" character). Each time a record is selected, its value is added to the list and each time it is

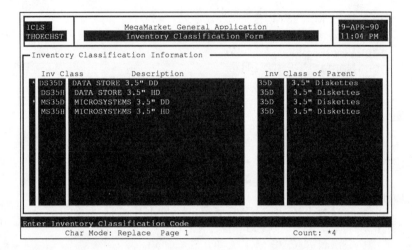

Figure 5.46 Multi-selection look-up form

deselected, the value is removed. Figure 5.47 shows the KEY-NXTFLD, STARIT, and UNSTARIT triggers for this process.

Exiting to SQL*Plus

Writing complex SQL within a trigger window can be difficult. We often exit from SQL*Forms and work within SQL*Plus on the necessary SQL. Once we have the SQL statement working we can add it to our form (by retyping or editing the INP file). This technique eliminates the frustration caused by debugging SQL statements executed in SQL*Forms.

5.7.4.6 Looping techniques. When we leave the form the field SELECTION_LIST is returned in a global variable to the calling form. Once this variable is received by the calling form it still must be parsed out into the individual codes. The trigger uses a looping technique within SQL*Forms. This technique is shown in Figure 5.48.

You will notice in a moment that the MINVSHIP form, which allows us to select the orders that came in on a given shipment, appears to use a similar technique for selecting the orders. The difference, however, is that the order records already exist and we must simply fill in the

Form Name: SLFVICLS
Block Name: SLFVICLS
Field Name: SELECTION
Trigger Level: Field
Trigger Name: KEY-NXTFLD

Step #1

```
#EXEMACRO CASE :SLFVICLS.SELECTION IS
   WHEN '' THEN EXETRG STARIT;
   WHEN OTHERS THEN EXETRG UNSTARIT;
END CASE;
```

Trigger Name: STARIT

Step #1

```
#EXEMACRO COPY '*' INTO :SLFVICLS.SELECTION;
```

Step #2

```
SELECT   :HEADER.SELECTION_LIST||
         RTRIM(:SLFVICLS.ICLS_CODE)||'|'
INTO     :HEADER.SELECTION_LIST
FROM     SYSTEM.DUAL
```

Trigger Name: UNSTARIT

Step #1

```
#EXEMACRO COPY '' :SLFVICLS.SELECTION;
```

Step #2

```
SELECT   SUBSTR(:HEADER.SELECTION_LIST, 1,
         INSTR(:HEADER.SELECTION_LIST,
         SLFVICLS.ICLS_CODE||'|')-1)||
         SUBSTR(:HEADER.SELECTION_LIST,
         :SLFVICLS.ICLS_CODE||'|')+
         LENGTH(:SLFVICLS.ICLS_CODE)+1)
INTO     :HEADER.SELECTION_LIST
FROM     SYSTEM.DUAL
```

Figure 5.47 Multi-selection look-up trigger (*Part 1*)

Form Name: SLFVICLS
Block Name: SLFVICLS ·
Trigger Level: Block
Trigger Name: PARSE_SELECTIONS

Step #1 Label: TOP

```
#EXEMACRO COPY GLOBAL.SELECTION_LIST
  INTO:HEADER.SELECTION_LIST;
  CASE :HEADER.SELECTION_LIST IS
    WHEN " THEN ENDTRIG;
    WHEN OTHERS THEN NULL;
  END CASE;
```

Step #2

```
SELECT  SUBSTR(:HEADER.SELECTION_LIST,1,
        INSTR(:HEADER.SELECTION_LIST,'|')-1,
        RTRIM(SUBSTR(:HEADER.SELECTION_LIST,
        INSTR(:HEADER,SELECTION_LIST,'|')+1))
INTO    :MINVFCLS.FCLS_ICLS_CODE,
        :HEADER.SELECTION_LIST
FROM    SYSTEM.DUAL
```

Step #3

```
#EXEMACRO NXTREC; GOSTEP TOP;
```

Figure 5.48 Multi-selection look-up trigger (*Part 2*)

shipment number. No SELECTION_LIST is necessary and the triggers STARIT and UNSTARIT just update and erase the shipment number for the current record.

5.7.4.7 Must-have relationships. Another situation that is often difficult to implement in SQL*Forms is a must-have relationship. If you remember our Entity/Relationship Diagram from Section 2.3, there were many cases where we said that one entity MUST HAVE one or more occurrences of another. For example, each SHIPMENT must have one or more

Pop-up windows in SQL*Forms 2.3

Another technique is often implemented with look-up forms such as these. In SQL*Forms 2.3, pop-up windows can be simulated to provide a very slick means of looking up a value. Because SQL*Forms 2.3 only refreshes the part of the screen that changes, when the look-up screen is small, the calling form can still be seen underneath the look-up form. The only problem with this is that CALL, CALLQRY, and NEWFRM each perform a hardware clear-screen before they call a new form and before they return. This can be circumvented by redefining the escape sequence associated with clearscreen in the CRT definition to do something that does not change the screen (to go to the HOME position, for example). Then, when you call the look-up form, it will appear to pop up on top of the current form.

orders. A shipment without any orders is impossible. If we build a traditional parent-child form with the shipment record in the top block and the many order records in the bottom block, we have a problem because there is nothing to prevent the user from committing a new shipment record without entering any orders. We solved this problem by reordering the blocks so that the order block will get committed before the shipment block. A PRE-UPDATE trigger in the order block assigns the primary key value to the shipment. In the shipment block, a PRE-INSERT fails if no shipment number has been assigned. In this way, no shipment record can be created unless at least one order has been committed. The triggers shown in Figure 5.49 accomplish this task.

5.7.4.8 Taking advantage of non-database fields. One other form that we implemented in our application gave us the opportunity to demonstrate how non-database fields can be used for interesting effects. In the MINVWMVE form pictured in Figure 5.50, there is only one database field on the screen.

This form allows us to create MINVMOVE records in a way that is somewhat more interesting than simply filling in the record. First, two warehouses are selected in the control block. When a facility number is entered, a POST-CHANGE trigger validates that the facility is a warehouse and moves the description to the CTRL_FACL_DESC field. Notice that the field is broken into two parts. The trigger shown in Figure 5.51

Form Name: SLFVICLS
Block Name: MINVORDR
Trigger Level: Block
Trigger Name: PRE-UPDATE

Step # 1

```
#EXEMACRO CASE :MINVSHIP.SHIP_NUM IS
          WHEN ' ' THEN
            NULL;
          WHEN OTHERS THEN
            CASE :MINVORDR.ORDR_SHIP_NUM IS
              WHEN ' ' THEN
                ENDTRIG;
            WHEN '0' THEN
                COPY :MINVSHIP.SHIP_NUM
                    INTO :MINVORDR.ORDR_SHIP_NUM;
                ENDTRIG;
            END CASE;
          END CASE;
```

Step # 2

```
SELECT  SHIP_SEQUENCE.NEXTVAL
INTO    :MINVORDR.ORDR_SHIP_NUM
FROM    SYSTEM.DUAL
```

Failure Message:
SYSTEM ERROR Unable to generate Shipment No;
Contact System Administrator.

Step # 3

```
#EXEMACROCOPY :MINVORDR.ORDR_SHIP_NUM
  INTO :MINVSHIP.SHIP_NUM;
```

Figure 5.49 "Must-have" relationship triggers

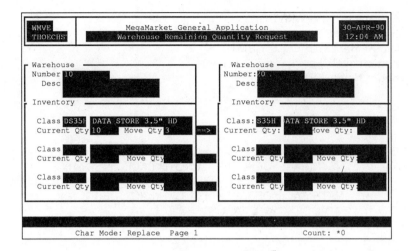

Figure 5.50 Warehouse movement form

takes the description and breaks it in half, making sure that it breaks on a space and not in the middle of a word.

Note that this "wrap around" effect only works when you are querying a field. It is impossible in SQL*Forms 2.3 or below to simulate word wrap with more than one field. When you get to the end of the first field, it is easy to take the word that you are typing and move it to the beginning of the next field, but it is impossible to position the cursor within the field to allow the typing to continue where it left off.

In the bottom block, we wanted to present the movement of inventory items in a more visually interesting way than the representation in the table. This was accomplished by using just one database field—the MOVE_ICLS_CODE field on the left. The POST-CHANGE trigger in Figure 5.52 fills in all of the related information in the record.

When an inventory class is chosen, it is simply printed twice under each warehouse and the number of items that currently exist for that warehouse is calculated. Notice that we accomplished both counts with a single SELECT statement by using the DECODE function. Because this table will be so large, it is likely that the time required by the two DECODE statements will outweigh the time required for a second SELECT statement. We will address this issue when we have more realistic data and when we do our other performance testing. (See Chapter 8 for more details.)

Form Name: MINVWMVE
Block Name: CTRL
Field Name: LEFT_FACL_NUM
Trigger Level: Field
Trigger Name: KEY-NXTFLD

Step # 1

```
SELECT    SUBSTR(FACL_DESC,1,
              INSTR(FACL_DESC,' ',21-LENGTH(FACL_DESC),1)),
              LTRIM(SUBSTR(FACL_DESC,
              INSTR(FACL_DESC,' ',21-LENGTH(FACL_DESC),1)))
INTO      FACL_DESC_1_L,FACL_DESC_2_L
FROM      MINVFACL
WHERE     FACL_NUM = :LEFT_FACL_NUM
AND       LENGTH(FACL_DESC) > 21
```

Note that 21 is the length of the FACL_DESC fields.

Figure 5.51 Word wrap trigger

The final triggers in this form that are of importance for creating our movement record are the POST-CHANGE triggers on the MOVE QTY fields. They are identical except that they apply in different directions. First they validate that no attempt is made to move more items than are available. Second, an arrow is copied into the middle field to illustrate the direction of the move. Next, the other quantity field is erased because items can only be moved in one direction. Finally, the appropriate FROM and TO facility numbers are added to the page 0 database fields. In this way, the user has filled in the movement record without having to explicitly type it in.

5.7.4.9 Outer joins. Another difficult situation in SQL*Forms is representing an outer join in a single form. This means that for a parent record, we want to show all of the possible children whether the records actually exist or not. Implementing the MINVWQTY form (which displays the available quantity of items for a given warehouse) presented this problem because for each warehouse, we wanted to show all of the items that a warehouse carries and the quantity of each currently in stock, even if that quantity were zero. This form is shown in Figure 5.53.

Form Name: MINVWMVE
Block Name: MINVMOVE
Trigger Level: Field
Trigger Name: POST-CHANGE

Step # 1

```
SELECT    SLFVICLS.ICLS_CODE,SLFVICLS.ICLS_DESC,
          SLFVICLS.ICLS_DESC,
          SUM(DECODE(MINVITEM.ITEM_FACL_NUM,
          :CTRL.LEFT_FACL_NUM,1,0)),
          SUM(DECODE(MINVITEM.ITEM_FACL_NUM,
          :CTRL.RIGHT_FACL_NUM,1,0))
INTO      MINVMOVE.RIGHT_ICLS_CODE,MINVMOVE.RIGHT_ICLS_DESC,
          MINVMOVE.LEFT_ICLS_DESC,MINVMOVE.LEFT_CURRENT_QTY,
          MINVMOVE.RIGHT_CURRENT_QTY
FROM      SLFVICLS,MINVITEM
WHERE     SLFVICLS.ICLS_CODE = :MINVMOVE.MOVE_ICLS_CODE
  AND     SLFVICLS.ICLS_CODE = MINVITEM.ITEM_ICLS_CODE
GROUP BY SLFVICLS.ICLS_CODE,SLFVICLS.ICLS_DESC
```

Figure 5.52 Taking advantage of non-database fields

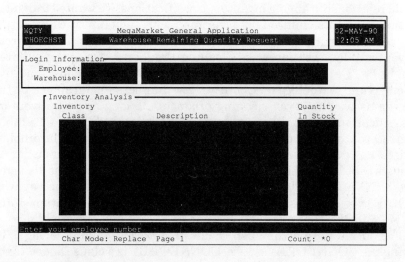

Figure 5.53 Warehouse movement form

Without a doubt, the most important decision to make was choosing the table to use as a base table for the bottom block. Again, since no updates are occurring on this form, choosing the right base table is only necessary so that we can view multiple rows in a given block. Generally, the choice for a base table is obvious. In this case, however, there were originally three candidates: MINVITEM, MINVFCLS, and SLFVICLS.

MINVITEM contains all of the individual inventory records. This is where the quantity for a given inventory class will be retrieved. Using this table as a base table is not quite appropriate, however, because it shows all inventory classifications rather than just those that apply to the given warehouse. We decided that we wanted this screen to display all of the inventory classes that were associated with a warehouse and the corresponding quantity (zero if there were none). By using the MINVITEM table, we would be showing one row for each item that actually exists in a warehouse, rather than one row for each inventory class that a warehouse handles.

We next considered the MINVFCLS table. This seemed like the appropriate choice because it contains records for each Warehouse/Inventory Classification combination. So, it appeared that a simple query with MINVFCLS as the base table would bring up each of the inventory classes that we wanted to count for the given warehouse. The POST-QUERY trigger shown in Figure 5.54 could then be used to actually select the number of items out there for this class.

This worked fine, but with one major exception. Because of the parent-child relationship among inventory classifications, we wanted to display a parent and its children on our screen with the quantities reflecting everything for a parent and its children. For example, if the parent inventory classification was "Cleaning Products," two of the children might be "Detergents" and "Sponges." If a given warehouse had five sponges and two detergents, both of these numbers should appear on the screen as well as seven cleaning products. As long as each inventory classification that applies (at all levels) is added to the MINVFCLS table, the records and quantities can be retrieved without trouble. The problem arises, however, when we try to order these rows. Since we want children classes to be listed under their parents, order is very important. By using the MINVFCLS table, however, ordering the rows in such a way with SQL*Forms becomes impossible because there is no information stored in MINVFCLS that distinguishes one as parent and one as child.

The only way to accomplish the desired parent-child ordering is by using the CONNECT BY clause. CONNECT BY is a clause added to the standard SQL commands by Oracle. It allows two columns in a table to

Form Name: MINVWQTY
Block Name: MINVFLCS
Trigger Level: Block
Trigger Name: POST-QUERY

Step #1

```
SELECT COUNT(*)
INTO :MINVFCLS.QTY
FROM MINVITEM
WHERE MINVITEM.ITEM_ICLS_CODE = :MINVFCLS.ICLS_CODE
AND MINVITEM.ITEM_FACL_NUM = :MINVITEM.FACL_NUM
```

Figure 5.54 Selecting quantities for inventory classes

be "connected" into a parent-child relationship. When a query is executed in this fashion, the table is essentially joined with itself over and over while ORACLE goes deeper and deeper in the hierarchy with each step. The syntax for the CONNECT BY clause is shown in Figure 5.55.

This says, "starting with rows that satisfy condition2, traverse the rows connecting the childcolumn of this row with the parentcolumn of the next row, displaying only those rows that meet condition1."

For us to accomplish this in our form, we need to use the table that contains the parent-child relationship, which is the SLFVICLS table. SQL*Forms allows us to use the CONNECT BY clause in the ORDER BY/WHERE CLAUSE of the Choose Block menu as long as we already have a WHERE clause. For our form, we need a where clause to access the MINVFCLS table and verify that we are only returning those classifications that are associated with the warehouse. This clause is shown in Figure 5.56.

There are many more triggers that we used in the MegaMarket application to provide a fully functional system. In this section we have pointed out the triggers that we felt represented some of the more important coding complexities in a production application.

```
SELECT column1, column
FROM tablename
WHERE condition1 is true
CONNECT BY PRIOR tablename.childcolumn = tablename.parentcolumn
START WITH condition2 is true
```

Figure 5.55 The CONNECT BY clause

Form Name: MINVWQTY
Block Name: SLFVICLS

Default WHERE/ORDER BY clause for QUERY:

```
WHERE  ICLS_CODE IN
          (SELECT FCLS_ICLS_CODE
           FROM MINVFCLS
           WHERE    MINVFCLS.FCLS_FACL_NUM =
                       :CTRL.EMPL_FACL_NUM)
CONNECT BY PRIOR ICLS_CODE = ICLS_ICLS_CODE
   START WITH
      (ICLS_CODE LIKE :SLFVICLS.ICLS_CODE
      AND :SLFVICLS.ICLS_CODE IS NOT NULL)
      OR
      (ICLS_ICLS_CODE IS NULL)
```

Figure 5.56 CONNECT BY in SQL*Forms

5.8 Conclusion

In this chapter we walked you through our entire online application development cycle. We began with specifications and standards and concluded with complex application forms. We hope that this mix of general information and very specific triggers and techniques helps you in your SQL*Forms application development. In the next section we will take a similar look at the development of reports for the MegaMarket application.

6

Building the Reports

6.1 Introduction

Now that the application forms are complete, we are ready to start developing the reports. A well-defined online system can alleviate many reporting needs. For example, the list field values forms described in Chapter 5 eliminate the necessity of code table reports. Other information, like summary data and time-based information, are best provided in periodic reports. ORACLE provides several tools for writing your reports: SQL*Plus, SQL*Report, SQL*ReportWriter, or a Pro*ORACLE program (using a 3GL with imbedded SQL). No single reporting tool is perfect for all applications and each has characteristics that make it appropriate for specific types of reports.

In this chapter, we will help you understand each of the tools so that you can decide which best satisfy your reporting needs. We will then take you through the report specification and design process, and finally show you the techniques we used to develop the MegaMarket reports.

6.2 Understanding SQL*Plus

In Chapter 4 we executed our application SQL scripts from within SQL*Plus to build our tables, views, and indexes. We also discussed how to write dynamic SQL routines to unload, and subsequently reload, data in application tables. Now we will see how to use SQL*Plus to develop reports. But first we will concentrate on understanding how SQL*Plus works in general, so we can easily apply our knowledge to the problem of reporting.

SQL*Plus is, to ORACLE, simply another program that issues SQL statements. In our discussion of SQL*Forms in Chapter 5, we noted that the only way to "talk" to ORACLE is through SQL. SQL*Forms is a program developed by Oracle to construct and issue SQL for the user. SQL*Plus, on the other hand, allows the user to issue his own SQL statements. The user issues a SQL statement to ORACLE and the values or results of the statement are returned from ORACLE.

As we saw in Chapter 3, ORACLE returns only raw data (the actual values that satisfy the request). Working within SQL*Plus, you can enhance the raw data by setting *environmental variables*. These variables are set to default values when you log in to SQL*Plus. For instance, the environmental variable HEADINGS is set to ON by default. Thus, when you issue a SQL statement, the column (or alias) headings are displayed above the raw data. There is another environmental variable called FEEDBACK, also set to ON by default, which causes the number of rows processed by each SQL statement to be displayed. Figure 6.1 demonstrates the result of using both of these default settings.

SQL*Plus provides environmental variables to allow you to tailor your SQL*Plus environment. You can change the setting for any variable

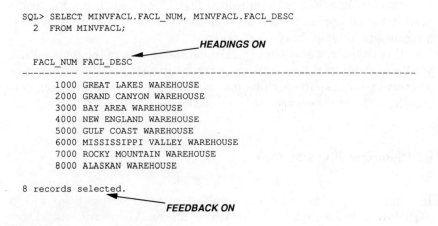

```
SQL> SELECT MINVFACL.FACL_NUM, MINVFACL.FACL_DESC
  2  FROM MINVFACL;
                                          HEADINGS ON
  FACL_NUM FACL_DESC
---------- ------------------------------------------------------------
      1000 GREAT LAKES WAREHOUSE
      2000 GRAND CANYON WAREHOUSE
      3000 BAY AREA WAREHOUSE
      4000 NEW ENGLAND WAREHOUSE
      5000 GULF COAST WAREHOUSE
      6000 MISSISSIPPI VALLEY WAREHOUSE
      7000 ROCKY MOUNTAIN WAREHOUSE
      8000 ALASKAN WAREHOUSE

8 records selected.
                          FEEDBACK ON
```

Figure 6.1 SQL*Plus formatting

using "SET VARIABLE VALUE" where VALUE is usually ON or OFF. To list the value of every environmental variable, type SHOW ALL.

Environmental Variables

Some of the environmental variables are not obvious in their effect but can be very useful. For instance, SPACE indicates the number of spaces to leave between columns. When creating a file to be sent to a different host computer it may be helpful to set this value to zero. Another pair of variables to keep handy are RECSEP and RECSEPCHAR. These variables define when a record separator is printed and what character to print (a record in SQL*Plus is one row of data). RECSEP and RECSEPCHAR can be set to EACH and some character like "_", respectively, to provide a visual break between each line of output.

You may find that you prefer to have some variables set every time you use SQL*Plus. You can create a file called "login.sql" to automate this process. SQL*Plus automatically executes this file when starting. Depending on your preferences, there are several environmental variables you may want to set. You may want to include "SET PAUSE Text PAUSE ON" to pause and display a message like "Press Return" after every screen full of data. This will prevent the SQL statement output from scrolling off the screen too quickly. Another statement you might include is "SET NUMWIDTH num" to set the display width of columns containing numbers. This is useful because a number wider than NUMWIDTH will display in scientific notation.

The SET commands can also be added to a SQL script to control the environment for the execution of that script. In our discussion of dynamic SQL discussion in Chapter 4, we created a SQL script with the following variables set:

```
SET ECHO OFF        (suppress the echoing of SQL commands)
SET FEEDBACK OFF    (suppress the SQL row count)
SET TERM OFF        (suppress terminal output)
SET HEADING OFF     (suppress the display of column headings)
```

Now we are ready to consider SQL*Plus as a reporting tool. Most reports, at the lowest level, are simply formatted raw data. SQL*Plus provides a series of commands to accomplish this formatting. There is a TTITLE command to display titles at the top of the page, a COLUMN command to specify column formats and column headings, a BREAK command to set breaks, and a COMPUTE command to perform calculations over columns and breaks.

Note that these SQL*Plus commands by themselves merely set the stage for the execution of a SQL statement. You can write a SQL*Plus script containing a TTITLE command, several COLUMN commands, and several COMPUTE commands, but executing this script will appear to do nothing (just like the setting of environmental variables). You can see the effect of SQL*Plus commands only when raw data is returned through the execution of a SQL statement. Hence, the SQL*Plus commands you specify are closely related to the SQL statement you will issue. For instance, you could specify that column TRAN_DATE have a heading of "Transaction Date." If your SQL statement specified SELECT TO_CHAR(TRAN_DATE, 'MM/DD/YY'), the column heading would *not* take effect, because SQL*Plus would not know that TRAN_DATE and TO_CHAR(TRAN_DATE, 'MM/DD/YY') are the same. SQL*Plus looks in the COLUMN definitions for an exact match of the SELECTed column. In this case, TRAN_DATE had a COLUMN definition but TO_CHAR(TRAN_DATE ...) did not. When using SQL*Plus commands such as COLUMN, BREAK, and COMPUTE, you should be careful to specify the exact SELECTed information.

Aliases

You can provide a column alias and use the alias in your SQL*Plus commands. For example, you could

```
SELECT TO_CHAR(TRAN_DATE, 'MM/DD/YY') "Tran Date"
FROM SYSTEM.DUAL
```

Then you can use "Tran Date" (including the double quotes) in any SQL*Plus command. But remember, you cannot use column aliases in SQL clauses such as GROUP BY or ORDER BY, because the ANSI-standard SQL syntax does not allow for alias substitution in these clauses.

We have been careful to identify a command as a SQL statement or a SQL*Plus command. This is a very important distinction, but how can you tell the difference? It helps to remember that SQL*Plus commands always manipulate the raw data returned from a SQL statement. Also, you can use SQL in any program (those written by Oracle and those written by you), but you can only use SQL*Plus commands within SQL*Plus. Think about this for a minute and consider whether the following commands are SQL or SQL*Plus:

1. BREAK ON *column*
2. ; (following a command)
3. SELECT *column list* FROM *table*
4. DESCRIBE *table*
5. / (on a line by itself)
6. COMMIT

If you decided that all of these are SQL*Plus commands except the SELECT (number 3) and COMMIT (number 6) statements, you were right! (Note that COMMIT was a SQL*Plus command in V5. It has since become an ANSI-standard SQL command.) We will be using SQL*Plus later in the chapter to develop the MegaMarket reports. Try to consciously differentiate between the commands while you review our reports.

6.3 Understanding SQL*ReportWriter

SQL*ReportWriter is a fairly sophisticated reporting tool. It allows you to modify column headings and column formats, define page breaks and summary information, and integrate textual information with the report. SQL*ReportWriter also provides a window interface to allow you to create reports that would be very difficult to create within SQL*Plus.

Although very different from SQL*Plus, SQL*ReportWriter is surprisingly similar to SQL*Forms. Both provide window interfaces, although the implementations are slightly different. SQL*ReportWriter provides a menu bar and SQL*Forms provides nested windows (although Version 3 of SQL*Forms also provides a menu bar). While using SQL*Forms we make a SELECTion to move down the window hierarchy and ACCEPT any changes to move up. In SQL*ReportWriter each menu bar choice represents the next level down the hierarchy. Thus, we make a SELECTion on the menu bar to define the level and ACCEPT any changes to move back to the menu bar.

The SQL*ReportWriter interface was designed to lead you through the process of developing a report. The choices on the menu bar along the top of the screen are listed in the order of use. You start out in

SQL*ReportWriter by providing a SQL statement via the QUERY menu bar choice. When you accept your SQL statement, the SQL*ReportWriter program reads the ORACLE data dictionary. Based on information in the dictionary, like column data types and column lengths, SQL*ReportWriter defines all of the information for a default report. You can then change the default report by choosing a menu bar option, such as FIELD, and changing information on that screen.

Another similarity between SQL*Forms and SQL*ReportWriter is that both insert information into their own database tables. Part of the installation process for these tools is the execution of a SQL script that creates the database tables for the product. The SQL*Forms tables begin with IAP while the SQL*ReportWriter tables begin with SRW. (Note that in Version 1.0 these tables began with FR.)

Another important similarity is that both tools create source code that must be GENERATEd prior to being EXECUTEd or RUN. The generation process creates executables on disk (in the developer's directory, minidisk, or whatever). The file extensions for these executables are FRM and REP for SQL*Forms and SQL*ReportWriter, respectively.

Now for the big differences. One critical distinction is that *changes made within SQL*ReportWriter are permanent*. SQL*Forms allows you to modify a form, run it, and then decide to discard the changes. This is possible because the SQL*Forms designer program (iad) makes changes within your workspace, not in the SQL*Forms tables. SQL*ReportWriter makes changes directly in the SQL*ReportWriter tables, therefore you can only undo changes within the current window.

Copying Reports

You may want to get in the habit of copying your SQL*ReportWriter report to a different name and making changes to the copy. This approach allows you to make modifications without destroying the original report.

Another main difference between the programs is that SQL*Forms builds the SQL statements that correspond to the formatted screen image. SQL*ReportWriter, on the other hand, asks the report developer to enter the actual SQL statements. In both cases, of course, the communication with ORACLE is via SQL.

There are several important concepts in SQL*ReportWriter that can be difficult to grasp, the first of which is the relationship between SQL statements. SQL*ReportWriter allows us to define one or more SQL statements in a report. Each SQL statement may be related to others, or it may not. For instance, there is no relationship between administrative offices (SGENOFFC) and transaction type codes (SLFVTTYP), but you could create a single SQL*ReportWriter report containing the columns from these unrelated tables.

More likely, you would want to combine information from related tables in a single report. For example, you might want to print each administrative office (SGENOFFC), the warehouses managed by that office (MINVWARE), and the stores managed by that office (MINVSTOR). As you know, you can use a join to retrieve information from more than one table. In SQL*ReportWriter, you can write a SQL join and use it as a single query. You can also write two individual SQL statements and specify the join criteria within SQL*ReportWriter by defining *parents* and *children*. A parent is an individual row in a table that may be related to one or more rows elsewhere (probably in another table). These other rows are referred to as the children. You can specify a parent query for each query in your report. Thus, you can define a parent, a child, and a grandchild, or you can define a parent and two children, and so on.

Remember that whether you write all of the SQL or you let SQL*ReportWriter write some of it, the SQL statement provided to ORACLE will be basically the same. SQL*ReportWriter will build WHERE clause predicates based on the information we provide. For example, if we build a "matrix" style report, we define three SQL statements. One SQL query represents the vertical information, the second represents the horizontal information, and the third represents the intersection cell (like a spreadsheet). SQL*ReportWriter will automatically append the necessary WHERE clause predicates to the intersection query.

The second tricky concept is that of a *group*. Each time we define a new SQL statement to be used in a report, SQL*ReportWriter defines a group. Each of the columns selected in the SQL statement are included in this group. The group itself has characteristics such as the number of lines to skip between rows returned, the number of spaces to leave between columns, label positioning, and print direction (for instance, print the rows down, as in SQL*Plus, or print the rows across as in our matrix example above). Basically, a group is a set of fields and all of the data for those fields. Consider the following queries and their groups:

```
Q1  SELECT * FROM MINVOFFC      G1  ALL COLUMNS OF Q1
Q2  SELECT * FROM MINVWARE      G2  ALL COLUMNS OF Q2
Q3  SELECT * FROM MINVSTOR      G3  ALL COLUMNS OF Q3
```

You can represent these queries with boxes of varying length and width, as in Figure 6.2.

The ordering of the groups specifies the print order. In this case G1, consisting of all of the administrative offices, prints first. G2, containing all of the warehouses, prints after G1. G3, composed of all stores, prints after G2. SQL*ReportWriter allows you to change the print order of the groups (in other words, you can move the boxes around on the page). For instance, you could print G3 first, followed by G1, followed by G2. You can also change the print relationship between two groups (more moving of the boxes). For instance, you could have G2 print *to the right of* G1 and G3 could print *below* G2.

We will discuss specific techniques for using SQL*ReportWriter later in Sections 6.4 and 6.5 when we define the MegaMarket reports.

6.4 Preparing to Write Report Specifications

The first step in developing reports is specifying them. You can usually begin with a report layout developed by the user. This layout might

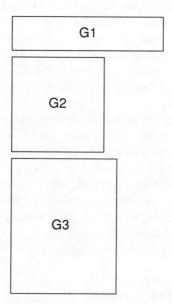

Figure 6.2 GROUPing

SQL*Report

The only other tool used for reporting prior to the introduction of SQL*ReportWriter was SQL*Report (usually referred to as RPT). SQL*Report was created over ten years ago as part of the first commercial release of the ORACLE RDBMS (Release 2). Thus, it is not a very robust reporting tool, nor is it very popular among developers. Instead, SQL*Report is a 3GL developed and supported by Oracle. SQL*Report has structures and verbs that any 3GL programmer can understand, verbs like GOTO and IF are main components of the language, and looping constructs are built in.

One of the main strengths of SQL*Report is also the main drawback. Everything done within SQL*Report uses SQL. For example, we can write a SQL*Report program containing the statement IF "&VAR1 > &VAR2". At program execution, SQL*Report will create the SQL statement SELECT 'X' FROM SYSTEM.DUAL WHERE &VAR1 > &VAR2. While this makes the SQL*Report program very portable, it can also make the program very inefficient. For ORACLE developers restricted to the OR-ACLE product set, SQL*Report was the only way to produce complex reports (prior to SQL*ReportWriter). These developers now have a choice.

However, there are two problems that may complicate the transition from SQL*Report to SQL*ReportWriter. First, there is no facility for converting a SQL*Report program into SQL*ReportWriter. The developer must rewrite the program using SQL*ReportWriter and this is not always a practical alternative to simply maintaining the original report. Second, consider batch processing (for instance, the creation of a regular process to summarize detailed financial information into a monthly report) that requires minimal reporting and maximum insert, update, and delete activity. It is often impossible to write these procedures within SQL*ReportWriter because of its limited procedural capabilities and restrictive insert, update, and delete functionality. A truly portable 3GL, such as SQL*Report or carefully written C, provides an alternative for such applications.

contain notes about totals, calculations, and headings. You then need to refine this information into report specifications. As with SQL*Forms, it can be difficult to devise a standard approach to the specification process.

Since a report is typically query-only, you can focus on what data is to be selected and how that data should be presented to the user. You can develop several sections for this information. These sections may be HEADER information including report and column headings, the main information in the report in the QUERY section, and SUMMARY information. And, with SQL*ReportWriter, you can quickly define a default report to be used as part of the specification.

6.4.1 Report design review

There are two main objectives of a report design review. The first is to determine the best tool for the report. Since each tool has benefits and drawbacks, using the right tool is critical to the performance, flexibility, and maintainability of the report.

The second objective of the review process is to make a preliminary assessment of performance requirements for the report. You need to assess the impact of running the report during peak hours versus suggesting off-peak scheduling. By considering these impacts early in the process mechanisms can be put in place to control execution of reports. For example, resource intensive reports can be restricted to specific times of day. In our application we specified that several small reports and any critical inventory reports could be run during peak hours. All others, mostly analysis reports, will be run overnight.

6.4.2 Creating standards for reports

Once again we need to consider standards prior to development. This is especially critical in reporting because there are several different tools available for development. Thus, although a different tool may be used for each report, the user should not be able to tell the difference. Standards enforce this consistency. Thankfully, reporting standards are fairly simple. You should consider coding standards (how to write SQL), naming conventions, and technique standards. You may also want to choose a standard heading for your reports.

6.4.2.1 SQL*Plus standards. SQL*Plus standards tend to be very concise. We start with naming conventions that are simple and consistent. We will call any parameter passed into SQL*Plus PARM_ and any non-database work field CTRL_.

Next we develop guidelines for writing SQL, with the goal of enhanced readability. We specify that table.column be used to identify each column and that the main verbs of the SQL statement (SELECT, FROM, WHERE, AND) be aligned. (Both of these guidelines were also part of our SQL*Forms standards.) Since each of our tools uses the same language—SQL—consistency across tools can be achieved.

The more difficult SQL*Plus standards deal with technique. For instance, we often need to create summary information in SQL*Plus. There are two basic ways to accomplish this. The first uses the SQL*Plus BREAK and COMPUTE commands. The second requires two queries, the first selecting the detail and the second selecting the totals, with a

```
SQL> RUN
    1  SELECT 1 DUMMY, TO_CHAR(MINVFACL.FACL_NUM), MINVFACL.FACL_DESC
    2  FROM   MINVFACL
    3  UNION
    4  SELECT 2 DUMMY, NULL, NULL
    5  FROM   SYSTEM.DUAL
    6  UNION
    7  SELECT 3 DUMMY, '-----','------------------------'
    8  FROM   SYSTEM.DUAL
    9  UNION
   10  SELECT 4 DUMMY, 'TOTAL', TO_CHAR(COUNT(MINVFACL.FACL_NUM))
   11  FROM   MINVFACL
   12* ORDER BY 1,2

TO_CHAR(MI FACL_DESC
---------- ------------------------------------------------------------
1000       GREAT LAKES WAREHOUSE
2000       GRAND CANYON WAREHOUSE
3000       BAY AREA WAREHOUSE
4000       NEW ENGLAND WAREHOUSE
5000       GULF COAST WAREHOUSE
6000       MISSISSIPPI VALLEY WAREHOUSE
7000       ROCKY MOUNTAIN WAREHOUSE
8000       ALASKAN WAREHOUSE


-----      ------------------------
TOTAL      8

11 records selected.
```

Figure 6.3 Customized totals

UNION of the results. Using a dummy field and an ORDER BY, we can force the totals to print after the detail. This technique works, but it can be difficult to read and maintain as you can see in Figure 6.3.

Some die-hard SQL wizards will tell you that they can write anything in SQL*Plus. While this is often true, the SQL can be extremely complex and practically impossible to maintain. As with all of the tools, we should strive to keep the SQL as simple as possible. Overly complex SQL in SQL*Plus report code is the sign of either a hacker at work or the selection of the wrong reporting tool.

6.4.2.2 SQL*ReportWriter standards. Standards for SQL*ReportWriter contain many components. First are naming conventions. Within SQL*ReportWriter there are many different types of objects each of which should have its own naming standards. Your naming standards document might include a section like the one shown in Figure 6.4.

Most of these naming conventions are fairly straightforward, but the field naming may need some explanation. If our report contains the SQL statement "SELECT EMPL_NAME_LAST||EMPL_NAME_FIRST FROM SGENEMPL" we would have one field in the report. SQL*ReportWriter tries to create intelligent field names based on the SQL provided. It eliminates miscellaneous characters, such as "_" and "|", and defines a field. In this report, the field would be called "EMPL_NAME_LAST_EMPL_NAME_FIRST." Obviously, in this case

Object	Naming Convention
QUERY (Single Table)	Q_TABLE
QUERY (Multi Table)	Q_TABLE1_TABLE2_...._TABLEN
QUERY (Header)	Q_HEADER
GROUP (Default)	G_ (default group name)
GROUP (Manually defined)	G_DESCRIPTIVE_NAME
FIELD (Database)	DATABASE_FIELD_NAME
FIELD (Database w/Func)	DESCRIPTIVE_NAME
FIELD (Non-Database/Hdr)	CTRL_DESCRIPTIVE_NAME
FIELD (Calculated)	CALC_DESCRIPTIVE_NAME
SUMMARY	SUMM_DESCRIPTIVE_NAME
PARAMETER	PARM_DESCRIPTIVE_NAME

Figure 6.4 Report naming conventions

the name is not so intelligent. We can prevent this from occurring by using column aliases, since SQL*ReportWriter will use the alias name as the field name. We can then add this guideline to our standards.

The second portion of our standards document deals again with how to write SQL, and contains the same requirements we specified earlier for SQL*Plus and in SQL*Forms.

The last portion of our standards document considers technique issues (in a similar fashion to the SQL*Plus technique issues). As we noted earlier, SQL*ReportWriter allows us to create joins by specifying parent-child relationships or by writing SQL to make the connections directly. Both of these will produce the same report output. When writing the join ourselves the SQL will (obviously) be more complex. We will also need to create an additional group for the query (one query with some fields in one group and some fields in another) to create breaks and totals and so on.

The trade-off tends to be one of performance versus maintainability and flexibility. Unfortunately, the performance side is hard to predict. That is, depending on the groups and totaling functions used, a SQL*ReportWriter join may be faster. However, there are an equal number of cases where writing our own join is faster. See Section 8.3.2 for more details on tuning SQL*ReportWriter reports.

6.5 Developing Report Skeletons

We created skeletons to be used to develop SQL*Forms applications. We developed these skeletons for two main reasons: consistency for the user and elimination of redundant work for the developer. We can use this same strategy for our reports. The only complication is that we must create a different skeleton for each tool. In our application these tools are SQL*Plus and SQL*ReportWriter. However, this technique can also be applied to a 3GL and SQL*Report.

6.5.1 SQL*ReportWriter skeleton

In SQL*ReportWriter we establish standard page headers and footers by creating a skeleton calledskelrpt.rep. This skeleton contains one query, called Q_HEADER, which is shown in Figure 6.5.

```
Action    Query    Group    Field    Summary    Text    Report    Parameter    Help
                              Query Settings
 ┌─────────────────────────────────────────────────────────────────────────────┐
 │ Query Name: Q_HEADER                                          Query  1 of 1   │
 │                         SELECT Statement                                      │
 │^│ SELECT  :MENU_RPT_NAME                          HEADER_CTRL_RPT_NAME,        │
 │ │         LPAD(' ',(50-LENGTH(:MENU_RPT_DESC))/2)||                           │
 │ │              :MENU_RPT_DESC                     HEADER_CTRL_RPT_DESC,        │
 │ │         TO_CHAR(SYSDATE)                        HEADER_CTRL_DATE,            │
 │ │         TO_CHAR(SYSDATE,'HH:MI PM')             HEADER_CTRL_TIME,            │
 │ │         USER                                    HEADER_CTRL_USER            │
 │ │ FROM    SYSTEM.DUAL                                                         │
 │v│                                                                             │
 ├─────────────────────────────────────────────────────────────────────────────┤
 │                        Parent-Child Relationships                             │
 │  Parent Query 1:                          Parent Query 2:                     │
 │                                                                               │
 │     Child Columns           Parent 1 Columns         Parent 2 Columns         │
 │^│                      │                        │                             │
 │v│                      │                        │                             │
 └─────────────────────────────────────────────────────────────────────────────┘
 Report Name: skelrpt                          <INSERT>            <LOV>
```

Figure 6.5 SQL*ReportWriter query screen

There are a few points to note about this query. First, the aliases we choose for our columns correspond to the names of the fields in our SQL*Forms application. In fact, the report header closely parallels the SQL*Forms form header down to the last detail, including the centering of the report description. This makes the transition from online applications to reports easier for developers.

Also notice the use of two variables, MENU_RPT_NAME and MENU_RPT_DESC. These are indicated with a colon because they are report parameters. Defaults of "SKEL" and "Skeleton Report" are provided for these parameters. Again, we are echoing the process of the SQL*Forms applications. The START_FORM trigger in the SQL*Forms skeletons copies in the global parameters APPL_NAME and APPL_DESC for use in the form heading. Similarly, the report name and description will be passed to SQL*ReportWriter from the online menu system. (For further information on these parameters, refer to Chapter 7.) The default values for the parameters allow for the execution of the report from outside the menu system.

The other part of the SQL*ReportWriter skeleton is the arrangement of the PAGE HEADER text object to print the header information the way we want it. This is unfortunately a cumbersome process. We would like to remove the printing of the header fields from G_HEADER BODY and place them into the page header, but when we attempt to do this we

Action	Query	Group	Field	Summary	Text	Report	Parameter	Help
				Summary Settings				1 of 2

	Summary Name	Field	Function	Data Type	Width	Display Format
^	CTRL_RPT_NAME	HEADER_CTRL_RPT_	Min	CHAR	4	
	CTRL_RPT_DESC	HEADER_CTRL_RPT_	Min	CHAR	50	
	CTRL_DATE	HEADER_CTRL_DATE	Min	CHAR	9	
	CTRL_TIME	HEADER_CTRL_TIME	Min	CHAR	8	
v	CTRL_USER	HEADER_CTRL_USER	Min	CHAR	8	

Report Name: skelrpt   <INSERT>   <LOV>

Figure 6.6 SQL*ReportWriter summary screen

get the message "frequency of … in text … is inconsistent." In order to be able to print something from a "lower level" on the page header (a page is defined in SQL*ReportWriter as "above" the group G_HEADER) we need to take a few counter-intuitive steps. We will create a SUMMARY for each field in the header group using the MIN function (since the minimum of a value is the value itself). Summary fields have no placement restrictions, so we can put them in the page header, as shown in Figure 6.6. Finally, we can define a PAGE FOOTER text object to print "Page: &PAGE" (a built-in SQL*ReportWriter variable) at the bottom of the page. Figure 6.7 shows this window.

6.5.2 SQL*Plus skeleton

Our SQL*Plus skeleton achieves the same goals as our SQL*ReportWriter skeleton: consistency and elimination of duplicated effort. The main function of the skeleton is to create the standard header for all SQL*Plus reports. By now, we should be familiar with the SQL statement shown in Figure 6.8 which is used to provide the information for this header.

Notice that we defined HEADER_CTRL_RPT_NAME as the alias of &1 and HEADER_CTRL_RPT_DESC as the alias of &2. These symbols

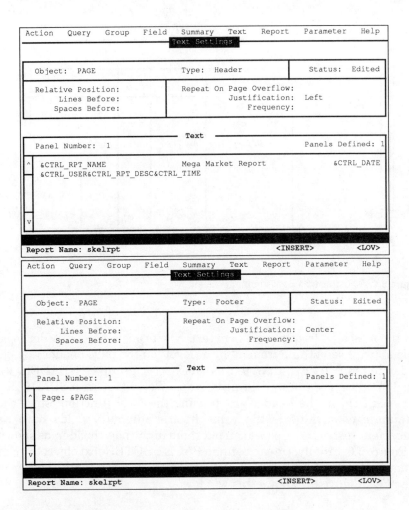

```
Action    Query    Group    Field    Summary    Text    Report    Parameter    Help
                                 Text Settings

  Object:  PAGE                   Type:  Header              Status:  Edited

  Relative Position:          Repeat On Page Overflow:
       Lines Before:                   Justification:  Left
       Spaces Before:                  Frequency:

                             ──── Text ────
  Panel Number:  1                                       Panels Defined:  1

^   &CTRL_RPT_NAME                    Mega Market Report              &CTRL_DATE
    &CTRL_USER&CTRL_RPT_DESC&CTRL_TIME



v

Report Name: skelrpt                              <INSERT>            <LOV>
```

```
Action    Query    Group    Field    Summary    Text    Report    Parameter    Help
                                 Text Settings

  Object:  PAGE                   Type:  Footer              Status:  Edited

  Relative Position:          Repeat On Page Overflow:
       Lines Before:                   Justification:  Center
       Spaces Before:                  Frequency:

                             ──── Text ────
  Panel Number:  1                                       Panels Defined:  1

^   Page: &PAGE



v

Report Name: skelrpt                              <INSERT>            <LOV>
```

Figure 6.7 SQL*ReportWriter text screen

(&1 and &2) are SQL*Plus parameters that will be passed to the report
from the online menu system. This is the same process we used for
SQL*Forms and SQL*ReportWriter. As with those tools, we need to
provide for the execution of the report from outside of the menu system.
We provided this functionality in SQL*Plus by using the DEFINE
command. This command allows us to place a default value into the
header variables CTRL_RPT_NAME and CTRL_RPT_DESC. The default value for these variables will only appear if no value is received

```
REM
REM     SQL statement to value all of the header information
REM
SELECT  '&1'                      HEADER_CTRL_RPT_NAME,
        '&2'                      HEADER_CTRL_RPT_DESC,
        TO_CHAR(SYSDATE)          HEADER_CTRL_DATE,
        TO_CHAR(SYSDATE,'HH:MI PM') HEADER_CTRL_TIME,
        USER                      HEADER_CTRL_USER
FROM    SYSTEM.DUAL;
```

Figure 6.8 SQL*Plus header statement

from the menu system (much like the DEFAULT INTO command for SQL*Forms globals).

We have the SELECT statement, but how do we provide this information for the page heading? In SQL*Plus the page header is defined using the TTITLE command. The only stumbling block is the use of SELECTed information in the TTITLE SQL*Plus command. We accomplish this using a special COLUMN clause called NEW_VALUE. This clause transfers SELECTed column data into SQL*Plus variables, which can then be used in the TTITLE command or anywhere else SQL*Plus variables are allowed.

For the skeleton page heading we use aliases in the SELECT statement and specify the aliases in the COLUMN commands. In our query, the NOPRINT column aliases shown in Figure 6.9 starting with "HEADER_CTRL_" place data into the SQL*Plus variables "CTRL_" via NEW_VALUE.

```
REM
REM     Assign default values for report name and description
REM
DEFINE CTRL_RPT_NAME = "SKEL"
DEFINE CTRL_RPT_DESC = "Skeleton Report"
REM
REM     Define the columns for use in report header
REM
COLUMN HEADER_CTRL_RPT_NAME     NOPRINT NEW_VALUE CTRL_RPT_NAME
COLUMN HEADER_CTRL_RPT_DESC     NOPRINT NEW_VALUE CTRL_RPT_DESC
COLUMN HEADER_CTRL_DATE         NOPRINT NEW_VALUE CTRL_DATE
COLUMN HEADER_CTRL_TIME         NOPRINT NEW_VALUE CTRL_TIME
COLUMN HEADER_CTRL_USER         NOPRINT NEW_VALUE CTRL_USER
```

Figure 6.9 SQL*Plus report headers and defaults

```
REM
REM    Define top title for each page and bottom title (page number)
REM
BTITLE CENTER 'Page: ' SQL.PNO        FORMAT 999
TTITLE LEFT       CTRL_RPT_NAME        -
       CENTER     'Mega Market Report'-
       RIGHT      CTRL_DATE            -
       SKIP 1                          -
       LEFT       CTRL_USER            -
       CENTER     CTRL_RPT_DESC        -
       RIGHT      CTRL_TIME            -
       SKIP 2
```

Figure 6.10 SQL*Plus titles

We are finally ready to define the top title using our SQL*Plus variables in the TTITLE command. In addition, we will define the bottom title using SQL.PNO (a supplied SQL*Plus variable) in the BTITLE command. Both of these commands are shown in Figure 6.10.

There are two other minor components to the SQL*Plus skeleton. First, we need to define our environment for the reports. We accomplish this by SETting the appropriate environmental variables, such as PAGESIZE and LINESIZE. Secondly, we place CLEARing functions at the bottom of the report to erase formatting variables (for example, COLUMNS and BREAKS) set during execution of the report.

Our SQL*Plus skeleton is fairly simple. Depending on your reporting needs, your skeleton may be more sophisticated. For example, you may consider developing a skeleton with standard COLUMN formats and headings for all possible database columns.

6.6 Building the Reports

We are now ready to build the reports for the MegaMarket system. Once again we can divide the reports into functional areas to allow each of us to work on different portions of the application. There are reports for store managers, reports for warehouse managers and employees, and reports for administrative office employees. One developer worked on the warehouse and administrative forms, so he will develop the store reports. Likewise, another developer worked on the store forms, so he will develop the warehouse and administrative reports. Switching responsibilities validates the work completed on the application and provides a fresh perspective.

Our reporting philosophy is to provide a core set of reports that are required for the business. Additional reports can be developed after the system is implemented. The justification for this thinking is that until the user learns the system, he does not really know what kind of additional reports he will need. Most reports can be written very quickly in SQL*Plus or SQL*ReportWriter after the user is comfortable with the overall system and information available.

6.6.1 SQL*Plus reporting techniques

Writing SQL*Plus reports is mainly an exercise in writing good SQL. In this section we will discuss some of the functionality of SQL*Plus that we can combine with a good understanding of SQL.

6.6.1.1 The BREAK command. Probably one of the most confusing areas of SQL*Plus is the use of the BREAK command. This command specifies to SQL*Plus the actions to take when the value in a column changes. For example, you may want to skip a line or force a page break. The BREAK command can be very powerful because it allows us to automatically provide nested breaks. You can specify a main BREAK on one column, a BREAK on a column within that column, and a BREAK on the completion of the report. Only one BREAK command is ever active, so multiple breaks must be written in a single command by providing the word BREAK and then a series of ON objects. At each break we can SKIP lines or PAGEs.

6.6.1.2 Eliminating the COMPUTE function name. At each of these breaks we can COMPUTE values. In the report shown in Figure 6.11, we provide a listing of the MINVMOVE information for each MegaMarket warehouse. We also COMPUTE a quantity summary. Notice that SQL*Plus prints asterisks and the function name (in this case "sum") with the COMPUTEd column when the break occurs. Many users do not like the "************" and the lowercase compute function name that appears in the report. You can eliminate these by using a non-printing column for the COMPUTE and the BREAK. For example, study the main statements in Figure 6.12 used to produce the report in Figure 6.11.

```
MOVE                          Mega Market Report            22-APR-90
THOECHST                    Inventory Movement Report         10:05 AM

Destination Inv Class   Inv Class Description            Quantity
----------- -----------  -------------------------------- --------
       1000 DT52D        DISKTECH 5.25" DD                     100
***********                                               --------
sum                                                            100


       2000 DS35D        DATA STORE 3.5" DD                    275
            DS52D        DATA STORE 5.25" DD                    60
            DT52D        DISKTECH 5.25" DD                     2000
            MS35D        MICROSYSTEMS 3.5" DD                   30
***********                                               --------
sum                                                           2365


       6000 DT52D        DISKTECH 5.25" DD                     150
            MS35H        MICROSYSTEMS 3.5" HD                  120
***********                                               --------
sum                                                            270


                         Page:          1
```

Figure 6.11 Movement report output

To eliminate the "sum" function name we made several modifications
to our report. First, we SELECTed the MOVE_FACL_NUM_TO column
twice with two different aliases: "Destination" and "Dest for Break." We
then defined the second column "Dest for Break" as a NOPRINT column.
Next, we changed the COMPUTE command to use "Dest for Break"
instead of "Destination." Finally, we changed the BREAK command to
break on both "Destination" and "Dest for Break." (Both of these values
will be the same, so the position of the break is unchanged.) Since the
BREAK column "Dest for Break" is not included in the report output, the
asterisks and function name are eliminated. The modified report is
shown in Figure 6.13.

6.6.1.3 Using DML statements in SQL*Plus. This report also required the
use of DML statements in a SQL*Plus report. The MINVMOVE rows are
created as a history of online changes to placement of inventory. For
instance, a store may ask for the delivery of 100 boxes of Data Store
double-sided disks from a specific warehouse. The warehouse employees
receive a nightly report listing the deliveries to be made. Once the report
is printed, the MOVEment rows should be deleted to reflect that the

```
REM
REM ---Begin Inventory Movement Report----
REM
COLUMN "Inv Class"                     FORMAT A11
COLUMN "Inv Class Description"         FORMAT A40      WORD_WRAP
COLUMN "Quantity"                      FORMAT 9999
COLUMN "Destination"                   FORMAT 9999999999
REM
BREAK ON "Destination" SKIP 2
COMPUTE SUM OF "Quantity" ON "Destination"
REM
SELECT MINVMOVE.MOVE_FACL_NUM_TO "Destination",
       MINVMOVE.MOVE_ICLS_CODE "Inv Class",
       SLFVICLS.ICLS_DESC "Inv Class Description",
       SUM(MINVMOVE.MOVE_QUANTITY) "Quantity"
FROM   MINVMOVE, SLFVICLS
WHERE  MINVMOVE.MOVE_FACL_NUM_FROM = &3
AND    MINVMOVE.MOVE_ICLS_CODE = SLFVICLS.ICLS_CODE
GROUP BY MINVMOVE.MOVE_ICLS_CODE, SLFVICLS.ICLS_DESC,
         MINVMOVE.MOVE_FACL_NUM_TO, MINVMOVE.MOVE_FACL_NUM_TO
ORDER BY 1;
```

Figure 6.12 Movement report script

```
REM
REM ---Begin Inventory Movement Report----
REM
COLUMN "Inv Class"                     FORMAT A11
COLUMN "Inv Class Description"         FORMAT A40      WORD_WRAP
COLUMN "Quantity"                      FORMAT 9999
COLUMN "Destination"                   FORMAT 9999999999
COLUMN "Dest for Break"                NOPRINT
REM
BREAK ON "Destination" ON "Dest for Break" SKIP 2
COMPUTE SUM OF "Quantity" ON "Dest for Break"
REM
SELECT MINVMOVE.MOVE_FACL_NUM_TO "Dest for Break",
       MINVMOVE.MOVE_FACL_NUM_TO "Destination",
       MINVMOVE.MOVE_ICLS_CODE "Inv Class",
       SLFVICLS.ICLS_DESC "Inv Class Description",
       SUM(MINVMOVE.MOVE_QUANTITY) "Quantity"
FROM   MINVMOVE, SLFVICLS
WHERE  MINVMOVE.MOVE_FACL_NUM_FROM = &3
AND    MINVMOVE.MOVE_ICLS_CODE = SLFVICLS.ICLS_CODE
GROUP BY MINVMOVE.MOVE_ICLS_CODE, SLFVICLS.ICLS_DESC,
         MINVMOVE.MOVE_FACL_NUM_TO, MINVMOVE.MOVE_FACL_NUM_TO
ORDER BY 2;
```

Figure 6.13 Movement report with double BREAK

movement took place (at least as far as the database is concerned). Thus, the last statement of the report shown in Figure 6.14 is a DELETE from the MINVMOVE table.

The risk we incur using this approach is that the report may not print properly. The printer may jam or run out of paper. Or the system may crash after the deletion but prior to print completion. On the opposite side, if we do not delete the rows automatically, we run the risk of duplication when the report runs the next night. You should consider these possibilities when designing this type of process. Our users prefer controlling the deletion of MINVMOVE records. So, we decided to split the process into two parts that are separate menu choices. The first prints the report and the second deletes the information in the MINVMOVE table.

6.6.1.4 SQL*Plus variables in SQL statements. One very strong feature of SQL*Plus is the ability to use SQL*Plus variables in SQL statements. SQL*Plus is the only Oracle tool where such a substitution can be made (because the SQL*Plus program substitutes the variables before sending to ORACLE, whereas the other tools force ORACLE to do the substitution). There is no restriction on what we can substitute, including column names and table names.

We used this technique in a productivity report for MegaMarket. This report provides a daily count of transactions per employee at each store. The "count of transactions" can be defined in two ways. It could be a count of individual items sold or a count of complete transactions regardless of the number of items in the transaction. We wanted our report to be able to handle both definitions of a transaction. Thus, we provided a SQL*Plus variable to hold the value DISTINCT or ALL. This variable determines whether we COUNT(ALL transactions) or COUNT(DISTINCT transac-

```
REM
REM    DELETE Movement Records for Warehouse
REM
DELETE FROM MINVMOVE
WHERE   MINVMOVE.MOVE_FACL_NUM_FROM = &&3;
REM
COMMIT;
```

Figure 6.14 Movement deletion

```
REM
REM   Main SELECT for Report
REM
SELECT '&3' HOLD_DISTINCT_OR_ALL,
       TRUNC(MINVTRAN.TRAN_DATE) "Tran Date",
       MINVFACL.FACL_DESC "Store Name",
       SGENEMPL.EMPL_NAME_LAST||' '||SGENEMPL.EMPL_NAME_FIRST "Employee Name",
       COUNT(&&DISTINCT_OR_ALL MINVTRAN.TRAN_NUM) "Trans"
FROM   MINVTRAN, SGENEMPL, MINVFACL
WHERE  MINVTRAN.TRAN_FACL_NUM_STOR = MINVFACL.FACL_NUM
AND    MINVTRAN.TRAN_EMPL_NUM = SGENEMPL.EMPL_NUM
AND    TRUNC(MINVTRAN.TRAN_DATE) BETWEEN '&4' AND '&5'
GROUP BY TRUNC(MINVTRAN.TRAN_DATE),
       SGENEMPL.EMPL_NAME_LAST||' '||SGENEMPL.EMPL_NAME_FIRST,
       MINVFACL.FACL_DESC
ORDER BY 1,2,4 DESC;
```

Figure 6.15 Transaction report statement

tions). Figure 6.15 shows the SQL statement we used. The value for &3
is resolved prior to making the SQL request to ORACLE. Thus we have
dynamically changed our report based on this parameter.

6.6.1.5 Spreadsheet-style reports using DECODE. A common request is to
create "denormalized" or spreadsheet-style reports. SQL expects to
return individual rows in a downward direction in the same fashion as
a table of columns and rows. Yet sometimes we need to create reports
where the individual rows go across instead of down. We can create
spreadsheet-style reports using the DECODE function. While this is
more SQL than SQL*Plus, it is usually needed in reporting and not in
online applications. (If we do need this functionality online we may need
to consider creating additional columns to store the data in a nonrelational fashion.) Note that DECODE is an ORACLE extension to
SQL. This means that the function is not ANSI-standard and will not be
available in other SQL-based RDBMSs.

The MegaMarket administrative office asked for a sales report that
provided six months worth of data on stores and transactions. The report
was defined to contain stores as the down column and the months
January thru June as the across columns. A second, virtually identical
report, was defined for the July through December sales interval. The
intersection cell was the dollar value of transactions (the sales) at the
store for the given month. Figure 6.16 shows a portion of the output from
the defined report.

This report requires a fairly complicated SQL statement. The complexity is a result of needing to produce a procedural result with a non-

```
DECD                      Mega Market Report                22-APR-90
THOECHST                Jan to June Sales Analysis             10:45 AM

    Store    January   February      March      April        May      June
----------- ---------- ---------- ---------- ---------- ---------- ----------
      9000  24880.33   62670.33   97850.22   92231.43  105322.32  105122.78
     10000  18660.24   47002.74   73387.66   69173.57   78991.73   78842.08
         .
         .
         .
         .
         .
         .
     28000  21770.3    54836.55   85618.95   80702.52   92157.05   91982.44


                              Page:          1
```

Figure 6.16 Transaction analysis report

procedural language. Figure 6.17 shows a more traditional, nonprocedural view of the result, starting with a simple SQL request.

This would give us the first column of information with the heading "January." We could then change the WHERE clause to equal '02' for February, then equal '03' for March, and so on. This process of replacing values is very procedural, yet SQL itself is not. If we created this report with six separate SQL statements, we would get six separate sets of

```
REM
REM   January Sales Figures
REM
SELECT MINVTRAN.TRAN_FACL_NUM_STOR "Store",
       SUM(MINVTRAN.TRAN_AMOUNT) "January"
FROM   MINVTRAN
WHERE  TO_CHAR(MINVTRAN.TRAN_DATE,'MM') = '01'
GROUP BY MINVTRAN.TRAN_FACL_NUM_STOR
ORDER BY 1;
```

Figure 6.17 Sales figures query

results. The best we could do would be to list one after another on the page. This is not good enough, because it does not meet the user requirements. So, we need a way to put the condition of the WHERE clause (the procedural test of IF) into the SELECT. In comes DECODE.

The DECODE function is the equivalent of an IF-THEN-ELSE structure within the SELECT list of the SQL statement. For this report we would say for each row (in English) "If the month of this row is January then add the amount to the January total" and "If the month of this row is February then add the amount to the February total" and so on. The syntax for the DECODE function specifies the two variables to be compared (in this case the TRAN_DATE and a specific numeric month value like '01'), the THEN operation, and the ELSE operation. Keep this in mind as you review Figure 6.18 which contains the statement we actually used for this report.

Suppose that after seeing this sales report, the users decided that the dates for the report should be variable. In other words, instead of fixed intervals of January through June and July through December, the report should be for "the last six months." This is a difficult request because the column month headings are hard-coded as aliases for each DECODE function in our SQL statement. Let's now look at satisfying this requirement.

```
REM
REM  Main SELECT for Sales Analysis Report
REM
SELECT MINVTRAN.TRAN_FACL_NUM_STOR "Store",
       SUM(DECODE(TO_CHAR(MINVTRAN.TRAN_DATE,'MM'),
               '01',MINVTRAN.TRAN_AMOUNT,0)) "January",
       SUM(DECODE(TO_CHAR(MINVTRAN.TRAN_DATE,'MM'),
               '02',MINVTRAN.TRAN_AMOUNT,0)) "February",
       SUM(DECODE(TO_CHAR(MINVTRAN.TRAN_DATE,'MM'),
               '03',MINVTRAN.TRAN_AMOUNT,0)) "March",
       SUM(DECODE(TO_CHAR(MINVTRAN.TRAN_DATE,'MM'),
               '04',MINVTRAN.TRAN_AMOUNT,0)) "April",
       SUM(DECODE(TO_CHAR(MINVTRAN.TRAN_DATE,'MM'),
               '05',MINVTRAN.TRAN_AMOUNT,0)) "May",
       SUM(DECODE(TO_CHAR(MINVTRAN.TRAN_DATE,'MM'),
               '06',MINVTRAN.TRAN_AMOUNT,0)) "June"
FROM   MINVTRAN
GROUP BY MINVTRAN.TRAN_FACL_NUM_STOR
ORDER BY 1;
```

Figure 6.18 Sales analysis report query

6.6.1.6 Dynamic column headings. Another powerful feature of SQL*Plus is the use of SQL*Plus variables for dynamic column headings. You can place a SQL*Plus variable as the alias for a column in a SELECT statement. When the column is printed the alias is used as the column

```
REM
REM     Define COL headings
REM
COLUMN CTRL_HEADING_MONTH1 FORMAT A9 NOPRINT NEW_VALUE
HEADING_MONTH1
COLUMN CTRL_HEADING_MONTH2 FORMAT A9 NOPRINT NEW_VALUE
HEADING_MONTH2
COLUMN CTRL_HEADING_MONTH3 FORMAT A9 NOPRINT NEW_VALUE
HEADING_MONTH3
COLUMN CTRL_HEADING_MONTH4 FORMAT A9 NOPRINT NEW_VALUE
HEADING_MONTH4
COLUMN CTRL_HEADING_MONTH5 FORMAT A9 NOPRINT NEW_VALUE
HEADING_MONTH5
COLUMN CTRL_HEADING_MONTH6 FORMAT A9 NOPRINT NEW_VALUE
HEADING_MONTH6
REM
REM     SELECT COL values into the Headings for the Report
REM
SELECT 'January'  CTRL_HEADING_MONTH1,
       'February' CTRL_HEADING_MONTH2,
       'March'    CTRL_HEADING_MONTH3,
       'April'    CTRL_HEADING_MONTH4,
       'May'      CTRL_HEADING_MONTH5,
       'June'     CTRL_HEADING_MONTH6
FROM   SYSTEM.DUAL;
REM
REM   ---Begin Report---
REM
SELECT MINVTRAN.TRAN_FACL_NUM_STOR "Store",
       SUM(DECODE(TO_CHAR(MINVTRAN.TRAN_DATE,'MM'),
                 '01',MINVTRAN.TRAN_AMOUNT,0)) "&&HEADING_MONTH1",
       SUM(DECODE(TO_CHAR(MINVTRAN.TRAN_DATE,'MM'),
                 '02',MINVTRAN.TRAN_AMOUNT,0)) "&&HEADING_MONTH2",
       SUM(DECODE(TO_CHAR(MINVTRAN.TRAN_DATE,'MM'),
                 '03',MINVTRAN.TRAN_AMOUNT,0)) "&&HEADING_MONTH3",
       SUM(DECODE(TO_CHAR(MINVTRAN.TRAN_DATE,'MM'),
                 '04',MINVTRAN.TRAN_AMOUNT,0)) "&&HEADING_MONTH4",
       SUM(DECODE(TO_CHAR(MINVTRAN.TRAN_DATE,'MM'),
                 '05',MINVTRAN.TRAN_AMOUNT,0)) "&&HEADING_MONTH5",
       SUM(DECODE(TO_CHAR(MINVTRAN.TRAN_DATE,'MM'),
                 '06',MINVTRAN.TRAN_AMOUNT,0)) "&&HEADING_MONTH6"
FROM   MINVTRAN
GROUP BY MINVTRAN.TRAN_FACL_NUM_STOR
ORDER BY 1;
```

Figure 6.19 Sales analysis report formatting

heading. Using this strategy for the sales report, our SELECT would look like the one in Figure 6.19.

We have solved half the problem by discovering that we can use SQL*Plus variables as our column headings. But how do we place the appropriate values into the headings? First, we need to determine how to change our DECODE to say "If the month of this row is six months ago then add the amount to the six months ago total" and so on for five months ago through one month ago. We start with one calculation, that for six months ago, as shown in Figure 6.20. This date calculation uses the current date (via SYSDATE) and subtracts x months at 30 days each (obviously this is just an approximation because not all months have 30 days, but for our purposes, it is sufficient). In this case x is 6 months. We can do the same calculation for 6 months through 1 month.

Now we are ready to place the appropriate column headings over the data. We might be tempted to place the date calculations we used above in the alias of our SELECT. This will cause an error because an alias between double quotes is not executed per se but taken literally. Thus, we place a dynamic value into the alias by using the NEW_VALUE clause in six COLUMN commands. (We used this clause to place data in the TTITLE command in Section 6.5.2—you may want to review that process now.) When we execute our SELECT the data value for the column is placed (via NEW_VALUE) into the SQL*Plus variable. Figure 6.21 shows these commands. Once the SQL*Plus variables contain the appropriate month names for the request, we can place the SQL*Plus variables into our SQL column aliases using "&&MONTH_HEADING1." Again, the SQL*Plus variable is substituted prior to being sent to ORACLE.

Is there another place in our SQL statement where we might use this technique? If you thought of the date calculation in each of our DE-CODEs, you were right. We could create six other SQL*Plus variables to hold the months for comparison in our DECODE. These variables are shown in Figure 6.22. This technique has two benefits—it makes the

```
SQL> RUN
  1  SELECT SYSDATE, TO_CHAR(SYSDATE-(30*6),'Month') "6 Months Previous"
  2* FROM    SYSTEM.DUAL

Today      6 Months Previous
---------- --------------------
22-APR-90  October
```

Figure 6.20 "6 Months Previous"

```
REM
COLUMN CTRL_HEADING_MONTH1 FORMAT A9 NOPRINT NEW_VALUE HEADING_MONTH1
COLUMN CTRL_HEADING_MONTH2 FORMAT A9 NOPRINT NEW_VALUE HEADING_MONTH2
COLUMN CTRL_HEADING_MONTH3 FORMAT A9 NOPRINT NEW_VALUE HEADING_MONTH3
COLUMN CTRL_HEADING_MONTH4 FORMAT A9 NOPRINT NEW_VALUE HEADING_MONTH4
COLUMN CTRL_HEADING_MONTH5 FORMAT A9 NOPRINT NEW_VALUE HEADING_MONTH5
COLUMN CTRL_HEADING_MONTH6 FORMAT A9 NOPRINT NEW_VALUE HEADING_MONTH6
REM
SELECT TO_CHAR(SYSDATE-(30*6),'Month') CTRL_HEADING_MONTH1,
       TO_CHAR(SYSDATE-(30*5),'Month') CTRL_HEADING_MONTH2,
       TO_CHAR(SYSDATE-(30*4),'Month') CTRL_HEADING_MONTH3,
       TO_CHAR(SYSDATE-(30*3),'Month') CTRL_HEADING_MONTH4,
       TO_CHAR(SYSDATE-(30*2),'Month') CTRL_HEADING_MONTH5,
       TO_CHAR(SYSDATE-(30*1),'Month') CTRL_HEADING_MONTH6
FROM   SYSTEM.DUAL;
REM
REM  ---Begin Report---
REM
SELECT MINVTRAN.TRAN_FACL_NUM_STOR "Store",
       SUM(DECODE(TO_CHAR(MINVTRAN.TRAN_DATE,'MM'),
                  TO_CHAR(SYSDATE-(30*6),'MM'),
                  MINVTRAN.TRAN_AMOUNT,0)) "&&HEADING_MONTH1",
       SUM(DECODE(TO_CHAR(MINVTRAN.TRAN_DATE,'MM'),
                  TO_CHAR(SYSDATE-(30*5),'MM'),
                  MINVTRAN.TRAN_AMOUNT,0)) "&&HEADING_MONTH2",
       SUM(DECODE(TO_CHAR(MINVTRAN.TRAN_DATE,'MM'),
                  TO_CHAR(SYSDATE-(30*4),'MM'),
                  MINVTRAN.TRAN_AMOUNT,0)) "&&HEADING_MONTH3",
       SUM(DECODE(TO_CHAR(MINVTRAN.TRAN_DATE,'MM'),
                  TO_CHAR(SYSDATE-(30*3),'MM'),
                  MINVTRAN.TRAN_AMOUNT,0)) "&&HEADING_MONTH4",
       SUM(DECODE(TO_CHAR(MINVTRAN.TRAN_DATE,'MM'),
                  TO_CHAR(SYSDATE-(30*2),'MM'),
                  MINVTRAN.TRAN_AMOUNT,0)) "&&HEADING_MONTH5",
       SUM(DECODE(TO_CHAR(MINVTRAN.TRAN_DATE,'MM'),
                  TO_CHAR(SYSDATE-(30*1),'MM'),
                  MINVTRAN.TRAN_AMOUNT,0)) "&&HEADING_MONTH6"
FROM   MINVTRAN
GROUP BY MINVTRAN.TRAN_FACL_NUM_STOR
ORDER BY 1;
```

Figure 6.21 New value and months (1)

SQL statement more readable and it improves the performance of the statement. See Chapter 8 for more on improving performance.

6.6.1.7 Passing parameters to SQL*Plus. We can define up to nine parameters by specifying &1 through &9 in our SQL*Plus script. When we execute the SQL*Plus report we can pass values into the parameters using "sqlplus user/pswd PARM_value1 PARM_value2." In Chapter 7 we

```
REM
COLUMN CTRL_MONTH1 FORMAT 9999999.00 NOPRINT NEW_VALUE MONTH1
COLUMN CTRL_MONTH2 FORMAT 9999999.00 NOPRINT NEW_VALUE MONTH2
COLUMN CTRL_MONTH3 FORMAT 9999999.00 NOPRINT NEW_VALUE MONTH3
COLUMN CTRL_MONTH4 FORMAT 9999999.00 NOPRINT NEW_VALUE MONTH4
COLUMN CTRL_MONTH5 FORMAT 9999999.00 NOPRINT NEW_VALUE MONTH5
COLUMN CTRL_MONTH6 FORMAT 9999999.00 NOPRINT NEW_VALUE MONTH6
REM
SELECT TO_CHAR(SYSDATE-(30*6),'MM')     CTRL_MONTH1,
       TO_CHAR(SYSDATE-(30*5),'MM')     CTRL_MONTH2,
       TO_CHAR(SYSDATE-(30*4),'MM')     CTRL_MONTH3,
       TO_CHAR(SYSDATE-(30*3),'MM')     CTRL_MONTH4,
       TO_CHAR(SYSDATE-(30*2),'MM')     CTRL_MONTH5,
       TO_CHAR(SYSDATE-(30*1),'MM')     CTRL_MONTH6
FROM   SYSTEM.DUAL;
REM
REM   ---Begin Report---
REM
SELECT MINVTRAN.TRAN_FACL_NUM_STOR "Store",
       SUM(DECODE(TO_CHAR(MINVTRAN.TRAN_DATE,'MM'),
               '&&MONTH1',MINVTRAN.TRAN_AMOUNT,0))  "&&HEADING_MONTH1",
       SUM(DECODE(TO_CHAR(MINVTRAN.TRAN_DATE,'MM'),
               '&&MONTH2',MINVTRAN.TRAN_AMOUNT,0))  "&&HEADING_MONTH2",
       SUM(DECODE(TO_CHAR(MINVTRAN.TRAN_DATE,'MM'),
               '&&MONTH3',MINVTRAN.TRAN_AMOUNT,0))  "&&HEADING_MONTH3",
       SUM(DECODE(TO_CHAR(MINVTRAN.TRAN_DATE,'MM'),
               '&&MONTH4',MINVTRAN.TRAN_AMOUNT,0))  "&&HEADING_MONTH4",
       SUM(DECODE(TO_CHAR(MINVTRAN.TRAN_DATE,'MM'),
               '&&MONTH5',MINVTRAN.TRAN_AMOUNT,0))  "&&HEADING_MONTH5",
       SUM(DECODE(TO_CHAR(MINVTRAN.TRAN_DATE,'MM'),
               '&&MONTH6',MINVTRAN.TRAN_AMOUNT,0))  "&&HEADING_MONTH6"
FROM   MINVTRAN
GROUP BY MINVTRAN.TRAN_FACL_NUM_STOR
ORDER BY 1;
```

Figure 6.22 New value and months (2)

will show you how we use this technique to pass information between SQL*Forms and SQL*Plus.

6.6.2 SQL*ReportWriter reporting techniques

Writing reports in SQL*ReportWriter is a process similar to the development of SQL*Forms applications. It begins with the definition of the SQL statements to be executed in the report and the relationships (if any) between those SQL statements. This creates a default report that can be reviewed with the user. You can then modify the default information to change field labels and add summaries and text.

Text Objects

Be sure to save the modification of text objects for last. The creation of summaries or changing of groups and queries will automatically affect the related text objects. Once altered, you may lose some of the automation provided by SQL*ReportWriter.

Comments

The report window of SQL*ReportWriter provides an area for comments. Be sure to use this area to document your report. In Chapter 9 you will see how to take advantage of this information.

6.6.2.1 Matrix-style reports. In the last section we saw how to create a spreadsheet-style report using the DECODE function. There is a similar capability built in to SQL*ReportWriter. Depending on the complexity and dynamic nature of the matrix report, you may decide that SQL*Plus is more appropriate. We defined a matrix-style report that listed inventory suppliers down the page, warehouses across the page, and the number

```
Report Name: MINVMTRX
Query Name: Q_SUPP

SELECT   MINVSUPP.SUPP_NUM, MINVSUPP.SUPP_DESC
FROM     MINVSUPP

Query Name: Q_WARE

SELECT   MINVWARE.FACL_NUM
FROM     MINVWARE

Query Name: Q_ORDR

Parent Query 1: Q_SUPP
   Child Column: ORDR_SUPP_NUM
   Parent Column:SUPP_NUM

Parent Query 2: Q_WARE
   Child Column: ORDR_FACL_NUM_WARE
   Parent Column: FACL_NUM

SELECT  MINVORDR.ORDR_FACL_NUM_WARE, MINVORDR.ORDR_SUPP_NUM,
   COUNT(MINVORDR.ORDR_NUM) "NUM OR ORDERS"
FROM     MINVORDR
GROUP BY MINVORDR.ORDR_FACL_NUM_WARE, MINVORDR.ORDR_SUPP_NUM
```

Figure 6.23 SQL*ReportWriter matrix report

of orders placed at the intersection. The definition of this default matrix report consisted of specifying the three SQL*Reportwriter queries shown in Figure 6.23.

Note that SQL*ReportWriter requires the SELECTion of any columns involved in a join. For instance, we do not want to print ORDR_SUPP_NUM or ORDR_FACL_NUM_WARE, yet we do need to use these columns in joins. Thus, we must select the columns and define them as non-printing in the field window. You do this by placing an "X" in the SKIP column for the fields.

The Q_ORDR query is the intersection information and is defined to SQL*ReportWriter to have two parent queries: Q_SUPP and Q_WARE. In the group window we define the three groups as members of a matrix by placing an "X" in the matrix column. Finally, we move to the field window to eliminate headings from all of the columns and determine the appropriate column sizes. We now have the simple default matrix-style report shown in Figure 6.24.

6.6.2.2 Printing only parents that have children. Another typical reporting requirement is to print a parent record and the matching children. If we define a report with this structure, SQL*ReportWriter will print all

```
MTRX                    MegaMarket Report                  22-APR-90
THOECHST          Facility/Order Analysis Report            08:31 AM


                    18000        19000        20000       21000
                 -----------  -----------  -----------  -----------
Market Supply Corp                                14          14
Compu-Disk            34
Floppy Disk World                   34           34
Office Vision                       14
                 -----------  -----------  -----------  -----------
                      34           48           48          14
```

Page: 1

Figure 6.24 Matrix report output

parents, including those with no children. You may instead want to define a report to print only parents that have children. For example, we defined a management report to print all administrative offices. For each administrative office we wanted to show the warehouses managed and the current inventory at each warehouse. We also wanted to show the stores managed and the current inventory at each store. Figure 6.25 shows a portion of this report.

In order to eliminate the printing of administrative offices that do not manage any warehouses or stores, we needed to define a parent query that SELECTs only those offices that are truly parents (i.e., they manage stores or warehouses). This query, shown in Figure 6.26, joins the parent and the child to eliminate any mismatches.

6.6.2.3 Eliminating column headings for children without any rows. The prior approach requires the parent-child join to occur twice, once explicitly in

```
ADMN                     MegaMarket Report                    22-APR-90
THOECHST              Facility Inventory Analysis             09:15 AM


   Office Num: 100
   Description: MegaMarket Headquarters


      Warehouse  Item Inventory      Store  Item Inventory
      ---------- --------------      ---------- --------------
           1000             38       18000             38
           3000             38       19000             23
           4000             42       20000             25
           5000             18
           6000             25                 --------------
           7000             40                             86
           8000             23

                  --------------
                            224




                         Page: 1
```

Figure 6.25 Administrative office report output

the parent query and again implicitly in the child query. A less resource intensive technique would be to eliminate the column headings for children without any rows. This can be achieved by adding the column NULL to the SELECT list for each of the child queries (in this case one for stores and one for warehouses). You then erase the label for both NULL fields and change the width to one character. Finally, create one group for each child and place the respective NULL field in the group. This technique eliminates the column headings because SQL*ReportWriter prints only the first field in a group that has no rows. Since this is the NULL field, one space will be printed.

Using NULL

There are many cases in SQL*ReportWriter where NULL fields, NULL groups, and NULL queries are required. For instance, you can define a Q_NULL with the statement "SELECT NULL FROM SYSTEM.DUAL" and use the query as a parent to change the print relationships of queries and groups. Keep this technique in mind if you find a situation where you feel that you cannot force the results you need. On a related note, you can define the datatype of the NULL field to be PRT. This will eliminate any spaces from printing for this field.

6.6.2.4 Using parameters. Using parameters in SQL*ReportWriter is a fairly simple exercise. We can refer to a SQL*ReportWriter variable with a colon when we are writing our SQL. When we accept the SQL statement, SQL*ReportWriter will automatically build a parameter variable. For example, we decided to allow the user of the report above to specify a particular administrative office to report on. To provide this functionality, we modified our query to include a parameter for the

Report Name: MINVADMN
Query Name: Q_OFFC

```
SELECT  TO_CHAR(SGENOFFC.OFFC_NUM) OFFC_NUM, SGENOFFC_DESC
FROM    MINVITEM, MINVFACL, SGENOFFC
WHERE   SGENOFFC.OFFC_NUM LIKE :PARM_OFFC_NUM
AND     SGENOFFC.OFFC_NUM = MINVFACL.FACL_OFFC_NUM_MGR
AND     MINVFACL.FACL_NUM = MINVITEM.ITEM_FACL_NUM
```

Figure 6.26 SQL*ReportWriter administrative office query

administrative office number, as shown in Figure 6.27. You can provide a default value for the parameter and define the parameter datatype via the parameter window of SQL*ReportWriter.

Using LIKE

You can make parameters more powerful by using a LIKE comparison instead of an equal to comparison in your WHERE clause. For example, we could define our SELECT in the example above to be WHERE OFFC_NUM LIKE :OFFC_NUM instead of WHERE OFFC_NUM = :OFFC_NUM. You could also default the value of :OFFC_NUM to the LIKE wildcard symbol "%". This strategy allows the same report to provide information about either a specific office or all offices, the trade-off with this technique is a performance loss on the specific office request. Refer to Chapter 8 for more details on tuning SQL statements.

When we execute the report a parameter entry window will appear by default. We can enter the administrative office number in this window. Parameters can also be passed directly into SQL*ReportWriter using the RUNREP facility. On the command line we can provide a value for the parameter in advance, specifying that we do not want to be prompted

```
┌─────────────────────────── Parameter Values ───────────────────────────┐
│                                                                          │
│  Parameter                          Value                                │
│  ───────────────────────────────────────────────────────────────────    │
│  Destination Type                   Screen                               │
│  File Name / Spool Device           minvadmn.lis                         │
│  Printer Description File           dflt                                  │
│  Number of Copies                   1                                    │
│  MENU_RPT_NAME                      ADMN                                  │
│  MENU_RPT_DESC                      Facility Inventory Analysis           │
│  Office Number                      100                                   │
│                                                                          │
│                                                                          │
│                                                                          │
│                                                                          │
│                                                                          │
│  Enter the desired value for each parameter.                             │
│  Report Name: minvadmn                              <INSERT>             │
└──────────────────────────────────────────────────────────────────────────┘
```

Figure 6.27 SQL*ReportWriter parameter screen

with the parameter window: "runrep paramform=no <PARM_NAME=value PARM_NAME=value>". You will see in Chapter 7 how this technique can be used to pass data between SQL*Forms and SQL*ReportWriter.

6.6.2.5 Dynamic ORDER BY. A typical user requirement in a report is to be able to view the information in one of several different ways. To implement this we need to define a dynamic ORDER BY within our report. The most common form of the ORDER BY clause is "ORDER BY column1, column2, ..." Another form of the ORDER BY uses a position reference of 1 for the first column in the SELECT list, 2 for the second column, and so on. There is one other valid parameter for the ORDER BY— a SQL expression. This form of the ORDER BY provides the flexibility needed for dynamic ordering. We can define a SQL expression for ordering with our old friend, the DECODE function. Figure 6.28 is an example of using DECODE in an ORDER BY clause.

We wanted to modify the MINVADMN report to allow the user to order the administrative offices by either the office number or office name. We can provide this functionality by adding a DECODE to the ORDER BY for our parent query. The DECODE checks a parameter (valued at runtime) that contains a "1" to specify ordering by office number or a "2" by office description. The parameter window is shown in Figure 6.29.

This SQL technique can be used in any of the SQL tools. For example, you can define a SQL*Forms application with a DECODE in the DEFAULT WHERE clause. This allows for dynamic ordering within your online application. The use of this technique is limited by the requirement of DECODE that all parameter values have the same datatype. You need to use a TO_CHAR conversion (as we did in Figure

Report Name: MINVADMN
Query Name: Q_OFFC

```
SELECT  TO_CHAR(SGENOFFC.OFFC_NUM) OFFC_NUM, SGENOFFC_DESC
FROM    MINVITEM, MINVFACL, SGENOFFC
WHERE   SGENOFFC.OFFC_NUM LIKE :PARM_OFFC_NUM
AND     SGENOFFC.OFFC_NUM = MINVFACL.FACL_OFFC_NUM_MGR
AND     MINVFACL.FACL_NUM = MINVITEM.ITEM_FACL_NUM
ORDER BY DECODE(:PARM_SORT,1,TO_CHAR(OFFC_NUM),OFFC_DESC)
```

Figure 6.28 Dynamic ordering in SQL*ReportWriter

```
┌─────────────────────────── Parameter Values ──────────────────────────┐
│ ┌──────────────────────────────┬──────────────────────────────────┐   │
│ │ Parameter                    │ Value                            │   │
│ ├──────────────────────────────┼──────────────────────────────────┤   │
│ │ Destination Type             │ Screen                           │   │
│ │ File Name / Spool Device     │ minvadmn2.lis                    │   │
│ │ Printer Description File     │ dflt                             │   │
│ │ Number of Copies             │ 1                                │   │
│ │ MENU_RPT_NAME                │ ADMN                             │   │
│ │ MENU_RPT_DESC                │ Facility Inventory Analysis      │   │
│ │ Office Number                │ %                                │   │
│ │ Sort(1=Off Num,2=Off Desc)   │ 1                                │   │
│ │                              │                                  │   │
│ │                              │                                  │   │
│ │                              │                                  │   │
│ │                              │                                  │   │
│ │                              │                                  │   │
│ └──────────────────────────────┴──────────────────────────────────┘   │
│ Enter the desired value for each parameter.                            │
│ Report Name: minvadmn                                   <INSERT>        │
└────────────────────────────────────────────────────────────────────────┘
```

Figure 6.29 Dynamic ordering parameters

6.29) if you try to order by either a number column or a character column. Beware that this conversion may destroy the accuracy of the sort.

6.7 Conclusion

In this chapter we took you through the process of writing reports using SQL*Plus and SQL*ReportWriter. With the completion of this process both the online and the offline portions of the application are ready for testing and tuning. Before moving on to these activities, however, we need to put our SQL*Forms applications and our reports together. The next chapter will explore the issues and problems you may face when integrating your application.

Pulling It All Together

7.1 Introduction

Although we have finished building the forms and reports that will make up our system, there's still quite a bit of work to be done before the MegaMarket Inventory Management System will be complete. The least tangible of these tasks is often referred to as "integration," a term that has been so grossly overused in the computer industry that it carries about as much meaning as terms like "user-friendly." Despite the countless development tasks that are grouped under the umbrella of "systems integration," we like to think that the term has its basis in the process of introducing a new system into an existing environment. We generally refer to this process simply as "pulling it all together." For lack of a better word, however, we will also often refer to this process as integration.

By "pulling it all together," we mean the tasks that will finally bring all of the separate pieces we have produced into one cohesive product that can communicate as well as possible with the systems (past, present, and future) that surround it. In this chapter we will discuss some of the steps that will help you to group your forms, reports, command files, old data, new data, old systems, and new systems into a consistent package. Some of these steps are general and can be applied to any system, while others are quite specific to the situation. Either way, they will help you provide the professional touch that distinguishes a simple collection of applications from a fully functional *system*.

7.2 Looking Back

If we take a moment to look back to the design of the MegaMarket system, we can see that many issues of "integration" were addressed at the outset. The Help and Menu systems that we built in Sections 5.6.1 and 5.6.3 help to pull our forms and reports together behind a single system interface. We also provide a consistent external interface across our forms through the use of the application skeletons and standards, as well as a consistent internal interface through the use of coding standards. Because we addressed many of these issues up front, we do not need to go back to complete them as part of the integration process. This benefit came about not by accident, but as a result of experience. It is much easier to integrate system components into a master plan as they are developed than to modify them to work together after the fact. Although it is not uncommon to wait until after the key components are built before addressing such issues, we urge you to plan ahead and integrate as you go along. Nonetheless, all the planning in the world won't solve every problem that needs attention before a system can go into production. Before we talk about some of the issues that we had to address during our integration phase, let's review some of the problems we avoided by planning ahead.

7.2.1 The menu system

One of the most common integration tasks of any system that has more than one SQL*Forms application is a front end interface that provides a uniform means of access to all of the applications. This is most often accomplished with a menu system. Several different tools are available for developing menus that link ORACLE applications together. Since each tool has unique benefits and problems, you should keep several things in mind when deciding which is right for you.

Perhaps the most important issue in choosing a method for building menus is flexibility. *Dynamic menus* are the most powerful because they can easily accommodate changes in application software such as the addition of forms and menus or the relocation of key files. Although "hard-coded" *static menus* are fast and easy to implement, they are much more difficult to support. Another important aspect of any menu system is the consistency of the interface. Navigating from one menu to another and through forms and reports should be simple and intuitive at each step of the way. This is largely accomplished by providing just a small subset of clearly defined functions that *work the same way everywhere.* The final aspect, which is important not only for menus but for all software, is portability. Integration of a unified collection of applications can ultimately grow into a unified collection of hardware and operating systems. Only software that has been designed to run on any platform will survive integration like this. We will discuss portability in more detail in Section 7.4 below, but first we will examine the options for menu systems.

7.2.1.1 SQL*Menu. Perhaps the most straightforward and flexible tool for developing menu systems that link ORACLE applications is the Oracle product SQL*Menu. Like all of the Oracle tools, SQL*Menu is based upon the RDBMS. Menu options, their functionality, and who can access them are stored in database tables and displayed through a flexible and intuitive graphical interface. Since the menu options depend on ORACLE data, the menus can be as flexible as the data itself. So, when a particular option is added or changed, the modification takes effect immediately throughout the system. This also makes the creation of menus very simple and fast. Additionally, security levels allow users to see only those options that apply to them. SQL*Menu can be used to access any ORACLE tools or operating system commands.

7.2.1.2 SQL*Forms dynamic menus. For our MegaMarket menu system we chose to use SQL*Forms. We did so because we were able to duplicate most of the flexibility and functionality of SQL*Menu without purchasing the additional software. We also did not want to be limited by the fact that not every user has SQL*Menu on their system. Also, by using our application skeleton to develop the menu forms, we were able to maintain a common interface between our menus and our forms. As you review the Menu system that we built in Section 5.6.3 take note of the fact that our menus are dynamic since both the choices available to the user and the location of the applications are stored in ORACLE tables. As a result, execution of any menu option is independent of application software location. With this architecture, we were able to accomplish our flexibility goals with only one sacrifice, the added development time required to build the menu forms. Because this menu architecture will be completely reusable in other systems, however, this was a sacrifice we were willing to make.

7.2.1.3 SQL*Forms static menus. A third alternative is building static menus with SQL*Forms. This is undoubtedly the most common type of menu system we see because they are so easy to produce. These menus are constructed by simply "painting" the menu options onto the boilerplate of a form. A single non-database field then allows for the input of a menu option number. A simple CASE statement on the KEY-NXTFLD (or any key) trigger with this form can then branch appropriately. Such a trigger is shown in Figure 7.1.

Although forms such as this one are very easy to build, they are rarely sufficient in large systems because of their inflexibility. Every time applications are added or deleted, all of the menu code must be changed. Static menus can also increase memory usage because running forms via CALLFRM "stacks" each menu form in memory as the user gets deeper into the hierarchy. With the dynamic method, the same menu form can simply be requeried. In Chapter 8, we will discuss other ways of avoiding such memory problems.

7.2.1.4 Non-ORACLE menu systems. Another menu strategy is to use a 3GL such as C or COBOL to control the calls to the various applications. This often provides the most flexible control over how the menus will look and operate, but the added programming is usually impractical and the

Form Name: SGENMENU
Trigger Level : Form
Trigger Name : KEY-NXTFLD

Step #1

```
#EXEMACRO  CASE :CTRL.OPTION_FIELD IS
            WHEN '1' THEN
              CALLFRM FIRSTFORM;
            WHEN '2' THEN
              CALLFRM SECONDFORM;
            WHEN '3' THEN
              EXIT;
            WHEN OTHERS THEN
              MESSAGE '*ERROR* Invalid Choice; Re-enter';
            END CASE;
```

Figure 7.1 Menu item selector trigger

system is far more difficult to maintain than a SQL*Forms or SQL*Menu application. Even minor changes to menus can require large programming efforts. Portability also becomes an issue once 3GLs come into play. Unlike custom-written 3GL programs, SQL*Forms and SQL*Menu will run anywhere ORACLE runs.

A final method is to use operating system command files to build simple menu systems. This alternative is sometimes acceptable for "quick and dirty" little menus to test functionality, but because menu functionality is greatly limited (and therefore probably inconsistent with our form interfaces) and because such command files have to be completely rewritten for each operating system to which the software is migrated, this option is not a good choice for production systems.

Once again, remember that by building our menu system from the start, we were able to plan ahead and resolve integration issues as they arose, rather than be forced to return after the fact to produce the menus. This helps us develop forms and menus that evolve together into an integrated system.

7.2.2 The help system

We were also able to plan ahead in the development of our help system. Very often, help systems are developed after the fact as a means of trying to "clean up" a system. Just as the programmer who comments code after it is finished asks "Wait a minute ... what was I doing here?" the developer who waits to develop the help system has to search for places where help might be needed. By planning ahead you can document difficult areas as you encounter them. In this way, the help system grows with the applications that it supports. Whether you choose to build a large and flexible help system like we did (see Section 5.6.1) or simply use the help features built into SQL*Forms is up to you. We do encourage you, however, to plan out and execute this aspect of integration right from the start.

7.2.3 An application skeleton

Although our principal motive for building the form and report skeletons in Sections 5.6.4 and 6.5 was to ease the development process, we can see now it also provided a means of enforcing consistency in the interface across the forms, menus, and reports. Consequently, there is no need to go back through our applications to "smooth" out the inconsistencies. This benefit is especially valuable because such smoothing is often neglected. It is not unusual for several different developers to work on their forms separately, each providing a unique "look and feel" in the user interface. Then, as deadlines approach, there is no time to go back and correct the inconsistencies. As a result, the users must learn to live with forms that operate in ways slightly different from one another. The irony is that when this happens, users will often accept the minor inconsistencies without complaining, but they won't come back to you for help with their next system. Since users will often assume that one inconsistency means many inconsistencies, they will lose confidence in you and your system.

Through these examples, we've seen that a little foresight can simplify the integration process, but in our system it is still far from complete. In the rest of this chapter, we will discuss how to bring things together even more tightly.

7.3 Calling Reports

Because all our screens are based on SQL*Forms, they can (and do) communicate with each other freely. The reports that we've constructed, however, are basically standalone procedures that are not naturally compatible with SQL*Forms applications. This, of course, is something we must remedy by pulling the reports into the menu and application structure. There are several approaches to accomplishing this task.

The first problem with creating a standard reporting interface is that each report type requires a different execution syntax. For example, SQL*Plus report command files can be executed by typing "sqlplus userid/password @reportname" while SQL*ReportWriter requires the execution of the "runrep" command. The user should, of course, be shielded from these inconsistencies by your interface. So, the first step in developing a reporting interface is establishing a standard calling convention.

The most flexible method is to build the reports into the application management system that we have already implemented. Remember that we built a table that stores the name and location of each SQL*Forms application (refer to Section 5.6.2 for details). We included in this table a column called APPL_TYPE_HCV to hold the application type. With all of our forms, the value of this column is either FRM or LFV. This tells us that the file referenced in that row is a SQL*Forms application. Similarly, we could add our reports to this table, specifying their types as SQL (SQL*Plus), SRW (SQL*Reportwriter), RPT (SQL*Report), or 3GL (3rd generation program). Our menu form could then be made more sophisticated, so that rather than always perform a CALL or NEWFRM, it can also execute an operating system command file using the SQL*Forms HOST command. This increased functionality would require that we add a field called HEADER.CTRL_COMMAND to our menu form and make the change shown in Figure 7.2.

HOST Macro

The HOST command is a macro function in SQL*Forms 2.3, so we can write our trigger this way. In earlier versions of SQL*Forms, the HOST command "#HOST :HEADER.CTRL_COMMAND;" must be placed in a separate user-named trigger and called from the CASE statement using EXETRG.

There is, of course, one major problem with this method: report parameters. This method assumes that the reports will run without user input. If user input is required, the report itself must prompt the user, but this is likely to lead to inconsistencies in report operation. For example, in SQL*Plus, user input is entered via SQL*Plus substitution variables (&variablename). Undefined variables produce the prompt "Enter value for *variablename*:" In SQL*Reportwriter, the parameter screen lists the SQL*Reportwriter variables that are undefined. SQL*Report's .ASK command allows the developer to customize the format for user input. As a result of these inconsistencies, this reporting interface is limited.

Since most operating systems provide a means of feeding user input into the reports (via shell scripts in UNIX, EXECS in VM, etc.), we can solve our parameter problem with an intermediary command file. This is accomplished by first constructing an operating system command file that will execute our report. This contains simply one line that calls our report with the appropriate tool (sqlplus, rpt, runrep, etc.). Once this command file is completed, we can modify it to allow for command line arguments. These arguments can then be "pumped" into the execution of the report as though the user typed them. (We will see an example of

Form Name: SGENMENU
Trigger Level: Form
Trigger Name : KEY-NXTFLD

Step #10

```
#EXEMACRO GOBLK CTRL;
            COPY :SGENMENU.MENU_DESC
              INTO GLOBAL.MENU_FORM_DESC;
            COPY :SGENMENU.MENU_APPL_NAME
              INTO GLOBAL.MENU_FORM_NAME;
            CASE HEADER.CTRL_APPL_TYPE_HCV IS
              WHEN 'LFV' THEN
                CALL &HEADER.CTRL_APPL_LOCATION;
                WHEN OTHERS THEN
                NEWFRM &HEADER.CTRL_APPL_LOCATION;
            END CASE;
```

BECOMES:

Step #10

```
#EXEMACRO GOBLK CTRL;
            COPY :SGENMENU.MENU_DESC
              INTO GLOBAL.MENU_FORM_DESC;
            COPY :SGENMENU.MENU_APPL_NAME
              INTO GLOBAL.MENU_FORM_NAME;
            CASE HEADER.CTRL_APPL_TYPE_HCV IS
              WHEN 'LFV' THEN
              CALL &HEADER.CTRL_APPL_LOCATION;
              WHEN 'FRM' THEN
              NEWFRM &HEADER.CTRL_APPL_LOCATION;
              WHEN 'SQL' THEN
              COPY 'sqlplus @'||:HEADER.CTRL_APPL_LOCATION
                INTO :HEADER.CTRL_COMMAND;
                HOST :HEADER.CTRL_COMMAND;
              WHEN 'SRW' THEN
              COPY 'runrep '||:HEADER.CTRL_APPL_LOCATION
                INTO :HEADER.CTRL_COMMAND;
                HOST :HEADER.CTRL_COMMAND;
              WHEN 'RPT' THEN
              COPY 'rpt '||:HEADER.CTRL_APPL_LOCATION
                INTO :HEADER.CTRL_COMMAND;
                HOST :HEADER.CTRL_COMMAND;
              WHEN '3GL' THEN
                COPY :HEADER.CTRL_APPL_LOCATION
                  INTO :HEADER.CTRL_COMMAND;
                  HOST :HEADER.CTRL_COMMAND;
            END CASE;
```

Figure 7.2 Alternative menu item selection trigger

this below.) In this way, we have constructed a means of executing the entire report with a single command line. As a result, we will be able to call it with a SQL*Forms HOST command.

SQL*Plus Command Line Parameters

Newer versions of SQL*Plus allow command line arguments, which are substituted in the SQL*Plus script for the variables &1, &2, and so on. Thus, if we created a SQL*Plus script called *my_script.sql* that included the following SQL statement:

```
SELECT *
FROM MINVITEM
WHERE ITEM_ICLS_CODE = '&1'
AND ITEM_FACL_NUM = &2
```

we could execute it by typing "sqlplus username/password @my_script MD35D 1000".

This method is fine if you have only a few small arguments and you are only using SQL*Plus scripts. Since the other tools operate differently, you may want to use our more general method when you plan to execute reports with more than one of the tools.

So, by taking advantage of the operating system command language, we can create SQL*Forms reporting applications that allow the user to provide report parameters through a familiar interface. There are many choices to be made, however, to determine how complex the SQL*Forms logic and operating system command files must be. First of all, should we build one SQL*Forms application that calls many different report programs, or should we build several forms, each of which calls a different report? Each method has advantages. A single SQL*Forms application that calls all the reports would certainly be easier to maintain, but it would also require more complex coding. Also, a single form would not easily accommodate the variable number of arguments required by each report. We have found that one SQL*Forms application for each report makes development more intuitive because there is no need to support the variable number of arguments across reports. It is often confusing to have a single form with many argument fields, only some of which apply to any given report.

You should also realize that this sort of reporting introduces portability problems. Because they are so directly tied to the syntax of the operating system language, the command files will need to be modified for each different one. For this reason, it is wise to avoid putting operating system specific code into trigger statements. You should not have to modify SQL*Forms applications when you move the system from one operating system to another. The way we avoid this is by placing the operating system specific code only in the command files. In the SQL*Forms triggers, then, you need only make a single, generic call to the command file.

For our report interface, we chose to build a single command file because we have a relatively small number of reports and because it provides us with a modular structure that can be easily modified when porting to another system. This program takes command line arguments which are mapped to the substitution variables in the reports, just as we described above. At the SQL*Forms end, we chose to develop a single SQL*Forms application for each report. Again, this is because we have a relatively small number of reports and we want each form to be customized to the particular report (titles, number of arguments, etc.). Although this solution requires the support of more applications, each application is simple and the users can clearly tell which report is being executed. This also means that we do not need to modify our menu application, because it will be calling SQL*Forms applications, rather than the reports themselves.

The first step in building this structure is the command file, the exact syntax of which depends upon your operating system. We have implemented ours to run under UNIX. Let's use the SQL*Plus Inventory Movement Report we described in Chapter 6 as our example. In it, we use four substitution parameters: the location of the report program, the four-character name of the report, the description of the report, and the facility number of the warehouse that is performing the movement. The first three parameters come from the SGENAPPL application management table, the fourth is specific to this report. Figure 7.3 shows the UNIX version of our command file, called "minvplus." This command file is executed by typing "minvplus *REPORT_LOCATION REPORT_NAME REPORT_DESC FACL_NUM.*" Note the use of the "<<" and "**END**" symbols in this file. This is a UNIX construct that will redirect input into the executing command file. Everything between the two "**END**" symbols will be forwarded into the file as though it were typed during execution.

Note also that we have hard-coded the userid and password into this command file. Although this practice may surprise you, we believe that it is acceptable in certain circumstances. First of all, the ORACLE userid

```
sqlplus -s report/adhoc @$1<<**END**
$2
$3
$4
**END**
```

Figure 7.3 SQL*Plus command file

REPORT that is referenced in the command file is one that we created especially for reporting. It is a CONNECT-only account that has SELECT only access to a subset of our tables. It would be impossible for someone to do any damage from this account because they cannot change or modify tables. This also provides a safe forum for "ad hoc" queries if our users choose to learn more about SQL (which we always encourage if sufficient training is available). Second, the operating system security is generally sufficient to keep this command file out of the hands of people who cannot use it. The people who can use it should already have accounts of their own anyway. Since most systems don't require more security, this is generally acceptable. If more security were in fact required, the command file could be written in a 3GL and compiled into executable code in which the password is well hidden. If this is still unacceptable (which should rarely be the case), the command file can simply prompt the user for the password before reconnecting to ORACLE. It seems that everyone's needs are different when it comes to sharing a single account. You should, of course, implement these command files so that they conform to any guidelines within your organization.

Command files like these can be implemented for any of the ORACLE reporting tools. Figure 7.4 shows the same command file (for UNIX) implemented for SQL*Reportwriter. Notice that there are additional operating system parameters in this command file since SQL*Reportwriter requires specification of both the parameter name and the parameter value. In this example $5 contains the name of the report parameter and $6 contains the value.

Once the command files for each reporting tool are ready, we add them to our SGENAPPL application table, specifying the full pathname. In this way, we can call the command file from a SQL*Forms application without worrying about the precise location.

The next step is to construct the forms that will call the reports. Because we are building a separate form for each report, each can accommodate the exact number of arguments. If no arguments are

```
runrep report=$1 userid=report/adhoc paramform=no
destype=$2 batch=$3 PARM_MENU_NAME=$4
PARM_MENU_DESC=$5 PARM_OFFC_NUM=$6
```

Figure 7.4 SQL*ReportWriter command file

required for a report, then no form is really necessary (it can be called directly from the menu, as explained above), but for the sake of consistency you should build a form for the report anyway. The code we will build into the form is much like what we used in the menu in Figure 7.2, except that no CASE logic is required and the SGENAPPL report location, name, and description are included. Our movement report form and the pertinent triggers are shown in Figure 7.5. Don't forget to use the application skeleton for these forms just like any others!

Note that our report screen includes an option that allows the user to choose how the report should be viewed. This argument to the command file can be as sophisticated as you like. For example, you might give them the option of displaying it on the screen or printing to whatever printer they select from a list (which you display from a table, of course).

Form Name: MINVMREP
Block Name: CTRL
Field Name: DISPLAY
Trigger Level : Field
Trigger Name : KEY-NXTFLD

Step #1

```
#EXEMACRO  COPY  'minvplus '||:HEADER.CTRL_APPL_LOCATION||' '||
                 'MOVE "'||:HEADER.CTRL_APPL_DESC||'" '||
                 :CTRL.WAREHOUSE_NUM
           INTO :CTRL.COMMAND;
           CASE :CTRL.DISPLAY IS
             WHEN 'Y' THEN
               HOST :CTRL.COMMAND;
             WHEN 'N' THEN
               HOST :CTRL.COMMAND NOSCREEN;
             WHEN OTHERS THEN
               MESSAGE "*ERROR* Enter Y or N';
                   ENDTRIG FAIL;
           END CASE;
```

Figure 7.5 Movement report form trigger

7.4 Portability Review

As a system approaches production, we must consider portability issues—questions of where the system will run. During the development process we were confined to one operating system platform (since it is generally impractical to attempt development of the same system on multiple machines simultaneously). If we encountered a task that required coding specific to our platform, we implemented it during our development. But because of ORACLE's portability the system can potentially be used on many different platforms. As a result, we decided to conduct a careful review to identify and document all potential portability issues. Any problems we find do not need to be corrected now, but they must be identified and documented to ease the work required if the application software is moved to another platform.

How can you identify portability problems? There are basically two places to look: ORACLE Version specific functions and operating system specific functions. Either of these can make a system incompatible with a new platform if you are not careful.

Since Oracle releases new versions of software frequently there will always be problems associated with running the same application throughout a large organization. If all of the tools on the various computers throughout an organization are always at exactly the same version, then all should be well. Keeping versions consistent in large environments, however, is a difficult task. Fortunately, all ORACLE software is upward compatible. Unless you develop an application with an advanced version and then run it using an older version, you should not encounter portability problems. But if you notice odd behavior when you move software to a new machine, remember that you should check all version numbers carefully. A very small upgrade on one machine can be all that it takes to cripple an application. Also remember that if you plan to build an application that will be distributed to users with potentially different versions of ORACLE, the application should be built using the earliest version they use, so that everyone can run it. Of course, we recommend that you use the most recent versions of all of the software whenever possible, but if you need a fully portable application you may find it easier to work entirely with a slightly older version to support more than one copy of the application code (e.g., support both a V2.3 SQL*Forms application and a V2.0 SQL*Forms application). Believe it or not, it is sometimes impossible to get everyone who may want to use the application to upgrade all of their software. This issue is especially crucial for an independent software developer who plans to sell the same application to several different ORACLE users.

Even more important than differences among software versions is the effect that operating system specific programming can have on portability. Whenever possible, you should avoid using any specific operating system commands in your applications. No matter how certain you are that the application will never be used on another operating system, the need always seems to arise eventually. If you prepare for this by writing your code with portability in mind, implementing the software on a new platform will be much simpler. The most common place for operating system conflicts to occur is with the HOST command in SQL*Forms applications.

HOST Portability

Since the HOST command spawns another process when it executes, there are problems with using it in single user environments. On PCs running MS-DOS, the problem has been fixed with the OHOST command. This command works just like HOST except that it allows you to execute another ORACLE connection by suspending the first one. On single-task VM machines, HOST cannot be used to make a second ORACLE connection.

Problems with HOST depend on the nature of the command. If you simply use it to call another program, then as long as that program exists on all your platforms, you'll have no problems. If, on the other hand, you take advantage of some operating system specific utility, you may encounter difficulties. For example, in UNIX, there is a utility called *grep* that allows you to search for a character string (or regular expression) in a given set of files. As with most UNIX utilities, grep has a syntax unlike that of any other operating system command. If you built a SQL*Forms application that constructed a grep statement and then ran it with the HOST command, you could encounter serious portability problems. When you moved the form to a VMS machine, you could probably rewrite that section of code using the *search* command, but the syntax is very different. But what if you decided to move your form to DOS which has no built-in string search facility? This simple HOST command could come back to haunt you.

Take advantage of ORACLE's portability—don't undermine it by using operating system specific commands everywhere. Remember, an application is only as portable as its least portable component. If you do need to write operating system specific code (as we did with our report-generating operating system command files in Section 7.3), now is the time to note the places where changes may be needed when the system is ported. Go through your forms and reports, looking for operating system commands, and simply note where each one is, the nature of the command, and why it would need changing. Don't bother trying to suggest actual changes at this point, because you don't know what the next operating system(s) will be. This list will then become part of the technical documentation, to become an invaluable resource when you or the next developer must migrate the application to a different operating system.

A final portability concern occurs when you need to move your application from a character-mode environment to a block-mode environment (or vice versa). Many of the SQL*Forms applications that you design for character mode will not execute properly in block mode. Refer back to Section 5.4 for a discussion of how character-mode and block-mode differ and their implications for SQL*Forms development.

7.5 Migrating Old Data

Since it is very rare that ORACLE is the first form of automation in an organization, there is almost always some electronic data already being used that must be *migrated* into the new system. We recommend that you make every effort to utilize existing data in your applications. A system that is delivered already full of data is always received with greater enthusiasm than an empty one.

You can also learn quite a bit from existing databases when you are designing new ones. If they found the data useful before, they'll probably find it useful in the future. Do not, however, restrict yourself to storing the data in the old format. As we saw in Chapter 2, the structural design of the new system should proceed independently of any existing systems. Since you can get any kind of data into ORACLE, there's no need to shape the tables to the old format. We have found that the integration phase is an appropriate time to migrate old data because the applications and the database are stable.

The method that you should choose for loading existing data into your tables depends on the nature of the data. If the old data is already in an ORACLE database and the table format has not changed, then the Oracle database import utility (imp) is probably the best choice. If the data is in a uniform flat file format (which can be generated by most other DBMSs), then the Oracle data loading tool, SQL*Loader, might be the solution. Finally, if the data is jumbled together in a file without much structure, a 3GL interface to ORACLE like Pro*C may be necessary to get the job done.

Using SQL*Loader

The SQL*Loader program and its predecessor ODL are part of the utility set provided with the RDBMS. (Other tools in this set include imp and exp and sqldba.) SQL*Loader allows both fixed and variable length records to be loaded into one or more database tables using a "control file" program. The program is written by a developer to provide mapping instructions for the SQL*Loader utility.

If you use SQL*Loader or a Pro* program we recommend that you move the data into intermediate tables "as is" (in the old format) and then move it into your tables using SQL. Unless the old data and your tables have the exact same format, using SQL as an intermediate step provides quite a bit more flexibility. Perhaps the most common example of this adaptability occurs when you have to normalize data into your tables. For instance, many flat file databases store data in one giant table. The flat file that holds this data has many rows and many fields in each row. If you decide to use this data in your tables, it will probably need to be stored in many different tables. Rather than write a sophisticated 3GL program that scans the data, building rows for several tables, making sure that no duplicates exist and that all foreign keys are properly assigned, you should simply load the whole thing into one big temporary table. Then, using SQL, you can insert records into your tables by using clever selections from this main table. When you are finished, simply drop the temporary table. The 3GL program required to normalize the data as it is loaded could be quite cumbersome, but the SQL to accomplish the task is usually straightforward. Also, since the program would probably be used only one time, the development effort is even further wasted.

During the development of our system, we discovered a need for migrating old data. One of our users was keeping track of employees and the different inventory classifications with his personal computer. He faithfully maintained a simple spreadsheet for each set of data. The employee spreadsheet was very much like our employee table. (In fact, we used it as a starting point when we identified the attributes of an employee.) We identified several fields that would provide good starting data for our employee table, but the inventory classification spreadsheet was not so conveniently organized. The main problem was that there was an excessive amount of duplication. Since it included the inventory item as well as the supplier, each item and each supplier appeared several times. Samples from the two spreadsheets can be seen in Figure 7.6.

After dumping these spreadsheets into ASCII files (a function provided by the spreadsheet software), we simply loaded each file into its own table using SQL*Loader. The spreadsheet software created files in

Adams	Jim	K	27	01/30/82	175-47-8294	
Jones	Margaret		12	11/12/84	843-23-8429	
Lopez	Mark	B	88	06/14/84	693-58-6991	
Carney	Patrick	F	29	04/10/87	520-03-2627	
Smith	Louis	G	16	04/23/79	765-87-1253	
Wilson	Marilyn	A	31	02/19/85	941-11-4521	
Matthews	William	R	41	03/12/86	776-98-2517	
Conners	Barney		32	06/07/88	893-00-2212	
Thomas	Mike	R	25	10/12/85	736-09-4538	
Malone	Carol	E	29	12/02/89	982-41-6934	
Matthews	Bill		41	03/12/86	776-98-2517	

DATA STORE 3.5" DD	FLOPPY DISK WORLD	
DATA STORE 5.25" DD	FLOPPY DISK WORLD	
DATA STORE 3.5" HD	FLOPPY DISK WORLD	
DATA STORE 5.25" HD	FLOPPY DISK WORLD	
DATA STORE 5.25" SD	FLOPPY DISK WORLD	
DISKTECH DD 5.25"	Computer Accessories, Inc.	
MICROSYSTEMS 3.5" DD	FLOPPY DISK WORLD	
MICROSYSTEMS 3.5" HD	FLOPPY DISK WORLD	
DATA STORE 5.25" DD	Computer Accessories, Inc.	
DATA STORE 5.25" HD	Computer Accessories, Inc.	
DATA STORE 5.25" SD	Computer Accessories, Inc.	
DISKTECH 5.25" HD	Computer Accessories, Inc.	
DISKTECH 5.25" DD	Computer Accessories, Inc.	

Figure 7.6 Spreadsheets to be loaded

variable field length format with each data value separated by a bar ("|") character. Figures 7.7 and 7.8 show samples from the ASCII files and the SQL*Loader control file that we used in this procedure.

Now we have two brand new temporary tables full of real data. But since the spreadsheet did not automatically validate the data the user entered, we do not know the "quality" of the data. Before we load it into our real tables, we must examine it and filter out invalid data.

First, we will look for imperfections in the data. We cannot overemphasize the importance of finding all flaws in the data. If the data was well maintained, this is generally not a problem, but any bad data

empl.dat
```
Adams|Jim|K|27|01/30/82|175-47-8294
Jones|Margaret||12|11/12/84|843-23-8429
Lopez|Mark|B|88|06/14/84|693-58-6991
Carney|Patrick|F|20|04/10/87|520-03-2627
Smith|Louis|G|16|04/23/79|765-87-1253
Wilson|Marilyn|A|31|02/19/85|941-11-4521
Matthews|William|R|41|03/12/86|776-98-2517
Conners|Barney||32|06/07/88|893-00-2212
Thomas|Mike|R|25|10/12/85|736-09-4538
Malone|Carol|E|29|12/02/89|982-41-6934
Matthews|Bill||41|03/12/86|776-98-2517
```

icls.dat
```
DATA STORE 3.5" DD|FLOPPY DISK WORLD
DATA STORE 5.25" DD|FLOPPY DISK WORLD
DATA STORE 3.5" HD|FLOPPY DISK WORLD
DATA STORE 5.25" HD|FLOPPY DISK WORLD
DATA STORE 5.25" SD|FLOPPY DISK WORLD
DISKTECH DD 5.25"|Computer Accessories, Inc.
MICROSYSTEMS 3.5" DD|FLOPPY DISK WORLD
MICROSYSTEMS 3.5" HD|FLOPPY DISK WORLD
DATA STORE 5.25" DD|Computer Accessories, Inc.
DATA STORE 5.25" HD|Computer Accessories, Inc.
DATA STORE 5.25" SD|Computer Accessories, Inc.
DISKTECH 5.25" HD|Computer Accessories, Inc.
DISKTECH 5.25" DD|Computer Accessories, Inc.
```

Figure 7.7 Data files to be loaded

that infects the new system can make its contents completely invalid. Since our new applications will not allow any invalid data to be entered into the system, this is only a concern when we are loading data created by some other application.

Indexes and Loading

You should create all indexes on a table after the data loading process is complete. This will greatly reduce the amount of time it takes to load the data and will improve the structure of the indexes.

Of course, the only way to ensure that all of the data is absolutely correct is to print out the files and review them carefully by hand. There are, however, a few techniques that can be used to quickly identify some

CONTROL FILE 1

```
LOAD DATA
INFILE empl.dat
REPLACE
INTO TABLE TEMPEMPL
FIELDS TERMINATED BY "|"
(EMPL_NAME_LAST,
 EMPL_NAME_FIRST,
 EMPL_NAME_MIDDLE,
 EMPL_NUM,
 EMPL_HIRE_DATE DATE "MM/DD/YY",
 EMPL_SOC_SEC_NUMBER)
```

CONTROL FILE 2

```
LOAD DATA
INFILE icls.dat
REPLACE
INTO TABLE TEMPFILE
FIELDS TERMINATED BY "|"
(ICLS_NAME   POSITION(01:40) CHAR,
 ICLS_SUPP   POSITION(42:70) CHAR)
```

Figure 7.8 SQL*Loader control files

kinds of problematic data. The first identifies duplicate rows. There are several techniques to eliminate duplications, one of which uses the COUNT function. The SQL statement shown in Figure 7.9 will create employee data from the temporary employee table with no duplications.

Of course, the number of columns listed in the correlated WHERE clause of this statement will affect the depth of duplication checking. The list should generally include just the primary key, but you may want to repeat the statement using other columns to check for duplicated names, etc. We decided to include just the primary key (EMPL_NUM).

SOUNDEX

By using the SQL SOUNDEX function, you can even check for duplication of values that *sound* the same:

```
SELECT TABLEA.NAME, TABLEB.NAME
FROM TABLEA, TABLEB
WHERE SOUNDEX(TABLEA.NAME) =
SOUNDEX(TABLEB.NAME)
AND TABLEA.ROWID <> TABLEB.ROWID
```

This SQL statement will list groups of names in the table that sound like one another (e.g. MARKS, MARX, MARCS, etc.).

Inserting the inventory classification data is more difficult, because each row of the temporary table has to fill rows in three of our tables (SLFVICLS, MINVSUPP, and MINVSCLS). This means that we will need one INSERT statement for each of these three tables. There are several problems with the insertion into the MINVICLS table.

First, we must not insert the same inventory classification more than once. This is solved by using the DISTINCT clause. We moved the

```
INSERT INTO SGENEMPL
SELECT *
FROM TEMPEMPL A
WHERE 2 > (SELECT COUNT(*)
  FROM TEMPEMPL B
  WHERE A.EMPL_NUM=B.EMPL_NUM))
```

Figure 7.9 Removing duplicates

inventory classes into another temporary table so that we would not have to deal with the duplicated classes from our original table. This was accomplished with the SQL statement in Figure 7.10.

Second, the primary key of SLFVICLS is a character, not a number (which could be incremented easily). Since there is no way to automatically assign meaningful primary key values and still maintain uniqueness, we decided that they must be assigned by hand. To make this easier, we added a column to our temporary table to accommodate this five character code. Then we updated each row, setting this new value to be the first five characters of the inventory class description. Next, we ran a SELECT statement to check for duplicate values, and we noted them. Finally, we created a quick default SQL*Forms application that allowed the duplicates to be fixed and the other values to be tailored by hand to improve any of the codes that didn't make sense. Once the duplicate rows in TEMPICLS are removed they are then simply INSERTed into SLFVICLS. The SQL statements used for this are shown in Figure 7.11.

```
INSERT INTO TEMPICLS (TEMPICLS.DESC)
   SELECT DISTINCT TEMPFILE.CLASS
   FROM TEMPFILE
```

Figure 7.10 Purging inventory classification data

```
ALTER TABLE TEMPICLS
ADD (CODE CHAR(5))

UPDATE TEMPICLS
SET TEMPICLS.CODE = UPPER(SUBSTR(TEMPICLS.DESC,1,5))

SELECT  A.DESC, B.DESC
FROM    TEMPICLS A, TEMPICLS B
WHERE   A.CODE = B.CODE
AND     A.ROWID <> B.ROWID

INSERT INTO SLFVICLS (ICLS_CODE, ICLS_DESC)
   SELECT  TEMPICLS.CODE, TEMPICLS.DESC
   FROM    TEMPICLS
```

Figure 7.11 Normalizing inventory classification data

Our next task was to move the supplier information into the MINVSUPP table. We used the SQL statement shown in Figure 7.12.

With the rows for those two tables created, we were finally ready to insert values into the intersection table MINVSCLS. The SQL statement in Figure 7.13 joined all of the necessary tables for this operation.

Although this seems like quite a few SQL statements to accomplish the simple task of loading in a flat file, it took far less effort than would a 3GL program to load and normalize the data. Carefully handling this process is critical to the integrity of your system, and using SQL generally reduces the chance of error.

7.6 Integrating Existing Systems

When a new system is put in place, it may have to be integrated with systems that already exist. If the existing systems are built in ORACLE or one of the RDBMSs with which ORACLE can communicate, then the integration process may be quite simple. If, on the other hand, you must achieve compatibility with a totally foreign system, direct integration can be very difficult. Because the tasks involved are intimately tied to the nature of the two applications, we cannot provide a single procedure you can follow in this area. We will, however, provide some guidelines and ideas to get you going in the right direction.

```
INSERT INTO MINVSUPP (SUPP_NUM,SUPP_DESC)
   SELECT  SUPPSEQ.NEXT,
           INITCAP(DISTINCT TEMPFILE.SUPP)
   FROM    TEMPFILE
```

Figure 7.12 Purging supplier information

```
INSERT INTO MINVSCLS (SCLS_SUPP_NUM, SCLS_ICLS_CODE)
   SELECT  MINVSUPP.SUPP_NUM, SLFVICLS.ICLS_CODE
   FROM    TEMP_TABLE, SLFVICLS, MINVSUPP
   WHERE   INITCAP(TEMPFILE.SUPP) =
           MINVSUPP.SUPP_DESC
   AND     TEMPFILE.CLASS = MINVICLS.ICLS_DESC
```

Figure 7.13 Normalizing supplier information

SQL*Connect

Oracle offers a set of utilities under the umbrella SQL*Connect for communication between an ORACLE RDBMS and a foreign DBMS. SQL*Connect products include interfaces to many popular DBMSs.

If you plan to integrate your system with another ORACLE database (or one of the other DBMSs with which ORACLE can communicate), then the technical aspects of integrating the two are relatively straightforward. Oracle's SQL*Net product allows ORACLE databases to communicate with each other transparently over most major network protocols. The details of this process are outside the scope of this discussion but we will return to questions of networking and distributed databases in Chapter 10.

Dirty Data

Remember that while your data is clean and well-validated, a system you are communicating with may not be so well maintained! When a user views data through your system, he will perceive it as your data. If the system with which you want to communicate is corrupt in any way, proceed with caution if you plan to present the data yourself.

Integration is more complicated with foreign applications that cannot communicate directly with ORACLE. Suppose your user has a budget or payroll system using (heaven forbid) a nonrelational database system, but still wants to present actual payroll information from that system along with employee information from your system. How is this best accomplished? Unfortunately, once again it depends almost entirely on the nature of the software used by the other system.

One of the best approaches is to implement a batch process that takes data from one system and updates tables in the other on a regular basis. In this way, the data is always available to your applications, but it may be slightly out of date. With a payroll system, this would not be impractical, because payroll information does not change that often. So, by creating a few tables for payroll information in your system and automating a process for loading them full of fresh data every day or every week, you can avoid the performance burden of an online system interface. In addition, when the foreign payroll system goes down, your system will still have data with which to work.

How can this process best be automated? You could choose to dump the data to ASCII files and load it like we did earlier in Section 7.5. This method is simple, but it requires not only several steps but also—in some cases—user intervention. If you want to fully automate the process, a more thorough option is to load the data with a 3GL program. Since such a program would be run over and over again, you can justify investing the programming time, and the added execution speed will be a bonus.

In our case, a user wanted to use his DOS-based spreadsheet software to do "what if" analysis of the transaction data. Essentially, this user wanted to take live ORACLE data and load it into his spreadsheet, where he could change it without harming the original. Our user also prepared stored payroll information using some custom software that he did not want to change. He wanted to view this data along with the employee information that is stored in the new system.

ORACLE for 1-2-3

This is something that we could easily accomplish using the ORACLE for 1-2-3 add-in tool, but our user was adamant about continuing to work within the familiar environment of his incompatible spreadsheet program. The Oracle add-in tool allows data from ORACLE to be SELECTed directly into a compatible spreadsheet. The user can also issue subsequent INSERTs, UPDATEs, and DELETEs to ORACLE.

Producing a data file based on our ORACLE tables for use in the spreadsheet was very simple. Since the spreadsheet software has a feature that allows it to load in ASCII files in a particular format, we simply produced such a file using ORACLE data and SQL*Report. We could have used a 3GL or a sophisticated SQL*Plus program to accomplish the same task, but SQL*Report is ideal for this. To automate the process, we built a simple UNIX command file that generates the report, starts the spreadsheet software, and executes a spreadsheet macro to load the file. From then on, the user simply treats the data as a spreadsheet without affecting the database. A segment of this SQL*Report is shown in Figure 7.14.

Using the employee payroll information in our ORACLE applications is slightly more involved. Since the payroll system software includes a reporting feature that produces external files, we were able to create ASCII files of the payroll data. The reporting capabilities of the payroll system were quite limited, however, and we were unable to format the

```
.REM
....column declares and print table define...
.REM
.DEFINE seltran
    SELECT MINVTRAN.TRAN_NUM, MINVTRAN.TRAN_EMPL_NUM,
        MINVTRAN.TRAN_ITEM_NUM, MINVTRAN.TRAN_DATE,
        MINVTRAN.TRAN_AMOUNT, MINVTRAN.TRAN_TTYP_CODE,
        MINVTRAN.TRAN_FACL_NUM_STOR
    INTO   TRAN_NUM, TRAN_EMPL_NUM, TRAN_ITEM_NUM, TRAN_DATE,
        TRAN_AMOUNT, TRAN_TTYP_CODE, TRAN_FACL_NUM_STOR
    FROM   MINVTRAN
..
.REM
.DEFINE body
    .PRINT tran_num
    ,
    .PRINT tran_empl_num
    ,
    .PRINT tran_item_num
    ,
    .PRINT tran_date
    ,
    .PRINT tran_amount
    ,
    .PRINT tran_ttyp_code
    ,
    .PRINT tran_facl_num_stor
    #NC
..
#T 1
.REPORT seltran body
```

Figure 7.14 Sample SQL*Report report

files to allow direct loading into our tables. As a result, we had to write a SQL*Loader program to load a temporary table and SQL*Plus statements that were smart enough to interpret the text file and insert the right data into the right tables. This process was very similar to the one we used in Section 7.5.

7.7 Moving the Software

Having finished writing all the programs to integrate our system, we are ready to move the software into the test environment. Remember the directory structure we set up before beginning development (refer to

```
cp devl/invmgtvl/batch/*.*     test/invmgtvl/batch
cp devl/invmgtvl/document/*.*  test/invmgtvl/document
cp devl/invmgtvl/form/*.*      test/invmgtvl/form
cp devl/invmgtvl/install/*.*   test/invmgtvl/install
cp devl/invmgtvl/report/*.*    test/invmgtvl/report
cp devl/sharedvl/batch/*.*     test/sharedvl/batch
cp devl/sharedvl/document/*.*  test/sharedvl/document
cp devl/sharedvl/form/*.*      test/sharedvl/form
cp devl/sharedvl/install/*.*   test/sharedvl/install
cp devl/sharedvl/report/*.*    test/sharedvl/report
```

Figure 7.15 UNIX staging command file

Figure 4.1 in Section 4.2). Up until now, we've been working in /softlib/ devl/invmgtv1 and /softlib/devl/sharedv1. These are the development directories for version 1 of the Inventory Management System and the Shared Software System. Now it is time to move the software into / softlib/test/invmgtv1 and /softlib/test/sharedv1, the test directories for the same application version. The directory structure under test is identical to the structure under devl. This equivalence makes copying the software simple. We developed the command file in Figure 7.15 to accomplish the task for us.

It is important that the software staging process be strictly regulated. A few guidelines will help you manage your software more effectively. First, *do not make changes to software in the test directories.* All changes should be made in the development area and then moved into the test area. Second, *do not move the software into the test directories after every small modification.* You should move all modified software into the test environment according to a defined schedule that is known to everyone working on the project, so the testers will know when they have new software to test. Third, *document all changes that are moved into the test area.* This helps the tester know exactly what aspects of the new version need to be checked.

7.8 Conclusion

Since we will discuss testing at length in Chapter 8, we will end our discussion of "pulling it all together" here. Because the process is so application-specific, we encourage you to look for methods of integrating your systems that we did not address. You will find that a little creativity and clever programming will help your system mesh seamlessly among those already in use. We know from experience that this will make life much easier on you and your users. Now we can begin the process of testing and tuning the MegaMarket system. In the next chapter we will provide insight into techniques for testing and tactics for tuning.

Testing and Tuning

8.1 Introduction

Testing and tuning are probably the most important, and the most difficult, parts of the application building process. Testing is a rigorous activity where the tester follows every possible path through the form or report in an attempt to expose bugs. Tuning, on the other hand, is more of an art where experience, instinct, and luck blend to reduce the response time and resource requirements, and increase the throughput of the overall system. Traditional lifecycle methodologies specify that testing of the individual program, the complete application, and ensemble of applications should follow the conclusion of the development effort. But few of these methodologies include a similar task for tuning the functionally complete application.

We have found that during integration testing we spend as much time tuning the application—and testing it again—as we spend on simple testing. Testing lends itself to this iterative process. As we diligently test all the possible paths through the application to eliminate any bugs that might exist, we create real data. When we convert data from existing systems (as we did in Chapter 7) we create more real data. The outcome of both activities is a large quantity of data. This provides the first opportunity to test our applications with anything more than a small amount of sample data. Code that used to execute almost instantaneously suddenly reveals hidden inefficiencies—not bugs or functionality problems, but poor performance resulting from improper tuning.

In this chapter we will provide a complete recipe for application tuning and testing. We will begin with an overview of how the ORACLE RDBMS operates; appreciating this is the key to skilled application tuning. We will then share our methods, tips, and tricks for tuning the application, discuss application testing, and explain what we did to maximize the performance of the MegaMarket application.

8.2 Inside the ORACLE RDBMS

There are many references in this book and in the ORACLE documentation to the ORACLE RDBMS, or the *kernel*. What is this nebulous entity called the ORACLE kernel? When we remove the shroud of mystery surrounding the kernel, you will probably be disappointed. Inside is merely a series of C programs (albeit extremely clever C programs) and a few assembly language routines (mostly operating system specific I/O and process control programs). Thus, your SQL requests to the kernel are nothing more than arguments or parameters to a C program.

A more important question than "what is the kernel?" is "how does it work?" Throughout this book we have tried to expand your understanding of each development tool. Now we will look at the most fundamental component of the database system. How does the kernel operate? How do we communicate with it and how does it give us back the data we request?

We know that we talk to the kernel (referred to simply as ORACLE throughout the rest of this section) exclusively in SQL. The steps involved in this communication process are straightforward. First, we write our SQL statement. This might be done through one of the Oracle tools (for instance, SQL*Forms or SQL*Plus) or through a Pro*ORACLE program you write. Once the SQL statement is written it must be issued to ORACLE and executed. Issuing the SQL statement alerts ORACLE that you have a request.

ORACLE allocates an area of memory, called a *cursor*, to communicate with you and to hold the result of the exchange. The Oracle tools allocate cursors for you, whereas a Pro*ORACLE program can allocate cursors explicitly by issuing DECLARE CURSOR statements. Each cursor is located within the ORACLE buffers in an area referred to as the program global area, or PGA. A separate PGA is allocated for each user logged into ORACLE. The PGA contains a number of open cursors up to a limit determined by the ORACLE startup parameter OPEN_CURSORS. Figure 8.1 is a simplified conceptual view of the PGA.

Note that the Oracle tools will return the error message "Max Open Cursors Exceeded" if you request a cursor beyond the number specified for OPEN_CURSORS. However, Pro*ORACLE programs will dynamically request additional cursors exceeding the OPEN_CURSORS limit as needed.

The implementations of the PGA and cursor memory allocation process are operating system specific (for example, in MVS a GETMAIN is used to obtain a chunk of memory). The initial size of a cursor is determined by another ORACLE startup parameter called CONTEXT_SIZE, whose default value ranges from 1024 to 4096 bytes.

Why "context" size instead of "cursor" size? Technically, the context (or a *context area*) is the actual memory area and the cursor is the *name* associated with that memory area. This distinction can be confusing, but

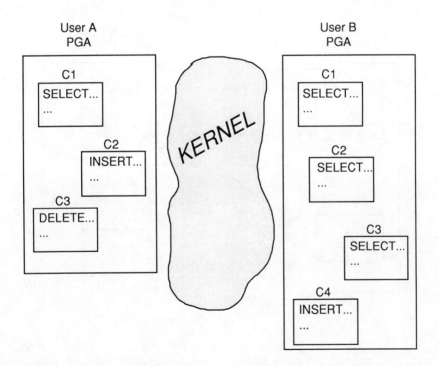

Figure 8.1 Conceptual view of PGA

fortunately it is not very important. A context area is a chunk of memory that can be allocated to one SQL statement (and thus one cursor) at a time. When that SQL statement is complete, the context area is free to be used by another SQL statement (another cursor). Thus, one context area can be used, over time, to satisfy many SQL statements (many cursors).

Regardless of the details, a chunk of memory called a cursor is reserved to satisfy your SQL request. Actually, things are not quite that simple, because there are really two cursors involved in this process. There is a cursor called the *user cursor* and there is a cursor inside the PGA called the *ORACLE cursor* (this is the cursor we have been discussing thus far). ORACLE will assign an ORACLE cursor for every user cursor opened. Thus, when a SQL statement is issued a user cursor is opened and assigned a pointer to an ORACLE cursor in the PGA. Figure 8.2 depicts this relationship.

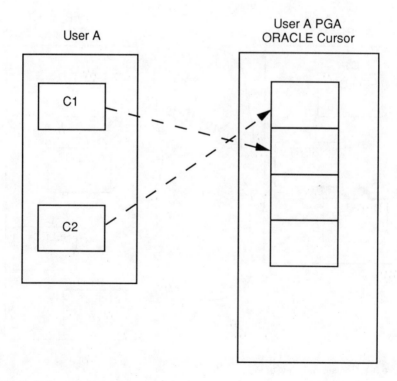

Figure 8.2 Cursor relationships

Once the ORACLE cursor and the user cursor are linked, the process works much like a mirror. First, the SQL request is placed into the user cursor and is *echoed*, or copied, into the ORACLE cursor. ORACLE then *parses* the SQL statement. Parsing starts with the binding of variables, which is a simple check to ensure that all of the user variables (such as :SCREEN_FIELD in SQL*Forms or &VAR in SQL*Plus) contain a value, as they should. An error message will be issued if any variable is undefined. Next, ORACLE validates the syntax of the SQL statement. Any syntax error, such as an extra comma or a missing FROM clause, will also cause an error message. Next, the objects in the FROM list are compared against the ORACLE data dictionary. This step checks for existence of the object, the object type (table, view, or synonym), and the user's privileges on the object. Finally, the attributes (data type and length) for each column for each object are determined.

View Overhead

ORACLE must determine if the object is a table or view owned by the requesting user or a synonym for a table owned by another user. If the object is a view ORACLE must read a data dictionary table containing the query for the view. Once the view query is read, it can be issued, parsed, and executed. This causes processing overhead (and therefore longer response time) for the query execution process.

Each of these checks represents one or more SQL queries generated by ORACLE to retrieve information from the data dictionary tables. To speed this process ORACLE will always look for the required information in special dictionary caches in memory before searching the data dictionary itself (see Section 8.3.1 for details on ORACLE memory structures).

The next major step in parsing is determining the access path to the data. This process, called *optimization*, includes determining available indexes and selecting the index or indexes to use. An understanding of the process used by the optimizer program will be a critical asset later in the tuning phase. We will explain the optimization process in greater detail throughout this chapter.

The end result of parsing and optimizing your SQL statement is something referred to as *meta code*. You can think of meta code as the compiled (or executable) version of your SQL statement. Specifically, meta code is the original SQL statement, combined with all the parsing and optimizing information, written in a fashion readable by ORACLE.

Column Prefixes

If the request is "SELECT * FROM TABLE" then ORACLE must read the data dictionary to determine the number of columns and the column names before determining the attributes of the columns. Similarly, if you execute a join as

```
SELECT  FACL_DESC, EMPL_NAME_LAST
FROM    SGENEMPL, MINVFACL
WHERE   EMPL_FACL_NUM = FACL_NUM
```

then ORACLE must determine the owning table (SGENEMPL or MINVFACL) for each column involved (FACL_DESC, EMPL_NAME_LAST, EMPL_FACL_NUM, and FACL_NUM). The coding standards we developed in Chapter 5 specify that the table name prefix all column names to avoid this extra work. A table alias can be used if the table names are very long. Once again, there is a trade-off between flexibility (if a column is added to the table) and the amount of work ORACLE does for you to resolve the SQL request. ORACLE's work is reflected in response time; yours is reflected in development and maintenance time.

Meta code gives ORACLE all of the information it needs to resolve the SQL request. And ORACLE can reuse the meta code for subsequent executions of the same SQL statement. Thus, each SQL statement is compiled at execution time, but only the first time it is issued. You can observe this easily in SQL*Forms. If you enter a block and press [EXECUTE QUERY], the SQL query will be parsed and executed. If you press [EXECUTE QUERY] a second time, the SQL query will be executed by reusing the meta code produced from the first query. The response time difference is usually noticeable.

In the next step, the meta code is placed into the ORACLE cursor, echoed back into the user cursor, and then executed. Execution begins with ORACLE determining the *active set* for the request. The active set is the entire list of rows that meet the criteria of the SQL statement.

ORACLE puts pointers to the first row of the active set into the user cursor and returns control to the user. If you choose to scroll through additional rows, each row pointer is passed from the ORACLE cursor and added to the user cursor. Figure 8.3 shows a conceptual depiction of each of the cursors as they would be seen at this point in the process.

Limiting the Active Set

Although you might not view all of the possible rows, ORACLE always determines all that qualify. The larger the active set, the slower the response from ORACLE. For example, if you are testing for existence of data (you are only interested in one row) you might issue a "SELECT 'X' FROM TABLE WHERE ROWNUM = 1". Although you will eventually see one row with this SQL statement, ORACLE must determine the set of rows that *could* be returned. In this case, the active set would include every row in the table!

Using Array Processing

By default ORACLE will move only one row pointer at a time between the ORACLE and user cursors. A feature called *array processing*, which is available in most of the Oracle programs, allows multiple rows to be placed in the ORACLE cursor and multiple row pointers to be passed between cursors. SQL*ReportWriter and SQL*Plus let you specify the size of arrays used to satisfy SQL requests; SQL*Forms has a fixed array size of 100 rows. The standard array size suggested by Oracle for use with all of the tools is 100 rows. However, we have found the optimal size depends on the row size for the data being returned and usually lies between 100 and 300.

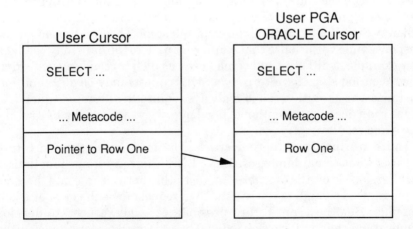

Figure 8.3 Passing row pointers between cursors

If the ORACLE cursor ever runs out of space, more memory will be needed to return all of the data. ORACLE will add memory to the existing ORACLE cursor in increments whose sizes are specified by the ORACLE startup parameter CONTEXT_INCR. (The default for this parameter is usually 4096 bytes.) This process will continue until either all of the rows have been queried or you decide to execute another SQL statement.

The next SQL statement might be a DML statement (insert, update, or delete), a new SQL statement, or the same SQL statement executed again. In each case the scenario is similar to that sketched above but not identical, since certain steps may be skipped. Try to imagine the process in each case, using the knowledge you have gained from this discussion.

8.3 Tuning SQL

The process we just outlined is based upon the execution of a single SQL statement, and every SQL statement is processed in the same manner. The essence of tuning SQL is to control this process by writing your SQL statements carefully.

Choosing how to write a SQL query can drive you crazy sometimes. In all but the simplest cases, you can get the same answer by asking the question in several different ways. Each way is correct and each query returns the same result, but one may perform faster than the others.

There are two reasons for the response time difference, and both can be blamed on the optimizer. Oracle's optimizer (like the SQL optimizers provided by most other vendors) is not sophisticated enough to notice when two queries are asking the same question. The first reason for the response time variation is that a different path to the data may be taken (for example, a different index may be used). The second reason is that the execution steps for alternative SQL requests may be different. For instance, the execution of a join always requires a different sequence of steps than does the execution of a subquery, even when the two return the same result.

You can expect that optimizers will be more intelligent in future releases of relational databases. (Indeed, Oracle is reworking the optimizer for Version 7 of the kernel.) In fact, the optimizer could become sophisticated enough to rewrite the SQL request to be the most efficient possible. But these are future possibilities, and we need to develop applications that perform well today. Thus, we must understand how the execution and optimization processes work in order to write efficient SQL statements.

8.3.1 Understanding query execution

There are really two interesting aspects of the execution of a SQL query: the process or steps taken to retrieve the data, and the determination of which indexes (if any) will be used to get the data. Understanding both parts will give you the ammunition needed to eliminate poorly performing SQL statements. This and the next section address these aspects in turn.

Execution of a simple, one table query will follow the parse and execute steps covered in the previous section. But there is a portion of that process that we intentionally glossed over: how the data is actually read and returned. This process can be very complex, so we will start at a high level and focus on the overall SQL execution flow. We will use the SQL statement in Figure 8.4 as the basis for the examples throughout this section.

This is a simple request for all the rows in the facility table (MINVFACL). ORACLE will resolve this request by first parsing the statement, then executing it and returning the first row of data. But where is the data for the row coming from?

Every row returned is read from a collection of memory buffers called the ORACLE *system global area* (the SGA). The SGA consists of buffers called *ORACLE blocks* that contain table data, indexes, and other memory structures. Each SGA buffer is 1024, 2048, or 4096 bytes (depending on the operating system).

The number of buffers is controlled by the ORACLE startup parameter DB_BLOCK_BUFFERS (simply BUFFERS in Version 5). The more buffers you specify, the more memory that will be allocated to the SGA and the more table data and indexes that will fit in memory at once.

```
SELECT  MINVFACL.FACL_NUM, MINVFACL.FACL_DESC
FROM    MINVFACL
```

Figure 8.4 SQL request for all rows in facility table

Adjusting DB_BLOCK_SIZE

One of the ORACLE startup parameters, DB_BLOCK_SIZE, allows you to change the ORACLE block size within your instance. If you are working on an IBM mainframe you might want to experiment with this parameter (since most IBM mainframes support large blocksize reads and writes).

Adjusting DB_BLOCK_BUFFERS

Adjusting the number of buffers specified can be a powerful tuning technique. Theoretically, if you had enough memory available, you could increase this parameter until the entire database would fit in memory. However, it is not quite that simple. With many operating systems, if one program (the ORACLE kernel, in this case) requires large amounts of memory, a memory request from another concurrent program might cause the first program to swap or page out. If this happens, ORACLE cannot do any work. Determine the available memory on your operating system so you can choose the number of buffers carefully.

How does the data for the facility table get into the SGA in the first place? When ORACLE is installed, at least one database file is created on a physical device (a disk drive). Additional database files can be created either at installation or at a later time. The number of database files and the size and location of each file are controlled by the ORACLE database administrator. Each database file contains physical database tables, indexes, and other database objects. One database file is distinctive because it contains the data dictionary—a collection of all the tables and indexes used by ORACLE.

The tables and indexes are created using the SQL statements CREATE TABLE and CREATE INDEX (discussed in section 3.3). Each table consists of one *data segment* and, optionally, one or more *index segments*. At the physical level, a data segment consists of one or more *data extents* and an index segment consists of one or more *index extents*. Each extent represents a set of contiguous ORACLE blocks within a file on a physical device. The various logical and physical components are shown in Figure 8.5

When a data request is made, ORACLE will search in memory (in the SGA) for the requested ORACLE block. If the data block is found in the SGA then it is returned to the user. (Remember that the data is returned

Using Tablespaces

The placement of the database files can have a significant effect on performance (especially on operating systems with relatively slow disk drives or systems that cause lots of disk I/O, like word processing applications). ORACLE provides a mechanism, called a *tablespace*, to map a logical grouping of tables to a physical file or files. Tablespaces can be used to separate objects and reduce contention for a disk drive or the connection to a set of disk drives. This will increase throughput and improve response time. For instance, you might want to separate the data segments of tables that will be frequently joined together, or you may want to separate a table's data segment from its index segment. To determine data and index segment placement (via tablespaces), you should analyze the SQL requests made by your applications. The only drawback of doing this is that the tablespace is also the unit of backup for your system. Thus, distribution of an application among tablespaces will make the backup and recovery process more complicated.

Note that in V5, the partition is analogous to the tablespace. The same strategy can be used for table separation, but a table's data segment cannot be separated from its index segment. Also, partition-level backup/recovery are not components of Version 5.

to the user via cursors, as discussed earlier.) If the data block is not in the SGA, then it must be read from the appropriate physical database file, placed into the SGA, and then returned to the user. This process continues for each data block needed to satisfy the SQL request. For example, if we assume that the facility table spans 20 data blocks, then 20 data blocks must be read into and out of the SGA. Although ORACLE might actually read several blocks into the SGA at one time, the process is always sequential conceptually.

What happens if the SGA is already full of data blocks and there is no empty space to put the next one read from disk? If the SGA is full, another block (more likely, several blocks) will be removed. If the removed blocks were modified they will also be written back to disk. ORACLE uses a "least recently used" (LRU) algorithm to determine which blocks will be removed. Each time a block is "touched" (read or changed by a user) the block is considered most recently used and is moved to the front of the queue. This technique ensures that frequently accessed blocks remain in the SGA.

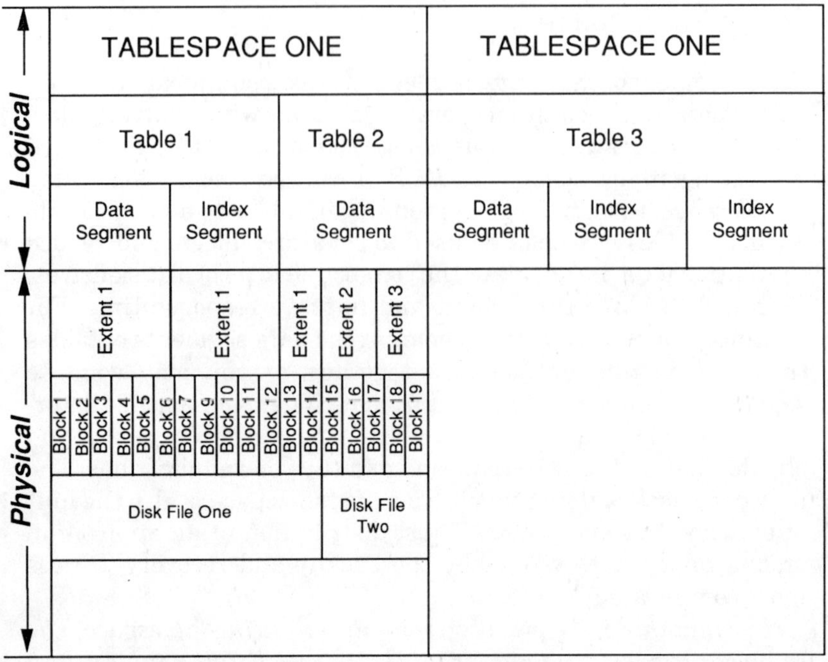

Figure 8.5 Logical and physical database components

ORACLE must know which block, or blocks, are needed by the user, so it considers the SQL request. In our example (Figure 8.4), ORACLE must read every data block in the facility table because we did not specify any criteria (there is no WHERE clause). The physical location of the first data block in the facility table is stored in the ORACLE data dictionary. This block, referred to as the *table data header block*, contains pointers to the data blocks that comprise the table. ORACLE can use this information to request every data block in the facility table. This process—reading the entire table into memory and processing it—is referred to as a *full table scan*. This is usually something we want to avoid, although in some situations we intentionally cause full table scans. We will analyze both of these cases in the next section.

Let's make our request slightly more complex, as shown in Figure 8.6, by asking for all facilities that do not have any inventory (i.e., those which have no entries in the inventory item table).

In our discussion of SQL in Section 3.2, we noted that a subquery is simply another list. ORACLE resolves the subquery and substitutes the

```
SELECT  MINVFACL.FACL_NUM, MINVFACL.FACL_DESC
FROM    MINVFACL
WHERE   MINVFACL.FACL_NUM NOT IN
   (SELECT MINVITEM.ITEM_FACL_NUM
    FROM    MINVITEM)
```

Figure 8.6 *Query 1*. SQL request for facilities with no inventory

values SELECTed into the parenthesis for the IN operator. Conceptually, this is a straightforward process, but the implementation is a little more complicated. To resolve this query, ORACLE must first literally execute the subquery. One part of the optimization process is to determine the *execution path*, or the series of steps that must be taken to reach the raw data. Note that the execution path does not consider whether all of the data is already in memory, whether the same request occurred two seconds ago, or whether indexes are available. Instead, it is a logical sequence of operations that will provide the desired result. The execution path for our example could be paraphrased as in Figure 8.7.

The main dilemma in this process is where to put the results of the first step. ORACLE needs to hold onto the values retrieved in step 1 in order to complete step 2. If the amount of data to be held is relatively small, ORACLE can place it in a work area in memory. The size of this work area is controlled by the ORACLE startup parameter SORT_AREA_SIZE.

If there is more data than the work area can hold, the results from the subquery are placed in an object called a *temporary data segment* (usually referred to as simply a temporary segment). ORACLE uses temporary segments to hold intermediate results, as in the subquery from Figure 8.6, and to sort data. The SQL operators that can cause ORACLE to use temporary segments include (but are not limited to) ORDER BY, GROUP BY, DISTINCT, IN, UNION, INTERSECT, and MINUS.

Temporary segments are allocated in the same way all other data segments are allocated: ORACLE will issue a CREATE TABLE statement on your behalf and generate INSERTs to put the data into this table. Yes,

1. SELECT the facility numbers from the ITEM table.
2. SELECT the appropriate facility numbers and descriptions from the FACL table.

Figure 8.7 Execution path for query

actual SQL INSERT statements! As we mentioned earlier, ORACLE is merely a set of C programs. These programs do not care where the SQL statements they execute come from. If a temporary segment is needed, the SQL statement CREATE TABLE must be used to create the temporary segment. And if rows are placed in the temporary segment, the SQL statement INSERT must be used. This is the simplest and most consistent approach.

When ORACLE issues the CREATE TABLE statement it must specify the storage parameters (such as the number of initial bytes for the data segment) and intended location of the temporary segment. The placement of a temporary segment is based on the USERID executing the SQL statement. Each USERID has a predefined pointer to a temporary segment tablespace (the default is the SYSTEM tablespace). You can change this default with the TEMPORARY TABLESPACE clause of the ALTER USER statement. The corresponding storage parameters used for creating temporary segments will be the default storage parameters for the tablespace that is used. These parameters can be changed with the ALTER TABLESPACE statement.

V5 TEMPTABLES

The storage and location of tables in Version 5 are controlled by space definitions. ORACLE uses a space definition called TEMPTABLES when creating any temporary table. You can ALTER this space definition to change the partition for temporary tables, the storage parameters, or both. Note that since temporary tables have no indexes, the parameters for the index initial size and increment size should be set to the minimum (3 ORACLE blocks) to avoid wasting storage.

You have no control over *whether* a temporary segment is used in a given situation. Likewise, its use does not automatically harm performance. However, you should understand what types of queries (in addition to the specific SQL operators) cause temporary segments to be built. This will allow you to make intelligent choices about the use of temporary segments as you write your queries.

Rewriting a query can significantly alter its execution path and overall response time. For example, can you think of a different way to phrase the NOT IN request from Figure 8.6 that we have been discussing? We came up with six other SQL statements (we'll number the first Version 1 and these new ones 2 through 7 for future reference) that will return

Temporary Segment Tablespace

You may want to separate your temporary segments from the other tables in the system by creating a tablespace just for temporary segments. You can control the storage for each temporary segment by altering the default storage for the temporary segment tablespace. Keep in mind when choosing those parameters that all temporary segments will use the same parameters. If you make the initial size very large, you will waste a great deal of space when smaller sorts are performed. Also remember that the tablespace storage parameters can be easily adjusted with the ALTER TABLESPACE statement. You can adjust these parameters to accommodate the creation of large indexes or the loading of large amounts of data.

the same result, and there are probably more that we didn't think of. ORACLE will follow a different execution path to the data for each of these queries. For the purpose of discussion, we will assume that the amount of data for all intermediate results requires temporary segments. Let's think about the steps ORACLE must take to resolve the various versions of the query, starting with Query 2 in Figure 8.8.

This request uses the MINUS operator to select all the facilities in the facility table and subtract, or eliminate, those in the inventory item table. To resolve this query ORACLE will execute the first subquery select and build a list containing the results, which will be held in a temporary segment. ORACLE will then execute the second subquery select and build a second list containing the results. The second list will be put into a second temporary segment. ORACLE can then use an

```
SELECT  MINVFACL.FACL_NUM, MINVFACL.FACL_DESC
FROM    MINVFACL
WHERE   MINVFACL.FACL_NUM IN
  (SELECT MINVFACL.FACL_NUM
   FROM    MINVFACL
   MINUS
   SELECT MINVITEM.ITEM_FACL_NUM
   FROM    MINVITEM)
```

Figure 8.8 *Query 2.* SQL phrasing alternative 2

algorithm for the MINUS operation to find the correct data using the two lists. Finally, ORACLE can select the data from the facility table based on the facility numbers returned from the subquery.

We could make the same request with Query 3, which uses an outer join, as shown in Figure 8.9.

This SQL statement joins the facility table with the inventory item table using the facility number key. The outer join specifies that if there is not a match in the item table for the facility number in the facility table, join the facility table to nothing (the plus sign means "add these in anyway"). The offbeat aspect of this query is that we are looking for only those rows in the facility table that do not have a matching row in the inventory item table—in other words, only those that were joined to nothing during the outer join. We specify that set of rows by specifying WHERE MINVITEM.ITEM_FACL_NUM IS NULL since in those cases ORACLE joined the facility table to nothing (in this case NULL).

In order to understand the process at a conceptual level, we will assume, for the moment, that none of these tables have any indexes. (We will consider the effect of indexes in the next section.) To resolve this join ORACLE will create a list of the selected columns and the join column for each table. In this case, ORACLE will build first a temporary segment containing FACL_NUM and FACL_DESC from the facility table, then a second temporary segment containing ITEM_FACL_NUM for the inventory item table. Finally ORACLE will use a routine called SORT/ MERGE (the details of which are not important for our discussion) to compare the lists in the temporary segments and find the result.

Query 4, shown in Figure 8.10, is very similar to Query 3. This example uses the join (again) and the NOT IN operator to determine the valid facility numbers.

To resolve this query ORACLE will scan the MINVITEM table to build a list containing all ITEM_FACL_NUMs. ORACLE will then process the join as discussed above and compare the subquery list of ITEM_FACL_NUMs against the joined tables to SELECT the FACL_NUM and FACL_DESC.

```
SELECT  MINVFACL.FACL_NUM, MINVFACL.FACL_DESC
FROM    MINVFACL, MINVITEM
WHERE   MINVFACL.FACL_NUM = MINVITEM.ITEM_FACL_NUM (+)
AND     MINVITEM.ITEM_FACL_NUM IS NULL
```

Figure 8.9 *Query 3.* SQL phrasing alternative 3

```
SELECT  MINVFACL.FACL_NUM, MINVFACL.FACL_DESC
FROM    MINVFACL, MINVITEM
WHERE   MINVFACL.FACL_NUM = MINVITEM.ITEM_FACL_NUM (+)
  AND   MINVFACL.FACL_NUM NOT IN
    (SELECT MINVITEM.ITEM_FACL_NUM
     FROM   MINVITEM)
```

Figure 8.10 *Query 4.* SQL phrasing alternative 4

The next three alternatives, Queries 5 through 7, use *correlated subqueries* to pass data from the main query to the subquery. The first, shown in Figure 8.11, checks for the existence of each facility number in the inventory item table and chooses only those that do not exist.

We can quickly identify this query as correlated because one of the columns specified in the subquery (MINVFACL.FACL_NUM) is a column from the main query. In other words, the table MINVITEM does not contain a column called MINVFACL.FACL_NUM. Often, the table in the main query is given an alias, such as X, which is then used in the subquery reference, as in Figure 8.12.

To resolve this query ORACLE must read the first row in the facility table to obtain MINVFACL.FACL_NUM. Then the subquery can be executed for that facility number. ORACLE will read every row in the facility table (a full table scan) to determine the result of the subquery.

In this case the correlated subquery will always return a result of either existence or nonexistence. ORACLE executes the subquery and places this binary answer in a buffer, since a temporary segment is not necessary to hold such a small result. However, this is not true of all correlated subqueries. For instance, consider Figure 8.13.

The correlated subquery here will be executed in much the same fashion as the prior example. ORACLE must read the first row in the facility table and pass the MINVFACL.FACL_NUM to the subquery.

```
SELECT  MINVFACL.FACL_NUM, MINVFACL.FACL_DESC
FROM    MINVFACL
WHERE   NOT EXISTS (SELECT MINVITEM.ITEM_FACL_DESC
                    FROM    MINVITEM
                    WHERE   MINVITEM.ITEM_FACL_NUM =
                            MINVFACL.FACL_NUM)
```
Figure 8.11 *Query 5.* SQL phrasing alternative 5

```
SELECT  X.FACL_NUM, X.FACL_DESC
FROM    MINVFACL X
WHERE   NOT EXISTS (SELECT MINVITEM.ITEM_FACL_DESC
                    FROM    MINVITEM
                    WHERE   MINVITEM.ITEM_FACL_NUM =
                            X.FACL_NUM)
```
Figure 8.12 Correlated subquery alias

```
SELECT  MINVFACL.FACL_NUM, MINVFACL.FACL_DESC
FROM    MINVFACL
WHERE   MINVFACL.FACL_NUM NOT IN
  (SELECT MINVITEM.ITEM_FACL_NUM
   FROM    MINVITEM
   WHERE  MINVITEM.ITEM_FACL_NUM = MINVFACL.FACL_NUM)
```
Figure 8.13 *Query 6.* SQL phrasing alternative 6

The subquery is then executed to select all of the inventory items that have the given facility number. ORACLE does not know in advance how many rows will be returned (in contrast to the EXISTS operation), so a temporary segment must be allocated to hold the results. This table will be used as the NOT IN list for the main query. ORACLE will delete all the rows from the temporary segment and insert a new set for every execution of the subquery. (Remember that for discussion we have assumed that the amount of data for all intermediate results requires temporary segments.)

Our last query, shown in Figure 8.14, is very similar to the other two correlated subqueries, but in this case we are selecting the count of the

```
SELECT  MINVFACL.FACL_NUM, MINVFACL.FACL_DESC
FROM    MINVFACL
WHERE   0 = (SELECT NVL(COUNT(*), 0)
            FROM    MINVITEM
            WHERE   MINVITEM.ITEM_FACL_NUM =
                    MINVFACL.FACL_NUM)
```
Figure 8.14 *Query 7.* SQL phrasing alternative 7

number of items in the item table for the given facility. If we do not find any items (0 = COUNT(*) for this facility) we select the facility.

The execution path for this query is the same as that for the other two correlated queries. Do you think that ORACLE will need a temporary segment for this query? If you said no, you were correct because ORACLE can use a buffer instead of a temporary segment to hold a finite value, such as the count of the number of rows in the inventory item table.

Writing efficient SQL is difficult because there are many different approaches that will obtain the same result. Our only general suggestion is to keep it simple. You can see from these examples that the execution path taken to the data is critical to the efficient processing of a query. We will look next at the other key performance variable in the execution process, the use of indexes.

8.3.2 Understanding the optimization process

When we create tables we have the option to create indexes on those tables. We must always create one unique index to enforce the primary key, but we can create additional indexes. These indexes are usually referred to as *access* or *performance* indexes since they are used to reduce the time required to access data (rather than to enforce data integrity, the reason for requiring a primary key).

Indexes are critical to the performance of an application. Database administrators are usually responsible for creating the appropriate indexes, but application developers are responsible for understanding indexes and ensuring that the indexes are utilized effectively by ORACLE. The communication between these project members about index requirements and usage will have significant impact on the success (or failure) of the entire system.

8.3.2.1 Single table optimization. Once a table has one or more indexes, how does ORACLE know to use them? As we mentioned, part of the ORACLE parsing process includes optimizing the query, or determining which indexes to use in the execution of the SQL statement. ORACLE will attempt to determine the optimal index usage for the given SQL statement.

The optimization process is actually quite straightforward: ORACLE analyzes the SQL statement to determine the available index(es), and then uses a ranking scheme to decide which one(s) to actually use. As an example, consider the slightly modified version of our original SQL example, shown Figure 8.15.

ORACLE will check whether a WHERE clause has been specified. If there is no WHERE clause—in other words, no search criteria—there is no optimization, and a full table scan must be performed. In our case there is a WHERE clause, so ORACLE will begin optimization by evaluating the WHERE clause predicates. The predicates are the criteria specifications that are grouped together with the AND and OR operators. In this example there is only one predicate: MINVFACL.FACL_DESC = UPPER('Bay Area Warehouse').

ORACLE will then execute a query against a data dictionary table that holds one row for every index in the system. It will issue a SELECT statement like the one in Figure 8.16. Note that the query that ORACLE issues against the index data dictionary table is always a full table scan. ORACLE has no mechanism for using an index to retrieve a row in the index table. (That would be using an index on an index!)

ORACLE may find no index on the column specified in the WHERE clause, and so perform a full table scan on the facility table. Or ORACLE may find that FACL_DESC has an index. If so, ORACLE can read the index to find UPPER('Bay Area Warehouse'). An ORACLE index is a B*-tree index which can be represented as a tree or a hierarchy as shown in Figure 8.17.

The index entry at the lowest level (described as a leaf node in Figure 8.17) within the index block contains the data value, FACL_DESC in this case, and an address to the data related to that key. This address is called (you guessed it) the *ROWID*. Every row in every table in every application

```
SELECT  MINVFACL.FACL_NUM, MINVFACL.FACL_DESC
FROM    MINVFACL
WHERE   MINVFACL.FACL_DESC = UPPER('Bay Area Warehouse')
```

Figure 8.15 A simple WHERE clause to optimize

```
SELECT  INDEX_NAME, INDEX_TYPE
FROM    INDEX_DATA_DICTIONARY_TABLE
WHERE   TABLE_NAME = 'MINVFACL'
AND     COLUMN_NAME = 'FACL_DESC'
ORDER BY INDEX_NAME
```

Figure 8.16 An internal data dictionary query

Index Balancing

ORACLE indexes are B*-tree indexes, which are by definition always balanced. This means that the number of steps to access any particular piece of data will be the same. There are obvious benefits of this approach, but it requires that the index be rebalanced whenever there are many inserts into the table. This is most necessary when all of the inserts occur at one "end" of the index. The rebalancing process can waste space and reduce the value of having the index. You should consider rebuilding indexes on critical tables on a regular basis (perhaps as part of an overall database reorganization procedure) to improve performance.

in each ORACLE instance is given a unique identifier called the ROWID. The ROWID is used to determine the data block to be read for the raw data. ORACLE "walks" through the index to find each ROWID that meets the WHERE predicate criteria.

But where does ORACLE perform this reading of the index? The process is similar to that for reading the data for the table. The address for the first index block (the index header block) is kept in the data dictionary table for indexes. ORACLE reads this block to find the addresses for the rest of the index blocks in the index. Each requested index block might be in memory; if not, it must be read from the database files into the SGA.

At this point ORACLE knows that the requested row exists and knows the FACL_DESC. To complete the execution of the query, ORACLE

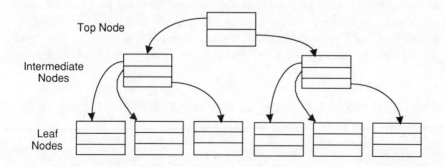

Figure 8.17 ORACLE B*-tree index

analyzes the columns in the SELECT list. The user requested the
FACL_DESC, which is known at this point, and the FACL_NUM, which
is not. Therefore, ORACLE uses the ROWID to access the specific data
block in the table and return the FACL_NUM.

This example considered a table with one index. However, a single
table can have multiple indexes, and ORACLE might use more than one
of them to retrieve data. For example, we might modify our query as
shown in Figure 8.18.

For this example, let's assume there are two indexes on the facility
table: a NON-UNIQUE index on FACL_NUM index and a NON-UNIQUE
index on FACL_DESC index. Considering the logical structure of an
index we know the FACL_NUM index will have a leaf entry of 1000 and
ROWID and the FACL_DESC index will have a leaf entry of "Bay Area
Warehouse" and ROWID. Remember that ROWID is a unique identifier
for the row. Therefore the ROWID specified in both indexes identifies the
same row and has the same value. Since the ROWIDs are the same,
ORACLE will resolve this request by finding the matching ROWID
entries for the given data values. This process is called an *index merge*.

Now suppose the FACL_NUM index is UNIQUE and the FACL_DESC
index is NON-UNIQUE. (In the prior example both indexes were NON-
UNIQUE.) ORACLE optimizes queries with a ranking scheme, whose
intent is to determine which index or indexes are most efficient. Figure
8.19 show the ranking list ORACLE uses for optimization. Note that
these rankings provide no guarantees for the optimization of queries, nor
will they be stagnant in future releases of the kernel. You should rely on
them only as a basis for writing efficient SQL.

Each WHERE clause predicate is evaluated for available indexes,
which are then ranked according to this scheme. The highest ranked
index is the one that will be used; if there is a "tie," then all the indexes
in the tie will be used after an index merge is performed. (We encountered
such a case earlier when we had two NON-UNIQUE indexes on
MINVFACL.) Using multiple indexes to resolve a request improves
performance, to a point. The diminishing returns are caused by the

```
SELECT  MINVFACL.FACL_NUM, MINVFACL.FACL_DESC
FROM    MINVFACL
WHERE   MINVFACL.FACL_DESC = 'Bay Area Warehouse'
  AND   MINVFACL.FACL_NUM = 1000
```

Figure 8.18 A two-predicate WHERE clause to optimize

overhead involved in the index merge process. The break-even point is reached somewhere between three and five indexes.

The ranking scheme makes assumptions about the attributes of a particular type of index or a particular WHERE clause SQL operator. For example, indexes can be either UNIQUE or NON-UNIQUE. As we know, defining an index as UNIQUE will ensure that all the data entries are unique. Since there is no duplication in the index ORACLE will either find the value or not, but will never find multiple entries in the index for the same value. In other words, once the requested value is found, ORACLE can stop reading the index. Thus, since they are likely to require fewer accesses, ORACLE considers UNIQUE indexes to be more efficient than NON-UNIQUE indexes. Consequently, in our example, ORACLE will use the UNIQUE index on FACL_NUM to access the facility table data.

The facility table could also have a UNIQUE index that contained two columns, FACL_NUM and FACL_DESC. This type of index is referred to as a *concatenated index*. The advantage of a concatenated index is that

Rank	Path
1	ROWID = Constant
2	Unique Indexed Column = Constant
3	Entire Unique Concatenated Index = Constant
4	Entire Non-unique Concatenated Index = Constant
5	Non-unique Indexed Column = Constant
6	Entire Concatenated Index >= Constant
7	Leftmost Concatenated Index Column = Constant
8	Unique Indexed Column BETWEEN Constant AND Constant *or* LIKE 'Constant%'
9	Non-unique Indexed Column BETWEEN Constant AND Constant *or* LIKE 'Constant%'
10	Unique Indexed Column > Constant *or* < Constant
11	Non-unique Indexed Column > Constant *or* < Constant
12	SORT/MERGE (Joins Only)
13	MAX(Indexed Column) or MIN(Indexed Column)
14	ORDER BY Entire Index
15	Full Table Scan

Figure 8.19 ORACLE optimizer ranking list

its values are pre-merged. (Remember the merge that ORACLE performed for the NON-UNIQUE index on FACL_NUM and the separate NON-UNIQUE index on FACL_DESC.) The index entries for this concatenated index would contain the FACL_NUM, the FACL_DESC, and the ROWID.

For the query in Figure 8.18, ORACLE would search the concatenated index for the requested FACL_NUM and FACL_DESC. If the index entry were found it would be returned to the user. Note that ORACLE does not need to read the facility table data to resolve this request—it was handled entirely through the index. Resolving a query in the index is usually efficient for two reasons. First, the index is always sorted whereas the data is much more randomly distributed. Second, the storage used for an index is much smaller (in most cases) than the storage for the entire table. Thus, fewer ORACLE blocks must be processed to return the data.

Indexes That Are Tables

There are a few cases in which it may be worthwhile to have the index replicate the entire table. For instance, some developers prefer to store all of the list field values data in one table to avoid the need for separate SQL*Forms applications. The tradeoff is the large size of this table. This table might have columns of LFV_TABLE_NAME, LFV_VALUE, and LFV_DESC. We would probably create a UNIQUE index on LFV_TABLE_NAME and LFV_VALUE. Yet, how many times do we ask for the LFV_VALUE without asking for the LFV_DESC? Almost never. ORACLE will need to read the table data for the LFV_DESC each time we request a LFV look-up. By creating a UNIQUE index on all three columns, we would "pre-sort" the data and eliminate the need to ever read the table data! It is true that space is wasted by storing the LFV_DESC in both places, but the reduction in access time is more important.

To continue this investigation, imagine that we issued the query in Figure 8.20 with our UNIQUE concatenated index.

```
SELECT  MINVFACL.FACL_NUM, MINVFACL.FACL_DESC
FROM    MINVFACL
WHERE   MINVFACL.FACL_NUM = 1000
```

Figure 8.20 Optimizing with a concatenated index

Once again, ORACLE could find the requested data using only the concatenated index. In this case ORACLE is given only the FACL_NUM in the WHERE predicate, so it will use only that portion of the index. But, since the index is concatenated, the FACL_DESC will also be stored in the index entry for facility 1000. This means that ORACLE can return both of the SELECTed columns from the concatenated index, without ever reading the table data.

V5 COMPRESSED INDEXES

Version 5 indexes can be either COMPRESSED or NON-COM-PRESSED (contrary to popular belief, COMPRESSED is the default). The purpose of compression is to reduce index storage requirements. Each index entry in a COMPRESSED index is passed through algorithms for FORWARD COMPRESSION and REAR COMPRESSION, when the index entry is created and each time it is referenced by a query. Due to the complexity of the REAR COMPRESSION algorithm, ORACLE must always read the data for the given ROWID to verify the accuracy of the decompression. Thus, queries using COMPRESSED indexes can *never* be resolved purely in the index. (For example, the prior HINT would not work with a COMPRESSED index.) Furthermore, the ranking for a COMPRESSED index is always lower than that of a NON-COM-PRESSED index. Version 6 indexes are FORWARD COMPRESSED only.

Would ORACLE be able to resolve the query in the index if we changed our WHERE predicated to WHERE FACL_DESC = UPPER('Bay Area Warehouse')? No, because a concatenated index is built to prohibit access by the "right hand" (or lower) column. The "left-most" column of the index must be specified for the index to be useful. This restriction occurs because the index tree is built based on the left-most portion of the index. If the value for that column is not given, the index cannot be used. Note, however, that a concatenated index of FACL_DESC and FACL_NUM is logically equivalent to a concatenated index of FACL_NUM and FACL_DESC.

The order of the columns within the index is only important for queries that do not specify all of the concatenated columns (for the reasons given above). A general rule is to make the most specific column the left-most column. This rule should be broken only when there will be frequent requests for the column or columns on the right. However, be careful that you do not duplicate indexes by specifying the same columns in a different order, since this is not necessary. Attempt to devise an index that will optimize the majority of your SQL requests. You can see from these discussions that there are two important issues to consider when creating indexes: the WHERE clause predicate that will be used and the SELECTed columns.

8.3.2.2 Multiple table optimization. The optimization process is basically the same, though more complex, when more than one table is involved. Consider the join in Figure 8.21. This join requests data from two columns in the facility table and two columns in the item table. The join predicate, in this example the last WHERE clause predicate, tells ORACLE how to match the data in the facility table with that in the item table. The indexes that are available for the join predicate on each table will determine how the join is resolved. ORACLE determines whether the join is *non-indexed, partially-indexed* (either FACL_NUM or ITEM_FACL_NUM indexed), or *fully-indexed* (both FACL_NUM and ITEM_FACL_NUM indexed).

We will first consider the simple case where there are no indexes on either table. Without any indexes ORACLE is forced to determine the path to the data without any solid information. Thus, ORACLE must perform a full table scan of both tables. The columns SELECTed and the ROWID from the item table and the same data from the facility table are placed in memory (in the sort area or a temporary segment). Figure 8.22 shows a view of this data.

Once the data is in memory ORACLE must decide which table to use for the matching process. The chosen table is called the *driving table* because it leads or drives the scanning process. In this example ORACLE has two alternatives for the driving table: to use the data in the facility table to match with the item table, or the data in the item table to match with the facility table. This matching process is called *SORT/MERGE*

```
SELECT  MINVFACL.FACL_NUM, MINVFACL.FACL_DESC,
        MINVITEM.ITEM_NUM
FROM    MINVFACL, MINVITEM
WHERE   MINVFACL.FACL_DESC = 'Bay Area Warehouse'
AND     MINVFACL.ITEM_NUM = MINVITEM.ITEM_FACL_NUM
```

Figure 8.21 Optimizing a join between facilities and items

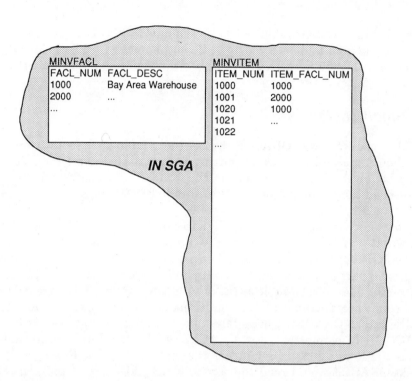

Figure 8.22 Sort areas in memory for a join

since both tables are sorted in memory and one is scanned to merge it with the other.

The choice of a driving table is very important. In many cases one table will be considerably larger than the other. If the larger table is used as the driving table then ORACLE must do more work to resolve the request, and more work always translates into longer response times. In the MegaMarket application, the facility table is relatively small and static. The user estimates a maximum of 800 facilities in the system and that items in the system will be very volatile and the volumes very large. We have received estimates well in excess of a million items per facility. In this case ORACLE's choice of a driving table will mean the difference between scanning millions of entries or 800 entries!

How does ORACLE determine the driving table? When ORACLE does not have enough information to choose the driving table (because there are no indexes or they are all equal) it will default to the *last* table specified in the FROM clause. In this example MINVITEM is specified last, so the item table is the driver. If we changed the FROM clause to "FROM MINVITEM, MINVFACL" then the facility table would be the driver.

Small Table Last

Because of the way ORACLE chooses the default driving table you should make a practice of putting the smallest table (smallest based on both the qualifiers in the WHERE predicate and the overall table size) as the last table in the FROM clause.

Now we will complicate matters by assuming there is a UNIQUE index on the FACL_NUM of the MINVFACL table. (The query remains the same.) ORACLE will evaluate the join predicate and now determine that the join is partially-indexed. A partially-indexed join will cause ORACLE to use the *non-indexed* table as the driving table. Using the non-indexed table may seem strange at first, but think for a moment about the path to the data. If ORACLE drove off the indexed table, it would read the first FACL_NUM using the index. ORACLE would then have to full table scan the item table, searching for the matching ITEM_FACL_NUM. Next ORACLE would read the second FACL_NUM, and again would have to full table scan the item table searching for a match. This process would cause the item table to be full table scanned 800 times, once for each FACL_NUM in the facility table index! If the item table were used as the driver instead, ORACLE would read the first ITEM_FACL_NUM and use the FACL_NUM index for the specified ITEM_FACL_NUM to determine if there is a match. Thus, driving off the non-indexed table is obviously a more efficient process.

Suppose we now created a NON-UNIQUE index on the ITEM_FACL_NUM of the MINVITEM table in addition to the existing UNIQUE index on the MINVFACL table. In this case the join is fully-indexed. This is almost desirable, since it avoids a full table scan of either table. You probably think that ORACLE will use the ranking scheme to determine the driving table. If this were so, the UNIQUE index would rank higher and MINVFACL would be the driver. Although this sounds perfectly logical, it is not accurate. ORACLE does not use the ranking scheme against the join predicate, because the type of index is really not important in the join process since all of the rows must be processed in any case. If there are 800 rows in the facility table, there are 800 unique index entries, each of which must be processed. The same reasoning applies to the item table.

ORACLE has no basis for determining the driving table for a fully-indexed join (as for the non-indexed join). Thus, ORACLE will again default to the *last* table in the FROM clause. To resolve our query ORACLE will scan the index for the MINVITEM table and evaluate each ITEM_FACL_NUM against the facility index.

These various cases lead us to offer the following join rules:

- ORACLE will use the last table in the FROM clause when the columns appear equal (for example, both sides of the join are non-indexed or both sides are indexed).
- ORACLE will drive from the non-indexed table when one side is indexed and the other side is not indexed.
- Both columns of the join predicate should be indexed unless one of the tables is very small.

Thus far we have been ignoring the other predicate in our sample SQL statement (Figure 8.21). In addition to the join predicate we specified the condition FACL_DESC = UPPER('Bay Area Warehouse'). Given any combination of the indexes we have discussed thus far, ORACLE will process every row in the facility table to check the facility description.

Suppose we created a NON-UNIQUE index on the FACL_DESC column. You can imagine that the quickest path to the data will start with the FACL_DESC index (rather than scanning every row in the facility table for a matching facility description). ORACLE will find the first matching entry in the FACL_DESC index and read the associated data (using ROWID) to find the FACL_NUM. ORACLE will then use the ITEM_FACL_NUM index for the appropriate item information. Since the FACL_DESC index is nonunique, ORACLE will repeat this process by continuing the index search for other matching facility descriptions.

Concatenated Indexes

We could have created a concatenated index on FACL_DESC and FACL_NUM. This technique would have allowed ORACLE to find the facilities based on the description. ORACLE could then determine the facility number directly from the index and avoid reading the data. Once again we have the desirable and efficient situation of ORACLE resolving a query in the index.

Now we'll modify our SQL request to include an additional WHERE clause predicate as shown in Figure 8.23. In addition, suppose we have created a UNIQUE index on ITEM_NUM in the inventory item table.

ORACLE will begin to analyze this request by determining that the join is fully-indexed. It will then consider the remaining predicates for the request. In this case ORACLE has two index choices, one on FACL_DESC and one on ITEM_NUM. This is where the ranking scheme becomes important. ORACLE will determine the rank of each of the available indexes on the facility table and then determine the rank of each of the available indexes on the item table. The table with the highest ranking index will be the driving table.

In the current example the item number index is UNIQUE, with a rank of two. The facility description index is NON-UNIQUE, with a rank of five. Thus, the item table will be the driving table. Suppose both indexes were NON-UNIQUE, or both were UNIQUE. In either case, the ranking would be equal and ORACLE would default to the last table in the FROM clause. Even if more WHERE clauses were added to the query, ORACLE would still systematically rank each index and select the one that ranks the highest on the "efficiency" scale.

8.3.3 SQL tuning techniques

Tuning SQL is half knowing the rules and half knowing the tricks. Some concepts are intuitive, but others must be learned. We often see those tips, culled from hard-earned experience, taped to the wall or the terminal screen. In this section we will take the scraps of paper off our walls and share them with you. Following are several "gotchas" and tips that should help shorten your SQL tuning learning curve.

Note that these recommendations are guidelines, not hard and fast rules that must be obeyed in all cases. Do not automatically assume that

```
SELECT  MINVFACL.FACL_NUM, MINVFACL.FACL_DESC,
        MINVITEM.ITEM_NUM
FROM    MINVFACL, MINVITEM
WHERE   MINVFACL.FACL_DESC = 'Bay Area Warehouse'
  AND   MINVITEM.ITEM_NUM = 1000
  AND   MINVFACL.ITEM_NUM = MINVITEM.ITEM_FACL_NUM
```

Figure 8.23 A three-predicate WHERE clause to optimize

a query with a "gotcha" needs to be changed, or that a tip should be applied to every possible situation.

8.3.3.1 Over-complicated SQL. The most common mistake in coding SQL is over-complication. Although the question might be complex, the request should still be readable. Look at your SQL statement. Can you readily determine what the question is? Can you put it into English? If not, ORACLE may have the same problem. We must try to simplify the request, *not* the question, as much as possible to reduce the chance of ORACLE misunderstanding or doing unnecessary work.

Compare Queries 1 and 6 (Figures 8.6 and 8.13) once again, noting their similarities. Both use the NOT IN operation to resolve the question asked. At first glance the queries almost look the same, but Query 6 is a correlated query and Query 1 is not. This is an important distinction and a prime example of inadvertent over-complication. Which do you think will perform better? Query 1 will create one temporary segment with one row for each ITEM_FACL_NUM and then resolve the main query. But since Query 6 is correlated, the subquery will be executed *once for every row* in the main query against the FACL table, resulting in poorer performance.

Another example involves Queries 1 and 4 (Figures 8.6 and 8.10). Do you see the over-complication? Query 4 is almost exactly the same as Query 1, except a join is used in the main query. Notice that we are SELECTing the FACL_DESC and the FACL_NUM from the FACL table, and we are determining the desired FACL_NUMs based on the NOT IN condition. Since we are not SELECTing any columns from the ITEM table and we are not using any columns for the WHERE clause, the join to the ITEM table is not needed! This is an easy trap to fall into, especially when experimenting with different versions of a SQL statement. We often include a table in a join, then change the technique and forget to eliminate the joined table. Always make sure that the tables joined are used in either the SELECT list or in an additional WHERE clause condition (beyond the join predicate).

8.3.3.2 Using SQL Functions. The FACL_NUM we have used throughout these examples is a system-assigned number (generated using a sequence called FACL_NUM_SEQ). What if our users wanted something more meaningful, like the state the facility is located in and the zip-code of the facility? They might claim this is easier to remember and more useful for locating the appropriate facility. This scheme would eliminate the FACL_ADDR_STATE column and change the FACL_NUM column to a character field of seven positions (we will ignore nine-digit zip-codes for simplicity) in the format ST99999 where ST is the two-character state abbreviation and 99999 is the zip-code.

A typical question might be to find out how many facilities are in a particular state. A query about Maryland could be phrased as in Figure 8.24. We have a unique index on the FACL_NUM column, so ORACLE will walk the index to find the FACL_NUMs starting with NY, right? Wrong! The index on FACL_NUM contains the entire key, not just the first two characters. The entire index tree is built on all seven positions, making it impossible for ORACLE to walk the index using only the first two positions. The only alternative for ORACLE is an expensive full table scan (those three dreaded words ...).

This example demonstrates that ORACLE will not use an indexed column that has been modified in any way. Look carefully at your SQL and the way data is stored in your database. We addressed some of these issues in the logical-to-physical design discussion in Section 2.5. As in this example, are you using intelligent keys? Are you storing a column as DATE when you always need the TIME as well?

We want to avoid situations like these at all costs. Sometimes we can use a SQL function on the variable (in this case 'MD') instead of the database column. For example, we can convert a variable into ORACLE date format rather than convert the ORACLE date column to the variable date format. This type of technique can be used in our current example by adding the LIKE operator, as shown in Figure 8.25.

Although this is a bit better than a full table scan, we have exchanged a UNIQUE index on the system-assigned number for a NON-UNIQUE

```
SELECT  COUNT(*)
FROM    MINVFACL
WHERE   SUBSTR(FACL_NUM,1,2) = 'MD'
```

Figure 8.24 SQL functions on an intelligent key

```
SELECT  COUNT(*)
FROM    MINVFACL
WHERE   FACL_NUM LIKE 'MD%'
```

Figure 8.25 The LIKE operator alternative

index on an intelligent key with a LIKE operation. The rankings of these requests is two and nine, so a better alternative would be to eliminate the intelligent key, or at the very least, to include a redundant indexed column on the state abbreviation.

8.3.3.3 Those pesky NULL operators. There are many columns in the database that allow null values; indeed, the only columns that are always required are primary keys. Beware, though, that the decision of making a column NOT NULL or NULL has many consequences. The first relates to the integrity of the data—will a row be valid without this column? This is important, but does not affect performance. The second consequence, however, directly impacts application performance.

When we define a column as NULL, we often use the operators IS NULL and IS NOT NULL in our SQL statements. These operators *never* use an index. This is primarily because ORACLE does not store NULL values in the index, so if we ask for those that are NULL, ORACLE cannot use the index for these values. Likewise, if we ask for those that are NOT NULL, ORACLE will know automatically that the NOT NULL entries are the whole index.

The ORACLE optimizer makes assumptions about the data when determining the optimal path. Consider the query in Figure 8.26.

This query counts all items remaining on the shelves of the store (those *not* in a transaction). ORACLE makes the broad assumption that a majority of the items will have a NULL transaction number. In a request for IS NULL, ORACLE assumes that you are selecting a majority of the data in the table. Likewise, if you request IS NOT NULL, ORACLE assumes that the majority of the item table has NOT NULL in the column. Thus, any index on ITEM_TRAN_NUM would be ignored. (Note that ORACLE would still use the facility number index for this request.)

The ORACLE optimizer is usually correct in its assumptions; the exceptions occur when we are searching for the minority items. For example, consider the case where there are one million rows in the item

```
SELECT  COUNT(MINVITEM.ITEM_NUM)
FROM    MINVITEM
WHERE   MINVITEM.ITEM_TRAN_NUM IS NULL
AND     MINVITEM.ITEM_FACL_NUM = 100
```

Figure 8.26 SQL request for NULLs

table and only ten have a NULL transaction number. Regardless of our SQL statement, we can never use an index to return the NULL rows. If the request for those minority rows is frequent and important you must find a way to avoid this situation. The only way is to make the column NOT NULL and place a standard "dummy" value into the column to represent a NULL value. Again we see the importance of the decisions made during logical-to-physical design.

8.3.3.4 Using the NOT operator. Another presumption made by the ORACLE optimizer is that a request for "NOT something" will also return a majority of the data. Since the index contains all of the values for the column, requests for NOT equal to a specific value includes every other entry in the index. Using an index to return every value but one is inefficient, so ORACLE will ignore the index. Consider Figure 8.27, a query that includes a NOT operator.

ORACLE will assume that there are many facility numbers in this table and that a majority of them will not equal 100. This will usually be true. However, there are occasions when only a few rows will qualify for this request. There is no way to force ORACLE to use the index with a NOT request; instead, in these cases we must try to rephrase the question. We could, for example, ask for all rows less than 100 and all rows greater than 100 as shown in Figure 8.28.

8.3.3.5 Watch out for OR. Up until the previous figure, all the queries we have reviewed so far have used AND operators in the WHERE clause.

```
SELECT  COUNT(MINVITEM.ITEM_NUM)
FROM    MINVITEM
WHERE   MINVITEM.ITEM_FACL_NUM NOT = 100
```

Figure 8.27 SQL request using NOT

```
SELECT  COUNT(MINVITEM.ITEM_NUM)
FROM    MINVITEM
WHERE   MINVITEM.ITEM_FACL_NUM > 100
OR      MINVITEM.ITEM_FACL_NUM < 100
```

Figure 8.28 The NOT query rephrased

What about the OR operator? The processing of the AND operator is simple to understand, but the OR operator is more difficult. The OR condition really causes two distinct sets to be returned together (logically it is very similar to the INTERSECT operator).

ORACLE cannot resolve a query containing an OR operator without doing some extra work. The query in Figure 8.29 represents a typical request made by MegaMarket management. Think about the processing for this query. It asks for the items with facility number 100 and the items with order number 1000, but not those that meet both criteria (those in facility 100 with an order number of 1000). This is the procedural way to think about the request; in fact, ORACLE must issue the request in a somewhat procedural way to get the proper results. ORACLE will actually transform the query into two requests similar to those in Figure 8.30 (note that the precise SQL statements that will be generated are difficult to predict).

There are two reasons the OR can cause a performance problem. First, ORACLE must take many steps to get to the data, as the amount of code in the pair of generated queries shows. Second, the unforeseen NOT operator might be turning off the index on the second request. The moral

```
SELECT  COUNT(MINVITEM.ITEM_NUM)
FROM    MINVITEM
WHERE   MINVITEM.ITEM_FACL_NUM = 100
  OR    MINVITEM.ITEM_ORDR_NUM = 1000
```

Figure 8.29 SQL request using an OR

First Request
```
SELECT  COUNT(MINVITEM.ITEM_NUM)
FROM    MINVITEM
WHERE   MINVITEM.ITEM_FACL_NUM = 100
```

Second Request
```
SELECT  COUNT(MINVITEM.ITEM_NUM)
FROM    MINVITEM
WHERE   MINVITEM.ITEM_ORDR_NUM = 1000
  AND   MINVITEM.ITEM_FACL_NUM <> 100
```

Figure 8.30 Optimizing an OR with two SQL statements

of the story is to beware of the OR operator, and to use it only when absolutely necessary.

These gotchas are not helpful to know without tips for getting around them. Many of these tips describe habits we encourage you to acquire. They may not always eliminate the particular performance problems, but they will reduce their chances of occurring.

8.3.3.6 When not to use indexes. Based on our analysis up to this point, you might conclude that we should force ORACLE to use an index for every request we make. This is *almost* true, but there are two specific cases in which you should not use indexes.

The first involves a very small table. Any table in the system that requires less than 20K of storage (5 ORACLE blocks on VM and MVS, 10 ORACLE blocks on most other systems) will usually not benefit from an index, since it is small enough to be handled easily in memory.

The second, less obvious case, can occur depending on the percentage of data being requested from a table. For example, reporting programs generally process large portions (sometimes more than 50 percent) of a table. There is a point in the index usage process after which walking the index is actually detrimental to performance. The point of diminishing returns is reached when the number of accesses to the index and the data is higher than that required for a full table scan. Oracle Corporation's "official" estimate of this point is around 20 percent, but we have found it to be closer to 40 percent. Thus, if your SQL request is likely to return more than 40 percent of the data in the table, don't use the index.

Remember that an index may still be needed for online applications and other requests. You might have to intentionally avoid using an existing index to optimize a SQL statement that returns a large percentage of the data. The easiest technique to "turn off" the index is to add zero to a number column (NUM_COLUMN + 0) or concatenate NULL to a character column (CHAR_COLUMN | | ").

8.3.3.7 Table ordering for joins. We mentioned this idea earlier in the discussion of join processing in Section 8.3.2.2., but the tip is worth repeating because of its enormous importance. The moral of the join story is that you should *always* make the smallest table (the one with the fewest rows to process, based on all predicates) the *last* table in the FROM clause, since there are many cases in which ORACLE will choose the last table for the driving table.

Consider our Query 3 (Figure 8.9) in this context. Is the table order correct? Of course it isn't—the inventory item table is huge (millions of rows), while the facility table is small and stable (less than 1000 rows). These tables should be switched to improve the performance of this query.

8.3.3.8 Using powerful functions like DECODE. There is one function in the SQL language supported by Oracle that is as powerful as it is underutilized: DECODE. Complex applications include many processes that are quite procedural. For example, we might need to report the total number of items sold each month. This type of request could be resolved in SQL by SELECTing the total sold for January, then SELECTing the total sold for February, and so on. That is, by issuing twelve SQL statements.

When we discussed reporting in Chapter 6, we used the DECODE function for this request. DECODE provides the functionality of a conditional test in the SELECT portion of the statement. Using DECODE we can SELECT all rows and place each row into the appropriate time slot based on the DECODE conditions. The DECODE function improves performance because it allows many SQL statements to be replaced by a single one, and we can almost guarantee better response times by reducing the number of SQL statements.

8.3.3.9 Embedded boilerplate. To embed boilerplate is to store display characters in a data field. A function must be applied to any column that is represented on the screen or in reports with boilerplate, such as a social security number or a phone number displayed with inserted hyphens. For example, to display a social security number we must SUBSTR the column into three pieces and concatenate a dash to each. As we mentioned earlier, applying a function to a column will prevent the use of the index on that column. The alternative we recommend is to store the boilerplate in the column with the data to allow the index to be utilized.

8.3.3.10 What to SELECT. Many SQL statements are simple existence, or binary, tests. The most common is a SELECT against SYS(TEM).DUAL (used mostly within SQL*Forms). This query is used to test for a true or false condition. When issuing these binary requests, we should consider our SELECT list carefully. For example, refer to Query 5 (Figure 8.11) once again. Note that the main query uses the EXISTS operator that always tests for a binary result, and notice that the subquery SELECTs the column ITEM_FACL_DESC.

Do we need the actual data in the ITEM_FACL_DESC column for this query? Are we presenting this data to the user? No—so we could easily change this request to SELECT 'X' (or SELECT NULL) from the MINVITEM table. This technique avoids the work ORACLE would do to return the actual data for the column, improving response time. This is especially useful if the column, ITEM_FACL_DESC in this case, is not part of the index. If the index on the table contained only ITEM_FACL_NUM, ORACLE would perform a full table scan to return data that is not used for anything!

8.3.3.11 What to COUNT. Many applications require a count of the number of rows of data that meet some criteria. Such a request usually requires some sort of scan, our choice is whether to scan the data or the index. Scanning the index is usually a better choice, but we can tell ORACLE what to do with our SQL statement. Consider the COUNT operation in Query 7 (Figure 8.14), which asks ORACLE to "COUNT(*)" on the MINVITEM table. This allows ORACLE to use the ITEM_FACL_NUM index to find the qualifying rows, but forces ORACLE to read the data. The alternative is to use "COUNT(MINVITEM.ITEM_FACL_NUM)," since this column is NOT NULL and *is* indexed. ORACLE can then scan the index for the count of the number of rows and avoid the data completely.

8.3.3.12 Using NEW_VALUE. Some SQL statements perform a subquery that calculates a "fixed" value, which may vary over time but remains constant during the execution of the query. An example is shown in Figure 8.31.

Here, the report date is a column in another table. ORACLE will resolve this subquery and use the value returned for the main query. Not much overhead is incurred in this case, but what if the subquery had to be executed many times, perhaps once per row in the main query? ORACLE would have to perform a great deal of extra work.

We can eliminate such subqueries for constant values within the SQL*Plus environment with the NEW_VALUE function. The subquery SELECT can be executed once and the results placed into a SQL*Plus

```
SELECT  SUM(MINVTRAN.TRAN_AMOUNT)
FROM    MINVTRAN
WHERE   MINVTRAN.TRAN_DATE =
  (SELECT SGENREPT.REPT_DATE
   FROM    SGENREPT
   WHERE  SGENREPT.REPT_NAME = 'EXAMPLE')
```

Figure 8.31 A subquery SELECTing a constant value

variable, which can then be used in the main query. Chapter 6 provides examples of the use of the NEW_VALUE function.

8.3.4 Using Oracle's SQL analysis tools

If all these details on the optimization and execution of SQL are confusing you, there is still hope! ORACLE provides two diagnostic tools, called EXPLAIN and TRACE, which provide specific performance information about your SQL statements to help you analyze and reformulate requests. Prior to Version 6, such SQL analysis tools either were not documented or did not exist, an omission from the ORACLE product that caused great frustration among application developers. Unable to verify that ORACLE was doing what they thought, developers were left guessing—and in many cases, left to wait until the application went into production to find out from users that a SQL statement was a poor performer. Thankfully, ORACLE no longer suffers from this omission. The following sections describe how to use and interpret information from the new performance tools.

(For some time, a proprietary TRACE tool for Version 5 was available to Oracle employees only. Although it is not always reliable, it does provide some helpful information. ORACLE decided to make the TRACE tool nonproprietary early in 1989, so we will cover it in Section 8.3.4.3.)

8.2.4.1 The EXPLAIN facility. Throughout this chapter we have discussed the execution paths followed by ORACLE to resolve SQL requests. The EXPLAIN facility simply shows the execution path (referred to as the PLAN) for a given SQL statement. With this tool you can verify your understanding of the execution path. Do not, however, rely completely on this tool, since many of the internal steps are excluded from the PLAN and some important information is not provided (for instance, determining the driving table in queries can be difficult). To tune effectively you still must understand the statement's execution path—without relying on any tools.

Using the EXPLAIN facility is very easy. You ask ORACLE to EXPLAIN a particular SQL statement. The explanation is placed into a database table, called the PLAN_TABLE, which is manually created as a table owned by the requester prior to this process. Figure 8.32 is a description of the PLAN_TABLE.

To review the results of the EXPLAIN, you query this table, just like any other database table. The information in this table uses a hierarchical relationship, similar to the one we used for the inventory classification table (SLFVICLS). You may want to take a moment to review the discussion of our data model in Section 2.3 before continuing.

In order to resolve your SQL request, ORACLE performs a series of actions, each of which depends on the completion of other actions. These dependency relationships are stored in the PLAN table. For our purposes we need to analyze the steps taken to resolve the SQL statement. We would like to review the steps in the order in which they would be

Column Name	Datatype
STATEMENT_ID	CHAR(30)
TIMESTAMP	DATE
REMARKS	CHAR(80)
OPERATION	CHAR(30)
OPTIONS	CHAR(30)
OBJECT_NODE	CHAR(30)
OBJECT_OWNER	CHAR(30)
OBJECT_NAME	CHAR(30)
OBJECT_INSTANCE	NUMBER(38)
OBJECT_TYPE	CHAR(30)
SEARCH_COLUMNS	NUMBER(38)
ID	NUMBER(38)
PARENT_ID	NUMBER(38)
POSITION	NUMBER(38)
OTHER	LONG

Figure 8.32 EXPLAIN PLAN table definition

```
REM
REM
REM  EXPLAIN  OUTPUT  SQL
REM
REM  Creator:  Nicole  and  Tim
REM  Created:  January  1990
REM
REM
COLUMN  OPERATION  FORMAT  A20
COLUMN  OPTIONS  FORMAT  A10
COLUMN  OBJECT_NAME  FORMAT  A15
COLUMN  OBJECT_TYPE  FORMAT  A15
REM
SELECT  NVL(OBJECT_NAME,  'SORT/TEMP  TABLE')  OBJECT_NAME,
   OBJECT_TYPE,  OPTIONS,  OPERATION
FROM  PLAN_TABLE
WHERE  PARENT_ID  IS  NOT  NULL
ORDER  BY  PARENT_ID  DESC,  POSITION;
```

Figure 8.33 SQL*Plus script for PLAN output

performed. The hierarchical definition of the PLAN_TABLE appears to complicate this simple presentation of the data. The SQL file in Figure 8.33 contains the query to present the execution steps in sequential order, as well some helpful formatting commands.

An example of the output from this SQL script is shown in Figure 8.34. The statement EXPLAINed is Query 1, the first of the SQL statements

```
SELECT  MINVFACL.FACL_NUM, MINVFACL.FACL_DESC
FROM     MINVFACL
WHERE  MINVFACL.FACL_NUM NOT IN
   (SELECT MINVITEM.ITEM_FACL_NUM
    FROM     MINVITEM)
```

OBJECT_NAME	OBJECT_TYPE	OPTIONS	OPERATION
MINVFACL		FULL	TABLE ACCESS
MINVITEM		FULL	TABLE ACCESS

Figure 8.34 EXPLAIN PLAN for Query 1

we have dissected in this chapter. (The SQL statement is repeated here for convenience.)

Query 1, as we noted earlier, contains a subquery that uses a temporary segment (or sort area) to hold intermediate results. Notice that the PLAN_TABLE does not show the steps taken for the subquery operations. Also note that both of the table accesses are full table scans. The SQL statement does not include a WHERE clause for MINVITEM, so this access must be performed using a full table scan. Do you know why the MINVFACL table is full table scanned? The NOT operator is the culprit here; as we discussed in Section 8.3.3.1, the NOT operator often disables the index.

The rest of our queries are more complex. Figure 8.35 lists the PLAN_TABLE data for Queries 2 through 7. You should review these queries and the EXPLAIN results to verify your understanding of the execution process.

8.3.4.2 The V6 TRACE facility. Figure 8.35 shows that a full table scan is performed on MINVFACL in almost all of our queries, and that a full table scan is performed on MINVITEM in some of our queries. But knowing that a full table scan is occurring is only half of the battle; you must still determine the cost of the full table scan. The TRACE facility provides the information you need to do this. TRACE provides very detailed timing information, breaking down the parsing process into the times used to parse the SQL statement, to execute the code, and to fetch the data. Each time information is further divided into CPU time and elapsed (real) time. (Note that these timings are only available if TIMED_STATISTICS is turned ON in the ORACLE startup parameters.)

TRACE can be turned on for all users and all SQL statements or for an individual user in an individual session. Using TRACE globally is generally not a good idea, since it causes every query to consume additional resources for tracing. Instead, turn TRACE ON and OFF by issuing the command "ALTER SESSION SET SQL_TRACE (TRUE or FALSE)." This command can be issued within any ORACLE tool, including SQL*Plus, SQL*Forms, and SQL*ReportWriter. SQL*Plus is the most common environment for TRACE, since an individual statement is usually the focus. Once the ALTER SESSION command is entered, each SQL statement issued is traced and the output placed in a file. The

Query 2

OBJECT_NAME	OBJECT_TYPE	OPTIONS	OPERATION
MINVFACL		FULL	TABLE ACCESS
MINVITEM_FK1	NON-UNIQUE	RANGE SCAN	INDEX
SORT/TEMP TABLE			NESTED LOOPS
MINVFACL		FULL	TABLE ACCESS
SORT/TEMP TABLE		UNIQUE	SORT
SORT/TEMP TABLE		UNIQUE	SORT
SORT/TEMP TABLE			MINUS

Query 3

OBJECT_NAME	OBJECT_TYPE	OPTIONS	OPERATION
MINVFACL		FULL	TABLE ACCESS
MINVITEM_FK1	NON-UNIQUE	RANGE SCAN	INDEX
SORT/TEMP TABLE		OUTER	NESTED LOOPS

Query 4

OBJECT_NAME	OBJECT_TYPE	OPTIONS	OPERATION
MINVFACL		FULL	TABLE ACCESS
MINVITEM_FK1	NON-UNIQUE	RANGE SCAN	INDEX
MINVITEM		FULL	TABLE ACCESS
SORT/TEMP TABLE		OUTER	NESTED LOOPS

Query 5

OBJECT_NAME	OBJECT_TYPE	OPTIONS	OPERATION
MINVFACL		FULL	TABLE ACCESS
MINVITEM_FK1	NON-UNIQUE	RANGE SCAN	INDEX

Query 6

OBJECT_NAME	OBJECT_TYPE	OPTIONS	OPERATION
MINVFACL		FULL	TABLE ACCESS
MINVITEM_FK1	NON-UNIQUE	RANGE SCAN	INDEX

Query 7

OBJECT_NAME	OBJECT_TYPE	OPTIONS	OPERATION
MINVITEM_FK1	NON-UNIQUE	RANGE SCAN	INDEX
MINVFACL		FULL	TABLE ACCESS
SORT/TEMP TABLE		GROUP BY	SORT

Figure 8.35 EXPLAIN PLAN for Queries 2 through 7

name and location of this file is specified in another ORACLE startup parameter called USER_DUMPS, whose value is operating system specific.

The data in the TRACE file is not useful before it is converted into a readable form. TKPROF, another program in the TRACE package, reads the TRACE output and creates a text file that we can analyze. TKPROF has several parameters for execution. One of the most useful controls the sorting of the TRACE file data. For example, the output from TKPROF can be sorted by EXECPU, which represents the amount of CPU time spent executing. These sorting options are very convenient, especially when analyzing an application containing hundreds of SQL statements.

Integrating TRACE and EXPLAIN

We can specify to TKPROF that we want each SQL statement that was TRACEed during the session to be EXPLAINed during TKPROF processing. This allows us to integrate the performance tools. Thus, we can turn on TRACE and issue a series of SQL statements without using EXPLAIN. We can later use the TRACE file to gather all the timing and executing details for each SQL statement, all the performance information we might need.

The output from TKPROF will vary in complexity depending on the level of detail specified. For example, Figure 8.36 is the output from the TRACE of Query 1 and the subsequent TKPROF. The query was executed during testing and integration when the facility table contained 25 rows and the inventory item table contained approximately 100,000 rows. Notice the entries in the file labeled *"recursive calls"* that capture the timing for SQL statements issued on your behalf against the data dictionary tables.

You can quickly see the cost of the full table scan on the MINVITEM table. The request took 0.002 CPU seconds to parse, 0.005 CPU seconds to execute, and 67.612 CPU seconds to fetch. The total CPU time was 67.619. The other versions of the query (2 through 7) used from 0.021 to 86.933 seconds of total CPU time. Remember, these are identical queries! This example should dramatize the critical importance of performance tuning to the success of an application.

8.3.4.3 The V5 TRACE facility. The Version 5 TRACE facility, as we noted earlier, was a proprietary tool until early 1989. This tracing tool was

```
count  = number of times OPI procedure was executed
cpu    = cpu time executing in hundreths of seconds
elap   = elapsed time executing in hundreths of secs
phys   = number of physical reads of buffers (from disk)
cr     = number of buffers gotten for consistent read
cur    = number of buffers gotten in current mode (usually for update)
rows   = number of rows processed by the OPI call

=============================================================================
SELECT MINVFACL.FACL_NUM, MINVFACL.FACL_DESC FROM MINVFACL WHERE
MINVFACL.FACL_NUM NOT IN (SELECT MINVITEM.ITEM_FACL_NUM FROM MINVITEM)
```

	count	cpu	elap	phys	cr	cur	rows
Parse:	1	2	2	0	0	0	
Execute:	1	5	26	1	0	2	0
Fetch:	1	67612	136724	56368	56521	50	2

```
=============================================================================
```

Figure 8.36 TRACE TKPROF output for Query 1

never intended for frequent use by the ORACLE user community; instead, it was used internally by the developers of the optimizer. Although we can obtain some very useful information from the Version 5 TRACE tool, beware of inaccuracies and plain bugs. Oracle does not and will not support the use of this tool. In fact, it was disabled in release 5.1.22 of the kernel so we will limit our discussion of the tool to an overview.

TRACE in Version 5 is similar to the tools available in Version 6. In some ways it is a combination of both the Version 6 TRACE and the EXPLAIN facilities. Version 5 TRACE allows you to TRACE one of two things (or both). You can TRACE "SQL" or you can TRACE "ACCESS". The ACCESS trace is a less sophisticated version of EXPLAIN. It provides detailed information on the access path used for the SQL statement, including queries against data dictionary tables. SQL tracing provides information about cursor usage. As we noted earlier, each SQL statement is placed into a cursor and parsed. Tracing SQL shows which SQL statement was parsed and which cursor was used.

Each of the C programs in the ORACLE optimizer checks a bit in memory to determine whether to display its activity. This bit is set OFF by default. We can turn it ON by using a special function, called TRACE, within a SQL statement. We use the function within SQL*Plus as shown in Figure 8.37.

We need to issue two select statements to turn ON/OFF both of the TRACE facilities. Did you notice we did not specify any FROM clauses? That is because ORACLE will turn the TRACE facility ON or OFF during the parsing of these SQL statements. Therefore we do not need

```
SELECT TRACE('ACCESS',1);      turn ACCESS tracing ON
SELECT TRACE('SQL',1);         turn SQL tracing ON
SELECT TRACE('ACCESS',0);      turn ACCESS tracing OFF
SELECT TRACE('SQL',0);         turn SQL tracing OFF
```

Figure 8.37 SQL statements to turn on V5 TRACE in SQL*Plus

a valid SQL statement. We will receive a parsing error, but the facility will be activated or deactivated nonetheless.

We can use those SQL statements (or variants) within all of the ORACLE programs. In some cases a valid SQL statement is important, so a FROM clause is needed. For example, we can create a KEY-STARTUP trigger in SQL*Forms to execute a SELECT. If we do not include the FROM clause, we will get an ORACLE error message (again, the TRACE function will still be activated).

SQL*Forms and V5 TRACE

Novice SQL*Forms users can gain valuable understanding of the forms program by using the SQL trace while running a form. You might consider choosing two KEY- triggers for TRACE; one which turns it on and one which turns if off. The TRACE details, including the number of cursors used by the form and the actual statements (in the actual order) executed in those cursors, are invaluable for tuning a complex SQL*Forms application.

In other cases, the ORACLE program validates the statement prior to sending it to the ORACLE optimizer. This validation process may consider the TRACE function to be invalid. SQL*ReportWriter, for instance, validates the SELECT entered in the QUERY window. To use TRACE in this ORACLE program we must specify the TRACE function in the WHERE clause, as in Figure 8.38.

```
SELECT 'X' FROM SYSTEM.DUAL
WHERE  TRACE('ACCESS',1) IS NOT NULL
AND    TRACE('SQL',1) IS NOT NULL
```

Figure 8.38 Turning on V5 TRACE in SQL*ReportWriter

Once TRACE is activated every SQL statement executed will cause information to be written to a file. Unlike the Version 6 TRACE facility, this file can be read without additional processing. The name and the location of the file, as with Version 6 TRACE, depend on the ORACLE startup parameter USER_DUMPS.

TRACE output can be difficult to read. You goal in using it should be to verify the process and indexes ORACLE is using to retrieve data. Half the battle in tuning is to understand the process ORACLE uses. This tool will help you in this effort, but remember that the information it provides is sometimes inaccurate.

8.3.5 Interpreting the tuning Information

So in Version 6 we can easily produce volumes of useful information for tuning SQL statements. But we must be careful about how we interpret all of these details! Many factors can affect the execution of a particular SQL statement. For example, the number of rows in the application tables can make a tremendous difference in our statistics. You may find that one technique is best for a small table joined with a large table but a completely different technique works best for a large table joined with a small one.

The first thing to remember is that timing information is very susceptible to other activities on the machine. For example, a CPU-intensive batch job might have been executing at the same time, or an end-user may have been issuing ad hoc queries. Since we seldom can control the entire machine, we should concentrate not on the absolute but on the *relative* timing information.

We also need to account for variations caused by parsing the SQL statement. (Remember that the first time the statement is issued it will be parsed, which uses extra time.) We can either ignore the initial timing information to account for the parsing or determine the actual parsing time using the Version 6 TRACE facility. A standard procedure is to execute the statement several times, perhaps ten, throw out the timings for the first execution (the parsing time), and the highest and lowest timings, and average the remaining seven timings to get an execution speed estimate.

8.3.6 A methodology for tuning SQL

We now have all of the ingredients and utensils to prepare a well-tuned system, but we are working without a recipe. This section describes the details of the methodology we use for tuning.

The first step is to isolate the SQL that is being executed. We can take all of the SQL, place it into a file, run that file through TRACE or EXPLAIN (or both), and make adjustments where needed. Most of the ORACLE tools make this process fairly easy. SQL*Forms places all of the SQL statements into a table called IAPSQLTXT. Every trigger in a form places information into this table. Each individual line of each trigger step is a separate row, and the default WHERE clause is stored in this table as well. Figure 8.39 shows the rows that would be in IAPSQLTXT if Query 1 was in a SQL*Forms trigger step.

The same representation is used for all trigger step entries, including #EXEMACRO and other SQL*Forms commands. In order to produce a file of all of the SQL statements in a form we need only query SQL from the IAPSQLTXT table. While making this selection we may also want to eliminate trivial statements, such as queries against DUAL. The SELECT in Figure 8.40 does this.

Saving to IAP Tables

Obviously, you can use this procedure only if your forms are saved into the SQL*Forms tables. Although saving forms during development is time consuming, you might consider saving all the application forms prior to tuning and testing. You can write an operating system command file to execute "IAC -i pgm user/pwd" for every INP file. You may also want to regenerate using "IAG pgm" at this point to ensure that your INP and FRM files are synchronized.

```
SQTNO   SQTLINE   SQTTEXT
-----   -------   ------------------------------------------------
    1         1   SELECT MINVFACL.FACL_NUM, MINVFACL.FACL_DESC
    1         2   FROM    MINVFACL
    1         3   WHERE   MINVFACL.FACL_NUM NOT IN
    1         4           (SELECT MINVITEM.ITEM_FACL_NUM
    1         5            FROM    MINVITEM)
```

Figure 8.39 IAPSQLTXT output of Query 1

```
SELECT  SQTTEXT
FROM    IAPSQLTXT
WHERE   SQTAPPID = &&APPL_ID
  AND   SQTNO NOT IN
    (SELECT SQTNO
    FROM    IAPSQLTXT
    WHERE (UPPER(SQTTEXT) LIKE '%#%'
    OR     UPPER(SQTTEXT) LIKE '%DUAL%')
    AND    SQTAPPID = &&APPL_ID)
```

Figure 8.40 SQL SELECT to produce SQL timing file

A similar procedure can be developed for every ORACLE tool. SQL*ReportWriter keeps the SQL used in the report in a table called SRW_QUERY (which was called FR_QUERY in version 1.0 of SQL*ReportWriter). Processing the SQL in a PRO*, SQL*Plus, or SQL*Report program is only a matter of deleting everything in the program except the SQL (in a *copy* of the original, of course).

Although we have now isolated all the SQL that is executed for the application, we must make some modifications before we can run it through SQL*Plus. First we need to eliminate any INTO clauses, which SQL*Plus does not recognize. Next, we may need to alter variables used by the application. For example, SQL*Forms uses names like :variable for its screen fields, so we must place a value into these variables to execute the same statement within SQL*Plus. We can make simple substitutions of "X" for character fields, 1 for number fields, and "01-jan-01" for date fields. Beware of mixing datatypes when using this technique, and remember that any manipulation of a column will prevent the use of the index on the column. This includes ORACLE internally using a TO_CHAR (or any other data conversion operator) on a column. Also keep in mind that analyzing index usage, not actual timing information, is the primary goal of this procedure. Timing data is useless since dummy variables substituted into the SQL statements will cause no rows to be returned in most cases.

Once we have made all of these modifications to the SQL, we are ready to execute and compile statistics. As we mentioned earlier, we may want to set some SQL*Plus environmental variables to control this process. We can specify a large PAGESIZE and LINESIZE, turn screen output off using TERMOUT, and spool all the results using SPOOL. Depending on the analysis we are performing, we may want to turn SQL*Plus TIMING

NEW_VALUE for Timing

We can often use NEW_VALUE to place values into variables for SQL*Plus. First, globally change :variable to &&variable using your text editor. Next, determine which columns represent the variables. Often the columns from one SELECT are the variables in the WHERE clause for another SELECT. We need to determine the queries that value each of the variables and specify "COLUMN hold_variable NEW_VALUE variable" for them. We also need to modify the associated SELECT to specify the column alias hold_variable. For example, suppose we have an application form that displays facility information at the top of the screen and all of the items assigned to that facility at the bottom of the screen. The first SQL statement for the form would be "SELECT * FROM MINVFACL" and the second SQL statement would specify:

```
SELECT  *
FROM    MINVITEM
WHERE   ITEM_FACL_NUM = :MINVFACL.FACL_NUM
```

Using our tuning methodology with these statements we would change the file as shown in Figure 8.41 to use NEW_VALUE for the :MINVFACL.FACL_NUM variable.

```
COLUMN HOLD_FACL_NUM NEW_VALUE FACL_NUM
REM
SELECT  MINVFACL.FACL_NUM HOLD_FACL_NUM,
        MINVFACL.*
FROM    MINVFACL;
REM
SELECT  MINVITEM.*
FROM    MINVITEM
WHERE   MINVITEM.ITEM_FACL_NUM = &&FACL_NUM;
```

Figure 8.41 Using NEW_VALUE in timing file

ON. In addition, at the end of the file we should reset the environmental variables and close the SPOOL file.

The quickest way to incorporate these variables into your tuning procedures is to put all of the needed SQL*Plus commands into a file that can be merged with the SQL script prior to execution. This technique works well and eliminates the possibility of forgetting an important parameter, such as SPOOL. (There are few things more frustrating during an intensive tuning effort.) Figure 8.42 shows a sample SQL tuning script.

Automated Tuning

This entire process could be automated with some creative programming. Depending on the resources available for tuning efforts, it may be worthwhile to write operating system programs for these procedures.

8.4 Tuning the Rest of the Application

Tuning SQL will definitely give you the best return on your invested effort. However, each ORACLE tool gives you choices that can affect

```
REM
REM  Timing SQL Script "Include" File
REM
REM
SET  PAGESIZE  1000
SET  LINESIZE  132
SET  TERMOUT  OFF
REM
SPOOL  timing.lis
REM
ALTER  SESSION  SET  SQL_TRACE  TRUE;
REM
REM
-----Place SQL Statements Here-----
REM
REM
SPOOL  OFF
REM
SET  TERMOUT  ON
ALTER  SESSION  SET  SQL_TRACE  FALSE;
EXIT
```

Figure 8.42 Environmental variables for SQL tuning script

performance and improve your applications. The following sections provide small lists of things to check and be sure to do (or not do).

8.4.1 Tuning SQL*Forms applications

SQL*Forms applications might seem impossible to tune at the first glance, but don't despair. There are several key areas to analyze and verify for efficient SQL*Forms applications. SQL*Forms applications are normally online query and update programs. Although they usually include some data entry screens, these are seldom the focus of high activity and rarely cause performance bottlenecks. The query and update processes are more likely to be sources of inefficiencies.

We discussed one SQL*Forms tuning technique in Section 5.4, which focused on the potential drawbacks of developing large multi-function applications. This is a classic example of how considering issues early in development can have a tremendous impact (and result in huge time and cost savings).

The rest of our tuning tips concern the methods used with the application code. As we review them, try to add them to your "mental library" of SQL*Forms techniques. *The primary goal should always be to reduce the amount of SQL used in the application.* There is a direct relationship between the performance of an application and the amount of work it does with the database. This makes perfect sense, given what we have learned about the work ORACLE does to answer queries. We need to provide maximum functionality with minimal interaction with the database.

What do you choose when given a choice between writing a SELECT statement and a MACRO? The correct answer is virtually always to use a MACRO. Whenever we issue a SELECT statement in SQL*Forms we must walk through the process outlined earlier in this chapter and interact with ORACLE. When we use a MACRO we are simply executing a C routine, so ORACLE doesn't need to open a cursor or parse any statements, it simply executes the command. Thus, one of the first steps in optimizing SQL*Forms applications is to replace unnecessary SELECT statements with MACROs.

Of course, not all SELECTs can be replaced. But, when we must use a SELECT we should attempt to make the statement as concise as possible and analyze and improve its efficiency.

Another "resource reducing" idea is to retrieve all of the necessary data the first time we access the table. For example, suppose we have a base table query, and that other columns in the table are used in related queries but are not needed on the screen. If we do not retrieve these values at query time we must get the data through a join, which is obviously inefficient. We can also use this technique to grab ROWID or other key data at query time.

A secondary SQL*Forms tuning goal is to reduce application memory usage. The steps taken during SQL execution are the same, regardless of the tool used to issue the statement. What this means is that every SQL statement in the SQL*Forms application will open a cursor for execution. A typical application will have 40 to 80 cursors open at one time. Remember that each cursor is the size of one ORACLE block (1024 to 4096 bytes).

Limiting OPEN_CURSORS

A startup parameter called OPEN_CURSORS limits the number of cursors that can be opened by any one user. The value of this parameter typically defaults to 50. It will not take long for developers to complain about the "Max Open Cursors" error messages, but you should resist the temptation to raise the parameter to the maximum just to avoid the complaints. Sloppy programming and SQL*Forms design can lead to an excessive number of open cursors. Very few well-written applications require more than 100 cursors, so keeping OPEN_CURSORS low will force the developer to rethink or rewrite some of his code and make it more efficient.

The size of the SQL*Forms executable (the FRM file) and the memory used by the cursors constitute the total memory used by the application. In some environments, this can be a serious constraint. So what do we do? First, we reduce the needed SQL (and therefore the cursors) to the minimum. If this is still not enough we have a second route. When we run the SQL*Forms application there is a switch we can provide on the command line, "-t," that will tell SQL*Forms to share *one* cursor for *all* requests rather than use a *separate* cursor for *each* request. (Note that SQL*Forms will still open separate cursors for base table operations of QUERY, INSERT, UPDATE, etc.) If you think about this you will see that the trade-off will be the additional parsing required. Using the same cursor for all requests means that each statement must be reparsed at each execution. Therefore we are trading memory usage (which might affect response time) for parsing time (which almost always affects response time).

Thankfully there is a happy medium. We can run the form with the switch and systematically open cursors for specific SQL statements. Each trigger step has an attribute (in the trigger step attribute window) called "Open Separate Cursor Data Area." We usually open cursors for those SQL statements that will be re-executed, such as POST-CHANGE or POST-QUERY, but we usually do not worry about DUAL table SELECTs.

The second memory issue involves the MACRO used to link SQL*Forms applications together. We can use CALL and CALLQRY to access (call) one application—the called application, from another application—the calling application. After exiting the called application we return to the calling application. The memory concern occurs because the calling application is kept in memory while we work in the called application. Not only the application but also all of its currently open cursors are kept in memory. The called application also opens cursors and uses more memory.

NEWFRM, on the other hand, does not keep the calling application in memory—the called application completely replaces the calling application. The difficulty lies in simulating the "return to the calling form" functionality of the CALL and CALLQRY macros. This can be achieved by writing KEY-EXIT logic to automatically NEWFRM back to the calling application. Refer to the trigger steps used in the MENU form (Section 5.6.5 and Figure 5.19) for the details of this process.

In the previous paragraphs we have focused on solving SQL*Forms performance problems by focusing on techniques used in a specific form. Improving response time problems, however, will require taking a look at the *overall demands on the processor*. If your system has a large number of SQL*Forms users (like our MegaMarket system) you should note that two different types of performance problems may occur. The first relates to the raw throughput of the system, the other considers response time. Poor throughput can be caused by any of the factors mentioned thus far and will usually be constant. Response time, however, is characterized by slow response in different places at different times. For example, a form may be efficient when interactive applications are running. As soon as a report or two are added to the mix, the form takes longer to process certain validations or modifications. Response time problems, unlike throughput problems, are usually resolved by determining the constrained resource (memory, I/O, etc.) and reducing the application requirements for that resource.

8.4.2 Tuning SQL*ReportWriter applications

There are not many specific tuning tips for the SQL*ReportWriter product. Again, reduce the amount of SQL in your programs, and make the remaining SQL as efficient as you can. Reports often return large amounts of data, so you will probably need to revise the SQL statements to eliminate the use of indexes.

SQL*ReportWriter's 4GL facilities allow you to write a join with one SQL statement or two SQL statements linked by the data captured in SQL*ReportWriter. These queries should execute identically, but as we have seen throughout this chapter, even a small change to a statement can be detrimental to performance. For reports that are executing with unacceptable response times, we suggest that you experiment with replacing the default functionality with hard-coded SQL statements.

8.5 Application Testing

Testing an application is usually a tedious and difficult process. Some organizations include a quality assurance group to alleviate this difficulty. Others have teams of dedicated testers. And still others have no special procedures for testing. Regardless of your situation, a minimal amount of testing must be performed by the application developer. We realize that most developers avoid proper testing regimens, but we will provide some tips to make it easier and less tedious.

One of the keys to good testing is the creation of large amounts of data. Unfortunately, most organizations cannot afford to have anyone (especially an application developer), spend time pouring data into the database. So how do we get the data into the system?

The best technique we know is to use a little SQL to create rows based on other rows. For example, suppose you INSERT ten rows into the MINVITEM table. Can you think of an easy way to use those rows to create other rows? Check your SQL against Figure 8.43 to see how close you came.

```
INSERT INTO MINVITEM
    (SELECT * FROM MINVITEM)
```

Figure 8.43 SQL to create test data

```
INSERT INTO MINVITEM
    (SELECT ITEM_SEQUENCE.NEXTVAL, ITEM_DESC,
            ITEM_ORDR_NUM, rest of columns
    FROM    MINVITEM)
```

Figure 8.44 SQL to create test data using sequence numbers

The only difficultly with this technique is that the key values for the new rows will be invalid. Starting with item numbers 1 thru 10, we would be attempting to insert 1 thru 10 again! We need to make one change to avoid this problem. We can take advantage of the sequence number generator to assign a new sequence number to each row in the ITEM table. The modified INSERT is shown in Figure 8.44.

V5 Test Data

A similar solution to this problem will work for Version 5 users. Think back to our discussion of the pseudo-column ROWNUM for the MENU form in Section 5.6.3. This column is assigned by ORACLE whenever a query is performed. In our example, the subquery would return ten rows with ROWNUM values from 1 to 10. We can use this to generate sequence numbers in a Version 5 database. The query would be very similar to the Version 6 query. Another similar technique is to initially insert the duplicate data and update it later to assign each row a unique number. Both of these SQL statements are shown in Figure 8.45.

```
INSERT INTO MINVITEM
    (SELECT ROWNUM + current_max, ITEM_DESC, ...
    FROM MINVITEM)

UPDATE MINVITEM
SET ITEM_NUM = ROWNUM
```

Figure 8.45 SQL to create test data for V5

We can use this technique to generate plenty of data for our tables, since the number of rows inserted each time will increase exponentially. Assuming we INSERT 10 rows initially, the first INSERT INTO AS SELECT FROM will create 10 more for a total of 20 rows, the second execution will create 20 more for a total of 40, and 40 more for a total of 80, and so on. After 15 executions by simply typing RUN in SQL*Plus we have created 327,680 rows! Altering hard-coded values for each execution can even make the data fairly realistic. Remember that since we will be using this data for performance tuning, we should attempt to make it as realistic as possible.

Once we have created, updated, deleted, and tested with a fair amount of data we should take a look at the data dictionary. We want to validate our assumptions about space usage at this point, so we should look for tablespace, index, and data fragmentation.

Another difficult question is how to test multiuser capabilities. One option, of course, is to ask a group of people to sit at their terminals and enter data. A better solution takes advantage of a rarely used facility in SQL*Forms for echoing keystrokes. This facility captures the keystrokes executed in a particular session, so they can be "replayed" at any time. In other words, you can have ghost users executing the same keystrokes from a file over and over again. The only pitfall with this technique is that the operating system's limitations can cause the forms to get out of synchronization with one another. Due to limited processor resources, one simulated operator may get ahead of the others. If concurrency is crucial, the PAUSE macro can be added into the SQL*Forms application to display the message "Press Any Key to Continue" for each iteration.

8.6 Tuning and Testing the MegaMarket Application

We have used the MegaMarket application as the basis for most of the examples in this chapter. We used the tuning techniques discussed throughout the chapter on the application. The first step was completed at the end of the last chapter when we moved all of the application forms and reports to the integrated testing environment. In our development process, this environment is called TEST and is a separate ORACLE instance from DEVL (refer back to Sections 4.2 and 4.3 for information on staging philosophies).

There are a few issues faced by the developers of the MegaMarket application that stretch beyond SQL tuning and program tuning. The main issue relates to the large number of users expected for the system and the tremendous amount of data that will ultimately be captured. We focused heavily on concurrency issues during testing, we leaned our design process toward efficient and concise applications, and we spent a great deal of time tuning both the ORACLE database and application. There is very little else that can be done from an application standpoint to address either of these issues. Unfortunately, the burden usually falls on the capacity of the processor and operating system to handle the application environment. Distributed processing and distributed databases provide some solutions to this bottleneck, so we will explore them in Chapter 10.

8.7 Conclusion

Now we will take a look at one of the loose ends that needs to be tied up before we have finished the application. Documentation is typically a dreaded task, but it is crucial to the success of an application. The next chapter introduces some techniques to make the process a little easier.

Documenting the System

9.1 Introduction

Although documenting an application may be the most dreaded task of the entire development process, it should never be avoided. Documentation not only helps the user understand how to use the application, but also helps you to better support the application by giving you all the information you will need to make future changes. Of all the application components described so far, documentation is the most difficult one to describe with step-by-step procedures. The primary reason for this is that taste will particularly govern the format and style behind application documentation. Also, since many companies already have guidelines and standards for application documentation, it could be counterproductive for us to tell you exactly how to write your documentation. Finally, there really is no single correct way to write application documentation. In view of these considerations, we will confine our discussion in this chapter to suggestions for preparing your documentation and techniques for using ORACLE to help ease the documentation burden.

9.2 Documentation Overview

There are several different types of application documentation and thousands of possible formats. Regardless of the specific format, most documentation falls into two categories: *user documentation* and *techni-*

cal documentation. The following two sections address the considerations for these two types of documentation.

9.2.1 User documentation

User documentation is vitally important to the success of an application. An application will not be a success if a user has difficulty operating it, whether because it is just hard to use or wasn't properly explained. It is critical to ensure that the user understands how the application functions and that a resource is available for questions when you are not. Good user documentation makes these things possible.

There are several issues to consider when you write your user documentation. First, remember that your documentation may be the first exposure a user will have to an ORACLE application (or even a computer application). The tone that you adopt should be simple enough that new users are not confused, but not so overly simple that important details are omitted. This line is often difficult to walk; inevitably, one user will complain that the documentation is too hard, while another will say that it is too easy. We have found that providing a basic introduction to each function followed by a detailed technical breakdown of the options available results in documentation that can serve users of all levels.

Second, try to arrange your user documentation around how the application will actually be used. A sterile alphabetical reference to all of an application's functions is not a very gentle introduction. It would be more effective to arrange the topics according to the logical progression of application use. For example, by taking the user through a complete insertion, query, update, and deletion cycle, you illustrate exactly how the entire application will be used. By discussing the functions that will actually be performed on a daily basis, you can probably cover 80% of the functionality most users will need. They can look up the other 20% in the function reference section of your documentation when needed.

Third, create a consistent, one-page summary of each screen and its functionality. By placing a picture of the screen at the top of the page, you help the user to find out easily exactly where he stands in the application. Below the picture, place a brief technical summary of the screen's purpose. Also include a detailed list of the important functions that can be performed from this form, along with a list of the forms that call this one and those that this one calls.

Online Help

We built a simple help system in conjunction with our SQL*Forms applications. This technique allowed for parallel creation of user documentation and the application code. Investment in the development of a sophisticated online help system can alleviate the burden (and difficulty) of developing documentation after the fact. Refer to section 7.2 for a discussion of our help system.

Fourth, include a more detailed reference to all function keys and menu options in the back of the user guide, along with cross-references to other parts of the documentation. This will serve as an index to the rest of the documentation, making the documentation a valuable ongoing resource. Remember, if they can't find the answer in the documentation easily, guess who will get a phone call ...

Finally, if your application allows the user to access the database tables directly through SQL*Plus for ad hoc queries, you should include detailed documentation of the tables, including column names and data types. Illustrations of the relationships between tables, in the form of diagrams and examples, will also be helpful to guide the user through joins and more complicated queries.

Good user documentation can significantly ease the burden of supporting your application. Most questions users ask about an application are simple, and can be answered in advance by thorough documentation.

9.2.2 Technical documentation

The technical documentation is as important to the developer as user documentation is to the user. It provides not only a detailed description of how the application was designed and built, but also all of the information necessary for application revisions. If user documentation answers the questions that arise in using the system, technical documentation answers those that arise in revising it. It also provides an excellent source for new applications by reducing the need to "reinvent the wheel." When you go on to build your next application, you will find the technical documentation from previous applications invaluable.

Again, the exact format that you choose for your technical documentation is up to you and the standards of your organization. There are a few features, however, that no technical documentation should be without.

First, all of the documentation that you prepared during the analysis and design of the application should be included as part of your final technical documentation. This includes Entity/Relationship diagrams, Data Flow diagrams, Functional decompositions, interview summaries, logical-to-physical design decisions, and module specifications. This material will not only provide a history of the application development, but will also act as a platform upon which further development can occur. A record of the decisions made during the design will be useful during subsequent development so that the same points do not have to be debated again.

Second, a thorough listing of all standards and guidelines followed during the development process should be included near the beginning of the technical documentation. These will constitute a roadmap to the application for people who are unfamiliar with it, by explaining the significance of particular table names, SQL*Forms triggers, and other application components. The technical documentation should always consider the developer who must implement changes long after your involvement with the application has ceased. Providing a detailed description of terms, coding standards, and naming conventions will help this developer immensely.

Third, detailed directions for recreating the database structures and operating environment must be outlined. They should include descriptions of the SQL scripts you used to build tables, indexes, and other database structures. This will aid in recovery, should the database be corrupted, as well as in migrating the application to other platforms.

Fourth, a complete listing of all tables, indexes, synonyms, forms, reports, SQL scripts, operating application programs, and 3GL programs should be compiled, along with references to current and past versions and physical locations. This list, which should also include a brief description of each item on it, will be one of the most extensively used pieces of your documentation. Its uses will include adding reports and integrating new applications with yours.

Fifth, the detailed screen layouts from the user documentation should be refined and included in the technical documentation. You should add a detailed breakdown of blocks, fields, triggers, and other important points about each form. This will give other developers the information necessary to make changes. It will also help when you come back after several months and need to understand your implementation decisions. Also, when you are working on your next application, this documentation will guide you to the interesting pieces of code you may want to use again.

SQL*Forms Comments

In Chapter 5 we suggested you use the comment fields on trigger steps, triggers, fields, blocks, and forms liberally. Careful and consistent entry of information into these windows is a quick source of technical documentation.

Sixth, the functionality and peculiar programming considerations behind all reports and programs should be documented to ease the process of making changes to them. This can be a cursory description or a detailed technical analysis, depending on the nature and size of the programs in question. As always, program and report code should be thoroughly commented to ensure maximum readability.

Finally, although it may be impractical to include it as part of the technical documentation, the source code to all the applications forms, reports, and programs should be grouped together and stored some-where. Having a printout accessible at all times is a real help when you're trying to track down a bug. In the next section, we'll see how to print some of the source code in more readable formats than those to which you are accustomed.

9.3 Easing the Technical Documentation Burden

Developers who are more hacker than human certainly detest the very thought of compiling technical documentation materials. There are, however, ways to get ORACLE to do some of the work for you. Since ORACLE has stored practically everything you need to know about your application in the data dictionary, we should be able to use the tools we've been discussing all along to display this information in a readable format. In this section, we will present some techniques for using the database itself as a documentation resource.

9.3.1 Documentation using CASE*Dictionary

The first way that ORACLE can be used as a documentation tool is through an application designed for that purpose. In the ORACLE tool set, that means the CASE tools. The principal CASE tool is

CASE*Dictionary, an ORACLE application that stores information about a data model. It is generally used during the early stages of design to help track entities, relationships, and attributes. (See Chapter 2 for a discussion of these concepts.) At that point in the process, it can not only help validate the data model, but also actually build the database tables. A wonderful side effect is that all of this information can then be unloaded from the CASE*Dictionary tables and used directly to document the database structure. Because the technical documentation should include information about the database design, the CASE*Dictionary output can give you a great head start on your documentation.

CASE*Dictionary provides many standard reports that are useful for technical documentation. Reports you might consider using include entities and attributes, tables and columns, domain definitions, and module information. Figure 9.2 is an example of the output from the table and column report and Figure 9.1 shows the domain definition report.

Documentation Applications

You may find that developing your own special applications to maintain application information is useful. For example, although we did not develop separate tables and forms strictly for the purpose of technical documentation, we did create the SGENAPPL table to help us manage our applications. By generating reports from this table, we can easily list all of the forms, reports, and command files in the application, along with their types and locations. You could create tables such as this with simple forms that allow you to maintain this sort of information yourself.

9.3.2 Documentation using the data dictionary

Another way to use ORACLE to get a jump on documentation is to take advantage of the data dictionary itself. The data dictionary, of course, is the set of tables that ORACLE uses to maintain the database structure. It stores information about tables, indexes, synonyms, users, and so on. It is a perfect source of technical information about your data structures because it is always updated automatically, so you can be confident that its contents reflect the current state of the environment. Since these

```
Date : 30-APR-90          ORACLE : CASE*Dictionary          Page :            1
                 DOMAIN DEFINITION FOR APPLICATION INVMGT VERSION 1


     NAME        : LAST NAME
     SUPERTYPE   : NAME

     DESCRIPTION : Last name of the contact

     ---ATTRIBUTE---------------------------COLUMN----------------------------
                                          |
       FORMAT    : CHAR                    |   DATA TYPE  : CHAR
       LENGTH    :     25                  |   MAX LENGTH :     25
       U.O.M.    :                         |

     OWNED BY APPLICATION INVMGT VERSION 1

     ---AVAILABLE TO--------ACCESS RIGHT-----------AUTHORITY/LEVEL--------------



       RESPONSIBILITY OF

     --------------------------------------------------------------------------

     DEFAULT VALUE :
     NULL VALUE    :

     DERIVATION :
     ------------


     ---DOMAIN VALUES----------------------------------------------------------
            VALUE    | HIGH VALUE  | ABBREVIATION |        MEANING
                     |             |              |
     --------------------------------------------------------------------------

     VALIDATION RULES :
     ------------------

     Any field based on this domain will end in _NAME_LAST

     --------------------------------------------------------------------------
```

Figure 9.1 CASE*Dictionary domain definition report (*Part 1*)

tables are tables like any others, they can be queried with standard SQL syntax. In this way, we can run reports that produce "snapshots" of our database environment.

The clearest example of a data dictionary query is simply "SELECT * FROM USER_TABLES." This query will list all of the tables owned by the current user. This is useful, but we can take the idea further with more complicated queries. For example, how would you do something as simple as print out each table in the application, along with its columns and datatypes? The easiest way to perform this task is to enter SQL*Plus, open a file to spool the output (using the SQL*Plus SPOOL command),

```
Date : 30-APR-90         ORACLE : CASE*Dictionary          Page :              2
                DOMAIN DEFINITION FOR APPLICATION INVMGT VERSION 1


     NAME       : FIRST NAME
     SUPERTYPE  : NAME

     DESCRIPTION : First name of the contact

     ---ATTRIBUTE---------------------------COLUMN-------------------------      -
                                   |
        FORMAT   : CHAR            |   DATA TYPE  : CHAR
        LENGTH   :    15           |   MAX LENGTH :    15
        U.O.M.   :                 |

     OWNED BY APPLICATION INVMGT VERSION 1

     ---AVAILABLE TO--------ACCESS RIGHT-----------AUTHORITY/LEVEL--------------


        RESPONSIBILITY OF

     ----------------------------------------------------------------------      -

     DEFAULT VALUE :
     NULL VALUE    :

     DERIVATION :
     -----------


     ---DOMAIN  VALUES---------------------------------------------------------
          VALUE   | HIGH VALUE  | ABBREVIATION  |        MEANING
                  |             |               |
     ----------------------------------------------------------------------      -

     VALIDATION RULES :
     ------------------

     Any field based on this domain will end in _NAME_FIRST

     ----------------------------.--------------------------------------------
```

Figure 9.1 CASE*Dictionary domain definition report (*Part 2*)

and then DESCRIBE each table. This would be quite cumbersome with many tables, because you would have to describe each one separately. A more flexible way to accomplish this task is shown in Figure 9.3.

These SQL statements run a query against the data dictionary that gives us the details of each table in exactly the format that we want. It also conveniently puts each table on a separate page. Other data dictionary reports can include indexes, synonyms, grants, and space usage. To list all the tables in the data dictionary that you can query in this fashion, simply execute the statement "SELECT * FROM DICTIONARY."

```
Date : 01 MAY 90                      ORACLE : CASE*Dictionary                                    Page   1

                    TABLE DEFINITION REPORT FOR APPLICATION INVMGT VERSION 1

   Table Name      |   Entities Implemented   | Start Rows | End Rows |   Space Name   | Display Title
---------------------------------------------------------------------------------------------------------
SGENEMPL             EMPLOYEE

   Comment :    Created from Entity EMPLOYEE by THOECHST on 11-DEC-89
   Description : This table contains all of the MegaMarket employee information.
                Both managers and non-managers are stored in this table. The
                employee information is maintained by the adminstrative offices.

Col
Seq (PK Seq) Column / In Index (Seq) Format  Size    Nulls ?   Initial Final        Description / Comment
---------------------------------------------------------------------------------------------------------
 1  ( 1) EMPL_NUM             NUMBER  (10,0)  NOT NULL                  COLUMN DEFINITION DERIVED FROM ATTRIBUTE NUM

 2  EMPL_FACL_NUM             NUMBER  (10,0)  NULL                      Facility where Employee Works

 3  EMPL_OFFC_NUM             NUMBER  (10,0)  NULL                      Admin Office where Employee Works

 4  EMPL_EMPL_NUM_MGR         NUMBER  (10,0)  NULL                      Number of Employee's Manager

 5  EMPL_NAME_FIRST           CHAR    (25)    NOT NULL                  Last Name of Employee

 6  EMPL_NAME_LAST            CHAR    (15)    NOT NULL                  First Name of Employee

 7  EMPL_NAME_MIDDLE          CHAR    (1)     NULL                      Middle Name of Employee

 8  EMPL_USERID               CHAR    (8)     NULL                      ORACLE Userid for Employee

 9  EMPL_HIRE_DATE            DATE    ()      NOT NULL                  Date Employee was Hired

10  EMPL_SOC_SEC_NUM          CHAR    (11)    NOT NULL                  Social Security Number of Employee

11  EMPL_TITLE                CHAR    (60)    NULL                      Title for Employee
```

Figure 9.2 CASE*Dictionary table and column definition report

```
REM
REM   SQL File to print Table Definitions
REM
REM   Creator:  Tim and Nicole
REM   Created:  April 1990
REM        .
SET FEEDBACK OFF
SET PAGESIZE 56
SET ECHO OFF
SET LINESIZE 80
REM
BREAK ON "Table" SKIP PAGE
REM
COLUMN "Type"      FORMAT A15
COLUMN "Table"     FORMAT A20
COLUMN "Column"    FORMAT A30
REM
REM
SELECT TABLE_NAME "Table", COLUMN_NAME "Column",
       DECODE(NULLABLE,'N','NOT NULL','NULL') "Null?",
       DATA_TYPE||'('||DECODE(DATA_TYPE,
                               'CHAR',DATA_LENGTH||')',
                        DATA_PRECISION||','||DATA_SCALE||')') "Type"
FROM   USER_TAB_COLUMNS
ORDER BY TABLE_NAME, COLUMN_ID;
```

Figure 9.3 SQL for table definition report

9.3.3 Documentation using tool tables

Another valuable documentation resource is available through ORACLE tools such as SQL*Forms, SQL*ReportWriter, and SQL*Plus. Each of these programs has a distinct set of database tables that can be used to save your work. These tables store all the information about each of your forms, reports, or menus and contain the most thorough description of your applications. You can take advantage of these tables to produce reports that will document almost all of your software.

9.3.3.1 SQL*Forms reports. For SQL*Forms applications, the only format even partially readable is the INP file. These files should be included in the technical documentation with the other source code listings, but they are so difficult to read that a better format is a virtual necessity. Depending on the quality of your report, you can produce a very understandable SQL*Forms description based on the IAP tables. Several reports that perform this function are available through ORACLE user groups and Oracle has even started distributing one with Version 6 on all platforms and 5.1C for DOS. If you do not want to list the entire SQL*Forms application, you can write your own specific reports. For example, you might wish to list each form along with all of the field names in the form. Figure 9.4 shows the query for this information. What you choose to list will depend on the nature of your documentation; just remember that all the information you need is yours for the asking in the IAP tables. Figure 9.5 lists the IAP tables.

9.3.3.2 SQL*ReportWriter reports. Another ORACLE tool that uses it own set of tables is SQL*Reportwriter. These tables are more complex than the IAP tables because SQL*ReportWriter considers each component of a report as a separate "object." For example, a query is an object and a field is a different object. Each object is assigned a unique identifier called ITEMID within the object type. The problem with this scheme is that the name of all objects are stored in a common table called SRW_STE. Notice the ITEMID field (and the lack of a name or description) in the four SRW tables listed in Figure 9.6.

Although there are ten tables that store report definitions, you should focus on the report, query, group, and field information. These tables hold most of the critical details of the report and provide a solid foundation for report documentation.

9.3.3.3 SQL*Menu reports. You can generate reports from the tables used by SQL*Menu just as with SQL*Forms and SQL*Reportwriter. Unless you have a very specific need, though, this should be unnecessary, since SQL*Menu has a built-in reporting feature that can produce detailed descriptions of any given menu hierarchy. These SQL*Menu reports produce not only textual descriptions of the menus, but also the SQL statements required to rebuild the menu structure, allowing you to easily migrate a menu application to another machine.

```
COL "Form Name"    FORMAT A10
COL "Form Title"   FORMAT A30
COL "Field Name"   FORMAT A30
REM
BREAK ON "Form Name" ON "Form Desc" SKIP PAGE
REM
SELECT APPNAME "Form Name", APPTITLE "Form Title",
       FLDNAME "Field Name"
FROM   IAPFLD, IAPAPP
WHERE  FLDAPPID = APPID
ORDER  BY APPNAME, FLDNAME;
```

Figure 9.4 SQL for form and field listing

Table	Column	Null?	Type
IAPAPP	APPID	NOT NULL	NUMBER(,)
	APPOWNER	NULL	CHAR(30)
	APPNAME	NOT NULL	CHAR(30)
	APPTITLE	NULL	CHAR(80)
	APPWKSIZE	NULL	NUMBER(,)
	APPVAUNIT	NULL	CHAR(6)

Table	Column	Null?	Type
IAPBLK	BLKAPPID	NOT NULL	NUMBER(,)
	BLKNAME	NOT NULL	CHAR(30)
	BLKDESC	NULL	CHAR(60)
	BLKHIDE	NULL	CHAR(1)
	BLKSEQ	NULL	NUMBER(,)
	BLKUNQKEY	NULL	CHAR(1)
	BLKCTRL	NULL	CHAR(1)
	BLKTOWNER	NULL	CHAR(30)
	BLKTNAME	NULL	CHAR(30)
	BLKNOREC	NULL	NUMBER(,)
	BLKNOBUF	NULL	NUMBER(,)
	BLKBLIN	NULL	NUMBER(,)
	BLKLNRC	NULL	NUMBER(,)
	BLKOBYSQL	NULL	NUMBER(,)

Table	Column	Null?	Type
IAPCOMMENT	CMTAPPID	NOT NULL	NUMBER(,)
	CMTBLK	NULL	CHAR(30)
	CMTFLD	NULL	CHAR(30)
	CMTTRGTYP	NULL	CHAR(30)
	CMTTRGSEQ	NULL	NUMBER(,)
	CMTLINE	NULL	NUMBER(,)
	CMTTEXT	NULL	CHAR(80)

Table	Column	Null?	Type
IAPFLD	FLDAPPID	NOT NULL	NUMBER(,)
	FLDBLK	NOT NULL	CHAR(30)
	FLDNAME	NOT NULL	CHAR(30)
	FLDSEQ	NULL	NUMBER(,)
	FLDTYPE	NULL	CHAR(7)
	FLDLEN	NULL	NUMBER(,)
	FLDDLEN	NULL	NUMBER(,)
	FLDQLEN	NULL	NUMBER(,)
	FLDBTAB	NULL	CHAR(1)
	FLDKEY	NULL	CHAR(1)
	FLDCKBLK	NULL	CHAR(30)
	FLDCKFLD	NULL	CHAR(30)
	FLDDFLT	NULL	CHAR(80)
	FLDDISP	NULL	CHAR(1)
	FLDPAGE	NULL	NUMBER(,)
	FLDLINE	NULL	NUMBER(,)
	FLDCOL	NULL	NUMBER(,)
	FLDPROMPT	NULL	CHAR(80)
	FLDPRABOV	NULL	CHAR(1)
	FLDPRRPT	NULL	CHAR(1)
	FLDENTER	NULL	CHAR(1)
	FLDQUERY	NULL	CHAR(1)
	FLDUPDATE	NULL	CHAR(1)
	FLDUPDNUL	NULL	CHAR(1)
	FLDMAND	NULL	CHAR(1)

Figure 9.5 IAP tables (*Part 1*)

	FLDFIXED	NULL	CHAR(1)
	FLDSKIP	NULL	CHAR(1)
	FLDHIDE	NULL	CHAR(1)
	FLDAUTOHLP	NULL	CHAR(1)
	FLDUPPER	NULL	CHAR(1)
	FLDLOVT	NULL	CHAR(61)
	FLDLOVC	NULL	CHAR(30)
	FLDLOW	NULL	CHAR(30)
	FLDHI	NULL	CHAR(30)
	FLDHELP	NULL	CHAR(80)

Table	Column	Null?	Type
IAPMAP	MAPAPPID	NOT NULL	NUMBER(,)
	MAPPAGE	NOT NULL	NUMBER(,)
	MAPLINE	NULL	NUMBER(,)
	MAPGRPH	NULL	CHAR(1)
	MAPTEXT	NULL	CHAR(132)

Table	Column	Null?	Type
IAPSQLTXT	SQTAPPID	NOT NULL	NUMBER(,)
	SQTNO	NOT NULL	NUMBER(,)
	SQTLINE	NULL	NUMBER(,)
	SQTTEXT	NULL	CHAR(80)

Table	Column	Null?	Type
IAPTRG	TRGAPPID	NOT NULL	NUMBER(,)
	TRGBLK	NULL	CHAR(30)
	TRGFLD	NULL	CHAR(30)
	TRGTYPE	NOT NULL	CHAR(30)
	TRGSEQ	NULL	NUMBER(,)
	TRGLABEL	NULL	CHAR(30)
	TRGSQL	NULL	NUMBER(,)
	TRGCURS	NULL	CHAR(1)
	TRGMVE	NULL	CHAR(1)
	TRGINV	NULL	CHAR(1)
	TRGROLL	NULL	CHAR(1)
	TRGSLAB	NULL	CHAR(30)
	TRGFLAB	NULL	CHAR(30)
	TRGMSG	NULL	CHAR(80)

Table	Column	Null?	Type
IAPTRIGGER	TRIGAPPID	NOT NULL	NUMBER(,)
	TRIGBLK	NULL	CHAR(30)
	TRIGFLD	NULL	CHAR(30)
	TRIGTYPE	NOT NULL	CHAR(30)
	TRIGDESC	NULL	CHAR(20)
	TRIGHIDE	NULL	CHAR(1)

Figure 9.5 IAP tables (*Part 2*)

9.3.4 Cross reference reports

The information in the data dictionary can be combined with the information in the tool tables to produce valuable documentation. We call this type of documentation *cross reference* since it references data

Table	Column	Null?	Type
SRW_FIELD	OWNER	NULL	CHAR(30)
	APPID	NOT NULL	NUMBER(9,0)
	ITEMID	NOT NULL	NUMBER(9,0)
	GROUPID	NOT NULL	NUMBER(9,0)
	SOURCE_QUERY	NULL	NUMBER(9,0)
	TARGET_POSITION	NULL	NUMBER(3,0)
	COMPUTE	NULL	CHAR(240)
	HEADING	NULL	CHAR(240)
	SKIP	NULL	CHAR(1)
	FIELD_ORDER	NULL	NUMBER(3,0)
	FORMAT_MASK	NULL	CHAR(40)
	WIDTH	NULL	NUMBER(3,0)
	DATATYPE	NULL	NUMBER(1,0)
	OPERATOR	NULL	NUMBER(2,0)
	RESET_GROUP	NULL	NUMBER(9,0)
	REPRINT	NULL	CHAR(1)
	RELATIVE_POS	NULL	NUMBER(1,0)
	LINES_BEFORE	NULL	NUMBER(3,0)
	SPACES_BEFORE	NULL	NUMBER(3,0)
	ALIGNMENT	NULL	NUMBER(1,0)

Table	Column	Null?	Type
SRW_GROUP	OWNER	NULL	CHAR(30)
	APPID	NOT NULL	NUMBER(9,0)
	ITEMID	NOT NULL	NUMBER(9,0)
	QUERYID	NULL	NUMBER(9,0)
	PAGE_BREAK	NULL	NUMBER(1,0)
	GROUP_ORDER	NULL	NUMBER(2,0)
	REPETITION	NULL	NUMBER(1,0)
	LINES_BEFORE	NULL	NUMBER(3,0)
	SPACES_BEFORE	NULL	NUMBER(3,0)
	INTER_ROW	NULL	NUMBER(3,0)
	INTER_FIELD	NULL	NUMBER(3,0)
	FIELD_HILITE	NULL	NUMBER(2,0)
	LABEL_HILITE	NULL	NUMBER(2,0)
	RELATIVE_POS	NULL	NUMBER(1,0)
	FIELDS_ACROSS	NULL	NUMBER(3,0)
	MULTI_PANEL	NULL	CHAR(1)
	MATRIX_FLAG	NULL	CHAR(1)
	LOCATE_LABELS	NULL	NUMBER(1,0)

Table	Column	Null?	Type
SRW_QUERY	OWNER	NULL	CHAR(30)
	APPID	NOT NULL	NUMBER(9,0)
	ITEMID	NOT NULL	NUMBER(9,0)
	PARENTID	NULL	NUMBER(9,0)
	MATRIX_PARENTID	NULL	NUMBER(9,0)
	QUERY_ORDER	NULL	NUMBER(2,0)
	QUERY	NULL	LONG(,)

Table	Column	Null?	Type
SRW_REPORT	APPID	NOT NULL	NUMBER(9,0)
	NEXT_ITEMID	NOT NULL	NUMBER(9,0)
	REPORT_NAME	NULL	CHAR(80)
	PAGE_HEIGHT	NULL	NUMBER(3,0)
	PAGE_WIDTH	NULL	NUMBER(3,0)
	LEFT_MARGIN	NULL	NUMBER(3,0)
	RIGHT_MARGIN	NULL	NUMBER(3,0)

Figure 9.6 SQL*ReportWriter tables (*Part 1*)

TOP_MARGIN	NULL	NUMBER(3,0)
BOTTOM_MARGIN	NULL	NUMBER(3,0)
VERSION	NULL	NUMBER(5,0)
MODIFIED_VERSION	NULL	NUMBER(5,0)
COMMENTS	NULL	LONG(,)
OWNER	NULL	CHAR(30)
MODIFIER	NULL	CHAR(30)
CREATE_DATE	NULL	DATE(,)
MODIFIED_DATE	NULL	DATE(,)
PARAM_TITLE	NULL	CHAR(80)
PARAM_HINT	NULL	CHAR(80)
PARAM_STATUS	NULL	CHAR(50)

Figure 9.6 SQL*ReportWriter tables (*Part 2*)

across all of the knowledge sources. Cross reference reports can be very useful, especially when you need to determine the effect of a proposed application change like renaming a database table. A report for this purpose might list each table and show every application (report or form) that uses the table. Figure 9.7 shows this cross reference report and the SQL statement that was used to produce it.

This report could also be made more detailed to provide a cross reference of columns and usage, which helps to gauge the effect of changing the size of a column or removing a column. An example column cross reference report and the SQL statement is pictured in Figure 9.8.

9.3.5 Data integrity reports

Integrity in a relational database can sometimes be difficult to control. Many of the integrity rules are dependent upon a conscientious developer, a thorough review team, and a dedicated tester. Clever reports can be used to try to capture some of the things that inevitably pass through the cracks. Keep in mind, however, that these reports can only be produced if the knowledge of application primary keys, foreign keys, and other integrity constraints were recorded in the data dictionary. We used referential integrity constraints when we created our tables, so we can write a report that shows each table and associated foreign key columns. Figure 9.9 is the SQL statement for this listing and a portion of the resulting report.

Any application that manipulates these tables should enforce the foreign key column relationships. Reports can be developed to compare this data dictionary information with the actual application trigger code, field attributes, and field validations in the forms to verify foreign key

```
REM
REM   TBLCROSS.SQL
REM   Cross Reference Report
REM   Lists each Table and the Applications that use the table
REM
REM   Creator: Tim and Nicole
REM   Created: April 1990
REM
SET PAGESIZE 56
SET FEEDBACK OFF
REM
COLUMN TABLE_NAME FORMAT A10  HEADING "Table Name"
COLUMN NAME       FORMAT A20  HEADING "Application Name"
COLUMN TYPE       FORMAT A5   HEADING "Tool"
REM
BREAK ON TABLE_NAME SKIP 2
REM
SELECT DISTINCT TABLE_NAME,
       UPPER(REPORT.NAME) NAME, 'SRW' TYPE
FROM   SRW_STE REPORT, SRW_STE QUERY, USER_TABLES
WHERE  REPORT.APPID = QUERY.APPID
AND    REPORT.TYPE = 1
AND    QUERY.TYPE = 2
AND    UPPER(QUERY.NAME) LIKE '%'||SUBSTR(USER_TABLES.TABLE_NAME,5,4)||'%'
UNION
SELECT DISTINCT TABLE_NAME,
       UPPER(IAPAPP.APPNAME) NAME, 'FORMS' TYPE
FROM   IAPSQLTXT, IAPBLK, IAPAPP, USER_TABLES
WHERE  (IAPAPP.APPID = IAPBLK.BLKAPPID AND
        SUBSTR(IAPBLK.BLKNAME,1,8) = USER_TABLES.TABLE_NAME)
OR     (IAPAPP.APPID = IAPSQLTXT.SQTAPPID AND
        IAPSQLTXT.SQTTEXT LIKE '%'||USER_TABLES.TABLE_NAME||'%')
AND    IAPAPP.APPOWNER = 'THOECHST'
ORDER BY 1, 2;
```

PRODUCES:

Table Name	Application Name	Tool
MINVFACL	MINVFLFV	FORMS
MINVFCLS	MINVSQTY	FORMS
	MINVSTOR	FORMS
MINVMOVE	MINVSMVE	FORMS
	MINVWMVE	FORMS
MINVORDR	MINVMTRX	SRW
	MINVORDR	FORMS
	MINVRLFV	FORMS
	MINVSHIP	FORMS
MINVSCLS	MINVSUPP	FORMS
MINVSHIP	MINVRLFV	FORMS
	MINVSHIP	FORMS

Figure 9.7 Cross reference report (*Part 1*)

MINVSUPP	MINVMTRX	SRW
	MINVSUPP	FORMS
MINVTRAN	MINVTRAN	FORMS
SGENAPPL	SGENAPPL	FORMS
SGENEMPL	SGENELFV	FORMS
	SGENEMPL	FORMS
SGENMENU	SGENMENU	FORMS
	SMENMAIN	FORMS
SGENOFFC	MINVADMN	SRW
	SGENOFFC	FORMS
	SGENOLFV	FORMS
SLFVICLS	MINVILFV	FORMS
	MINVWQTY	FORMS
	SLFVICLS	FORMS
SLFVTTYP	SLFVTTYP	FORMS

Figure 9.7 Cross reference report (*Part 2*)

enforcement. Any discrepancies or missing triggers can be noted for investigation. For example, Figure 9.10 shows the SQL required to check for the existence of SQL statements that will enforce referential integrity within SQL*Forms (these triggers are POST-CHANGE, POST-FIELD, and KEY-NXTFLD).

9.4 Documenting Reference Tables and Data

Reference tables require special documentation because we need to include both the structure of the table and the data within the table. There are several ways to produce this documentation. We could, of course, simply export the table once using the ORACLE export utility (exp) and then import it when needed. However, if we used this technique the export file itself could not be used as a documentation source and it could not be modified in any way (for example, if we need to change the data before it is reloaded). There are at least two good alternatives that

```
REM
REM   COLCROSS.SQL
REM   Cross Reference Report
REM   Lists each Column and the Applications that use the Column
REM
REM   Creator: Tim and Nicole
REM   Created: April 1990
REM
SET PAGESIZE 56
SET FEEDBACK OFF
REM
COLUMN COLUMN_NAME FORMAT A20 HEADING "Column Name"
COLUMN TABLE_NAME  FORMAT A10 HEADING "Table Name"
COLUMN NAME        FORMAT A20 HEADING "Application Name"
COLUMN TYPE        FORMAT A5  HEADING "Tool"
REM
BREAK ON COLUMN_NAME ON TABLE_NAME SKIP 2
REM
SELECT DISTINCT COLUMN_NAME, TABLE_NAME,
       UPPER(REPORT.NAME) NAME, 'SRW' TYPE
FROM   SRW_STE REPORT, SRW_STE FIELD, USER_TAB_COLUMNS
WHERE  REPORT.APPID = FIELD.APPID
AND    REPORT.TYPE = 1
AND    FIELD.TYPE = 4
AND    UPPER(FIELD.NAME) LIKE '%'||USER_TAB_COLUMNS.COLUMN_NAME||'%'
UNION
SELECT DISTINCT COLUMN_NAME, TABLE_NAME,
       UPPER(IAPAPP.APPNAME) NAME, 'FORMS' TYPE
FROM   IAPSQLTXT, IAPFLD, IAPAPP, USER_TAB_COLUMNS
WHERE  (IAPAPP.APPID = IAPFLD.FLDAPPID AND
       IAPFLD.FLDNAME = USER_TAB_COLUMNS.COLUMN_NAME)
OR     (IAPAPP.APPID = IAPSQLTXT.SQTAPPID AND
       IAPSQLTXT.SQTTEXT LIKE '%'||USER_TAB_COLUMNS.COLUMN_NAME||'%')
AND    IAPAPP.APPOWNER = 'THOECHST'
ORDER BY 1, 2;
```

PRODUCES:

Column Name	Table Name	Application Name	Tool
EMPL_EMPL_NUM_MGR	SGENEMPL	SGENEMPL	FORMS
EMPL_FACL_NUM	SGENEMPL	MINVSMVE	FORMS
		MINVSQTY	FORMS
		MINVTRAN	FORMS
		MINVWQTY	FORMS
		SGENELFV	FORMS
		SGENEMPL	FORMS
EMPL_HIRE_DATE	SGENEMPL	SGENEMPL	FORMS
EMPL_NAME_FIRST	SGENEMPL	SGENELFV	FORMS
		SGENEMPL	FORMS
EMPL_NAME_LAST	SGENEMPL	SGENELFV	FORMS
		SGENEMPL	FORMS
EMPL_NUM	SGENEMPL	MINVSMVE	FORMS
		MINVSQTY	FORMS
		MINVTRAN	FORMS
		MINVWQTY	FORMS
		SGENELFV	FORMS
		SGENEMPL	FORMS

Figure 9.8 Sample column cross reference report (*Part 1*)

EMPL_OFFC_NUM	SGENEMPL	SGENELFV	FORMS
		SGENEMPL	FORMS
EMPL_SOC_SEC_NUMBER	SGENEMPL	SGENELFV	FORMS
		SGENEMPL	FORMS
EMPL_TITLE	SGENEMPL	SGENEMPL	FORMS
EMPL_USERID	SGENEMPL	SGENEMPL	FORMS
FACL_ADDR_CITY	MINVFACL	MINVFLFV	FORMS
		MINVSTOR	FORMS
		MINVWARE	FORMS
	MINVSTOR	MINVFLFV	FORMS
		MINVSTOR	FORMS
		MINVWARE	FORMS
	MINVWARE	MINVFLFV	FORMS
		MINVSTOR	FORMS
		MINVWARE	FORMS
FACL_ADDR_FAX_NUMBER	MINVFACL	MINVSTOR	FORMS
		MINVWARE	FORMS
	MINVSTOR	MINVSTOR	FORMS
		MINVWARE	FORMS
	MINVWARE	MINVSTOR	FORMS
		MINVWARE	FORMS
FACL_ADDR_PHONE_NUMBER	MINVFACL	MINVSTOR	FORMS
		MINVWARE	FORMS
	MINVSTOR	MINVSTOR	FORMS
		MINVWARE	FORMS
	MINVWARE	MINVSTOR	FORMS
		MINVWARE	FORMS
FACL_ADDR_STATE	MINVFACL	MINVFLFV	FORMS
		MINVSTOR	FORMS
		MINVWARE	FORMS
	MINVSTOR	MINVFLFV	FORMS
		MINVSTOR	FORMS
		MINVWARE	FORMS

output continues ...

Figure 9.8 Sample column cross reference report (*Part 2*)

```
REM
REM    Select all Foreign Key References
REM
SET PAGESIZE 56
SET FEEDBACK OFF
REM
COLUMN TABLE_NAME  FORMAT A10 HEADING "Table Name"
COLUMN COLUMN_NAME FORMAT A30 HEADING "Column Name"
COLUMN FK_NAME     FORMAT A10 HEADING "FK Table"
REM
BREAK ON TABLE_NAME SKIP 1
REM
SELECT USER_CONS_COLUMNS.TABLE_NAME,
       USER_CONS_COLUMNS.COLUMN_NAME,
       FK.TABLE_NAME FK_NAME
FROM   USER_CONS_COLUMNS, USER_CONSTRAINTS, USER_CONSTRAINTS FK
WHERE  USER_CONSTRAINTS.CONSTRAINT_NAME = USER_CONS_COLUMNS.CONSTRAINT_NAME
AND    USER_CONSTRAINTS.R_CONSTRAINT_NAME = FK.CONSTRAINT_NAME
AND    USER_CONSTRAINTS.CONSTRAINT_TYPE = 'R'
ORDER BY 1, 2;
```

PRODUCES:

```
Table Name Column Name                         FK Table
---------- ----------------------------------  ----------
MINVFACL   FACL_OFFC_NUM_MGR                    SGENOFFC

MINVFCLS   FCLS_FACL_NUM                        MINVFACL
           FCLS_ICLS_CODE                       SLFVICLS

MINVITEM   ITEM_FACL_NUM                        MINVFACL
           ITEM_ICLS_CODE                       SLFVICLS
           ITEM_ORDR_NUM                        MINVORDR

MINVMOVE   MOVE_FACL_NUM_FROM                   MINVFACL
           MOVE_FACL_NUM_TO                     MINVFACL
           MOVE_ICLS_CODE                       SLFVICLS

MINVORDR   ORDR_FACL_NUM_WARE                   MINVFACL
           ORDR_ICLS_CODE                       SLFVICLS
           ORDR_SHIP_NUM                        MINVSHIP
           ORDR_SUPP_NUM                        MINVSUPP

MINVSCLS   SCLS_ICLS_CODE                       SLFVICLS
           SCLS_SUPP_NUM                        MINVSUPP

MINVSHIP   SHIP_FACL_NUM_WARE                   MINVFACL
           SHIP_SUPP_NUM                        MINVSUPP

MINVTRAN   TRAN_EMPL_NUM                        SGENEMPL
           TRAN_FACL_NUM_STOR                   MINVFACL
           TRAN_ITEM_NUM                        MINVITEM
           TRAN_TTYP_CODE                       SLFVTTYP

SGENEMPL   EMPL_EMPL_NUM_MGR                    SGENEMPL
           EMPL_FACL_NUM                        MINVFACL
           EMPL_OFFC_NUM                        SGENOFFC

SGENMENU   MENU_APPL_NAME                       SGENAPPL

SLFVICLS   ICLS_ICLS_CODE                       SLFVICLS
```

Figure 9.9 Sample data integrity report

```
REM
REM    INTEGRITY.SQL
REM    This report selects the names of all forms that
REM    do not enforce a foreign key reference
REM
REM    Creator:   Tim and Nicole
REM    Created:   April 1990
REM
SET PAGESIZE 56
SET FEEDBACK OFF
REM
TTITLE CENTER "Fields Missing Foreign Key Reference Triggers" SKIP 2
REM
COLUMN FORM  FORMAT A10 HEADING "Form Name"
COLUMN FIELD FORMAT A30 HEADING "Field Name"
REM
SELECT DISTINCT UPPER(APPNAME) FORM, FLDNAME FIELD
FROM    USER_CONS_COLUMNS, USER_CONSTRAINTS, USER_CONSTRAINTS FK,
        IAPFLD, IAPAPP
WHERE   IAPAPP.APPID = IAPFLD.FLDAPPID
AND     USER_CONSTRAINTS.CONSTRAINT_NAME = USER_CONS_COLUMNS.CONSTRAINT_NAME
AND     USER_CONSTRAINTS.CONSTRAINT_TYPE = 'R'
AND     USER_CONSTRAINTS.R_CONSTRAINT_NAME = FK.CONSTRAINT_NAME
AND     IAPFLD.FLDNAME = USER_CONS_COLUMNS.COLUMN_NAME
AND NOT EXISTS
        (SELECT 'X' FROM IAPSQLTXT, IAPTRG
         WHERE  IAPTRG.TRGTYPE IN ('POST-CHANGE','POST-FIELD','KEY-NXTFLD')
         AND    IAPSQLTXT.SQTTEXT LIKE '%'||FK.TABLE_NAME||'%'
         AND    IAPTRG.TRGSQL = IAPSQLTXT.SQTNO
         AND    IAPTRG.TRGFLD = IAPFLD.FLDNAME
         AND    IAPSQLTXT.SQTAPPID = IAPAPP.APPID
         AND    IAPFLD.FLDAPPID = IAPAPP.APPID);
```

PRODUCES:

```
                Fields Missing Foreign Key Reference Triggers

Form Name   Field Name
----------  ------------------------------
MINVSUPP    SCLS_ICLS_CODE
```

Figure 9.10 Sample SQL*Forms integrity report

provide more flexibility. The first is a report that creates a SQL script full
of the INSERT statements that would refill the table when necessary.
Using this method you can even generate the CREATE TABLE statement as part of your script. (This is, for all intents and purposes, what
CASE*Dictionary does when it is used to create tables.) We described
this method as a hint in Section 4.9.

The creation of the dynamic SQL files is a relatively simple task if you
create a customized report for each table. Once all the tables are created
and loaded, however, it would be better to have a single utility that
produced scripts for all load files for all of the tables. We recommend a
report that generates a SQL*Loader control file that can rebuild the
table and reload the data. Such a file is far easier to construct for all

```
.REM
.REM    SQL*Report Program
.REM    to create SQL*Loader CTL file
.REM
#DT 1 1 80 #
.REM
.DECLARE TABLE_NAME      A8
.DECLARE COLUMN_NAME     A50
.REM
.DEFINE sel_columns
        SELECT COLUMN_NAME
        INTO   COLUMN_NAME
        FROM   USER_TAB_COLUMNS
        WHERE  TABLE_NAME = &TABLE_NAME
..
.REM
.REM  Create Control File Header Information
.REM
.DEFINE body
        #S 2
        LOAD DATA #NC
        INFILE
        .PRINT TABLE_NAME
        #CONCAT
        .dat
        #NC
        INTO TABLE
        .PRINT table_name
        #NC
        FIELDS TERMINATED BY "," #NC
        (
        .REPORT sel_columns column_body column_head
        ) #NC
..
.REM
.REM  List each Column
.REM
.DEFINE column_head
        .PRINT column_name
..
.REM
.DEFINE column_body
        , #NC
        .PRINT column_name
..
.REM
#T 1
.ASK "Please enter table name: " TABLE_NAME
.body
#TE
```

Figure 9.11 Report to create SQL*Loader file

tables based on the data dictionary. Also, SQL*Loader control files are easier to modify than dynamic SQL when the data changes. A portion of the report used to create SQL*Loader control files is shown in Figure 9.11.

9.5 Conclusion

The application is finally developed, tested, tuned, and documented. Our project's lifecycle is complete—and we are ready to start over and enhance the MegaMarket application. We hope that sharing our development experiences have provided ideas and insight for yours.

Chapter 10, our final chapter, explores some areas outside the application development process. These include distributed processing, archiving, and executive information systems. We will also touch on some of the new Oracle product releases that may affect your development process. For example, SQL*Forms 3.0 and SQL*Menu 5.0 significantly change the way you present information to the user (but do not change the application development process).

10

Additional Development and Software Topics

10.1 Introduction

Although we've discussed many topics so far, there are a few more issues we should consider. These topics may or may not apply to your application development effort, but you should think about them regardless. Many of these topics could fill volumes by themselves, but we will just present a brief introduction to each—enough information to help you evaluate the issues during your development process. We will begin with distributed processing and distributed databases, continue with security, archiving, and auditing, move into ad hoc reporting databases and executive information systems, and close with an overview of the Oracle products that you can expect to see in the near future.

10.2 Distributed Processing

Over the past ten years computer technology has advanced at an incredible pace, but the size and amount of information being stored and managed has grown even faster. The result is that databases are large and getting larger and applications are complex and becoming more complex.

Consider the circumstances of the MegaMarket application. The initial release of the application will be installed at the stores and warehouses managed by 10 administrative offices (one in each region of the country), managing a total of 50 warehouses and 250 retail stores. The remaining administrative offices, 50 in all, are to be brought online during the next five years. The MegaMarket application and the ORACLE databases reside on a large mainframe computer located at MegaMarket corporate headquarters, which most end users will access from their desktop personal computers. How can we manage such a large application and provide acceptable response time to our end users?

The logical solution would be to implement a distributed architecture. As a first step, we can move the MegaMarket applications down to the personal workstations and leave the database on the mainframe. This arrangement is called distributed processing, and is also referred to as a client-server architecture. The client in this case is the personal computer and the server is the mainframe that houses the ORACLE databases. The key benefit of this architecture is that the personal computer is no longer acting as a dumb terminal, but actually executes the application code. The mainframe database server is only accessed to resolve database requests. Thus, much of the processing load is offloaded from the mainframe and distributed among the personal computers.

SQL*Net is the Oracle software that resides on both sides of the connection between client and server. The SQL*Net program on the client passes SQL requests to the SQL*Net program on the server, using any of the several network protocols that Oracle supports for distributed processing. We can't speak of SQL*Net without speaking of the specific protocol for the product. For instance, SQL*Net for NetBIOS and SQL*Net for TCP/IP are two different versions of the SQL*Net program for two different operating systems.

We decided to distribute the MegaMarket application in the first year of implementation. To accomplish this, we developed a methodology for downloading and controlling the code that will reside on the personal computers. This code includes both the application code (both initial releases and maintenance releases) and the Oracle code (all of the tools we use in our application).

In this case, deciding where to put each component of the software was relatively simple. You may find that your environment includes more hardware and software considerations. When trying to decide what software (and consequently what tasks) should be run on each machine in the network, you should consider what each of the machines does best. For example, the mainframe handles many users and lots of disk space effectively, while it is not very good at providing a fast and graphical user interface. The personal computer, on the other hand, cannot handle many users, but can interact with the user graphically and quickly. This is why we decided to let the mainframe handle the database functions, while the PC handles the applications. You should be able to apply similar reasoning to the hardware configuration in your organization.

10.3 Distributed Databases

Distributing the application will temporarily alleviate the processing requirements for the MegaMarket system, but the long-term expansion of the user base and the size of the database itself will eventually make this solution unacceptable. Although the application processing has been offloaded, the large number of users accessing the database will cause the mainframe to slow down as well. The next step we can take is to distribute both the application and the data. For example, we could move some parts of the data to either other mainframes or all the way down to the personal computers. We could also introduce minicomputers and distribute the data across multiple machines. The architecture choices are almost unlimited—as is the complexity that will result. Distributing data, unlike distributing processing, is a big step to take.

We developed an overall plan for distributing the MegaMarket data to be executed following the implementation of distributed processing. We decided that two years after the initial implementation, we will distribute region-specific data to separate processors, thus moving the data closer to the end users and reducing the likelihood of performance bottlenecks on the mainframe. To do this, we will explore the use of SQL*Server, the ORACLE RDBMS for the OS/2 Server. This product is an important addition to the Oracle product line because it brings a full Version 6.0 implementation of the ORACLE RDBMS to the more manageable personal computing environment. Since it can also be connected to larger machines, it provides a very practical solution to the problem of database distribution.

We still must develop many difficult administrative procedures before we can implement this architecture. We must determine the process for reporting across all of the regional processors as well as how to assign sequence numbers across processors. And how do we handle the movement of a supplier to another region or the movement of items from a warehouse in one region to a warehouse in another region? Solving these problems will require a very sophisticated distributed database. Although Version 6.0 of the ORACLE RDBMS lacks many of the necessary features, Version 7.0 will include them. Version 7.0 is discussed in Section 10.9.7.

Distributed databases are definitely the future of information management—the key word being *future*. The complexity of the network and the complications of rolling transactions up to a host and processing mass distributed requests mean that a new generation of software will be necessary. Take heart, because the standards that have been and are still being defined within the database industry should enable you to distribute existing databases very easily once the technology is secure. You will not need to start over by any means.

Process and *Data Distribution*

Remember that distributing the data and distributing the processing are not mutually exclusive. It is also common that a combination of the two is most appropriate. For example, you may have minicomputers in each region with the database distributed across them. Then each user can access these databases from their personal computers thus distributing the processing as well. The technology for such a setup is really no different from using just one of the methods.

10.4 Security Management

The ORACLE RDBMS provides some facilities for security management. These facilities fall into two general categories: authorizing the userid and password of anyone that can connect to the database, and restricting the data (tables and views) that are accessible by each userid for insert, update, delete, and query. Together, these features usually meet all of the security needs of an application.

Our application uses the ORACLE security management features to control the user environment. We use GRANT commands to create individual userids and to determine the privileges of the user. Since our application covers a broad geographic area, we use the WITH GRANT OPTION version of the GRANT statement. This feature allows us to distribute the control and maintenance of userids to individuals in the various administrative offices.

Each new user must first be given a password and then be GRANTed access to the appropriate application tables. Because of the large number of tables in our application, executing the GRANT statements can be tedious and maintaining the privileges can be even more difficult. We chose an approach that is based on the concept of *user roles*. Each user is classified—given a role—according to table security requirements. Two SQL scripts are developed—one containing all of the appropriate GRANT statements and another with the corresponding REVOKE statements—for each role. When a new user is added to the system, the security administrator in the administrative office classifies the user and executes the appropriate SQL script. Version 7.0 of the RDBMS will provide for roles in the database itself (see Section 10.9.6 for details).

We used a similar philosophy at the application level. We modified our menu system written in SQL*Forms (described in Section 5.6.3) to query a security table to determine the menu selections that should be displayed for each individual userid. Thus, we can make available all of an application (all of its forms and reports) or only certain pieces of it (some of its forms and reports). The role assigned to a user by the security administrator with the GRANT scripts will determine his role in our menu system. (You could use SQL*Menu to provide the same functionality.)

10.5 Auditing

Security often overlaps the area of auditing. Auditing in ORACLE terms means the recording of activity within the RDBMS. For instance, we may choose to audit any DELETE statements issued against the transaction table, or any unsuccessful attempts to connect to the RDBMS. This type of audit is useful for monitoring a specific activity.

Another possibility is the creation of a true audit trail which records every change that occurs in the database, including the values before and after each change. For example, we might record that a user changed the city for an employee from "San Francisco" to "Oakland." The type of functionality that stores both of these values must be written into the application. Several approaches can be used to accomplish this; one straightforward one is to create an audit database that contains all of the tables in the application. You could then write triggers into each application to force any row that is modified to be written to the audit database. Remember that any type of auditing requires extra processing within the application, which will degrade the performance of the system.

10.6 Archiving

The issue of archiving, or moving data offline to permanent storage, is usually ignored until the later stages of application development. This is typical because the distinctions between online and offline data are difficult to determine prior to the implementation of the system. The user requirements and expectations are very difficult to determine. The key question that must be answered is "How long must the application data be kept online?" Unfortunately, users will almost always answer "forever," and will not understand the cost of this choice until response time is affected.

The archiving process typically requires the development of programs that regularly extract data from the production database and store it offline. In reviewing our archiving requirements, we realized that the MegaMarket database provided no facilities for an extract. We had no way of knowing when a row was last updated and therefore no way of knowing which data was ready for archiving. To correct this oversight, we had to go back and add a "last modified" column to every table in the database. This gives us a way of removing data from the production database when it reaches a certain age, which is calculated by comparing its last modification data with the current date. To implement this, of course, we had to go back and modify all of our applications to record the date in the "last modified" column. This omission obviously caused us to lose a great deal of development time.

Another decision related to archiving is the process of "de-archiving" the data. For archived data to be useful, there must be a mechanism for bringing the data back into the production database. This portion of the process requires very careful preparation to eliminate the possibility of overlaying production data or creating integrity errors. One solution is to load the archived information into a separate temporary archive database, so that queries can simply be run against this database without destroying the integrity of the production data.

10.7 Executive Information Systems

Although systems built with SQL*Forms and SQL*Reportwriter are usually easy to use, sometimes they need to be simplified for casual or "executive" users. Because such users rarely want to modify the data, but do need to see it presented in a straightforward format, a separate set of applications is often built to meet these particular needs. These applications are called *executive information systems*. Although these users do not need a separate database, they do need a special set of applications designed with their particular needs in mind.

Several Oracle tools can effectively be used to develop executive information systems. The most obvious is SQL*Forms. It is not difficult to build a form that permits only queries and that provides summary or high-level information rather than the detailed, itemized data that might typically be used by a staff member. Such forms can even be sufficiently automated so that appropriate queries are performed with little or no direction from the user.

The Oracle tool that is perhaps most suited to the job of executive information systems, though, is ORACLE for the Macintosh. When Oracle ported the RDBMS to the Apple Macintosh, they implemented the entire kernel on the Mac as for any other platform. They did not, however, bring the tools with the kernel. (For portability reasons, the tools will be included in a future release.) Rather than bringing SQL*Forms and SQL*Reportwriter (tools designed for character mode environments) to the graphic operating environment of the Mac, they decided to take advantage of the application development tools already available on the Mac, the most important of which is HyperCard.

HyperCard, an Apple product that comes with every Macintosh, is basically an application development tool for people who know nothing about programming. It is an object-oriented development environment that allows the user to integrate fields, "buttons," text, and graphics together through the use of an English-like language called HyperTalk. HyperTalk programs are simply "scripts" that control what happens when the mouse is clicked on a button, when a key is typed in a field, and so on. Oracle has provided the capability of adding SQL to HyperTalk scripts. So now these scripts can query the database, manipulate the results, and display them on the screen amid HyperCard graphics.

With these capabilities, an intuitive, mouse-driven application can query ORACLE data and display it along with pictures and sound. All of this together provides an ideal environment for the executive who wants to click the mouse a few times and then view up-to-the-minute data in summary and graphical formats.

10.8 Reporting Databases

One of the strongest selling points of a relational database is that the end user can learn to write SQL queries on an "ad hoc" basis. Natural language interfaces and executive information systems make it even easier for users to extract information at will, but there are costs associated with providing all of this functionality directly to the end user. Knowing what we learned in Chapter 8 about performance and full table scans, would you let an end user loose on your production system? This is a common data processing dilemma. We want to provide a system that meets the users' needs, but we must also exercise a degree of control over the users' information requests to prevent a query from bringing the entire mainframe to a crawl.

One solution is to create a separate reporting database (preferably on a separate processor) for ad hoc requests. Such a database would be created from the production data and updated on a regular basis. An end user can issue any request to this database at any time without affecting the performance of the online production system. The drawback of this solution is that the reporting data is no longer "real time," but only as current as the last reporting database update. While this may seem at first glance like a prohibitive drawback, we have found that most users find the reporting database solution fully acceptable.

A similar approach is to develop a set of tables in the production database that contain summary information. This information can be continually maintained by the production applications or can be created each day during a nightly update. End user requests almost always involve mostly summary statistical data; this approach provides that information without draining the resources of the production system.

10.9 Future Oracle Software

In this section, we will briefly cover some of the Oracle products that were in development or were still quite new when we wrote the book (early 1990).

10.9.1 PL/SQL

One of the difficult aspects of using SQL is that most of us are more familiar with procedural than nonprocedural programming languages. In procedural languages like C or COBOL, we give each instruction in the order that it is to occur, "Do this, then do that, and if this is true then do something else ..." In SQL, on the other hand, we use a single statement to say, "Find the rows that satisfy some criteria and change a column value to the result returned from selecting some row from this table." We are more used to if-then logic and looping than we are to the nonprocedural syntax found in SQL. As a result, SQL can be difficult to grasp at first. The difficulty is not with SQL, however, but with how we are used to thinking. We look for procedural solutions to problems and then get frustrated when we can't make SQL do the job. It is common for people in this situation to resort to a 3GL with which they feel more comfortable. To help address this need and to help provide a common ground for integration between the development tools, Oracle introduced a product called *PL/SQL* with Version 6.0 of the RDBMS. PL/SQL is a procedural extension to SQL. This means that you can utilize standard procedural constructs (like if-then logic, looping, local variables, and so on) along with SQL.

PL/SQL doesn't increase the functionality of SQL itself, but it does give you a new tool to use with SQL so you don't have to resort to a 3GL. More important, though, is the fact that PL/SQL has been integrated into the tool set so that you can use it in SQL*Plus, SQL*Menu, SQL*Forms and almost anywhere else. As you can imagine, this improves the flexibility of these tools by giving them ways to manipulate the data returned by SQL statements, something SQL alone cannot do. Another powerful benefit of PL/SQL is increased performance. Without PL/SQL, even simple comparisons and functions required individual database calls. For example, in SQL*Forms, in order to check if a field value is equal to 37, we must execute the SQL statement in Figure 10.1 and check to see whether or not it succeeds.

```
SELECT 'X'
FROM SYSTEM.DUAL
WHERE :fieldname = 37
```

Figure 10.1 Conditional logic in SQL

```
IF :fieldname = 37
THEN
   ...
ELSE
   ...
END IF;
```

Figure 10.2 Conditional logic in PL/SQL

With PL/SQL, we can simply use the code in Figure 10.2. This makes the actual comparison faster, but more importantly, it allows you to group statements together. Each PL/SQL block is treated as a single statement. The result is that many SQL statements as well as if-then logic and looping can be combined into a single statement and sent to the database. The performance gains are greatest when each SQL statement must pass through SQL*Net over a network to the database server.

PL/SQL statements are combined into logical blocks that are enclosed by BEGIN and END. Each PL/SQL or SQL statement in one of these blocks is terminated with a semicolon. You'll find that the syntax for PL/SQL is not unlike that of Pascal. Local variables can be declared within blocks and most of the SQL functions can be used in PL/SQL expressions. We will see how PL/SQL is integrated with the other tools in the following sections, but for now you can get a feel for PL/SQL from an example. The PL/SQL block shown in Figure 10.3 could be typed right into SQL*Plus and would INSERT rows into the table *tablename*.

```
BEGIN
  FOR i IN 1..100 LOOP
    IF (i = 16
      OR
       i BETWEEN 75 AND 85)
    THEN
      INSERT INTO tablename
        VALUES(sequencename.NEXTVAL, 'Counter Value:
          '||TO_CHAR(i));
    END IF;
  END LOOP;
END;
```

Figure 10.3 Sample PL/SQL block

10.9.2 SQL*Forms 3.0

Of all the new products being released in 1990, SQL*Forms 3.0 is perhaps the most exciting. Because SQL*Forms is the most widely used of the application development tools, a revised version has been anxiously awaited. Since SQL*Forms 3.0 offers so many new features, we won't be able to describe them all here, but we will mention some of the highlights.

First, SQL*Forms 3.0 is upwards compatible, so you will be able to use your existing applications. They will, of course, not take full advantage of the new features. For example, there is a new format for triggers in SQL*Forms 3.0, but you can still continue to write your triggers in the Version 2.0 format. We think that you will quickly adapt to the new format, and that you will prefer it to the old one eventually.

The most significant changes in SQL*Forms 3.0 are for the developer. Not only is the triggering syntax more flexible and powerful, but simply navigating the Designer is much easier. The entire structure of the Designer has been broken down into a set of pull-down menus so that with just a few keystrokes you can get to any spot in the form you are working on. Many locations can be reached directly via function keys as well. Once you become familiar with the menus, you'll discover that you can move around very quickly. Another important change to the layout is that form, block, field, and trigger information can always be displayed in one of two formats. First, you can view several at a time in a matrix format (similar to a multi-row block listing). This is very convenient when you are making a few changes to several different fields or triggers. Since most such listings will contain several columns, you can scroll horizontally as well as vertically. You can, however, always change the display with a single keystroke and see a particular object in full screen format (similar to a single-row block listing). This works well when you are making many changes to a single object. You will probably switch between formats quite often depending on exactly what sort of change you are making. Figure 10.4 shows the matrix screen format as it appears in the new Designer.

Many small features that may go unnoticed have been added to make life easier for developers. Field attributes are listed in a small pop-up window that is very simple to use. Whenever you leave a screen, your place is saved, so that when you return, the cursor is positioned where you left off. (This only applies within a session, of course.) This feature makes debugging triggers easier because you can edit a trigger, execute the form, and then return to your trigger with a single keystroke. The [NXTBLK] and [PRVBLK] keys work in the screen painter so that you

```
Action  foRm  Block  Field  Trigger  Procedure    Image  Help  Options
                              ▒▒▒▒▒▒▒▒▒▒
┌─────────────────────────────────────────────────────────────────────────┐
│                    Seq     Data        Select    Fld   Qry   Dis         │
│    Field Name      Num     Type      Attributes  Len   Len   Len    X    │
│  ▒▒▒▒▒▒▒▒▒▒▒        1     CHAR         ( * )      15    15    15    1     │
│  FIELD2             2     CHAR         ( * )      15    15    15    66    │
│  FIELD3             3     CHAR         ( * )      50    50    50    16    │
│  FIELD4             4     NUMBER       ( * )      10    10    1     1     │
│                                                                          │
│                                                                          │
│                                                                          │
│                                                                          │
│ ▒▒▒▒▒▒▒▒▒▒▒▒▒▒▒▒                                                     >   │
├──────────────────────────────────────────────────────────────────────────┤
│ ▒▒▒▒▒▒▒▒▒▒▒▒▒▒▒                                                           │
│Frm: FAA_PILOT    Blk: HEADER      Fld: FORMNAME    Trg:          <Rep>    │
└──────────────────────────────────────────────────────────────────────────┘
```

Figure 10.4 SQL*Forms 3.0 Designer

don't have to leave the painter and then come back just to switch blocks. You can navigate up and down the form hierarchy with the new [ZOOM IN] and [ZOOM OUT] function keys. For example, if you have the multiple block listing on the screen, you can position the cursor on a block and press [ZOOM IN] to list all of the fields in that block. Pressing [ZOOM IN] again would show all of the triggers for a field. [ZOOM OUT] brings you out of the hierarchy in the same fashion. You can also copy objects (fields, triggers, etc.) between forms or within a single form. By pressing the appropriate function key, you get a window that asks for a source (user, form, block, field, trigger) and a destination. The copy is then made instantly. These and other navigation features (among others) make moving about the Designer simple and efficient.

The next important feature of SQL*Forms 3.0 is the new way in which triggers are handled. At long last, the trigger editor is a full text editing window with wraparound. More important, though, is the new trigger format. SQL*Forms 3.0 triggers are based on PL/SQL. All of the macros from SQL*Forms 2.3 are still available, but now they are used as PL/SQL procedures (these are called *packaged procedures*). So every trigger has just one step, but it can be an entire PL/SQL script that performs IF-THEN checks, looping, packaged procedures, your own procedures, and so on. You can even maintain local PL/SQL variables in triggers if you like. Figure 10.5 is a simple Version 3.0 trigger that demonstrates how

```
BEGIN
  SELECT STATE_DESC
  INTO :fieldname1
  FROM STATE
  WHERE STATE_CODE = :fieldname2;

  IF :fieldname1 = 'AZ'
  THEN
    NEXT_BLOCK;
    EXECUTE_QUERY;
  ELSE
    GO_BLOCK('blockname');
    :fieldname3 := SUBSTR(:fieldname1,1,5);
  END IF;

EXCEPTION
  WHENEVER NO_DATA_FOUND
    MESSAGE('*ERROR* Invalid state code.');
    RAISE FORM_TRIGGER_FAILURE;
END;
```

Figure 10.5 SQL*Forms 3.0 trigger

PL/SQL is used in a form. Notice that the names for the packaged procedures are different from the macro names in SQL*Forms 2.3, but that they are more intuitive.

Whenever you leave the trigger editor, SQL*Forms will try to compile your PL/SQL for you. At this point, it checks your syntax, validates your SQL, and tells you if field references are incorrect or ambiguous. This improves development productivity because you don't have to wait until form generation or execution to discover simple errors.

PL/SQL routines can also be put into your own procedures that reside at the top level of the form, and can be called from any level within the form. This modular approach is a good way to maintain your forms because it simplifies moving modules between forms. More importantly, however, we will see that in Version 7.0 of the RDBMS, these procedures can be compiled once and then stored in the database to minimize storage and maximize performance.

Another important feature of SQL*Forms 3.0 is that it literally does much of your work for you. For example, when creating default blocks, you can specify that a parent-child relationship exists between two blocks, as well as which field is the common key. SQL*Forms 3.0 will then write all of the triggers in the parent block for complete block coordination. Lists of values have also been made much easier—to create one, you merely specify the title and position of the pop-up window and a SELECT statement that defines what should be listed. Thus, you can list virtually anything in the lookup window, since the SELECT statement can be as sophisticated as you like (even including DECODE or CONNECT BY). Whenever the user enters the field during execution, the symbol <LIST> automatically appears in the bottom right corner of the screen. When the user presses the [LIST FIELD VALUES] key, a pop-up window displays the results of your SELECT statement. This window also includes a field in which LIKE comparisons can be made to narrow the list and find a particular value more quickly. When the user presses COMMIT, the values are copied into the fields listed in the INTO clause of your SELECT statement. This can really add flare to applications, but it is not the only way that SQL*Forms 3.0 uses pop-up windows. For any character field, a pop-up editor window can be defined that allows the user to modify the field's value with a full-featured text editor that can even do string searches. This is particularly useful because SQL*Forms 3.0 supports LONG data types, so, you can now define a field that can contain thousands of characters and give the user an editor to modify its contents. You can also create your own pop-up windows. Each page in a form can be given a view that represents the "window" in which it will be displayed; then, when you go to a field on the page, it pops up on the screen. You can choose to keep it on the screen or have it disappear when leaving the page. You can also control these pop-ups from within triggers.

Finally, SQL*Forms 3.0 has a few new general features that are very helpful. There is a function key called [MENU] that displays a pull down menu bar across the top of the screen during execution. This menu can be either the default (which contains all of the SQL*Forms execution functions like [EXEQRY] or [NXTBLK]) or a SQL*Menu 5.0 menu of your own design. You can imagine the power that this offers, because, as we will see in the next section, SQL*Menu 5.0 applications that are called from SQL*Forms this way can use many of the packaged procedures available in triggers. So these menus can modify field values, call other forms, or execute your own procedures. SQL*Forms 3.0 also offers a very complete help system. Like all of the new tools, its help system has keyword search to help you quickly find the information you need. It also

Preparing for SQL*Forms 3.0

One way that you can prepare for SQL*Forms 3.0 is to take advantage of the integrity constraints available in the Version 6.0 table creation syntax (refer to Figure 4.8 for an example of these constraints). Although the database will not enforce these constraints until Version 7.0, you can have SQL*Forms 3.0 automatically build the triggers required to enforce them. SQL*Forms 3.0 can also use them to recognize the join conditions when it is building the block coordination triggers between two tables. These constraints not only help you document the relationships between your tables, but they will ease the development burden when SQL*Forms 3.0 is available.

allows you to place a "bookmark" on a particular help screen so that you can jump back to it with a single keystroke later. There are also many new SYSTEM variables available in SQL*Forms 3.0. For example, a new variable called SYSTEM.LAST_QUERY contains the query that was last executed including the query criteria entered by the user. This is extremely useful for two reasons. First, you can place this variable into a field to help yourself debug a form by looking at the queries SQL*Forms is building. Second, you can place this variable into a command file that is then sent to SQL*Plus. This allows you to use SQL*Forms as a dynamic report-generating tool and saves the user the trouble of printing the screens whenever he wants to save a query.

10.9.3 SQL*Menu 5.0

Like SQL*Forms 3.0, SQL*Menu 5.0 is a new version of an existing tool. We did not use SQL*Menu in our application because it is not as widely available to developers as SQL*Forms. That should change with Version 5.0. Because it is integrated with the rest of the tools and much easier to use than before, SQL*Menu 5.0 will become a very valuable tool in future development efforts.

The first important feature of SQL*Menu 5.0 is the consistency of the application development interface. It operates just like the SQL*Forms 3.0 Designer (with pull-down menus, two different display formats, zoom in, zoom out, and other features). This consistency makes learning SQL*Menu 5.0 very easy. A sophisticated menu can be constructed for an application in a matter of minutes.

Menu applications created with SQL*Menu can run on top of other programs and call forms, reports, other menus, or operating system commands. This makes it easy to create a consistent user interface for the execution of all programs in an application. SQL*Menu 5.0 supports three different menu styles: *pull-down, full screen,* and *Lotus-type.* The particular style, however, is not part of the menu definition, so any menu can be executed in any of the different styles. For example, when menus are executed from within SQL*Forms 3.0, they run in pull-down mode.

Security is also handled in a new way in SQL*Menu 5.0. Earlier versions used security *levels*; the developer could define multiple levels of access and give particular menu options a minimum level. Any user assigned to that level or a higher one would see the option on his menu. In SQL*Menu 5.0, security is handled with groups or *roles.* Now each menu item and each user are explicitly assigned to one or more roles; if a user is in the right group for a menu option, he can access it. Roles permit a more flexible and realistic division of responsibility throughout the menu hierarchy. The use of roles is also more consistent with the security directions that will be taken by Version 7.0 of the RDBMS (see Section 10.8.6).

When you define a menu item in SQL*Menu, you associate it with either another menu or an action to be performed. These actions can include calls to SQL*Forms, SQL*Reportwriter, SQL*Plus, or any of the other ORACLE tools, operating system commands, or SQL*Menu macros. Most importantly, though, you can use single- and multiple-step PL/SQL procedures in your SQL*Menu applications. These PL/SQL blocks can also be put into modular procedures that can be called from any of your items. With Version 7.0 of the RDBMS, these procedures will be compiled and stored in the database for general use. With all of these options, the function performed by an individual menu item can be very simple or very complex.

When SQL*Forms 3.0 and SQL*Menu 5.0 are linked together, you can use the two in tandem to give applications a professional, polished look. As we mentioned in the previous section, a SQL*Forms 3.0 application can have an associated menu that is shown at the top of the screen during execution of the form when the [MENU] key is pressed. The PL/SQL procedures called from the selections in such menus can reference objects in the form and call many of the packaged procedures offered in SQL*Forms 3.0.

10.9.4 The CASE*Tools

CASE*Dictionary, CASE*Designer, and CASE*Generator are three Oracle products that help to automate the task of developing a database design within the ORACLE RDBMS environment. These aren't really "future" tools, because they are available on many platforms already, but since CASE*Designer requires a bitmapped interface, the complete set is only now becoming widely used. (See Chapter 2 for more on data modeling.)

CASE*Dictionary is the main component of the CASE tool set. It is a collection of tables and SQL*Forms applications that store information about a database design in an ORACLE database so that the model can be easily validated and documented. Since the information that is stored in CASE*Dictionary can be accessed by multiple users, it is ideal in large development efforts for managing every detail of a database design. Once the data entry is complete, not only can reports be generated, but the SQL scripts used to create the actual tables and indexes can be produced automatically.

CASE*Designer is a graphical interface to CASE*Dictionary that provides the analyst with bitmapped graphics tools that produce the relevant diagrams and maintain the data in CASE*Dictionary. Instead of using SQL*Forms to enter or modify CASE*Dictionary information, the analyst can use CASE*Designer to simply draw Entity/Relationship diagrams, Function Hierarchies, and Data Flow Diagrams using a mouse and intuitive object-oriented drawing tools. CASE*Designer can, of course, print these diagrams so they can be made part of the design documentation.

Finally, CASE*Generator is a new tool that can produce sophisticated SQL*Forms applications based on the information in CASE*Dictionary. After all of the analysis and design data has been entered into CASE*Dictionary, CASE*Generator uses it to construct SQL*Forms applications that include complex triggers to support the validation described in CASE*Dictionary and maintain key relationships. These applications are not intended to be a final product, but they provide an excellent starting point and really only need to be customized to suit particular needs.

The CASE tools help to manage large database development efforts in a complete, organized way. They are easy to use, they help you to make sure that no steps have been skipped, and they can even give you a head start on the development of your SQL*Forms applications.

10.9.5 ORACLE*Graphics

ORACLE*Graphics is a tool that provides a brand new way of viewing ORACLE data. Through a bitmapped environment, you can create complex graphs of ORACLE data that can be displayed in color and modified automatically as the data changes. This sort of interface is brand new for ORACLE users, and it represents a departure from the sterility of text-only data display (caused by the need for complete portability restricting users to character- and block-mode terminals). This product is not portable to all machines that run ORACLE, but it will be an extremely powerful tool for users with the hardware to support it. Remember, though, that you can use SQL*Net to talk with *any* ORACLE database.

ORACLE*Graphics utilizes a bitmapped menu and windowing environment to display *charts*. A chart has two components: a tabular and a graphic representation of some data. A data table (which resembles a spreadsheet but lacks the data manipulation functionality of a spreadsheet program) is used as a place to organize the data that will be graphed. A data table can be filled in by hand, from an external file, or, more importantly, with the results of a SQL statement. Once the table is populated, its contents can be modified or graphed in bar, column, scatter, and pie (among others) formats. These graphs can viewed in full color and edited to change shades, patterns, text and so on.

When the data table in an ORACLE*Graphics chart is populated from the database, the SQL statement that retrieves the data can be *linked* to the chart. Then, whenever the chart is updated, the SQL will be reexecuted and the latest data displayed. Updates to the chart can be issued explicitly or set with a timer to occur periodically. You can even set thresholds for individual chart values that cause the color or pattern of the associated graphic component to change when the value crosses the threshold. Using this feature, you can make charts into unique, animated graphical representations of ORACLE data.

Also built into ORACLE*Graphics is a *page layout* environment that allows you to mix one or more charts with text data, static text, and pictures to create unified visual displays. And charts that are part of such layouts can maintain their link to the database and be automatically updated.

In our application, we could easily use ORACLE*Graphics to show inventory levels at different stores. A map could be used that had a picture of each store on it. In each store, a bar chart could represent the current inventory level of a chosen item. As inventory levels change, the chart would reflect this giving us a visual way of seeing product movement.

10.9.6 ORACLE Version 7.0

Version 7.0 will be the next major release of the ORACLE RDBMS. Many of the Version 7.0 features are still on the drawing board as we write, but some will definitely be included. The first advantage of the Version 7.0 database will be improved performance. Every release of the RDBMS has provided additional performance enhancements. These enhancements will come through modifications to the optimizer (which was not changed in Version 6.0). Another feature will be the implementation of referential integrity. Version 6.0 allows for the documentation of integrity constraints (for instance, noting that a column is a foreign key); Version 7.0 will enforce these rules at the database level to help prevent the entry of invalid data through any application.

Full distributed database capabilities will also be incorporated into Version 7.0, including the two-phase commit which will let a single transaction update more than one table. (This will help us with the problem described in Section 3.2.5 of distinguishing a logical transaction from a physical one.) This will also allow for the distribution of all operations (query, insert, update, and delete). Version 6.0 only allows for the distribution of queries.

Version 7.0 will also provide for *stored procedures*. This means that PL/ SQL procedures will be compiled and then stored in the database. These procedures will either be called explicitly by an application or they will be tied to database events (an update to a table, for example). So, you will be able to produce sophisticated data validation procedures and make sure they get executed whenever data is added to the table.

Finally, Version 7.0 will offer greatly improved security features. Not only will it allow for the definition of user roles at the database level, but the database auditing procedures will be improved, and the database administration functions will be made more granular so that the giving administration privileges is not an all or nothing proposition. (For you security buffs, these features will make Version 7.0 of the RDBMS compliant with level C2 of the Trusted Database Interpretation of the Orange Book security standards document.)

10.10 Conclusion

In the last section of this chapter, we attempted to give you a glimpse of what to expect from future Oracle products. This is, of course, only the tip of the iceberg because Oracle's product line is expanding rapidly into office automation, manufacturing, finance, and many other areas. We hope this discussion will help you determine the direction of your database systems development efforts by showing you Oracle's own directions.

We hope that this book has shown you how to structure your ORACLE development projects and taught you a few tricks for implementing interesting applications. It is important to remember that what we have presented is just a beginning—you should experiment with our ideas to develop methods that suit your individual needs. You may find that much of what we have discussed can fit right into your own projects, while other things will just trigger new ideas. We wish you the best of luck with all of your development efforts and we hope that we've been able to help you through some of the rough spots.

Development Checklist
for an ORACLE Application

☐   1   Create the data model
☐   2   Create the physical model
         Refine relationships (1:1, 1:M, M:M)
         Make physical implementation choices
☐   3   Define the software management environment
☐   4   Define the ORACLE environment
☐   5   Determine naming conventions
☐   6   Define an application goal
☐   7   Determine environment creation strategy
☐   8   Develop SQL*Forms standards
☐   9   Write SQL*Forms specifications
☐ 10   Perform forms design review
☐ 11   Create skeleton forms
         Application Skeleton
         List Field Values Skeleton
☐ 12   Develop utility subsystems
         Menu system
         Help system
☐ 13   Build the default forms
☐ 14   Review form layout with users
☐ 15   Complete the forms
☐ 16   Unit test the forms
☐ 17   Develop report standards
☐ 18   Write report specifications

❑ **19** Perform report design review
❑ **20** Create skeleton reports
❑ **21** Build the reports
❑ **22** Unit test the reports
❑ **23** Interface reports and forms
❑ **24** Perform portability review
❑ **25** Migrate old data
❑ **26** Test the integrated applications
❑ **27** Tune the integrated system
❑ **28** Complete the documentation
         User documentation
         Technical documentation

MegaMarket Forms Standards

Creator: Nicole and Tim
Created: September, 1989

—Change Log—

DESCRIPTION	DATE	NAME
Original Standards	Sept 89	Nicole and Tim
Added Message Formats	Sept 89	Nicole
Changed CODE flds in CTRL blk	Oct 89	Nicole
Changed Field Positions	Oct 89	Tim

Introduction

Following are guidelines for the development of SQL*Forms in the MegaMarket application. These guidelines describe cosmetics, naming conventions, operational guidelines, and coding standards for all SQL*Forms applications.

Naming Conventions

- All form, block, field, trigger names will be capitalized
- All form names will follow the file naming conventions
- All database block names will be the name of the base table
- Any second block with the same base table will be base_table2
- The standard header information block will be HEADER

- All non-database block names will be CTRL
- All database field names must be the database field name
- All non-database fields (except those in the CTRL block) will be CTRL_field_function
- All CTRL fields for CODE input will be YZZZFUNC_XXXX_DESC (for auto LFV automation)
- All CTRL fields for DESC display will be CTRL_XXXX_DESC
- Any second field with the same name (function) will be CTRL_field_function2 (such as CTRL_DATE2)
- All user-named triggers follow these guidelines:

COORD_PAGEn	coordinate blocks on a page n
COPY_	copy field(s) to other field(s)
DATE_	date conversions
GLOBALS_	global field manipulations
START_	form initialization functions

Messages

- All Function Key references will be the FUNCTION name
- All Function Key references will be capitalized
- All trigger failures will provide a message in this format:
  TYPE Short message; What to do.
  (where TYPE is ERROR, WARNING, SYSTEM ERROR)
  Example:
  ERROR Invalid transaction type code; press LIST VALUES for valid transaction types.
- Most fields will provide AUTOHELP in the following format:
  Enter field function; values/format/other help.
  Example:
  Enter transaction type code; press LIST FIELD VALUES for valid transaction types.

Cosmetics

- All forms will contain the standard header (see operation stds)
- All blocks will be enclosed in a "box" of graphics
- The first line of the box will be a left justified desc of the block function (like index cards)
- All labels for fields will be mixed case
- All labels will capitalize first letter of each word

- All labels will be aligned
  - Small Label: Very Big Label:
  - Tiny Label: Medium Label:
- All labels for single-row displays will be to the left
- All labels for multi-row displays will be above and to the left

Operation (Skeletons)

Two skeleton forms have been developed that provide standard triggers. These skeletons must be used as a basis for every form.

The main triggers provided in the application skeleton are:

KEY-HELP	to access SQL*Forms help
KEY-F0	to access the dynamic help subsystem
KEY-LISTVAL	to automate calling list value forms
KEY-OTHERS	to turn off ALL keys at the form level
KEY-?	to turn on always needed keys (KEY-EXIT, for instance)

The main triggers provided in the list values skeleton are:

KEY-HELP	to access SQL*Forms help
KEY-F0	to access the dynamic help subsystem
KEY-EXIT	to exit and return global value
KEY-MENU	to exit without global value
KEY-OTHERS	to turn off ALL keys at the form level
KEY-?	to turn on always needed keys (KEY-NXTFLD, for instance)

Due to KEY-OTHERS, certain keys must be specified, if needed, at the block level. For example, SCRUP and SCRDOWN are only useful in multi-row displays. Add these triggers based on your needs.

The skeleton names are:
  SKELAPP for applications
  SKELLFV for list field values forms

These forms are in the forms database and the \softlib\devl directory. To use the forms, either copy the skeleton to your form name and LOAD into SQL*Forms or LOAD your form name from the skeleton. Be careful to not destroy the skeletons!

Operation (Application Form Function)

- All forms will be queried on a page-by-page basis
- All subsequent blocks on a page will be automatically queried
- All blocks will only be queried when moving forward (pg2 to pg3)
- All forms will have a main "key" block on which form is based
- The remaining blocks on the form will be coordinated with the "key" block
- The "key" block will have complete functionality (entqry, etc)
- All code fields will display at least 30 chars of the code field desc next
- The code field will be displayed without a label

Operation (Look-up Form Function)

- All look-up forms will be used for both query and input
- All blocks will be automatically queried at startup
- All DESC fields will display at least 40 characters

Coding

- The HEADER block will be the first block in the form
- If a CTRL block is used, it will be the second block
- All Column references in SQL will be prefaced with the table name
- All Screen Field references will be prefaced with the block name
- Case statements and user-named triggers are preferred over branching between steps (except when using GOSTEP)
- All trigger steps used in branching will have a meaningful name
- All SQL will be capitalized
- All SQL SELECT statements will be aligned as follows:

```
SELECT  TABLE1.COL1, TABLE2.COL2, TABLE1.COL1,....
        TABLE2.COL2....
INTO    :BLOCK1.FLD1, :BLOCK1.FLD2, :BLOCK1.FLD3,
        :BLOCK1.FLD4....
FROM    TABLE1, TABLE2....
WHERE   PREDICATE1
AND     PREDICATE2
.....
```

- All CASE statements will be capitalized and aligned as follows:

```
#EXEMACRO CASE :BLOCK.FIELD IS
  WHEN 'VALUE1' THEN
    MACRO1; MACRO2;
  WHEN 'VALUE2' THEN
    MACRO1; MACRO2; MACRO3;
  WHEN OTHERS THEN MACRO1;
END CASE;
```

MegaMarket Naming Conventions

Following are the naming conventions for the MegaMarket application. These conventions must be followed to allow other developers to use your applications; please follow them.

Non-ORACLE Objects

All file names will be eight characters long to allow for portability of the application (VM and MS-DOS are restricted to eight characters). The file names will be in the format Xyyyzzzz.ext as follows:

X   is the *application title*
   Example:
      M for all MegaMarket applications
yyy   is the *subapplication within the application*
   Examples:
      INV for Inventory applications
      GEN for General applications
      MEN for Menu applications
      LFV for "Lookup" applications
zzzz   is the *function within the subapplication*
   Examples:
      SHIP for shipment function
ext   is an *extension specific to the particular tool used*
   Examples:
      FRM for SQL*Forms
      REP for SQL*ReportWriter

ORACLE Objects

Table Names: Xyyyzzzz
Xyyyzzzz are the same as the file naming conventions
associative all associative tables (many-to-many relationships) will
contain the abbreviations that describe the relationship
Examples:
MINVSUPP is the prime table
MINVICLS is the prime table
MINVSCLS is the associative table

Column Names: zzzz_DESCRIPTION
zzzz is the 4-character abbreviation of the table description from the
table name
DESCRIPTION is the description of the field.
foreign keys all foreign key column descriptions will be the primary
key's column name.
Examples:
SUPP_NUM is the primary key
zzzz_SUPP_NUM is the foreign key
ICLS_CODE is the primary key
zzzz_ICLS_CODE is the foreign key

Index Names: Xyyyzzzz_PKn
Xyyyzzzz_FKn
Xyyyzzzz_ACn
PK is a primary key index (unique)
FK is a foreign key index
AC is an access index
n is the number of the index (beginning with 1)

Domains

NAME	Description	Datatype
ADDR	Address information	
ADDR_CITY	City	CHAR(30)
ADDR_STREETn	Street line n	CHAR(40)
CODE	Table based look-ups	CHAR[2]
DATE	Date information	DATE[1]
DESC	Description	CHAR(30)
HCV	Hard-coded values	CHAR[2,3]
IND	Indicator (Y/N/null)	CHAR(1)
NAME	Name information	
NAME_FIRST	First name	CHAR(20)
NAME_LAST	Last name	CHAR(60)
NUM	System-generated keys	NUM(9)
QUANTITY	Quantity	NUM(3)
TIME	Time information	DATE[1]

1. Standard Oracle date format, including time.
2. Size will vary.
3. Any column that will have predefined values that are NOT stored in a minor table.

MegaMarket Tables

Table	Column	Null?	Type
MINVFACL	FACL_NUM	NOT NULL	NUMBER(10)
	FACL_DESC	NOT NULL	CHAR(60)
	FACL_EMPL_NUM_MGR		NUMBER(10)
	FACL_OFFC_NUM_MGR	NOT NULL	NUMBER(10)
	FACL_TYPE_HCV	NOT NULL	CHAR(1)
	FACL_ADDR_STREET1	NOT NULL	CHAR(40)
	FACL_ADDR_STREET2		CHAR(40)
	FACL_ADDR_CITY	NOT NULL	CHAR(30)
	FACL_ADDR_STATE	NOT NULL	CHAR(2)
	FACL_ADDR_ZIP	NOT NULL	CHAR(10)
	FACL_ADDR_PHONE_NUMBER		CHAR(10)

Table	Column	Null?	Type
MINVFACL	FACL_ADDR_FAX_NUMBER		CHAR(10)
	FACL_NO_OF_CUSTOMERS		NUMBER(9)
	FACL_SQUARE_FOOTAGE		NUMBER(8)

Table	Column	Null?	Type
MINVFCLS	FCLS_FACL_NUM	NOT NULL	NUMBER(10)
	FCLS_ICLS_CODE	NOT NULL	CHAR(5)

Table	Column	Null?	Type
MINVITEM	ITEM_NUM	NOT NULL	NUMBER(10)
	ITEM_ORDR_NUM	NOT NULL	NUMBER(10)
	ITEM_ICLS_CODE	NOT NULL	CHAR(5)
	ITEM_FACL_NUM	NOT NULL	NUMBER(10)
	ITEM_TRAN_NUM		NUMBER(10)
	ITEM_COMMENT		CHAR(60)

Table	Column	Null?	Type
MINVMOVE	MOVE_ICLS_CODE	NOT NULL	CHAR(5)
	MOVE_FACL_NUM_FROM	NOT NULL	NUMBER(10)
	MOVE_FACL_NUM_TO	NOT NULL	NUMBER(10)
	MOVE_QUANTITY	NOT NULL	NUMBER(10)
	MOVE_COMMENT		CHAR(60)

Table	Column	Null?	Type
MINVORDR	ORDR_NUM	NOT NULL	NUMBER(10)
	ORDR_ICLS_CODE	NOT NULL	CHAR(5)
	ORDR_SUPP_NUM	NOT NULL	NUMBER(10)
	ORDR_SHIP_NUM	NOT NULL	NUMBER(10)
	ORDR_FACL_NUM_WARE	NOT NULL	NUMBER(10)
	ORDR_DATE	NOT NULL	DATE

Table	Column	Null?	Type
MINVSCLS	SCLS_SUPP_NUM	NOT NULL	NUMBER(10)
	SCLS_ICLS_CODE	NOT NULL	CHAR(5)

Table	Column	Null?	Type
MINVSHIP	SHIP_NUM	NOT NULL	NUMBER(10)
	SHIP_SUPP_NUM	NOT NULL	NUMBER(10)
	SHIP_FACL_NUM_WARE	NOT NULL	NUMBER(10)
	SHIP_DATE	NOT NULL	DATE

Table	Column	Null?	Type
MINVSTOR	FACL_NUM	NOT NULL	NUMBER(10)
	FACL_DESC	NOT NULL	CHAR(60)
	FACL_OFFC_NUM_MGR	NOT NULL	NUMBER(10)
	FACL_EMPL_NUM_MGR		NUMBER(10)
	FACL_TYPE_HCV	NOT NULL	CHAR(1)
	FACL_ADDR_STREET1	NOT NULL	CHAR(40)
	FACL_ADDR_STREET2		CHAR(40)
	FACL_ADDR_CITY	NOT NULL	CHAR(30)
	FACL_ADDR_STATE	NOT NULL	CHAR(2)
	FACL_ADDR_ZIP	NOT NULL	CHAR(10)
	FACL_ADDR_PHONE_NUMBER		CHAR(10)

Table	Column	Null?	Type
MINVSTOR	FACL_ADDR_FAX_NUMBER		CHAR(10)
	FACL_NO_OF_CUSTOMERS		NUMBER(9)

Table	Column	Null?	Type
MINVSUPP	SUPP_NUM	NOT NULL	NUMBER(10)
	SUPP_DESC	NOT NULL	CHAR(60)
	SUPP_ADDR_STREET1	NOT NULL	CHAR(40)
	SUPP_ADDR_STREET2		CHAR(40)
	SUPP_ADDR_CITY	NOT NULL	CHAR(30)
	SUPP_ADDR_STATE	NOT NULL	CHAR(2)
	SUPP_ADDR_ZIP	NOT NULL	CHAR(10)
	SUPP_ADDR_PHONE_NUMBER		CHAR(10)
	SUPP_ADDR_FAX_NUMBER		CHAR(10)

Table	Column	Null?	Type
MINVTAB	TNAME	NOT NULL	CHAR(30)
	TABTYPE		CHAR(9)
	CLUSTERID		NUMBER

Table	Column	Null?	Type
MINVTRAN	TRAN_NUM	NOT NULL	NUMBER(10)
	TRAN_EMPL_NUM	NOT NULL	NUMBER(10)
	TRAN_ITEM_NUM	NOT NULL	NUMBER(10)
	TRAN_DATE	NOT NULL	DATE
	TRAN_AMOUNT	NOT NULL	NUMBER(7,2)
	TRAN_TTYP_CODE	NOT NULL	CHAR(2)
	TRAN_FACL_NUM_STOR	NOT NULL	NUMBER(10)

Table	Column	Null?	Type
MINVWARE	FACL_NUM	NOT NULL	NUMBER(10)
	FACL_DESC	NOT NULL	CHAR(60)
	FACL_OFFC_NUM_MGR	NOT NULL	NUMBER(10)
	FACL_EMPL_NUM_MGR		NUMBER(10)
	FACL_TYPE_HCV	NOT NULL	CHAR(1)
	FACL_ADDR_STREET1	NOT NULL	CHAR(40)
	FACL_ADDR_STREET2		CHAR(40)
	FACL_ADDR_CITY	NOT NULL	CHAR(30)
	FACL_ADDR_STATE	NOT NULL	CHAR(2)
	FACL_ADDR_ZIP	NOT NULL	CHAR(10)
	FACL_ADDR_PHONE_NUMBER		CHAR(10)

Table	Column	Null?	Type
MINVWARE	FACL_ADDR_FAX_NUMBER		CHAR(10)
	FACL_SQUARE_FOOTAGE		NUMBER(8)

Table	Column	Null?	Type
SGENAPPL	APPL_NAME	NOT NULL	CHAR(4)
	APPL_TYPE_HCV		CHAR(3)
	APPL_OWNER_HCV		CHAR(1)
	APPL_TOOL_HCV		CHAR(3)
	APPL_LOCATION	NOT NULL	CHAR(60)

Table	Column	Null?	Type
SGENEMPL	EMPL_NUM	NOT NULL	NUMBER(10)
	EMPL_NAME_LAST	NOT NULL	CHAR(25)
	EMPL_NAME_FIRST	NOT NULL	CHAR(15)
	EMPL_USERID		CHAR(8)
	EMPL_NAME_MIDDLE		CHAR(1)
	EMPL_FACL_NUM		NUMBER(10)
	EMPL_OFFC_NUM		NUMBER(10)
	EMPL_EMPL_NUM_MGR		NUMBER(10)
	EMPL_HIRE_DATE	NOT NULL	DATE
	EMPL_SOC_SEC_NUMBER		CHAR(11)
	EMPL_TITLE		CHAR(60)

Table	Column	Null?	Type
SGENHBLK	HBLK_FRM	NOT NULL	CHAR(30)
	HBLK_BLK	NOT NULL	CHAR(30)
	HBLK_TEXT_LINE_NUM	NOT NULL	NUMBER(10)
	HBLK_TEXT	NOT NULL	CHAR(60)

Table	Column	Null?	Type
SGENHFLD	HFLD_FRM	NOT NULL	CHAR(30)
	HFLD_BLK	NOT NULL	CHAR(30)
	HFLD_FLD	NOT NULL	CHAR(30)
	HFLD_TEXT_LINE_NUM	NOT NULL	NUMBER(10)
	HFLD_TEXT	NOT NULL	CHAR(60)

Table	Column	Null?	Type
SGENHFRM	HFRM_FRM	NOT NULL	CHAR(30)
	HFRM_TEXT_LINE_NUM	NOT NULL	NUMBER(10)
	HFRM_TEXT	NOT NULL	CHAR(60)

Table	Column	Null?	Type
SGENHTXT	HTXT_HELP_NUM	NOT NULL	NUMBER(10)
	HTXT_TEXT_LINE_NUM	NOT NULL	NUMBER(10)
	HTXT_TEXT	NOT NULL	CHAR(60)

Table	Column	Null?	Type
SGENMENU	MENU_NAME		CHAR(4)
	MENU_APPL_NAME		CHAR(4)
	MENU_MENU_NAME_PARENT		CHAR(4)
	MENU_DISPLAY_NUMBER		NUMBER(2)
	MENU_DESC	NOT NULL	CHAR(60)

Table	Column	Null?	Type
SGENOFFC	OFFC_NUM	NOT NULL	NUMBER(10)
	OFFC_DESC	NOT NULL	CHAR(60)
	OFFC_ADDR_STREET1	NOT NULL	CHAR(40)
	OFFC_ADDR_STREET2		CHAR(40)
	OFFC_ADDR_CITY	NOT NULL	CHAR(30)
	OFFC_ADDR_STATE	NOT NULL	CHAR(2)
	OFFC_ADDR_ZIP	NOT NULL	CHAR(10)
	OFFC_ADDR_PHONE_NUMBER		CHAR(10)
	OFFC_ADDR_FAX_NUMBER		CHAR(10)

Table	Column	Null?	Type
SLFVICLS	ICLS_CODE	NOT NULL	CHAR(5)
	ICLS_ICLS_CODE		CHAR(5)
	ICLS_DESC	NOT NULL	CHAR(60)

Table	Column	Null?	Type
SLFVTTYP	TTYP_CODE	NOT NULL	CHAR(2)
	TTYP_DESC	NOT NULL	CHAR(60)

Sample MegaMarket
Form Design Document

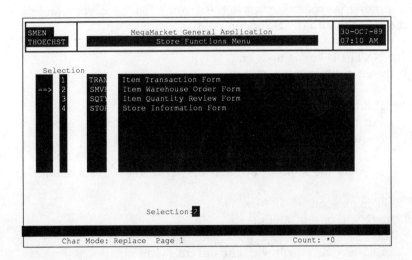

```
SMEN              MegaMarket General Application        30-OCT-89
THOECHST             Store Functions Menu               07:10 AM

    Selection
          1    TRAN  Item Transaction Form
    ==>   2    SMVE  Item Warehouse Order Form
          3    SQTY  Item Quantity Review Form
          4    STOR  Store Information Form




                      Selection: 2

        Char Mode: Replace   Page 1              Count: *0
```

Form Name: SMEN
Called By: Startup
Calls: All top level forms called by the menu

Description

This form is the main menu form. It lists all of the menu items from
SGENMENU. If the selected menu item references another menu,

then this form requeries itself at another menu level. This form represents the main point of entry for the Inventory Management System.

Pseudo Code Description

Upon entry:
 Fill in the form name, form title, and date field of the top block;
 Query the menu items that are at the top level (no parent menus);
 Put "1" into the Selection field;
 Put "==>" next to the first option;

If the NXTREC or PRVREC are pressed then move the "==>" up or down accordingly and increment or decrement the value in the Selection field;

If a number is typed then move the arrow to that posistion and put the number into the Selection field;

If the NXTFLD key is pressed:
 If the current item is a menu:
  Then
   Put the current menu name into global;
   Put the new menu name into a dummy;
   Requery based on the dummy field;
  Else
   Execute the appropriate CALL, CALLQRY, OS command, etc.

If EXIT is pressed:
 If there is a parent menu:
  Then
   Requery this form with the parent menu id;
  Else
   EXIT SQL*Forms

If anything else is pressed, do nothing.

Index

Active set, limiting, 231
Aliases, used in SQL*Plus, 164
ALTER command, 70
APPL form, SQL*Forms and, 101–103
Application building
  attributes, 12–13
  CASE*Method, 1011
  data model development, 10–11
  entities, 11–12
  relationships, 13–15
  See also Online application
    construction.
Application skeleton, 111
Application tables
  & & substitution, 73
  building, 68–74
  sizing, 67–68
  SQL to generate SQL, 73–74
Archiving, 312
Asterisk, used in SELECT statement,
  37–38
Attributes
  attribute list, 13, 15
  changing field attributes, 129
  domain of, 12–13
  entities and, 12–13
  table columns and, 19
Auditing, in RDBMS, 311

BLOCK DESCRIPTION field, 98
Blocks, 82–83
  BLOCK DESCRIPTION field, 98
  block names, 95
  DEFINE BLOCK window, 98, 123, 124
  in Designer program, 84, 85–86
  table data header block, 236
Boilerplate, 84
  embedded boilerplate, 261
  validating fields of, 131–135
BREAK command, 179

Calling reports, 202–211
CASE*Dictionary, documentation using,
  287–288, 291

CASE*Method, 10, 11
CASE statement, commas in, 137
Code
  CODE field, 117–118, 122, 137–138
  code library, 127–128
  reusable code, 133
Coding standards, 96
Column definitions
  numbers vs. characters, 31
  in physical model, 29–33
Column list, of INSERT statement, 45,
  46
COMMENTS function, 97, 287
Commit function, logical transaction
  concept of, 48
COMPUTE function name, eliminating,
  179–180
Computer Aided Systems Engineering
  (CASE), 10
CONNECT BY clause, 158
Context area, cursor as, 226
Correlated sub-query, 44, 241–243
COUNT operation, 262
CREATE INDEX statement, 234
CREATE statement, 87
  synonyms and, 49, 50–51
  tables and, 49
  views and, 49, 50
CREATE TABLE statement, 49–50, 234,
  237–238
  WHERE clause in, 49
Cross reference reports, 295, 297,
  298–299
Cursor
  as area of memory, 226–228
  limiting, 277
  ORACLE cursor, 228–229
  user cursor, 228–229

Database construction
  building application tables, 68–74
  documentation, importance of, 62
  domain definition, 64–65
  goal clarification, 66–67

instance layer, 59, 62
naming conventions, 62–64
naming for lookups, 64
ORACLE development environment, 58–62
sizing application tables, 67–68
software development standards, 65–66
software management, 55–58
synonyms in, 61
Data control, in SQL, 51–52
Data definition
  CREATE TABLE statement, 49–50
  RENAME command, 50–51
Data dictionary
  documentation using, 288–291
  of ORACLE, 37
Data extents, 234
Data Flow Diagrams, 11
  See also Entity/Relationship Diagram (ERD).
Data manipulation functions
  commit/rollback functions, 48
  DELETE statement, 47–48
  INSERT statement, 45–46
  SELECT statement, 36–45
  UPDATE statement, 46–47
Data model
  development of
    attributes, 12–13, 15
    CASE*Method, 11
    Data Flow Diagrams, 11
    Entity/Relationship Diagram (ERD), 11, 13, 15, 17
    Function Hierarchies, 11
    relationships, 13–15
  entities, 11–12
  logical-to-physical design, 18, 27, 32
  physical model
    column definitions in, 29–33
    table relationships in, 22–29
  use of, 18–21
Data segment, 234
Datatypes, of attributes, 12–13, 33, 45, 49
DECODE function, 183–185, 261
DEFAULT WHERE clause, 139
DEFINE option, 87
DELETE clause, WHERE clause in, 47–48
Design consideration
  block-mode terminals, 93
  portability, 93

Designer program
  blocks in, 84, 85–86
  saving vs. generating, 86–91
  screen painter, 84–86
  of SQL*forms, 81, 82–86, 91
  windows in, 82–84
Dirty data, 219
DISCARD option, 88
Display in Menus, trigger attribute, 114
Distributed databases, 309–310
Distributed processing, 307–309, 310
Documentation
  cross reference reports, 295, 297, 298–299
  data integrity reports, 297, 299
  documentation applications, 288
  online help, 285
  reference tables and data, 299, 303, 305
  technical documentation, 283–284, 285–287
  user documentation, 283, 284–285
  using CASE*Dictionary, 287–288, 291
  using data dictionary, 288–291
  using tool tables, 292–294
Domain, of attributes, 12–13, 64–65
DROP command, 51, 88
Dynamic vs. static menus, 198

Either/or relationships, 145–146
Entities
  attributes of, 12–13
  defining for ERD, 11–12
  major/minor entities, 11, 12
  relationships between, 13–15, 19
  STATE entity, 11–12
  tables, creating from, 19
  TRANSACTION TYPE entity, 12
Entity/Relationship Diagram (ERD), 11, 13, 15, 17
  defining attributes for, 12–13
  defining entities for, 11–12
  example of, 17
  physical ERD, 32
  relationship between entities, 13–15
  use of, 18
Environmental variables, in SQL*Plus, 163
Error messages, 94
Execution path, 237
EXPLAIN facility, 263–266
  integrating with TRACE facilities, 268
Extra relationships. See Redundant relationships

FILE option
  DISCARD option, 88
  DROP option, 88
  GENERATE option, 88
  RENAME option, 88
  SAVE AS option, 88
  SAVE option, 88
Foreign key, 20–21, 23, 31
  NULL foreign key, 31
  as primary key, 33
Form operation standards, 96–97
FRM file, 80, 81, 88
FROM clause, 39–40, 41
  as predicate statement, 42
  small table last rule, 252
Function Hierarchies, 11
Function keys
  core triggers and, 112, 114
  defined in ORACLE, 84
  Display in Menus attribute, 114
  skeletons and, 112–113
  trigger actions and, 100–101

GENERATE option, 88
GLOBAL variables, 98, 100, 108, 113,
  114–117
GRANT command, 51–52

Help system, 201
  AUTOHELP facility, 94, 95
  online help, 285
  SQL*Forms, 98–101
HOST command, portability of, 210

IAP tables, saving to, 272
Indexes
  access (performance) indexes, 243
  compressed indexes, 249
  concatenated indexes, 247, 248, 253
  creation of, 234
  index balancing, 245
  index merge, 246
  index segments, 234
  leaf mode of, 244
  and loading, 215
  multiple table optimization and,
    250–254
  NULL searches and, 31
  single table optimization and, 145–150
  as tables, 248
  when not to use, 260
INP file, 80–81, 88
  editing, 81, 133

INSERT statement, 46
  building application tables, 72
  column list in, 45, 46
  INSERT clause, 46
  SELECT statement used with, 46
  SQL*Forms and, 79
  values list of, 45, 46
Instance of database
  database administrator and, 59
  networking software for, 62
  owner as boundary for, 59
  production/development
    considerations, 61–62
Integration. See Systems integration
Integrity issues, 24, 25, 30–31, 32
Interface consistency, systems
  integration and, 198–199
Intersection table, 19–20
IS NULL operator, 41, 42

Joins, table ordering for, 260–261

Kernel, description of, 226

Languages (computer)
  non-procedural language of
    SQL*Forms, 78–79
  pros/cons for online applications, 77
Leaf node, of index entry, 244
Least recently used (LRU) algorithm,
  235
LIKE operator, 41, 42, 194
List field values (LFVs)
  forms, 122–124, 139
  skeletons, 111–112, 117–118
LIST option, 87
LOAD option, 87–88
Logical model, physical model
  relationship, 18, 21
Logical-to-physical design, 18, 27, 32
Logical transaction concept of commit/
  rollback functions, 48
Lookup form
  definition of, 64
  naming for, 64
Looping techniques, 150–152

Macros
  CALL macro, 101, 110, 111
  CALLQRY macro, 101, 102, 110, 111,
    119–122
  DEFAULT macro, 113
  HOST macro, 203

MENU macro, 98
MESSAGE macro, 112
NEWFRM macro, 101, 110, 111
undocumented macros, 142
Many-to-many relationship, 13, 15, 19
MAY BE relationship, 14, 29–30
Menu systems
  dynamic vs. static menus, 198
  interface consistency and, 198–199
  MENU macro, 98
  non-Oracle systems, 200–201
  for SQL*Forms, 103–111, 199, 200
  SQL*Menu, 199
  triggers and, 108, 110
MODIFY option, 87
Multi-column primary keys, 31
Multi-line forms, 126
Multi-selection look-up forms, 148–150
Must-have relationships, 152–153

Naming conventions, 62–64, 94–95, 117
Nested select statements, used in
    WHERE clause, 43–44
NEW_VALUE function, for
Non-database field, uses of, 153–156
Non-procedural language, of
    SQL*Forms, 78–79
NOT operator, 258
NULL field, using for report
    construction, 193
NULL operators, 257–258
NULL searches, indexes and, 31
NULL values, 30–31
  NULL foreign key, 31
  NULL searches, 31
  NVL function and, 30
  online application construction, 128
Numbers vs. characters, in column
    definitions, 31
NVL function, NULL values and, 30

One-to-many relationship, 13, 14–15, 20
One-to-one relationship, 13, 14, 19
Online application construction
  boilerplate, validating fields of,
    131–134
  CASE commas, 137
  changing field attributes, 129
  code library, generic functions and,
    127–128
  creating skeleton forms, 97–122
  default application forms, 124–127
  either/or relationships, 145–146

exiting to SQL*Plus, 150
faking database change, 144–145
INP file, editing, 133
list field value (LFV) forms, 122–124,
    139
looping technique, 150–152
multi-line forms, 126
multi-selection look-up forms, 148–150
must-have relationships, 152–153
non-database field
  query on, 135
  uses of, 153–156
NULL values, 128
query-only blocks, 128–130
running totals, 141–144
sequence number generation, 139
standardization for, 93–97
tracking time, 130–131
undocumented macros, 142
user exits, 137–138
validation triggers, developing,
    135–137
See also Application building;
  SQL*Forms.
Operating systems, for software
    management, 56
Optimization
  multiple optimization table, 250–254
  process of, 243
  single table optimization, 243–250
  of SQL statement, 229
ORACLE for 1-2-3, 220
ORACLE
  CASE*Method methodology, 10
  Data Dictionary of, 37
  DECODE function of, 183–185
  EXPLAIN facility, 263–266
  function key conventions, 84
  future software, 315–325
  ORACLE startup parameters, 232,
    234, 237
  query processing in, 37–44
  SQL*Forms used with, 79
  SQL and, 35–36
  SYSTEM.DUAL table, 40
  technical advantages of, 4–5
  TRACE facilities, 266
  versions used, 4
ORDER BY clause, 123, 124
OR operator, 258–260
Output table, 38, 40–41, 45
Owner, as database boundary instance,
    59

Parameters
  dynamic ORDER BY, 195–196
  ORACLE startup parameters, 232,
    234, 237
  passing to SQL*Plus, 188–189
  SPOOL parameter, 273, 274, 275
  SQL*Plus command line parameters,
    205
  using LIKE, 194
  using NULL, 193
Parsing SQL statement, 229
Performance vs. flexibility, in physical
    model, 24
Physical Entity/Relationship Diagram,
    32
Physical model
  column definitions in, 29–33
  implementation strategies, 24–25,
    28–29
  logical model relationship, 18, 21
  performance vs. flexibility in, 24
  physical ERD, 32
  process of construction, 18, 21, 32
  SQL*Forms applications and, 22, 25,
    27
  SQL complexity requirements and, 22
  table relationships in, 22–29
Portability
  design considerations, 93
  of HOST command, 210
POST-CHANGE triggers, 139
Predicate of statement, FROM clause as,
    42
PRE-INSET triggers, 139
PRE-QUERY trigger, 135
Primary key, 19, 20–21, 23
  foreign key as, 33
  multi-column primary keys, 31
Pro*ORACLE, 226
Prototypes, SQL*Forms, 97
  See also Physical model.

Query processing
  correlated sub-query, 44, 241–243
  in ORACLE, 37–44
  query-only blocks, 128–130
  sub-query, in SELECT statement, 43
  using PRE-QUERY trigger, 135
  view overhead and, 229
  See also Data manipulation functions.
Quiet mode, 95

Redundant relationships, 27–28

Reference tables and data,
    documentation of, 299, 303, 305
Relational database management system
    (RDBMS), definition of, 1
Relationships
  either/or relationships, 145–146
  extra/redundant relationships, 27–28
  foreign key for, 20–21
  many-to-many relationship, 13, 15, 19
  MAY BE relationship, 14, 29–30
  one-to-many relationship, 13, 14–15,
    20
  one-to-one relationship, 13, 14, 19
RENAME command, 50–51, 88
Report construction
  BREAK command, 179
  children without rows, eliminating
    column headings for, 192
  COMPUTE function name,
    eliminating, 179–180
  dynamic column headings, 186–188
  matrix-style reports, 190–191
  parameters
    dynamic ORDER BY, 195–196
    passing to SQL*Plus, 188–189
    using LIKE, 194
    using NULL, 193
  printing only parents with children,
    191–192
  reporting skeletons, 173–178
  spreadsheet-style reports, using
    DECODE, 183–185
  SQL*ReportWriter
    comments area in, 190
    reporting techniques for, 189
    text objects in, 190
  SQL statements, SQL*Plus variables
    in, 182–183
  using SQL*Plus, 161–165
    aliases used in, 164
    DML statements in, 180–182
    environmental variables, 163
    reporting techniques, 179
  using SQL*ReportWriter, 165–168
  writing report specifications
    creating standards, 170
    design review, 170
    SQL*Plus standards, 171–172
    SQL*Report, 169
Reusable code, 133
REVOKE command, 52
Rollback function, logical transaction
    concept of, 48

ROWID address, 244, 245–246
ROWNUM function, 108, 109–110
  SELECT statements and, 109–110
Rows buffered option, 125, 127
RUN option, 87

SAVE AS option, 88
SAVE option, 88
Saving, to IAP tables, 272
Saving vs. generating
  Designer program, 86–91
    in SQL*Forms, 86–91
Security management, 310–311
SELECT statement
  asterisk used in, 37–38
  FROM clause, 39–40, 41
  nested select statement, 43–44
  period used in, 38
  ROWNUM and, 109–111
  select list, 37, 38–40, 41
  sub-query in, 43
  SYSTEM.DUAL table, 40
  for testing/tuning applications,
    261–262
  used with INSERT statement, 46
  WHERE clause, 37, 38, 40–45, 49
Sequence number generation, 139
SET clause, 47
Skeletons
  application skeleton, 111, 201–202
  core triggers and, 112
  function keys and, 112–113
  list field values (LFV) skeletons,
    111–112, 117–118
  skeleton forms, 97–98, 111–122
Small table last rule, in FROM clause,
  252
Software management
  moving to test environment, 221–222
  operating systems, 56
  SQL*Forms application for, 58
  staging directories, 56, 57
  strategies for, 56–58
SOUNDEX function, 216
SPACE clause, for sizing application
  tables, 67–68
SPOOL parameter, 273, 274, 275
Spreadsheet-style reports, using
  DECODE, 183–185
SQL*Connect, 219
SQL*Forms
  & used in, 102–103
  APPL form and, 101–103
  application-specific techniques, 141

AUTOHELP facility, 94, 95
boilerplate, validating fields of,
  131–135
changing field attributes, 129
CODE field in, 117–118, 122
code library, generic functions and,
  127–128
COMMENTS function, 97
for database construction, 64, 66, 70
default application forms, 124–127
Designer program, 81, 82–86, 91
design review of, 92–93
either/or relationships, 145–146
exiting to SQL*Plus, 150
faking database change, 144–145
HELP system, 98–101
INP file, editing, 133
INSERT statement and, 79
list field value (LFV) forms, 122–124,
  139
looping techniques, 150–152
menu system for, 103–111
modules of, 79–82
moving fields, 85
multi-selection look-up forms, 148–150
must-have relationships, 152–153
non-database field, 135
  uses of, 153–156
non-procedural syntax of, 78–79
NULL values and, 128
operation prototypes, 97
outer joins, 156–160
pop-up windows in, 153
query-only blocks, 128–130
quiet mode, 95
reusable code, 133
ROWNUM function, 108, 109–110
running totals, 141–144
saving vs. generating, 86–91
sequence number generation, 139
skeleton forms, 97–98, 111–122
for software management, 58
standardization of, 93–97
SUBSTR function, 119
TRACE facilities and, 270
tracking time, 130–131
tuning SQL*Forms applications,
  276–279
undocumented macros, 142
user exits, 137–138
writing specifications for, 91–92
SQL*Loader, 72
SQL*Net, 62
SQL*Plus, 72, 73

aliases used in, 164
environmental variables in, 163
exiting to, 150
passing parameters to, 188–189
reporting standards, 171–172
reporting techniques and, 22, 25, 179, 161–165
using DML statements, 180–182
variables in SQL statements, 182–183
SQL*Report Writer
comments area in, 190
copying reports, 166
for report construction, 165–168
reporting techniques for, 172–173, 189
text objects in, 190
tuning SQL*ReportWriter applications, 279
SQL*Loader, 212–214
SQL to generate SQL, 73–74
SQL Language Reference Manual, The, 53, 3942
SQL script, 68
Staging directories, 56, 57
Standardization, reporting standards creation of, 170
SQL*Plus standards, 171–172
SQL*ReportWriter standards, 172–173
Standardization of SQL*Forms
coding standards, 96
error messages, 94
form operation standards, 96–97
importance of, 94
naming conventions, 94–95, 117
placement of user-named triggers, 95–96
Structured Query Language (SQL)
building application tables with, 68–74
data control in, 51–52
data definition
CREATE TABLE statement, 49–50
RENAME command, 50–51
data manipulation functions
commit/rollback functions, 48
DELETE statement, 47–48
INSERT statement, 45–46
SELECT statement, 36–45
UPDATE statement, 46–47
overcomplicated SQL, 255
reducing in application, 276
SQL tuning methodology, 272–275
SQL tuning techniques, 232, 233–243, 254–255

using SQL functions, 255–257
Sub-query
correlated sub-query, 44
SELECT statement, 43
SUBSTR function, 119
Synonyms
CREATE statement and, 49, 50–51
in database construction, 61
private synonym, 61
public synonym, 61
SYSTEM.DUAL, 40, 113
System global area 9GA), 233, 234, 235
Systems integration
application skeleton, 201–202
calling reports, 202–211
existing systems, 218–221
help system, 201
indexes and loading, 215
menu systems, 198–201
migrating old data, 211–218
moving software to test environment, 221–222
SOUNDEX function, 216
using SQL*Loader, 212–214

Tables
attributes as columns for, 19
base table, 82–83
building application tables, 68–74
CREATE statement and, 49
driving table, 250
entities, creating from, 19
foreign key, 20–21, 23, 31
IAP tables, saving to, 272
indexes as, 248
intersection table, 19–20
many-to-many relationship, 19
one-to-many relationship, 20
one-to-one relationship, 19
output table, 38, 40–41, 45
physical model relatioñships, 22–29
primary key, 19, 20–21, 23
renaming, 50–51
SELECT statement and, 37, 49
sizing application tables, 67–68
table data header block, 236
TEMPTABLES, 238
using tablespaces, 235
Temporary data segment, 237, 238
TEMPTABLES, 238
Testing/tuning applications, 279–282
adjusting buffers, 234
column prefixes, 230
embedded boilerplate, 261

interpreting tuning information, 271
joins, table ordering for, 260–261
limiting active set, 231
limiting cursors, 277
meta code use, 229–230
NOT operator, 258
NULL operators, 257–258
optimization
    multiple table optimization,
    250–254
    process of, 243
    single table optimization, 243–250
    SQL statement, 229
OR operator, 258–260
over-complicated SQL, 255
parsing SQL statement, 229
SQL tuning methodology, 232,
    254–255, 272–275
    query execution for, 233–243
    timing data, 273, 274
tuning SQL*Forms applications,
    276–279
tuning SQL*ReportWriter
    applications, 279
using array processing, 231
using COUNT operation, 262
using DECODE function, 261
using EXPLAIN facility, 263–266
using NEW_VALUE, function,
    262–263
using SELECT statement, 261–262
using SQL functions, 255–257
using tablespaces, 235, 239
using TRACE facilities, 266–271
view overhead, query processing and,
    229
without indexes, 260
Text objects, in SQL*ReportWriter, 190
TRACE facilities
integrating with EXPLAIN facility,
    268
SQL*Forms and, 270
for testing/tuning applications,
    266–271

Triggers
    core triggers and skeletons, 112, 113,
    115–117
    DEFINE TRIGGER window, 97
    Display in Menus attribute, 114
    function keys and, 100–101
    menu system and, 108, 110
    MESSAGE macro to define, 112
    placement of, 95–96
    skeleton forms and, 98
    standardization of names, 95
    user-named triggers, 95–96
    using PRE-QUERY trigger, 135
    using SQL*Forms macros, 101–103
    validation trigger, 133, 135–137
    word wrap trigger, 156

UPDATE statement
    SET clause, 47
    WHERE clause in, 46–47
User cursor, 228–229
User-exits, 77, 137–138
User-named triggers, 95–96

Validation trigger, 133, 135–137
Values list, of INSERT statement, 45, 46

WHERE clause, 38, 40–45
    in CREATE TABLE statement, 49
    in DELETE clause, 47–48
    nested select statements used in,
    43–44
    operators used in, 41–42
    in UPDATE statement, 46–47
Windows
    BLOCK OPTIONS window, 125, 126
    DEFINE BLOCK window, 98, 123, 124
    DEFINE TRIGGER window, 97
    DEFINE window, 114
    in Designer program, 82–84
    FIELD ATTRIBUTES window, 125
    pop-up windows, 153
Word wrap, trigger for, 156

Special Offer

Because the MegaMarket application is so large, it was impossible for us to include all of the application code that we developed in the text of this book. We have prepared a diskette that you can purchase if you are interested in looking at the application more closely or testing it yourself. The diskette is MS-DOS formatted and includes:

- SQL*Forms INP files (for SQL*Forms 2.3): Application screens, Dynamic Menu System, and Dynamic Help System
- SQL*Plus creation scripts and reports
- SQL*ReportWriter reports
- SQL*Report reports
- codeval() user exit (written in Pro*C)

In addition, you will receive enlarged copies of key documentation elements, including:

- The Entity/Relationship Diagram
- The Development Checklist

To order, send a check for $20, payable to *Guide to ORACLE*, to:

Guide to ORACLE
Post Office Box 5877
Bethesda, MD 20824 USA

Please specify 3.5" or 5.25" format. We also welcome any other comments you may have about the book, although we cannot guarantee a written personal response.

Please note that the application modules distributed on this diskette are for didactic purposes only. In most cases, we only implemented those portions that were pertinent to the discussion in the book. **These modules do not constitute a production application.** *You are, however, free to use any of this code as part of your own applications.*